A·N·N·U·A·L E·D·I·T·I·O·N·S

Educating Exceptional Children

05/06

Seventeenth Edition

D1409241

EDITOR

Karen L. Freiberg

University of Maryland, Baltimore County

Dr. Karen Freiberg has an interdisciplinary educational and employment background in nursing, education, and developmental psychology. She received her B.S. from the State University of New York at Plattsburgh, her M.S. from Cornell University, and her Ph.D. from Syracuse University. She has worked as a school nurse, a pediatric nurse, a public health nurse for the Navajo Indians, an associate project director for a child development clinic, a researcher in several areas of child development, and a university professor. Dr. Freiberg is the author of an award-winning textbook, *Human Development: A Life-Span Approach*, which is now in its fourth edition. She is currently on the faculty at the University of Maryland, Baltimore County.

McGraw-Hill/Dushkin

2460 Kerper Blvd., Dubuque, IA 52001

Visit us on the Internet
http://www.dushkin.com

Credits

1. **Inclusive Education**
   Unit photo—© Getty Images/Ryan McVay
2. **Early Childhood**
   Unit photo—© Getty Images/SW Productions
3. **Learning Disabilities**
   Unit photo—© Getty Images/PhotoLink
4. **Speech and Language Impairments**
   Unit photo—© Getty Images/PhotoLink/D. Berry
5. **Developmental Disabilities**
   Unit photo—© Getty Images/Vicky Kasala
6. **Emotional and Behavioral Disorders**
   Unit photo—© Getty Images/Rob Melnychuk
7. **Vision and Hearing Impairments**
   Unit photo—© CORBIS/Royalty-Free
8. **Multiple Disabilities**
   Unit photo—© Getty Images/Patrick Clark
9. **Orthopedic and Health Impairments**
   Unit photo—© CORBIS/Royalty-Free
10. **Giftedness**
    Unit photo—© Getty Images/Geostock
11. **Transition**
    Unit photo—© Getty Images/Photodisc Collection

Copyright

Cataloging in Publication Data
Main entry under title: Annual Editions: Educating Exceptional Children. 2005/2006.
1. Educating Exceptional Children—Periodicals. I. Freiberg, Karen L., *comp.* II. Title: Educating Exceptional Children.
ISBN 0–07–310363–2   658'.05   ISSN 0198–7518

Seventeenth Edition

Cover image © Geostock/Getty Images and Eyewire
Printed in the United States of America   1234567890QPDQPD987654   Printed on Recycled Paper

Editors/Advisory Board

Members of the Advisory Board are instrumental in the final selection of articles for each edition of ANNUAL EDITIONS. Their review of articles for content, level, currentness, and appropriateness provides critical direction to the editor and staff. We think that you will find their careful consideration well reflected in this volume.

Preface

In publishing ANNUAL EDITIONS we recognize the enormous role played by the magazines, newspapers, and journals of the public press in providing current, first-rate educational information in a broad spectrum of interest areas. Many of these articles are appropriate for students, researchers, and professionals seeking accurate, current material to help bridge the gap between principles and theories and the real world. These articles, however, become more useful for study when those of lasting value are carefully collected, organized, indexed, and reproduced in a low-cost format, which provides easy and permanent access when the material is needed. That is the role played by ANNUAL EDITIONS.

America is a land of diverse attitudes about special education of students with unique requirements and/or different characteristics. Many Americans embrace the concept "all men are created equal," (political correctness would now have this say "all people"). The rest of this famous quotation from the U.S. Declaration of Independence qualifies the statement, "That they are endowed by their Creator with certain inalienable rights; that among these are life, liberty, and the pursuit of happiness." From colonial days equal education was embraced by the American people. By the early nineteenth century free public schools were instituted for all children supported by local taxes with additional support from the government. By the end of the twentieth century free and appropriate public education, in the least restrictive environment, with individualized education programs for students with unique requirements, was U.S. law. The costs of maintaining specialized education programs in public schools has soared. This has caused some Americans to question the entitlements of the U.S. Declaration of Independence.

In April of 2003 the U.S. House of Representatives, (Committee on Education) approved a bill which would make it easier to exclude children with mental or emotional disorders from public schools. Immediately, disability advocacy groups organized a campaign to urge opposition to this bill.

Should children with special needs attend school with students without such requirements? The issue is far from settled.

This compendium of articles about children who need, and benefit from, special educational services, may serve as a counter-balance against the voices calling for reactionary reform. Is the elimination of any kind of so called favored treatment (supportive assistance) for children with exceptionalities a correction of past misguided education? Where do you stand on this issue? Our current lack of funds for education will require some changes. To what extent will more efficient use of financial resources necessitate the elimination of services? What services should go first? Will belt tightening have any positive effects?

A new and burgeoning field, biotechnology, may have an answer for our future: no children born with exceptionalities. Is this science-fiction or a real possibility?

The Human Genome Project's completion allowed us to decode the human genome. This means that we have knowledge of the sequencing of CATG (cytosine, adenine, thymine, guanine), the chemicals that form DNA. It means that we can replace strands of DNA (genes) with altered CATG sequences. It means that we can alter human development!

Should twenty-first century scientists be allowed to alter genes? Who will pay for resequencing of CATG to bring about new behaviors? Will human cloning be allowed to prevent the birth of any human with a disability? Will test tube fertilization, genome inspection, and genetic correction be used as an alternative means of preventing the birth of so-called "imperfect" beings? These and other questions are likely to lead to contentious debates for many years to come.

A near future answer to individuals with exceptionalities will be to replace dysfunctional body parts with new body parts generated from stem cells. In the United States, George W. Bush's administration, with its strong pro-life stance, infuriated many scientists by suggesting that a stem cell (a fertilized egg a few days old) is already a human life. If a stem cell is a human life, can it be transformed into some type of replacement tissue to cure diabetes, autism, asthma, epilepsy, or attention deficit disorder? Many are arguing that an embryo on a Petri dish is not a human life, while the same embryo attached to a woman's uterine lining is a life. This thorniest of human ethical dilemmas is yet to be resolved.

In homes where families are raising children with disabilities or conditions of exceptionality, the above questions have special poignancy. Where should the balancing fulcrum be placed between challenges and cautions?

Annual Editions: Educating Exceptional Children 05/06 includes articles discussing the pros and cons of educational reform and special education. It explains how IDEA, (the Individuals with Disabilities Education Act) is being implemented in all areas of special education. Selections have been made with an eye to conveying information, giving personal experiences, offering suggestions for implementation, and stimulating meaningful discussions among future parents and teachers.

To help us improve future editions of this anthology, please complete and return the postage-paid article rating form on the last page. Your suggestions are valued and appreciated.

Karen Freiberg

Karen Freiberg
Editor

Contents

UNIT 1
Inclusive Education

Four articles present strategies for establishing positive interaction between students with and without special needs.

UNIT 2
Early Childhood

Three unit articles discuss the implementation of special services to preschoolers with disabilities.

The concepts in bold italics are developed in the article. For further expansion, please refer to the Topic Guide and the Index.

UNIT 3
Learning Disabilities

The assessment and special needs of students with learning disabilities are addressed in this unit's four selections.

The concepts in bold italics are developed in the article. For further expansion, please refer to the Topic Guide and the Index.

UNIT 4
Speech and Language Impairments

In this unit, two selections examine communication disorders and suggest ways in which students can develop their speech and language.

UNIT 5
Developmental Disabilities

Three articles in this section discuss concerns and strategies for providing optimal educational programs for students with developmental disabilities and Down's syndrome.

The concepts in bold italics are developed in the article. For further expansion, please refer to the Topic Guide and the Index.

UNIT 6
Emotional and Behavioral Disorders

Ways to teach emotionally and behaviorally disordered students are discussed in the unit's four articles.

UNIT 7
Vision and Hearing Impairments

Two selections discuss the special needs of visually and hearing impaired children within the school system.

The concepts in bold italics are developed in the article. For further expansion, please refer to the Topic Guide and the Index.

UNIT 8
Multiple Disabilities

The implications of educational programs for children with multiple impairments are examined in this unit's three articles.

UNIT 9
Orthopedic and Health Impairments

In this unit, three articles discuss how health problems and mobility impairments have an impact on a child's education.

The concepts in bold italics are developed in the article. For further expansion, please refer to the Topic Guide and the Index.

UNIT 10
Giftedness

Three articles examine the need for special services for gifted and talented students, assessment of giftedness, and ways to teach these students.

UNIT 11
Transition

The three articles in this section examine the problems and issues regarding transitions within school or from school to the community and workforce.

The concepts in bold italics are developed in the article. For further expansion, please refer to the Topic Guide and the Index.

The concepts in bold italics are developed in the article. For further expansion, please refer to the Topic Guide and the Index.

Topic Guide

This topic guide suggests how the selections in this book relate to the subjects covered in your course. You may want to use the topics listed on these pages to search the Web more easily.

On the following pages a number of Web sites have been gathered specifically for this book. They are arranged to reflect the units of this *Annual Edition*. You can link to these sites by going to the DUSHKIN ONLINE support site at *http://www.dushkin.com/online/*.

ALL THE ARTICLES THAT RELATE TO EACH TOPIC ARE LISTED BELOW THE BOLD-FACED TERM.

Assessment
1. Standards for Diverse Learners
8. Providing Support for Student Independence Through Scaffolded Instruction
9. Reading Disability and the Brain
10. Successful Strategies for Promoting Self-Advocacy Among Students With LD: The LEAD Group
11. Group Intervention: Improving Social Skills of Adolescents with Learning Disabilities
12. Language Differences or Learning Difficulties
16. Inscrutable or Meaningful? Understanding and Supporting Your Inarticulate Students
17. Psychiatric Disorders and Treatments: A Primer for Teachers
25. Using Technology to Construct Alternate Portfolios of Students With Moderate and Severe Disabilities
28. Trick Question
29. Understanding the Young Gifted Child: Guidelines for Parents, Families, and Educators
30. Cultivating Otherwise Untapped Potential
31. Teaching Strategies for Twice-Exceptional Students
34. Choosing a Self-Determination Curriculum

Autism
14. The Secrets of Autism
16. Inscrutable or Meaningful? Understanding and Supporting Your Inarticulate Students

Brain diseases and disorders
9. Reading Disability and the Brain
28. Trick Question

Cognitive maturation
10. Successful Strategies for Promoting Self-Advocacy Among Students With LD: The LEAD Group

Collaboration
1. Standards for Diverse Learners
4. An Interview With Dr. Marilyn Friend
7. The Itinerant Teacher Hits the Road: A Map for Instruction in Young Children's Social Skills
12. Language Differences or Learning Difficulties
17. Psychiatric Disorders and Treatments: A Primer for Teachers
22. Using Tactile Strategies With Students Who Are Blind and Have Severe Disabilities
23. Making Inclusion a Reality for Students With Severe Disabilities
24. Training Basic Teaching Skills to Paraeducators of Students With Severe Disabilities
25. Using Technology to Construct Alternate Portfolios of Students With Moderate and Severe Disabilities
32. Transition Planning for Students With Severe Disabilities: Policy Implications for the Classroom

Computers
13. Young African American Children With Disabilities and Augmentative and Alternative Communication Issues
20. Classroom Problems That Don't Go Away
25. Using Technology to Construct Alternate Portfolios of Students With Moderate and Severe Disabilities

Conflict resolution
6. Building Relationships With Challenging Children
11. Group Intervention: Improving Social Skills of Adolescents with Learning Disabilities
17. Psychiatric Disorders and Treatments: A Primer for Teachers
18. Making Choices—Improving Behavior—Engaging in Learning
19. The Importance of Teacher Self-Awareness in Working With Students With Emotional and Behavioral Disorders
20. Classroom Problems That Don't Go Away

Creativity
5. Music in the Inclusive Environment
16. Inscrutable or Meaningful? Understanding and Supporting Your Inarticulate Students
28. Trick Question
29. Understanding the Young Gifted Child: Guidelines for Parents, Families, and Educators
30. Cultivating Otherwise Untapped Potential

Cultural diversity
1. Standards for Diverse Learners
12. Language Differences or Learning Difficulties
13. Young African American Children With Disabilities and Augmentative and Alternative Communication Issues
21. A Half-Century of Progress for Deaf Individuals
30. Cultivating Otherwise Untapped Potential

Developmental disabilities
14. The Secrets of Autism
15. Citizenship and Disability
16. Inscrutable or Meaningful? Understanding and Supporting Your Inarticulate Students
25. Using Technology to Construct Alternate Portfolios of Students With Moderate and Severe Disabilities
32. Transition Planning for Students With Severe Disabilities: Policy Implications for the Classroom

Early childhood education
5. Music in the Inclusive Environment
6. Building Relationships With Challenging Children
7. The Itinerant Teacher Hits the Road: A Map for Instruction in Young Children's Social Skills
9. Reading Disability and the Brain
29. Understanding the Young Gifted Child: Guidelines for Parents, Families, and Educators

Elementary school
3. Attitudes of Elementary School Principals Toward the Inclusion of Students With Disabilities
8. Providing Support for Student Independence Through Scaffolded Instruction
9. Reading Disability and the Brain
10. Successful Strategies for Promoting Self-Advocacy Among Students With LD: The LEAD Group
18. Making Choices—Improving Behavior—Engaging in Learning
26. Mobility Training Using the MOVE Curriculum: A Parent's View
28. Trick Question

World Wide Web Sites

The following World Wide Web sites have been carefully researched and selected to support the articles found in this reader. The easiest way to access these selected sites is to go to our DUSHKIN ONLINE support site at *http://www.dushkin.com/online/*.

AE: Educating Exceptional Children 05/06

The following sites were available at the time of publication. Visit our Web site—we update DUSHKIN ONLINE regularly to reflect any changes.

General Sources

Consortium for Citizens With Disabilities
http://www.c-c-d.org

Included in this coalition organization is an Education Task Force that follows issues of early childhood special education, the president's commission on excellence in special education, issues of rethinking special education, 2001 IDEA principles, and many other related issues.

Family Village
http://www.familyvillage.wisc.edu/index.htmlx

Here is a global community of disability-related resources that is set up under such headings as library, shopping mall, school, community center, and others.

National Information Center for Children and Youth With Disabilities (NICHCY)
http://www.nichcy.org/index.html

NICHCY provides information and makes referrals in areas related to specific disabilities, early intervention, special education and related services, individualized education programs, and much more. The site also connects to a listing of Parent's Guides to resources for children and youth with disabilities.

National Rehabilitation Information Center (NARIC)
http://www.naric.com

A series of databases that can be keyword-searched on subjects including physical, mental, and psychiatric disabilities, vocational rehabilitation, special education, assistive technology, and more can be found on this site.

President's Commission on Excellence in Special Education (PCESE)
http://www.ed.gov/inits/commissionsboards/whspecialeducation/

The report stemming from the work of the PCESE, *A New Era: Revitalizing Special Education for Children and Their Families,* can be downloaded in full at this site.

School Psychology Resources Online
http://www.schoolpsychology.net

Numerous sites on special conditions, disorders, and disabilities, as well as other data ranging from assertiveness/evaluation to research, are available on this resource page for psychologists, parents, and educators.

Special Education Exchange
http://www.spedex.com/main_graphics.htm

SpEdEx, as this site is more commonly known, offers a wealth of information, links, and resources to everyone interested in special education.

Special Education News
http://www.specialednews.com/disabilities/disabnews/povanddisab031200.html

This particular section of this site discusses the problems of coping with both poverty and disability. Explore the rest of the site also for information for educators on behavior management, conflict resolution, early intervention, specific disabilities, and much more.

UNIT 1: Inclusive Education

Institute on Disability/University of New Hampshire
http://iod.unh.edu

This site includes Early Childhood, Inclusive Education, High School and Post-Secondary School, Community Living and Adult Life, Related Links, both state and national, and information on technology, health care, public policy, as well as leadership training and professional development.

Kids Together, Inc.
http://www.kidstogether.org

Based on the IDEA law about teaching children with disabilties in regular classrooms, this site contains all the information on inclusion you might need to know.

New Horizons for Learning
http://www.newhorizons.org

Based on the theory of inclusion, this site is filled with information on special needs inclusion, technology and learning, a brain lab, and much more, presented as floors in a building.

UNIT 2: Early Childhood

Division for Early Childhood
http://www.dec-sped.org

A division of the Council for Exceptional Children, the DEC advocates for the improvement of conditions of young children with special needs. Child development theory, programming data, parenting data, research, and links to other sites can be found on this site.

Institute on Community Integration Projects
http://ici.umn.edu/projectscenters/

Research projects related to early childhood and early intervention services for special education are described here.

National Academy for Child Development (NACD)
http://www.nacd.org

The NACD, an international organization, is dedicated to helping children and adults reach their full potential. Its home page presents links to various programs, research, and resources into such topics as learning disabilities, ADD/ADHD, brain injuries, autism, accelerated and gifted, and other similar topic areas.

Special Education Resources on the Internet (SERI)
http://seriweb.com

SERI offers helpful sites in all phases of special education in early childhood, including disabilities, mental retardation, behavior disorders, and autism.

UNIT 3: Learning Disabilities

Children and Adults With Attention Deficit/Hyperactivity Disorder (CHADD)
http://www.chadd.org

CHADD works to improve the lives of people with AD/HD through education, advocacy, and support, offering information that can be trusted. The site includes fact sheets, legislative information, research studies, and links.

The Instant Access Treasure Chest
http://www.fln.vcu.edu/ld/ld.html

Billed as the Foreign Language Teacher's Guide to Learning Disabilities, this site contains a very thorough list of resources for anyone interested in LD education issues.

Learning Disabilities Association of America (LDA)
http://www.ldanatl.org

The purpose of the LDA is to advance the education and general welfare of children of normal and potentially normal intelligence who show handicaps of a perceptual, conceptual, or coordinative nature.

Learning Disabilities Online
http://www.ldonline.org

This is a good source for information about all kinds of learning disabilities with links to other related material.

OHSU Center on Self Determination
http://cdrc.ohsu.edu/selfdetermination/education/moving/ communitysolutions.html

The community solutions project described at this site focused on the unique needs of minority adolescents with disabilities as they transitioned from high school to adulthood.

Teaching Children With Attention Deficit Disorder
http://www.kidsource.com/kidsource/content2/add.html

This in-depth site defines both types of ADD and discusses establishing the proper learning environment.

UNIT 4: Speech and Language Impairments

Issues in Emergent Literacy for Children With Language Impairments
http://www.ciera.org/library/reports/inquiry-2/2-002/2-002.html

This article explores the relationship between oral language impairment and reading disabilities in children. The article suggests that language impairment may be a basic deficit that affects language function in both its oral and written forms.

Speech and Language Disorders Fact Sheet
http://www.nichcy.org/pubs/factshe/fs11txt.htm

This online publication of the National Dissemination Center for Children With Disabilities offers much useful information, including resources, organizations, and discussions of incidence, characteristics, educational implications, and how technology can help children with speech and language disorders.

Speech Disorders WWW Sites
http://www.socialnet.lu/handitel/wwwlinks/dumb.html

A thorough collection of Web sites, plus an article on the relationship between form and function in the speech of specifically language-impaired children, may be accessed here.

UNIT 5: Developmental Disabilities

Arc of the United States
http://www.thearc.org

Here is the Web site of the national organization of and for people with mental retardation and related disabilities and their families. It includes governmental affairs, services, position statements, FAQs, publications, and related links.

Disability-Related Sources on the Web
http://www.arcarizona.org/dislnkin.html

This resource's many links include grant resources, federally funded projects and federal agencies, assistive technology, national and international organizations, and educational resources and directories.

Gentle Teaching
http://www.gentleteaching.nl

Maintained by the foundation for Gentle Teaching in the Netherlands, this page explains a nonviolent approach for helping children and adults with special needs.

UNIT 6: Emotional and Behavioral Disorders

Educating Students With Emotional/Behavioral Disorders
http://www.nichcy.org/pubs/bibliog/bib10txt.htm

Excellent bibliographical and video information dealing with the education of children with emotional and/or behavioral disorders is available at this site.

Pacer Center: Emotional Behavioral Disorders
http://www.pacer.org/ebd/

Active in Minnesota for 8 years in helping parents become advocates for their EBD children, PACER has gone on to present workshops for parents on how to access aid for their child, explain what a parent should look for in a child they suspect of EBD, prepare a behavioral intervention guide, and link to resources, including IDEA's Parnership in Education site, and much more./

UNIT 7: Vision and Hearing Impairments

Info to Go: Laurent Clerc National Deaf Education Center
http://clerccenter.gallaudet.edu/InfoToGo/index.html

Important for parents and educators, this Web site from Gallaudet University offers information on audiology, communication, education, legal, and health issues of deaf people.

The New York Institute for Special Education
http://www.nyise.org/index.html

This school is an educational facility that serves children who are blind or visually impaired. The site includes program descriptions and resources for the blind.

UNIT 8: Multiple Disabilities

Activity Ideas for Students With Severe, Profound, or Multiple Disabilities
http://www.palaestra.com/featurestory.html

The Fall 1997 issue of the *Palaestra* contains this interesting article on teaching students who have multiple disabilities. The complete text is offered here online.

Severe and/or Multiple Disabilities
http://www.nichcy.org/pubs/factshe/fs10txt.htm

This fact sheet offers a definition of multiple disabilities, discusses incidence, characteristics, medical, and educational implications, and suggests resources and organizations that might be of help to parents and educators of children with severe impairments.

UNIT 9: Orthopedic and Health Impairments

Association to Benefit Children (ABC)
http://www.a-b-c.org

ABC presents a network of programs that includes child advocacy, education for disabled children, care for HIV-positive children, employment, housing, foster care, and day care.

An Idea Whose Time Has Come
http://www.boggscenter.org/mich3899.htm

The purpose of community-based education is to help students in special education to become more independent. Here is an excellent description of how it is being done in at least one community.

Resources for VE Teachers
http://www.cpt.fsu.edu/tree//ve/tofc.html

Effective practices for teachers of varying exceptionalities (VE) classes are listed here.

UNIT 10: Giftedness

The Council for Exceptional Children
http://www.cec.sped.org/index.html

This page will give you access to information on identifying and teaching gifted children, attention-deficit disorders, and other topics in gifted education.

National Association for Gifted Children (NAGC)
http://www.nagc.org/home00.htm

NAGC, a national nonprofit organization for gifted children, is dedicated to developing their high potential.

UNIT 11: Transition

National Center on Secondary Education and Transition
http://www.ncset.org

This site coordinates national resources, offers technical assistance, and disseminates information related to secondary education and transition for youth with disabilities in order to create opportunities for youth to achieve successful futures.

We highly recommend that you review our Web site for expanded information and our other product lines. We are continually updating and adding links to our Web site in order to offer you the most usable and useful information that will support and expand the value of your Annual Editions. You can reach us at: *http://www.dushkin.com/annualeditions/.*

UNIT 1

Inclusive Education

Unit Selections

1. **Standards for Diverse Learners**, Paula Kluth and Diana Straut
2. **Trends in the Special Education Teaching Force: Do They Reflect Legislative Mandates and Legal Requirements?**, Elizabeth Whitten and Liliana Rodriguez-Campos
3. **Attitudes of Elementary School Principals Toward the Inclusion of Students With Disabilities**, Cindy L. Praisner
4. **An Interview With Dr. Marilyn Friend**, Mary T. Brownell and Chriss Walther-Thomas

Key Points to Consider

- What conditions are needed to teach using a standards-based curriculum?

- How have professional teaching preparation practices been altered by IDEA?

- Why do the majority of school principals still have negative feelings about inclusive education?

- How important is collaboration between regular education and special education teachers?

 **Links: www.dushkin.com/online/**
These sites are annotated in the World Wide Web pages.

Institute on Disability/University of New Hampshire
  http://iod.unh.edu
Kids Together, Inc.
  http://www.kidstogether.org
New Horizons for Learning
  http://www.newhorizons.org

A huge strength of American schools is the dedication and motivation of its professional teachers. Weaknesses include inadequate social, emotional, and financial support, provision of more inservice education, and the wherewithal for continuing education. Teachers need all the help they can get, to be the best they can possibly be, and to feel appreciated!

This unit on Inclusive Education highlights what's good in special education, and includes some suggestions for ways it can be improved.

Regular education teachers are expected to know how to provide special educational services to every child with an exceptional condition in their classroom, despite not having had course work in special education. The numbers of students with exceptionalities who are being educated in regular education classes are increasing annually. During its 28 years in existence, the Individuals with Disabilities Education Act (IDEA) has reduced the numbers of special needs students being educated in residential centers, hospitals, homes, or special schools to less than 5 percent. Children who once would have been turned away from public schools are now being admitted in enormous numbers. Without adequate preparation and support, regular education teachers feel overwhelmed. Their abilities to educate all of their students, those with and those without disabilities, suffer grave consequences.

The trend toward inclusive education necessitates more knowledge and expertise on the part of all regular education teachers. Educating children with exceptionalities can no longer be viewed as the job of special-education teachers. This trend also mandates knowledge about collaboration and advisory activities on the part of all special educators. Teamwork is essential as special education and regular education are becoming more and more intertwined.

Public schools have an obligation to provide free educational services in the least restrictive environment possible to all children who have diagnosed conditions of exceptionality. Although laws in Canada and the United States differ slightly, all public schools have an obligation to serve children with exceptional conditions in as normal an educational environment as possible. Inclusive education is difficult. It works very well for some students with exceptionalities in some situations and marginally or not at all for other students with exceptionalities in other situations.

For inclusion to succeed within a school, everyone must be committed to be part of the solution: superintendent, principal, teachers, coaches, aides, ancillary staff, students, parents, and families. Special education teachers often find their jobs involving much more than instructing students with special needs. They serve as consultants to regular education teachers to assure that inclusion is meaningful for their students. They collaborate with parents, administrators, support personnel, and community agencies as well as with regular education teachers. They plan curriculum and oversee the writing of Individualized Family Service Plans (IFSPs), Individualized Education Plans (IEPs), and Individualized Transition Plans (ITPs). They schedule and make sure that services are provided by all team-involved persons. They keep up with enormous amounts of paperwork. They update parents even when parents are too involved, or not involved enough. They keep abreast of new resources, new legal processes, and new instructional techniques. They make projections for the futures of their students and set out ways to make good things happen. They also struggle to be accountable, both educationally and financially, for all they do.

The term "least restrictive environment" is often mistakenly understood as the need for all children to be educated in a regular education classroom. If students can learn and achieve better in inclusive programs, then they belong there. If students can succeed only marginally in inclusive education classrooms, some alternate solutions are necessary. A continuum of placement options exists to maximize the goal of educating every child. For some children, a separate class, or even a separate school, is still optimal.

Every child with an exceptional condition is different from every other child in symptoms, needs, and teachability. Each child is, therefore, provided with a unique individualized education plan. This plan consists of both long- and short-term goals for education, specially designed instructional procedures with re-

lated services, and methods to evaluate the child's progress. The IEP is updated and revised annually. Special education teachers, parents, and all applicable service providers must collaborate at least this often to make recommendations for goals and teaching strategies. The IEPs should always be outcome-oriented with functional curricula.

The first article in this unit discusses standards-based curriculum. The inclusion education movement has contributed to some very diverse classroom climates, where standards-based curricula must be flexible and developmental. There is no longer such a thing as a "grade" where one lesson-plan fits all, even in rural areas. Teaching to standards requires careful assessments, access to different levels of meaningful content, and assistance from all stakeholders in education—parents, teachers, and community members.

The second selection, "Trends in the Special Education Teaching Force," describes the changes in preparation of teachers between 1987 and 2000 to comply with the demands of IDEA and its aftermath.

The third article reports how school principals feel towards students with disabilities. A principal has prime responsibility for a school. The title's ending "pal" suggests a friendship. A principle (ending ple) is a basic truth or an ethical standard. Should a principal of a principled school show favoritism towards students who are easy to educate? Can leaders be intolerant of some of the persons over whom they have charge?

The last selection in this Inclusion Unit is an interview with an expert on inclusive education for students with disabilities. Dr. Marilyn Friend discusses what it takes to make collaboration of regular education and special education work. She answers questions about the challenges as well as the resources for success.

Standards for Diverse Learners

*Standards-based lessons create rich and challenging
learning experiences for all students.*

Paula Kluth and Diana Straut

Education standards receive much attention these days from political leaders, parents, and educators. Many of these stakeholders are concerned about what the standards movement means for the pluralistic classroom.

What kind of diversity exists in U.S. classrooms? Every kind.

- Students are no longer either Catholic, Jew, or Protestant; in fact, the fastest growing religion in the United States is Islam (Hodgkinson, 1998).

- Most of the 5.3 million U.S. students with disabilities spend some part of their day in classes with nondisabled students (Kaye, 1997).

- By 1995, bilingual programs were operating in nearly 200 U.S. schools (Rethinking Schools, 1998).

- At least one-third of the school-aged population in the United States is nonwhite (Marlowe & Page, 1999).

- 43 million people in the United States move every year (Hodgkinson, 1998), creating an increasingly mobile student population.

In addition, trends such as multicultural education, antitracking pedagogy, inclusive education, dual bilingual programs, magnet schools, and multi-age classrooms are contributing to the rich diversity of U.S. schools.

The standards movement will have little meaning if it cannot respond to the needs of all these students. Can we develop standards *and* make curriculum, instruction, and assessment responsive to learning differences?

Five Conditions

Doing so is not only possible, but vitally important; every student must be able to participate in standards-based education. To make standards inclusive, however, educators must support and cultivate five conditions.

- *Standards are developmental and flexible.* Standards should not be a one-size-fits-all approach to education. A student cannot and should not be expected to know and do exactly the same things as his or her peers. Developmental and flexible standards provide different students in the same classroom with opportunities to work on a range of concepts and skills according to individual abilities, needs, and interests (Reigeluth, 1997).

By adopting a personalized approach, teachers can use standards to "allow a range of acceptable performance" so that

> all students may continue to work toward student-outcome goals such as graduation or literacy, but within each goal area knowledge and skill standards may vary based on student-ability levels. (Geenen & Ysseldyke, 1997, p. 222)

For example, students can share how to solve an arithmetic problem in many ways. Some students may use sign language or communication boards to show understanding, others may write a paragraph explaining the process, and still others may express their knowledge through drawings. In addition, students in the same classroom can focus on problems that range in complexity, with some students describing the process for reducing fractions and others designing and explaining binomial equations.

To teach standards effectively in a diverse classroom, educators need to adapt the curriculum to meet the individual needs of learners and make alternatives available for instructional materials, teaching strategies, curricular goals, learning environments, instructional arrangements, and lesson formats (Udvari-Solner, 1996). For example, some students might use protractors and a compass to study obtuse and acute angles, whereas others may need to use a geometry software program. Experiential projects that encourage vocalizing and moving can meet the needs of active students who like to get out of their seats, investigate problems, and manipulate materials.

Some teachers believe that implementing adaptations in a standards-based classroom will diminish curriculum and instruction. The opposite is true. Creative adaptations can make curriculum more relevant, make abstract concepts more concrete, and connect the instructor's teaching style more effectively to students' different learning styles (Udvari-Solner, 1996). The following lesson illustrates how rich and challenging standards-based lessons can be for students with various learning profiles.

> Mr. Lee drafted daily lessons based on the standards he was teaching. For example, Mr. Lee decided to read every other chapter of [a historical novel] aloud to the students. They would read the opposite chapters in partners. He also decided to use learning centers with cooperative groups. Each center focused on an aspect of World War II and engaged students via one of the multiple learning styles. For example, one

of the centers involved journal writing, based on actual diaries from the Holocaust. Another center focused on geography and involved mapping the progress of war based on listening to actual radio broadcasts recorded during World War II. (Fisher & Roach, 1999, p. 18)

Mr. Lee's careful planning and conscientious design of the curriculum and instruction invites all learners to participate in an engaging and age-appropriate curriculum and also responds to a variety of learning styles. Mr. Lee's classroom does not expect one size to fit all students.

- *Standards require a wide range of assessment tools.* Professional literature and the popular media have linked standards with high-stakes testing. Standards and testing, however, are not the same. Educators must separate testing from the standards in conversations, in the design of curriculum, and in classroom instruction.

We believe that high-stakes assessment models are harmful and exclusive. Under the guise of accountability, several U.S. states and some individual school districts have implemented standardized testing programs that sort, eliminate, or stratify students from kindergarten through 12th grade. When students struggle with standardized tests, we only find out that they cannot perform effectively with such an assessment tool. When students do achieve high test scores, we do not necessarily know that they have learned more, learned better, or become more skilled or knowledgeable. These tests provide plenty of information about how skilled students are at taking standardized tests on a given day, but the tests do not provide much information about whether students have actually met the standards.

Standards do need some type of consistent and comprehensive assessment system, however. The most effective way to gather information about what students know and are able to do is to use a range of data collection strategies, including portfolios, interviews, observations, anecdotal records, self-evaluation questionnaires, journals, and learning logs (Lopez-Reyna & Bay, 1997; Pike & Salend, 1995). Students charged with explaining the ideas embodied in the Declaration of Independence, for example, could demonstrate their understanding by interviewing a peer, participating in a group skit, or writing an essay on the topic.

Kentucky has resisted high-stakes testing and has found a way to include all students in the formal assessment process (Kearns, Kleinert, & Kennedy, 1999). Most students in Kentucky undergo both traditional and alternative assessments. Students with significant disabilities participate in the statewide assessment by working on alternative portfolios that are tailored to their needs and strengths. Kentucky designed this range of assessments because many students struggle with traditional assessments and, more important, because a reliance on one kind of assessment does not provide a meaningful analysis of any student's abilities or progress.

In contrast to standardized measures, authentic assessments offer a fuller picture of student learning because they relate directly to what students are learning, are continuous and cumulative, occur during actual learning experiences, are collaborative, and clearly communicate proficiency to all stakeholders (Pike, Compain, & Mumper, 1994; Pike & Salend, 1995; Valencia, 1990). And because standards ask students to perform a range of competencies, we need a range of assessments to measure the learning of these competencies.

- *Standards allow equitable access to meaningful content.* If there were some alternative to standards that could ensure that all students—regardless of learning profile, race, ethnicity, or proficiency in English—had access to challenging academic content, then perhaps we could dismiss the standards movement. The truth is that we have not done a good job of giving all students—particularly those students with unique learning characteristics—access to an appealing, thought-provoking, and stimulating curriculum.

For example, Reese, a student with significant disabilities, works in an inclusive general education 4th grade classroom. While the general education students work in small groups to investigate fossils, Reese sits in the corner of the classroom and completes a counting worksheet with a paraprofessional.

Had Reese been expected to participate in a standards-based curriculum, he could be meeting his individual goals of "interacting appropriately with peers" and "classifying objects by at least three different characteristics." At the same time, he would have the opportunity to use interesting materials, work with peers, and learn about geography and history. Sorting fossils into categories or building a model di-

nosaur with a cooperative group would be both more meaningful and more content-based than filling in a worksheet that taught no science and did nothing to include Reese in the classroom community.

A set of standards, articulated across the state or district, can give parents, teachers, and administrators a common language for talking about student goals and progress. More crucial, attention to a set of common outcomes can serve as a challenge to view students as capable and to respect them with an appropriately rigorous curriculum.

- *It takes a community to implement standards.* Teaching to the standards is part of classroom teachers' responsibilities, but it is not their job alone. Teachers should receive assistance from all stakeholders in the school and community.

Collaboration among general and special educators can provide students with more opportunities to address the standards and to practice related skills. All students benefit from the different teaching approaches, instructional styles, and perspectives offered by two or more educators working in the same classroom (Cook & Friend, 1995).

The standards movement can provide teachers with a compass for crafting a rich curriculum and appropriate instruction.

Teaming across classrooms can also bring students closer to mastering the standards. For example, one physical education teacher helps kindergarten students recognize shapes by asking students to name the shapes of tumbling mats, hula-hoops, and floor scooters. While students learn new skills like hopping, galloping, and following rules, they are also engaged in an impromptu, cross-curricular, standards-based lesson with almost no up-front planning from the classroom teacher.

Teachers are not the only adults who can support a standards-based curriculum. The school secretary, recess monitor, lunchroom aides, teaching assistants, and family visitors can help. In one school, a custodian practices spelling words with students as they wait in line for lunch. Imagine the benefit of this fun exchange.

Students, the most important stakeholders in the standards movement, often know the least about implementing standards. Teachers should share information about standards in ways that students can understand; students are more likely to hit targets when they can see them (Strong, Silver, & Perini, 1999). Acting as allies in their own learning, students can develop personal strategies for meeting standards, and older students can even assist in developing standards-based lessons.

• *Standards are a catalyst for other reforms.* Some proponents of standards market them as the savior of public education, and many hope that this singular initiative will solve a wide range of educational and societal ills. At the same time, misconceptions about standards—as one-size-fits all, inequitable monsters that subject students and teachers to high-stakes tests—are creating a backlash that could reduce educators' commitment to designing learning opportunities for all students.

Standards are not the only route to educational excellence, but they can help us address the most pressing issues that stand in the way of students having a quality educational experience. For standards to work, schools need caring learning communities; skilled and responsive teachers; adequate financial, human, and material resources; effective partnerships with families; and concerned and visionary leadership. The standards movement should motivate political leaders to work for increased funding, smaller class sizes, better staff development opportunities, increased teacher planning time, and more social supports in schools, such as counselors and family liaisons.

The standards movement can provide teachers with a compass for crafting a rich curriculum and appropriate instruction, offering new opportunities and setting high expectations for all students in the multicultural, heterogeneous, dynamic classrooms of the 21st century.

References

Cook, L., & Friend, M. (1995). Coteaching: Guidelines for creating effective practices. *Focus on Exceptional Children, 28*(3), 1–15.

Fisher, D., & Roach, V. (1999). *Opening doors: Connecting students to curriculum, classmates, and learning.* Colorado Springs, CO: PEAK Parent Center.

Geenen, K., & Ysseldyke, J. E. (1997). Educational standards and students with disabilities. *The Educational Forum, 61*(1), 220–229.

Hodgkinson, H. L. (1998). Demographics of diversity for the 21st century. *The Education Digest, 64*(1), 4–7.

Kaye, H. S. (1997). Education of children with disabilities. *Disability Statistics Abstracts, 19.* San Francisco: Disability Statistics Center.

Kearns, J. F., Kleinert, H. L., & Kennedy, S. (1999). We need not exclude anyone. *Educational Leadership, 56*(6), 33–38.

Lopez-Reyna, N. A., & Bay, M. (1997). Enriching assessment: Using varied assessments for diverse learners. *Teaching Exceptional Children, 29*(4), 33–37.

Marlowe, B. A., & Page, M. L. (1999). Making the most of the classroom mosaic: A constructivist perspective. *Multicultural Education, 6*(4), 19–21.

Pike, K., Compain, R., & Mumper, J. (1994). *New connections: An integrated approach to literacy.* New York: Harper Collins.

Pike, K., & Salend, S. J. (1995). Authentic assessment strategies: Alternatives to norm-referenced testing. *Teaching Exceptional Children, 28*(1), 15–20.

Reigeluth, C. M. (1997). Educational standards: To standardize or to customize learning? *Phi Delta Kappan, 79*, 202–206.

Rethinking Schools. (1998). Number of language-minority students skyrockets. *Rethinking Schools Online, 12.* Milwaukee, WI: Rethinking Schools. Available: www.rethinkingschools.org/Archives/12_03/langsid.htm

Strong, R., Silver, H., & Perini, M. (1999). Keeping it simple and deep. *Educational Leadership, 56*(6). 22–24.

Udvari-Solner, A. (1996, July). Examining teacher thinking: Constructing a process to design curricular adaptations. *Remedial and Special Education, 17*, 245–254.

Valencia, S. (1990). A portfolio approach to classroom reading assessment: The why, whats, and hows. *The Reading Teacher, 43*(4), 338–340.

Authors' note: An expanded version of this article will appear in *Access to Academics for ALL Students* by P. Kluth, D. Straut, & D. Biklen (Eds.) (Mahwah, NJ: Lawrence Erlbaum Associates Publishers, in press).

Paula Kluth (pkluth@syr.edu) and **Diana Straut** (dmstraut@syr.edu) are Assistant Professors of Teaching and Leadership, Syracuse University, 150 Huntington Hall, Syracuse, NY 13244.

Trends in the Special Education Teaching Force: Do They Reflect Legislative Mandates and Legal Requirements?

by Elizabeth Whitten and Liliana Rodriquez-Campos

Introduction

Over the past decade several changes have evolved in special education teacher education, as well as reform movements throughout all aspects of the field of education, requiring appropriate and effective curriculum and instruction for students with disabilities in inclusive environments.[1] This type of movement has created the need to redefine the roles of special education teachers and prepare them to assume different roles. Although the Individuals with Disabilities Education Act (IDEA) of 1997 requires schools to include students with disabilities in the general education classroom to the maximum extent possible with appropriate support, teacher-preparation programs are struggling to keep up with the increasing need for special education teachers who reflect "best teaching practices" in educating students with disabilities. To be successful in least-restrictive settings, students need professionals prepared to provide the necessary support.[2] To meet these challenges teacher-preparation programs across the nation are modifying and redeveloping their programs.[3]

Although many researchers have made observations and predictions regarding the trends for special education in the next century, this article, based on a national survey, investigated trends across the nation in the special education teaching force.[4] The survey was administered in four waves (1987–88, 1990–91, 1993–94, and 1999–2000). The data were analyzed to determine if there were specific trends in the special education teacher population over the past decade. The identified trends include type of teaching assignments, diversity, training, certification, service delivery, and collaboration among personnel.

Teaching Assignment. Educational trends in special education teaching assignments reflect current legislation mandating inclusive education. An increasing number of students with disabilities are receiving their education in the general education classroom.[5] Teaching in isolation is rapidly coming to a close, and general education teachers are finding more and more students with disabilities in their classrooms for a larger portion of the day.[6] Special education teachers find themselves less often in segregated classrooms and more frequently in support roles to the general education classroom and teacher. Inclusive service-delivery models have been credited with decreasing the number of special education referrals.[7] If this trend continues, fewer students will be identified with disabilities because their needs will be met in the general education setting with special education support.

Teacher Diversity. The diversity in today's classroom is steadily increasing.[8] African, Hispanic, and Asian Americans comprise one-third of the U.S. population, and one-third of total school enrollment will be culturally diverse as well.[9] Substantial evidence shows overrepresentation of racial and ethnic groups in special education. Harry found a higher percentage of African American, Hispanic, and Asian American students in special education than in general education.[10] Regardless of student diversity in special education, the vast majority of special education teachers are Anglo American and speak only English.[11] In 1995 the percentage (14%) of special education teachers representing diverse backgrounds was less than half the percentage (32%) representing the diversity of students receiving special education services.[12] One of the barriers to addressing the needs of multicultural students receiving special education services is the lack of multicultural special education teachers.[13] Teachers from diverse cultural backgrounds provide students of diversity with role models as well as translators. Thus, special education personnel preparation programs will ideally recruit more teachers from culturally diverse backgrounds to provide students of diversity with an "intercultural understanding and communication."[14]

Teacher Preparation. Given the increasing demand for special education teachers, personnel preparation programs have found it necessary to intensify their use of time and resources. As a result many alternative programs now encourage teachers to complete certification requirements while they are employed, and distance education personnel preparation programs are available for teachers living in remote areas.[15] Such innovative preparation programs have increased the number of degrees and certified special education teachers and will most likely continue to provide career opportunities for potential special education teachers. Such programs include those operating at the University of West Virginia, the University of Kentucky, Fayetteville State University, the University of North Carolina, and Western Michigan University.[16]

Service Delivery. For many decades students with disabilities have received educational instruction in segregated settings, ranging from self-contained classrooms to resource rooms. The underlying assumption for specialized instruction has been that students with disabilities cannot be successfully instructed in the general education classroom, even with appropriate support.[17] Federal mandates, however, require schools to include students with disabilities in instruction with their nondisabled peers to the maximum extent possible.[18] Several researchers have found that teachers are not adequately prepared for inclusion.[19] Additionally, general and special education teachers are not certain of their roles in fully including students with disabilities. As a result the trends do not reflect the demands of federal laws mandating inclusive environments for students with disabilities. Lombardi and Ludlow suggest that special education may be the answer to many of our school problems.[20] Individual instruction significantly reduces documented school problems such as truancy, behavior problems, and low student achievement.[21] Teachers and teacher educators will need preparation and retooling to stay abreast of the needed changes in service delivery.

Collaboration among Personnel. Educators face significant challenges in today's diverse classroom.[22] To meet the educational needs of students with disabilities and those at risk academically or behaviorally, educators need to collaborate and to share their expertise. Collaborative skills require training and practice. Teacher preparation programs in general education typically require pre-service teachers to take a three-credit course on working with students with disabilities, and such a course does not involve preparation in collaboration or teaming.[23] Nevertheless, most general educators are teaching students with disabilities with minimal or no special education support in their classrooms.[24] General education teachers are well aware of the traditional practice of pulling students with disabilities from the general education classroom and providing them instruction in a segregated classroom with special education teachers. General educators are now expected to accept these same students into their classroom without receiving adequate preparation on how to instruct them or how to collaborate with support personnel. Nevertheless, special education teachers are expected to provide supportive services to general education so that students with disabilities can be successfully included in general education classrooms. Likewise, special education teachers infrequently have training in collaboration that would allow them to provide supportive services.

Purpose of the Study. This study of four waves of surveys conducted by the NCES describes how the characteristics of the special education (SPED) teaching force have evolved over the years. The details of the survey will be explained below. The survey data collected by NCES offer an excellent opportunity for determining whether the trend characteristics of SPED teachers are aligning with federal legislation regarding students with disabilities.

Sample, Data Source, and Weighting. The data for this study were extracted from the Schools and Staffing Survey (SASS) conducted by the NCES. The SASS is a national survey of school principals, schoolteachers, and local educational authorities. Given the nature of this article, the study used data collected from special educators who worked in public schools.

The data were analyzed from four SASS surveys conducted in 1987–88, 1990–91, 1993–94, and 1999–2000. Therefore, this study is a particular kind of longitudinal study called a *trend study.* In other words, by analyzing the national data from four rounds of the survey, we are able to discuss the trend of the relationship between the rhetoric and reality related to expectations for SPED teachers.

Actual and weighted samples for regular and special education teachers are shown in Table 1. The actual sample sizes of SPED teachers were 4,307 for SASS 1987–88; 5,054 for SASS 1990–91; 5,288 for SASS 1993–94; and 4,753 for SASS 1999–2000. Again, the subsamples of SPED teachers were not representative; hence, weights were applied in order for weighted samples to be representative of SPED teachers at the national level. As a result, the weighted samples of SPED teachers were 239,786 for SASS 1987–88; 273,956 for SASS 1990–91; 270,101 for SASS 1993–94; and 329,167 for SASS 1999–2000.

Results: Teaching Assignment. Data related to the special educator's current teaching assignment and school level are displayed in Table 2. The SPED teachers assigned to teach students with learning disabilities have shown the highest percentage throughout the years studied in this article. However, this percentage dipped from 47.3 in 1987–88 to 27.4 in 1990–91 to 27.2 in 1993–94, and then rose again to 28.9 in 1999–2000. Between the 1987–88 and 1999–2000 school years, the percentage of special educators assigned to teach students with mental retardation decreased from 19.4 to 6.3. The percentage of special educators assigned to teach students with emotional disturbance dipped from 9.4 in 1987–88 to 6.7 in 1993–94, and then rose to 8.6 in 1999–2000. For teachers assigned to work with speech- or hearing-impaired students, the percentage decreased from 12 in 1987–88 to 7.3 in 1993–94, and then increased to 8.7 in 1999–2000. The percentage of special educators assigned to teach general special education rose from 29.6 in 1990–91 to 33.6 in 1993–94 and decreased to 31.7 in 1999–2000. Furthermore, the percentage of special educators assigned to teach other types of special education options decreased from 11.9 in 1987–88 to 3.5 in 1999–2000.

Teacher Diversity. The longitudinal national data displayed in Table 3 indicate that the population of special

Table 1
Actual and weighted sample sizes:
A comparison across 1987–88, 1990–91, 1993–94, and 1999–2000

	1987–88		1990–91		1993–94		1999–2000	
	Regular	SPED	Regular	SPED	Regular	SPED	Regular	SPED
Actual sample	40,593	4,307	46,705	5,054	47,105	5,288	42,086	4,753
Weighted sample	2,323,204	239,786	2,559,488	273,956	2,561,293	270,101	2,984,781	329,167

Table 2
Special education teaching assignment:
A comparison across 1987–88, 1990–91, 1993–94, and 1999–2000 (in percentages)

	1987–88	1990–91	1993–94	1999–2000[3]
Current teaching assignment				
Learning disabilities[1]	47.3	27.4	27.2	28.9
Mental retardation	19.4	9.8	9.5	6.3
Emotional disturbance	9.4	8.3	6.7	8.6
Speech and hearing impairment[2]	12.0	8.7	7.3	8.7
Special education, general	NA	29.6	33.6	31.7
Deaf and hard-of-hearing	NA	2.3	2.1	1.2
Visually handicapped	NA	1.0	0.6	0.2
Orthopedically impaired	NA	1.0	0.5	0.4
Mildly handicapped	NA	2.2	2.8	5.0
Severely handicapped	NA	3.1	2.4	2.3
Autism	NA	NA	NA	1.0
Developmentally delayed	NA	NA	NA	0.9
Early childhood special education	NA	NA	NA	1.2
Traumatically brain-injured	NA	NA	NA	0.0
Other special education	11.9	6.7	7.3	3.5
Total	100.0	100.0	100.0	100.0
School level[4]				
Pre-kindergarten	13.5	16.5	5.9	4.6
Elementary	76.4	77.3	47.8	48.0
Middle/junior high	57.2	60.1	42.0	35.3
Senior high	43.3	49.5	29.2	28.1

[1] For the years 1987–88 and 1999–2000, this item was called "Learning disabled." However, for the years 1990–91 and 1993–94, this item was called "Specific learning disabilities."

[2] For the years 1987–88 and 1999–2000, this item was called "Speech and hearing impairment." However, for the years 1990–91 and 1993–94, this item was called "Speech/Language impaired."

[3] For the years 1999–2000 the term "Visually handicapped" was called "Visually impaired," the term "Mildly handicapped" was called "Mildly/moderately disabled," and term "Severely handicapped" was called "Severely/profoundly disabled."

[4] Since it is possible for a respondent to check two or more options (e.g., both kindergarten and elementary), the total percentage across the four school levels do total more than 100%.

educators has become more diversified by race. Therefore, the results reveal the general expectation that educators should reflect the increasingly diversified student population. Specifically, the data indicate an increasingly higher percentage of minority special educators in our schools. Accordingly, special educators of Hispanic origin showed the highest percentage of increase, from 2.2 in 1987–88 to 3.8 in 1999–2000. This increase was small in comparison to the expectation and the trend of diversity in student body.

Between the 1987–88 and 1999–2000 school years, the percentage of Asian or Pacific Islander special educators rose from 0.9 to 1.5. The combination of special educators who are American Indian, Aleut, or Eskimo first dipped in percentage from 1.2 in 1987–88 to 0.7 in 1990–91 and then rose to 1.3 in 1999–2000. However, the percentage of black special educators increased from 9.5 in 1987–88 to 9.6 in 1990–91 and then decreased to 9.2 in 1999–2000. Furthermore, the percentage of special educators of white origin rose from 88.4 in 1987–88 to 89.9 in 1993–94, and

Table 3

Special education teacher diversity:
A comparison across 1987–88, 1990–91, 1993–94, and 1999–2000 (in percentages)

	1987–88	1990–91	1993–94	1999–2000
Race				
Asian or Pacific Islander	0.9	1.0	1.0	1.5
American Indian, Aleut, Eskimo	1.2	0.7	0.8	1.3
Black	9.5	9.6	8.2	9.2
White	88.4	88.7	89.9	88.0
Hispanic origin				
Yes	2.2	2.5	3.2	3.8
No	97.8	97.5	96.8	96.2

Table 4

Special education teacher preparation:
A comparison across 1987–88, 1990–91, 1993–94, and 1999–2000 (in percentages)

	1987–88	1990–91	1993–94	1999–2000
Educational attainment by SPED teachers				
Bachelor's degree	99.8	99.9	99.3	99.7
Master's degree	54.1	55.6	54.0	53.9
Ed. specialist/professional diploma	10.3	7.8	7.5	4.7
Doctorate degree	0.6	1.2	1.0	0.5
Concentration in SPED				
Major	41.5	44.5	43.1	42.7
Minor	18.0	18.9	8.1	7.4
Certification	97.1	96.0	96.5	93.3

decreased to 88 in 1999–2000. In summary, the data on race show that the population of SPED teachers has become slightly more diversified.

Teacher Preparation. The results shown in Table 4 indicate that SPED teachers are a highly educated group. Between the 1987–88 and 1999–2000 school years, more than 99% of the population of special educators had earned bachelor's degrees. The percentage of special educators who had master's degrees rose from 54.1 in 1987–88 to 55.6 in 1990–91 and decreased to 54 in 1993–94 to 53.9 in 1999–2000. In addition, results show that the percentage of special educators who have educational specialist or professional diplomas decreased from 10.3 in 1987–88 to 4.7 in 1999–2000. Furthermore, the percentage of special educators who have doctoral degrees rose from 0.6 in 1987–88 to 1.2 in 1990–91 and decreased to 0.5 in 1999–2000.

Between 1987–88 and 1999–2000 almost all the special educators had certification in the SPED field, although this percentage decreased from 97.1 to 93.3 (see Table 4). However, the percentage of special educators with a major in the SPED field rose from 41.5 in 1987–88 to 44.5 in 1990–91 and decreased to 43.1 in 1993–94 to 42.7 in 1999–2000. Furthermore, the percentage of special educators with a minor in the SPED field increased from 18 in 1987–

88 to 18.9 in 1990–91, and then decreased to 8.1 in 1993–94 to 7.4 in 1999–2000. While more than half the special education teachers did not identify majors in special education, the overwhelming majority holds state-level special education certification. This is due to the varying requirements regarding degrees and certifications held by each state and university.

Table 5 shows the types of certification held by special educators from the 1987–88 to the 1999–2000 school years. Particularly, the regular or standard state certification displayed the highest percentage across the years studied in this article. This percentage rose from 86.1 in 1987–88 to 86.9 in 1990–91 and decreased to 85 in 1999–2000. For temporary, provisional, or emergency certification, the percentage of special educators decreased from 7.5 in 1987–88 to 5.8 in 1999–2000. Additionally, the percentage of special educators with probationary certification increased from 3.2 in 1987–88 to 3.3 in 1990–91 and then decreased to 2.5 in 1999–2000.

Service Delivery. The results in Table 6 display service delivery for elementary and secondary special educators. For the elementary level, results show that the percentage of special educators in collaborative teaching classes rose from 2.0 in 1987–88 to 11.2 in 1993–94 and decreased to 8.5 in 1999–2000. The percentage of special ed-

Table 5

Type of certification held by special education teachers:
A comparison across 1987–88, 1990–91, 1993–94, and 1999–2000 (in percentages)

	1987–88	1990–91	1993–94	1999–2000
Type of certification				
Regular/standard state certification	86.1	86.9	86.1	85.0
Temporary/provisional/emergency certification	7.5	5.8	7.3	5.8
Probationary certification	3.2	3.3	1.8	2.5
Other	0.3	0.0	1.3	0.0
Missing	2.9	4.0	3.5	6.7
Total	100.0	100.0	100.0	100.0

Table 6

Special education teacher service delivery:
A comparison across 1987–88, 1990–91, 1993–94, and 1999–2000 (in percentages)

	1987–88	1990–91	1993–94	1999–2000
Elementary				
Collaborative teaching	2.0	4.1	11.2	8.5
Resource room or pull-out class	46.8	48.0	42.1	46.8
Departmentalized instruction	4.2	3.4	7.0	5.6
Self-contained class	47.0	43.6	38.9	38.4
Elementary enrichment class	NA	1.0	0.8	0.7
Total	100.0	100.0	100.0	100.0
Secondary				
Collaborative teaching	5.9	7.9	8.4	10.3
Resource room or pull-out class	19.3	24.9	22.0	23.9
Departmentalized instruction	37.5	33.8	35.6	39.4
Self-contained class	37.3	33.3	34.0	26.4
Elementary enrichment class	NA	0.1	0.1	NA
Total	100.0	100.0	100.0	100.0

ucators in resource rooms increased from 46.8 in 1987–88 to 48.0 in 1990–91 and then decreased to 46.8 in 1999–2000. The percentage of special educators in departmentalized instruction classes rose from 4.2 in 1987–88 to 7.0 in 1993–94 and decreased to 5.6 in 1999–2000. Furthermore, the percentage of special educators in self-contained classes decreased from 47.0 in 1987–88 to 38.4 in 1999–2000.

In service delivery for the secondary level, the results in Table 6 show that between the 1987–88 and 1999–2000 school years, the percentage of special educators in collaborative teaching classes rose from 5.9 to 10.3. Additionally, the percentage of special educators in resource rooms increased from 19.3 in 1987–88 to 23.9 in 1999–2000. On the other hand, the percentage of special educators in departmentalized instruction classes decreased from 37.5 in 1987–88 to 33.8 in 1990–91 and then increased to 39.4 in 1999–2000. Further, the percentage of special educators in self-contained classes dipped from 37.3 in 1987–88 to 26.4 in 1999–2000. Although the service-delivery options for students with disabilities reflect the legis-

lative changes toward inclusion, the data clearly show that schools are using separate settings for the majority of instruction to students with disabilities.

Collaboration among Personnel. Data in Table 7 indicate how special educators perceive collaborative efforts among personnel, as well as the shared beliefs and values among colleagues. Special educators were asked to rate their perceptions on a 4-point scale, with 1 meaning *strongly agree* and 4 meaning *strongly disagree*. Only the percentages of those who responded *strongly agree* were reported on the tally. In regard to collaborative efforts among personnel, the results show that special educators' positive perceptions on this issue went down for all three certifications. Specifically, for special educators with regular or standard state certifications, the percentage decreased from 30 in 1987–88 to 4.3 in 1999–2000. For special educators with a probationary certification, the percentage dipped from 1.2 in 1987–88 to 0.1 in 1999–2000. Furthermore, from the 1987–88 to the 1999–2000 school years, the percentage of special educators with temporary, provisional, or emergency certification decreased from 2.5 to 0.1.

Table 7

**Percentage of SPED teachers who strongly agreed that there was collaboration among staff:
A comparison across 1987–88, 1993–94, and 1999–2000**

	1987–88	1993–94	1999–2000
Collaborative effort among personnel			
Regular/standard state certification	30.0	22.0	4.3
Probationary certification	1.2	0.5	0.1
Temporary/provisional/emergency certification	2.5	1.2	0.1
Shared beliefs and values among colleagues			
Regular/standard state certification	28.3	20.0	3.0
Probationary certification	0.9	0.5	0.1
Temporary/provisional/emergency certification	1.9	0.8	0.1

In regard to shared beliefs and values among colleagues, the data indicate that special educators' positive perceptions on this issue also went down for teachers of all three types of certification. The percentage of special educators with regular or standard state certification decreased from 28.3 in 1987–88 to 3.0 in 1999–2000. For special educators with probationary certification, the percentage decreased from 0.9 in 1987–88 to 0.1 in 1999–2000. Furthermore, from 1987–88 to 1999–2000, the percentage of special educators with temporary, provisional, or emergency certification dipped from 1.9 to 0.1. This data indicate that with increased inclusion, collaboration between general education teachers and special education teachers is no longer merely an option. Teachers should be adequately prepared to engage in effective collaboration.

Conclusion

The data presented in the results section indicate that trends found in the special education teaching force in recent years reflect changes in federal mandates and society in general. Although the process of retooling our special education personnel preparation programs and preparing teachers in-service is slow and arduous, the data indicate movement toward more inclusive service delivery. The percentage of special education teachers in today's schools has increased while assigning teachers to specific disability areas has decreased. These data reflect that schools are taking a more noncategorical approach to meeting the needs of students with disabilities as well as those students at risk academically or behaviorally. Additionally, delivery of services to students with disabilities is more inclusive: higher percentages of students receive services in resource rooms than in any other situation, and collaborative teaching has increased while self-contained classrooms have decreased. Nevertheless, teachers are not responding favorably to the need to collaborate with other school staff, which may indicate the limited training they have received in collaboration as well as the additional time needed for effective collaboration.

Although the diversity of the special education teaching force has increased slightly, it has not equaled the diversity of the students receiving special education services. The data indicate an increase in Asian American and Eskimo teachers, with the highest increase in teachers of Hispanic origin. We cannot be satisfied with the current state of diversity in our multicultural special education teachers.

The overwhelming majority of special education teachers have bachelor's degrees and more than half hold master's degrees. Eighty-five percent report that they have special education certification, and only 6.1% are on temporary or probationary certification. These data are inconsistent with state reports of increased demand for qualified special education teachers.

In summary, the data of the study reveal predictable trends in the special education teaching force. Throughout the years, special education teachers have: (a) maintained high levels of educational attainment; (b) slightly increased the diversity of the teaching force; (c) moved to more inclusive teaching; (d) focused increasingly on individual instruction rather than disability; and (e) increased the need to engage in continuous collaboration with general education teachers. Educators should not be satisfied with the current state of special education until they have established a climate that seamlessly supports inclusive teaching, mulitculturalism, and collaboration among staff.

Notes

1. D. P. Britzman, "Teacher Education in the Confusion of Our Times," *Journal of Teacher Education* 51 (May/June 2000): 200–205.

2. Individuals with Disabilities Education Act (IDEA) of 1997, P.L. 105–17, 20, U.S.C. SS 1400 ed seq.

3. B. Bateman, "Learning Disabilities: The Changing Landscape," *Journal of Learning Disabilities* 25 (1992): 29–36; and C. Walter-Thomas, L. Korinek, V. McLauglin, and B. Williams, *Collaboration for Inclusive Education: Developing Successful Programs* (Needham Heights, Mass.: Allyn and Bacon, 2000).

4. T. P. Lombardi and B. L. Ludlow, *Trends Shaping the Future of Special Education* (Bloomington, Ind.: Phi Delta Kappa

Educational Foundation, 1996); J. McLeskey, D. Henry, and M. Axelrod, "Inclusion of Students with Learning Disabilities: An Examination of Data from Report to Congress," *Exceptional Children* 66 (1999): 55–66; and S. Vaughn, S. Moody, and J. Schulman, "Broken Promises: Reading Instruction in the Resource Room," *Exceptional Children* 64 (1998): 211–225.

5. U.S. Department of Education. *The Condition of Education 2000, in Brief* (Washington, D.C.: Author: 2001).

6. N. Reinhillar, "Co-teaching: New Variations on a Not-so-new Practice," *Teacher Education and Special Education* 19 (1996): 37–47.

7. Walter-Thomas et al., *Collaboration for Inclusive Education.*

8. G. Cartledge and S. A. Loe, "Cultural Diversity and Social Skill Instruction," *Exceptionally 9*, nos. 1 and 2 (2001): 33–46; and A. G. Leasvell, M. Cowart, and R. W. Wilhelm, "Strategies for Preparing Culturally Responsive Teachers," *Equity and Excellence in Education* 32 (1999): 64–71.

9. C. A. Utley, K. C. Delquadri, F. E. Obiakor, and V. A. Mims, "General and Special Educators' Strategies for Multicultural Students," *Teacher Education and Special Education* 23 (2000): 34–50.

10. B. Harry, "Making Sense of Disability: Low-income Puerto Rican Parents' Theories of the Problem." *Exceptional Children* 59 (1992): 27–40, and B. Harry, *The Disproportionate Representation of Minority Students in Special Education: Theories and Recommendations* (Alexandria, Va.: National Association of State Directors of Special Education, 1994).

11. Utley et al., "General and Special Educators' Strategies."

12. L. H. Cook and E. E. Boe, "Who Is Teaching Students with Disabilities?" *Teaching Exceptional Children* 28 (1995): 70–72.

13. Utley et al., "General and Special Educators' Strategies."

14. Ibid.

15. T. Berkeley and B. Ludlow, "Meeting the Needs of Special Student Populations in Rural Locales," in A. J. DeYoung (ed.), *Rural Education: Issues and Practice* (New York: Garland, 1991), and S. Howard, M. Ault, H. Knowlton, and R. Swall, "Distance Education: Promises and Cautions for Special Education," *Teacher Education and Special Education* 15 (1992): 275–283.

16. R. L. Ludlow and J. S. Platt, "Developing Practicum Supervision Skills in Colleague Teachers," in *Alternative Futures for Rural Special Education* (Proceedings of the National Rural Special Education Conference 1988) (ERIC Document Reproduction Service No. ED 299 749); D. Cross, B. Collins, and J. Schuster, *Training Rural Educators in Kentucky* (Lexington, Ky.: University of Kentucky, Department of Special Education, 1991); V. J. Dickens and C. J. Jones, "Regular/Special Education Consultation: A Teacher Education Training Strategy for Implementation," *Teacher Education and Special Education* 13 (1990): 221–224; E. Whitten and J. Dynak, *Transdisciplinary Collaboration Preparation Program* (Kalamazoo, Mich.: Western Michigan University, Department of Special Education, 1998); and W. Wiener and E. Whitten, *Visual Impairments and Orientation and Mobility Training Preparation Program* (Kalamazoo, Mich.: Western Michigan University, Department of Special Education and Department of Blind Rehabilitation, 2000).

17. M. Will, "Educating Children with Learning Problems: A Shared Responsibility," *Exceptional Children* 53 (1986): 411–415.

18. Individuals with Disabilities Education Act (IDEA) of 1997.

19. Britzman, "Teacher Education."

20. Lombardi and Ludlow, *"Trends Shaping the Future."*

21. T. P. Lombardi, D. L. Nuzzo, K. D. Kennedy, and J. Foshay, "Perceptions of Parents, Teachers, and Students Regarding an Integrated Education Inclusion Program," *High School Journal* 77 (April/May 1994): 161–168.

22. M. W. Bahr, E. Whitten, L. Dieker, C. E. Kocarek, and D. Manson, "A Comparison of School-Based Intervention Teams: Implications for Educational and Legal Reform," *Exceptional Children* 66 (1999): 67–83.

23. C. K. Ormsbee and K. D. Finson, "Modifying Science Activities and Materials to Enhance Instruction for Students with Learning and Behavior Problems" *Intervention in School and Clinic* 36, no. 1 (2000): 10–14.

24. R. Coombs-Richardson and J. Mead, "Supporting General Educators' Inclusive Practices," *Teacher Education and Special Education* 24 (2001): 383–390.

Elizabeth Whitten, Ph.D., is chair of the Department of Educational Studies and a faculty member in special education at Western Michigan University.

Liliana Rodríguez-Campos, Ph.D., is a faculty member in evaluation at Western Michigan University.

From *Educational Horizons*, Spring 2003, pp. 138-145. © 2003 by Elizabeth Whitten and Liliana Rodriguez-Campos. Reprinted by permission.

Attitudes of Elementary School Principals Toward the Inclusion of Students With Disabilities

CINDY L. PRAISNER
Educational Consultant

A survey of 408 elementary school principals was conducted to investigate relationships regarding attitudes toward inclusion, variables such as training and experience, and placement perceptions. Results indicate that about 1 in 5 principals' attitudes toward inclusion are positive while most are uncertain. Positive experiences with students with disabilities and exposure to special education concepts are associated with a more positive attitude toward inclusion. Further, principals with more positive attitudes and/or experiences are more likely to place students in less restrictive settings. Differences in placement and experiences were found between disability categories. Results emphasize the importance of inclusionary practices that give principals positive experiences with students of all types of disabilities as well as provide principals with more specific training.

Over the last 2 decades, inclusion has become a critical part of the reform effort to improve the delivery of services to students with disabilities by focusing on the placement of these students in the general education setting. In an inclusive school, general education does not relinquish responsibility for students with special needs, but instead, works cooperatively with special education to provide a quality program for all students. This new arrangement for providing services has created challenges for many education professionals including the principal.

The role of the school principal has been dramatically changed to include additional duties, personnel, and paperwork. Principals are now expected to design, lead, manage, and implement programs for all students including those with disabilities (Sage & Burrello, 1994). Administrators are called upon to:

promote visions and values, and to support and encourage positive action on the part of students, teachers, parents, and community members. Other new administrative roles include identifying and articulating the needs of inclusive schools and providing an important link between the schools and the larger community. (Falvey, 1995, p. 10)

For such whole-school reform, a principal's leadership is seen as the key factor to success (Hipp & Huffman, 2000). Therefore, to ensure the success of inclusion, it is important that principals exhibit behaviors that advance the integration, acceptance, and success of students with disabilities in general education classes.

According to Goodlad & Lovitt (1993), the decision to develop an inclusive school depends largely upon leaders' values and beliefs. Leaders demonstrate their beliefs and priorities by the following:

- How they make and honor commitments.

- What they say in formal and informal settings.

- What they express interest in and what questions they ask.

- Where they choose to go and with whom they spend time.

- When they choose to act and how they make their actions known.

- How they organize their staff and their physical surroundings (Nanus, 1992, pp. 139-140).

As the leader in the school, the principal directly influences "resource allocations, staffing, structures, information flows, and operating processes that determine what shall and shall not be done by the organization" (Nanus, 1992, p. 142). Due to their leadership position, principals' attitudes about inclusion could result in either increased opportunities for students to be served in general education or in limited efforts to reduce the segregated nature of special education services. Therefore for inclusion to be successful, first and foremost, the school administrator must display a positive attitude and commitment to inclusion (Evans, Bird, Ford, Green, & Bischoff, 1992; Rude & Anderson, 1992).

... to ensure the success of inclusion, it is important that principals exhibit behaviors that advance the integration, acceptance, and success of students with disabilities in general education classes.

Although there has been some research and discussion regarding the importance of principals' attitudes toward inclusion, there is very little that identifies the present state of those attitudes. There is even less research that attempts to identify the influences that develop attitudes toward inclusion or determine the impact principals' attitudes have on placement perceptions. The earlier studies are also complicated by mixed groups, low numbers, unclear or outdated definitions, and small geographic area representation. This study (Praisner, 2000) was conducted to provide additional research, specifically focusing on principals and inclusion, using a more current definition and conceptual framework. Three research questions guided this study:

1. What are the attitudes of elementary principals toward the inclusion of students with severe/profound disabilities in the general education setting?

2. What is the relationship between principals' personal characteristics, training, experience and/or school characteristics and their attitudes toward inclusion?

3. What is the relationship between principals' perceptions of appropriate placements for students with different types of disabilities and their attitudes and experiences?

METHODOLOGY

SAMPLE

The sample consisted of 408 elementary school principals randomly selected from the Commonwealth of Pennsylvania. They represented schools that enrolled elementary-level students only, normally grades kindergarten through 6. The schools were of varying sizes ranging from less than 250 to over 1,000 students, and the average class size ranged from 10 to over 40. Most schools (47.1%) identified between 6%-10% of the student body as students with disabilities and represented varying degrees of inclusion.

INSTRUMENT

The Principals and Inclusion Survey (PIS) was designed to determine the extent to which variables such as training, experience, and program factors were related to principals' attitudes. Additionally, the impact of those attitudes on perceived most appropriate placements for students with disabilities was measured. The PIS has four sections: (a) demographics, (b) training and experience, (c) attitudes toward inclusion, and (d) principal beliefs about most appropriate placements. (A copy of the survey is available from the author.)

The demographics of the school were measured in Section I. Two questions addressing the school included the number of all students in the building and the average class size. Additionally, two questions focusing on students with disabilities included the approximate percentage of students with individualized education programs (IEPs) in the building (excluding gifted), and the approximate number of students with IEPs in the building that are included in regular education classrooms for at least 75% of their school day (excluding gifted).

Section II had 13 questions designed to gather data on variables that could potentially influence a principal's attitude toward inclusion. Questions pertaining to the principal included (a) age, (b) gender, (c) years of full-time regular education teaching experience, (d) years of full-time special education teaching experience, (e) years as an elementary school principal, (f) number of special education credits in formal training, (g) number of inservice hours in inclusive practices, (h) certification in special education, (i) number of relevant content areas in formal training, and (j) personal experience with an individual with a disability outside school settings. Two program factors, existence of a mission statement that includes a vision for inclusion and a specific plan to deal with crisis involving students with special needs, were also included. To ensure the validity of this section, the content was based on a review of inclusion literature to identify those factors that might relate to education professionals' attitudes toward inclusion. Additionally, a panel of four experts reviewed the questions. The final question in this section was presented as a chart to elicit an overall impression of the types of experiences principals had with individuals from each disability category. Principals were asked to rate their experiences from negative to positive or no experience with each disability category. Additionally, an overall Experience Score was calculated for each principal based upon an aggregation of those ratings for all 11 categories. The disability categories used included (a) specific learning disability, (b) mental retardation, (c) serious emotional disturbance, (d) blindness/visual impairment, (e) deafness/hearing impairment, (f) speech and language impairment, (g) other health impairment, (h) physical disability, (i) multihandicap, (j) autism/pervasive developmental disorder, and (k) neurological impairment.

In Section III, the 10 questionnaire items of the Superintendents' Attitude Survey on Integration (SASI), adapted by Stainback (1986) from the Autism Attitude Scale for Teachers (Olley, Devellis, Devellis, Wall, & Long, 1981), were used to measure attitude toward inclusion for students with severe/profound disabilities. For each statement concerning an aspect of inclusion for students with severe/profound disabilities, the respondent answered on a 5-point Likert scale with the following options: strongly agree, agree, uncertain, disagree, strongly disagree. For each principal, individual item scores and a total Attitude Score were determined. Stainback addressed the validity of this section through a panel of experts and the reliability coefficient was reported as 0.899 for this series of questions.

Section IV was designed to measure principals' perceptions about the most appropriate placements for students of different disability categories. For each disability category, the respondent chose 1 of 6 different placements that he or she believed to be most appropriate for that type of student. The placement options were as follows: (a) special education services outside the regular school, (b) special class for most or all of school day, (c) part-time special class, (d) regular education class instruction and resource room, (e) regular education class instruction for most of the day, and (f) full-time regular education with support. Based upon the responses, an Inclusiveness Score for each principal was determined as well as average responses for each disability category. The validity of this section was founded on the currently available options and categories as identified by the Commonwealth of Pennsylvania through special education services as defined by the Individuals with Disabilities Education Act (IDEA 1990) and subsequent Regulations (34 CFR Part 300).

The survey, consisting of 28 questions, was mailed to 750 elementary principals randomly chosen for the study. Each participant received a packet that included a cover letter requesting his or her participation, a survey, a stamped addressed postcard, and a stamped return envelope. The postcard containing identifying information was mailed separately when the survey was completed to allow for a second mailing and to ensure the anonymity of the respondents. The return rate was 54% after two mailings.

DATA ANALYSIS

Descriptive statistics were used to analyze the data, present data summaries, and to examine the relationships among the variables. Frequency distributions and percentages were computed for each variable of the survey. For the experience question, the frequency distribution and percentages were determined for each experience type across all disabilities as well as for each disability category. The frequencies and percentages were reported for each placement across all disabilities as well as for each disability category in Section IV. Central tendency data were calculated for the question on formal training topics and for the Attitude Score. Additionally, a Pearson-Product Moment Correlation (PPMC) or a Point-Biserial Correlation (PBC) was computed between each variable and the attitudes of the elementary principals to determine if there was a significant relationship at the .05 level of significance.

RESULTS

ATTITUDES OF ELEMENTARY PRINCIPALS TOWARD INCLUSION

One purpose of this investigation was to determine the attitudes of elementary principals toward the inclusion of students with special needs. The principals' attitudes were measured using Section III of the Principals and Inclusion Survey. The total score from this section had a possible range from 10 to 50, where lower scores indicated less favorable attitudes while higher scores indicated more favorable attitudes toward inclusion. Scores ranged from 14 to 50 with a mean of 34.8, a standard deviation of 7.0, a median of 36, and a modal score of 38. In this sample, 21.1% of the principals were clearly positive about inclusion and 2.7% were negative. The Attitude Scores for 76.6% of the respondents were within the uncertain range, not strongly positive or negative but generally skewed toward a positive attitude.

Responses to the specific items of the attitude scale indicate that most principals agree with the idea of inclusion when it is phrased in a generic and unregulated manner. However, less favorable attitudes arise when the wording becomes specific and implies mandatory compliance rather than voluntary participation. This disparity in the item responses seems to account for the large number of Attitude Scores that were within the uncertain range.

CORRELATES OF PRINCIPALS' ATTITUDE TOWARD INCLUSION SCORES

The research questions in Section II were designed to explore the relationship between variables potentially asso-

TABLE 1
Correlations Coefficients Between Dependent Variables and Attitude Score

Variable	n	r	r_{pb}
Experience score	408	0.35	**
Number of specific topics	408	0.22	**
Inservice hours	407	0.18	**
Special education credits	408	0.09	*
Age	406	-0.07	
Years teaching regular education	407	-0.05	
Years teaching special education	406	-0.02	
Years as elementary principal	408	0.01	
Gender	408		0.01
Special education certification	408		-0.01
Crisis plan	404		-0.01
Personal experience	402		-0.05
Vision	398		-0.03

* $p = .05$. ** $p < .05$.

ciated with principals and their attitudes toward inclusion. A PPMC coefficient was computed for those variables that were continuous (e.g., years of experience, age, credits in training) while the PBC was computed for the dichotomous variables such as gender and certification in special education. The probability level for statistically significant results was defined as an alpha of at least .05. Significant positive correlations were found between attitude toward inclusion and the number of special education credits ($r = 0.09$), inservice hours ($r = 0.18$), specific topics taken ($r = 0.22$), and the Experience Score ($r = 0.35$). Table 1 displays correlation coefficients for all variables.

The Experience Score was calculated by summing each individual's responses for the type of experience with students from all disability categories. Each of the 11 disability categories was rated on a scale from -2 for negative experience to 2 for positive experience, yielding a possible total score range from -22 to 22. Therefore, the higher the Experience Score, the more positive the principal's experiences across all categories. There was a significant correlation ($r = 0.35$) between the Experience Score and Attitude Score; that is, the more positive an individual's overall experiences with individuals with disabilities, the more positive the attitude.

The type of specific topics important to special education and inclusion included in preparation programs was also investigated. Data were collected by number of topics taken as well as the specific topic covered in the principals' formal training such as courses, workshops, and/or significant portions of courses (10% of content or

more). With a possible range of 0 to 14, the mean number of topics taken was 6.23 with a standard deviation of 3.28 and a modal score of 4. Only 2% of the principals had taken all of the topics surveyed. There was no single topic that had been taken by all principals. As shown in Table 2, most principals participated in training on special education law (83.6%), the characteristics of students with disabilities (77.7%), and behavior management (62%). Few received instruction in life skills (13.2%), family intervention (15.7%), eliciting parent and community support for inclusion (16.2%), or had participated in field-based experiences with actual inclusion activities (18.4%).

The number of inservice training hours in inclusive practices and the number of special education credits in formal training that a principal had completed were also significantly related to the Attitude Score (see Table 1). Specifically, the more hours and credits taken the more positive the attitude toward inclusion.

PLACEMENT PERCEPTIONS

When analyzing placements across disabilities, the most appropriate placements selected by the principals were distributed across the entire continuum of services. Full-time regular education with support was chosen most often (29.6%) and special education services outside regular education school least (6.0%). All of the options in regular education settings (full-time with support, for most of the day, or with resource room) accounted for 59.9% of the placements chosen.

TABLE 2
Specific Topics Covered in Preparation Programs by Topic (n= 408)

By Topic	f	%
Special education law	341	83.6
Characteristics of students with disabilities	317	77.7
Behavior management class for working with students with disabilities	253	62.0
Fostering teacher collaboration	237	58.1
Teambuilding	219	53.7
Change process	215	52.7
Supporting and training teachers to handle inclusion	198	48.5
Crisis intervention	196	48.0
Academic programming for students with disabilities	184	45.1
Interagency cooperation	122	29.9
Field-based experiences with actual inclusion activities	75	18.4
Eliciting parent and community support for inclusion	66	16.2
Family intervention training	64	15.7
Life skills training for students with disabilities	54	13.2

ATTITUDES AND PLACEMENT PERCEPTIONS

To explore the possible relationship between attitude and placement perceptions, a PPMC coefficient was calculated between the Attitude and Inclusiveness Scores. The Inclusiveness Score was calculated based upon a value between 1 and 6 given for the range of placements from most to least restrictive. Total scores ranged from 11 (most restrictive) to 66 (most inclusive). A significant positive relationship between attitude and inclusiveness was found ($r = 0.37$, $p < .05$). Thus, the more positive the attitude toward inclusion, the more inclusive the placements selected. It should be noted that 11 individuals declined to answer Section IV, which yielded the Inclusiveness Score, because they felt placement decisions should be made on an individual basis only and not on a general case.

RELATIONSHIP BETWEEN EXPERIENCE AND PLACEMENT

A PPMC was computed between the Experience score and the Inclusiveness score. A significant positive correlation between experience and inclusiveness was obtained ($r = 0.34$, $p < .05$). Thus, the more positive the experiences with students with disabilities the more likely the principal was to choose less restrictive settings. This relationship was also found for every disability category although the strength of the association varied.

DIFFERENCES ASSOCIATED WITH DISABILITY CATEGORY

Two differences were identified between disability categories. First, the perceived most appropriate placements varied considerably depending upon the disability category. Least restrictive placements in regular education were chosen most often for the categories of speech and language impairment (93.7%), physical disability (87.4%), other health impairment (84.9%), specific learning disability (81.9%), deaf/hearing impairment (74.5%), and blind/visual impairments (71.9%). Regular education settings were chosen less frequently for serious emotional disturbance (20.4%) and autism (30.1%).

The most segregated settings of special education services outside regular education schools and special classes were chosen by more than half of the respondents for serious emotional disturbance (63.6%) and autism/pervasive developmental disorder (49.8%). Approximately one third of respondents would place students with mental retardation (29.4%), neurological impairment (36.9%), or multihandicaps (39.1%) in such restricted settings. Other disability categories such as specific learning disability (1.8%) and speech and language impairment (1.6%) resulted in almost no responses in these two settings. Part-time special education and regular education class and resource room options were chosen largely for students with specific learning disability (62.0%) and mental retardation (59.7%).

The second difference found between disability categories was responses for types of experiences with students with disabilities. The category of serious emotional disturbance was the only category that had a large number of somewhat negative to negative experiences (51.4%). No experience accounted for only 4% of its responses. A high percentage of no experience responses was recorded for neurological impairment (36.5%), blind/visual impairment (36.1%), multihandicap (36.0%), autism/pervasive developmental disorder (28.3%), and deaf/hearing impairment (27.8%).

DISCUSSION

Inclusion has become a critical part of the reform effort to improve the delivery of services to students with disabilities by focusing on the placement of these students in general education classes. The literature on inclusion has identified a number of roles and responsibilities for principals that are necessary to create and sustain successful inclusion settings. However, the degree to which administrators support change efforts is often determined by the attitudes and values they hold. Therefore, if inclusion is to be a feasible alternative to more segregated placements, its success will depend heavily upon the readiness and willingness of general education administrators to make decisions that will provide appropriate opportunities for students with special needs to remain in general education (Ayres & Meyer, 1992).

This study was conducted to improve our understanding of principals' attitudes toward inclusion, the factors related to attitudes, and their potential impact upon the placement of students with disabilities. The findings demonstrate the importance of principals' attitudes in the inclusion of students with disabilities. Three areas related to attitudes toward inclusion warrant additional research and focus: (a) factors related to placement perceptions, (b) role of experience with students with disabilities, and (c) types of training in inclusive practices.

FACTORS RELATED TO PLACEMENT PERCEPTIONS

Although placement decisions for students with disabilities are made by each student's IEP team, the behavior and perceptions of the principal strongly influence placement decisions. Furthermore, a principal's support is necessary for the successful implementation of inclusion. As shown in this study, principals with more positive attitudes toward inclusion were more likely to believe that less restrictive placements were most appropriate for students with disabilities. McAneny (1992) reported a similar relationship between attitude and placement decisions regarding mainstreaming. The moderate strength of this finding emphasizes the importance of principals' attitudes toward inclusion. With such a powerful impact on programming, it is important that attitudes and attitude development become an integral part of the evaluation and professional development process for building administrators.

The disability category or label that a student carries was also related to the recommended placement. Students with serious emotional disturbance, autism/pervasive developmental, mental retardation, neurological impairment, and multihandicaps were particularly likely to be placed in a more restrictive setting. Evidently, ele-

mentary school principals believe that certain disability categories, such as those without emotional or social needs and who tend to "fit in" academically, are more appropriate for inclusive settings. This is in stark contrast to the idea of full inclusion where everyone has an opportunity to be educated within the general education setting. In 1998, Barnett and Monda-Amaya also found that principals generally viewed inclusion as most appropriate for students with mild disabilities. These results are commensurate with data included in the Twenty-Second Annual Report to Congress (Office of Special Education Programs, 2000), which indicated a disparity across disability categories with students with significant disabilities in more restrictive settings. Consequently, extra attention needs to be paid to these groups to facilitate increased inclusion.

ROLE OF EXPERIENCE

The type of experiences with students with disabilities proved to be important; the more positive the experiences, the more positive a principal's attitude was toward inclusion. This finding supports previous research (Villa, Thousand, Meyers, & Nevin, 1996; Wisniewski & Alper, 1994) that showed experience with individuals with disabilities is related to positive attitudes toward inclusion. However, this study and others (McAneny, 1992; Villa et al.) found no significant relationships between attitude and years of experience in regular education, special education, or elementary administration. It seems apparent that the nature of experiences in a school setting and not the amount of experience, is connected to attitudes toward inclusion.

Inclusion has become a critical part of the reform effort to improve the delivery of services to students with disabilities by focusing on the placement of these students in general education classes.

The types of experiences principals had with students with disabilities varied by the disability category, although most experiences were categorized as somewhat positive to positive or having had no experience. Students with serious emotional disturbance were an exception with almost equal percentages of positive and negative experiences. In order to change the perceptions of principals toward groups such as serious emotional disturbance, autism/pervasive developmental disorder, and/or multihandicaps, it is essential to provide principals with positive experiences with individuals from all disability categories.

Positive experiences with students with disabilities were also associated with placement. The more positive the experiences with students with disabilities the more those principals chose less restrictive placements. This relationship was found for all of the disability categories including serious emotional disturbance and autism. Therefore, although some students with disabilities might not be seen as initially suited for general education, with more positive experiences, principals seem to become more open to including all students.

TYPES OF TRAINING

Preparation programs and inservice training programs for principals need to address inclusion as part of their required curriculum. As shown in this study, exposure to special education concepts through special education credits and inservice training were related to a more positive attitude toward inclusion. There is no previous research that specifically relates special education credits to attitude; therefore, additional research is needed to validate this particular finding. However, Hegler (1995) and Stoler (1992) found a relationship between inservice hours and attitude for administrators; and the literature emphasizes the importance of special education coursework for the development of more positive attitudes (Greyerbiehl, 1993; Hyatt, 1987, Valesky & Hirth, 1992).

This study shows that for these principals, preparation programs provided them with only a small part of the knowledge base deemed by experts in special education as important to the implementation of inclusion. The majority of principals had taken only 4 to 6 of the 14 identified topics. General special education information such as characteristics of disabilities, special education law, and behavior management may be adequately covered, but specific topics that address actual strategies and processes that support inclusion seem to be lacking. Patterson, Bowling, and Marshall (2000) support these findings and conclude that principals are ill-trained for inclusion and special education leadership.

The lack of specific training in special education topics is not surprising, considering the amount of coursework that is necessary to receive a degree in administration. These topics are important, however, as they were related to a principal's attitude toward inclusion. The more topics that principals had as part of their formal training such as courses, workshops, and/or significant portions of courses (10% of content or more), the more positive their attitudes were toward inclusion. Further research is necessary to replicate the relationship between training content and attitudes as well as to determine which specific topics are important for principal preparation. The reality is that school administrators need to take part in the development and implementation of inclusion programs and therefore need to be adequately prepared to do so.

LIMITATIONS

A concern with this study is its focus on only one state and on only elementary principals. Although this may weaken the scope of the research, it was deemed necessary to restrict the sample in order to reduce the number of variables and thereby provide clearer results. Additionally, the use of the full inclusion perspective, the inclusion of students with severe/profound disabilities, in the attitude scale may have reduced the "strength" of positive attitudes toward inclusion. However, this perspective was utilized as it was most likely to polarize responses and thereby produce statistically significant findings. Finally, another limitation results from the assumption that all principals work under the same conditions. In practice, a principal's level of control and ability to experiment may be influenced by legal requirements, district policies, and other specific issues that vary by setting.

IMPLICATIONS FOR RESEARCH AND PRACTICE

The findings of this study demonstrate the importance of principals' attitudes for the successful inclusion of students with disabilities. The elementary principals' placement perceptions were, in part, related to their attitudes toward inclusion. Therefore, when school districts hire and/or evaluate elementary principals, consideration of their attitudes toward inclusion should be an integral part of the process. An awareness of factors related to attitude is also necessary to assist principals in developing a favorable attitude toward inclusion.

INVESTIGATE CATEGORY DIFFERENCES

The results of this research establish that principals have different experiences and perceptions of appropriate placements depending upon the student's disability category. Placement decisions are made based upon these beliefs and experiences and therefore certain disability groups are not given equal opportunity to be placed in general education classes. In order to change the perceptions of principals toward groups like serious emotional disturbance, autism/pervasive developmental disorder, and/or multihandicaps, it is essential to provide principals with positive experiences with individuals from *all* disability categories. Also, successful environments should be evaluated to determine the skills and strategies necessary for the inclusion of each disability group. Additionally, a more indepth look at principals' specific perceptions of each disability group would be beneficial.

IMPROVE PRINCIPAL PREPARATION

Too often, principals who are prepared well to administer general education programs are made responsible for a broad range of special education programs in areas in which they have had minimal training and/or experience (Anderson & Decker, 1993). Preparation programs and inservice training programs for principals need to address inclusion as part of their required curriculum. Principals require specific training that is designed to meet their needs as building administrators, especially regarding their leadership role in inclusion. This study shows that general special education information such as characteristics of disabilities, special education law, and behavior management may be adequately covered. However, specific topics that address actual strategies and processes that support inclusion are lacking. University and college preparation programs as well as inservice training components should be carefully examined to determine how to include more of the topics identified in Table 2 in their current offerings.

Professional development opportunities within the district should also include opportunities to observe and take part in the successful inclusion of students with disabilities through the support of the director of special education, teaching staff, and outside consultants. Including principals as integral team members will enable them to develop an understanding for the individual needs of students as well as the skills and strategies necessary to make inclusion work. In addition, whenever possible, principals should be provided a mentor or peer partner to assist them with the development or improvement of inclusive practices.

ENSURE POSITIVE EXPERIENCES

The findings of this study emphasize the importance of implementing quality inclusion programs and not "dumping" students with disabilities into general education classes. They also suggest that care must be taken in establishing inclusion settings in resistant environments. To do so, the special education and general education staff in each educational environment must strive to collaboratively develop the knowledge and skills required to identify and articulate their particular needs. Experiences with students with disabilities must be carefully crafted to increase the number of positive encounters that principals have with these students. Additionally, principals should be given opportunities to observe and model administrator and teacher behaviors in successful inclusion settings.

Too often, principals who are prepared well to administer general education programs are made responsible for a broad range of special education programs in areas in which they have had minimal training and/or experience (Anderson& Decker, 1993).

REFERENCES

Anderson, R. J., & Decker, R. H. (1993). The principal's role in special education programming. *National Association of Secondary School Principals Bulletin, 77*(550), 1-6.

Ayres, B., & Meyer, L. H. (1992). Helping teachers manage the inclusive classroom. *School Administrator, 49*(2), 14-21.

Barnett, C., & Monda-Amaya, L. E. (1998). Principals' knowledge of and attitudes toward inclusion. *Remedial and Special Education, 19*(3), 181-192.

Evans, J. H., Bird, K. M., Ford, L. A., Green, J. L., & Bischoff, R. A. (1992). Strategies for overcoming resistance to the integration of students with special needs into neighborhood schools: A case study. *CASE in Point, 7*(1), 1-15.

Falvey, M. (1995). *Inclusive and heterogeneous schooling.* Baltimore, MD: Brookes.

Goodlad, J. I., & Lovitt, T. C. (Eds.). (1993). *Integrating general and special education.* New York: Merrill.

Greyerbiehl, D. (1993). *Educational policies and practices that support the inclusion of students with disabilities in the general education classroom.* Charleston, WV: West Virginia Developmental Disabilities Planning Council.

Hegler, K. L. (1995, April). *The "What, why, how and if" of inclusion processes in rural schools: Supporting teachers during attitude and teaching behavior change.* Paper presented at the 73rd Annual International Convention of the Council for Exceptional Children, Indianapolis, IN.

Hipp, K. A., & Huffman, J. B. (2000, April). *How leadership is shared and visions emerge in the creation of learning communities.* Paper presented at the 81st Annual meeting of the American Educational Research Association, New Orleans, LA.

Hyatt, N. E. (1987). Perceived competencies and attitudes of a select group of elementary school administrators relative to preparation and experience in administering special education programs (Doctoral dissertation, College of William and Mary, 1987). *Dissertation Abstracts International, 48(02A),* 361.

Individuals with Disabilities Education Act of 1990, 20 U.S.C. §1401.

Individuals with Disabilities Education Act Regulations, 34 C.F.R. Part 300.

McAneny, F. X. (1992). The impact of school principals attitudes toward mainstreaming on student referrals. (Doctoral dissertation, Temple University, 1992) *Dissertation Abstracts International, 53(10A),* 3495.

Nanus, B. (1992). *Visionary leadership: Creating a compelling sense of directions for your organization.* San Francisco: Jossey-Bass.

Office of Special Education Programs, United States Department of Education. (2000). *To assure the free and appropriate public education of all children with disabilities: Twenty-second annual report to Congress on the implementation of the Individuals with Disabilities Education Act.* Washington, DC: U.S. Government Printing Office. (ERIC Document Reproduction Service No. ED 444 333)

Olley, G., Devellis, R., Devellis, B., Wall, J., & Long, C. (1981). The autism scale for teachers. *Exceptional Children, 47,* 37-38.

Patterson, J., Bowling, D., & Marshall, C. (2000). Are principals prepared to manage special education dilemmas? *National Association of Secondary School Principals Bulletin, 84*(613), 9-20.

Praisner, C. L. (2000). Attitudes of elementary school principals toward the inclusion of students with disabilities in general education classes. (Doctoral dissertation, Lehigh University, 2000). *Dissertation Abstracts International, 61(07),* 2661.

Rude, H. A., & Anderson, R. E. (1992). Administrator effectiveness in support of inclusive schools. *CASE in Point, 7*(1), 31-37.

Sage, D., & Burrello, L. (1994). *Leadership in educational reform: An administrator's guide to changes in special education.* Baltimore, MD: Brookes.

Stainback, G. H. (1986). Attitudes of division superintendents toward the integration of students with severe and profound handicaps into educational programs in regular schools (Doctoral Dissertation, University of Virginia, 1986). *Dissertation Abstracts International, 48(05A)*, 1172.

Stoler, R. D. (1992). Perceptions of regular education teachers toward inclusion of all handicapped students in their classrooms. *Clearing House, 65*(1), 60-62.

Valesky, T. C., & Hirth, M. A. (1992). Survey of the states: Special education knowledge requirements for school administrators. *Exceptional Children, 58*, 399-406.

Villa, R. A., Thousand, J. S., Meyers, H., & Nevin, A. I. (1996). Teacher and administrator perceptions of heterogeneous education. *Exceptional Children, 63*, 29-45.

Wisniewski, L., & Alper, S. (1994). Including students with severe disabilities in general education settings: Guidelines for change. *Remedial and Special Education, 15*(1), 4-13.

CINDY L. PRAISNER, Educational Consultant, Colchester, Connecticut.

An Interview With... Dr. Marilyn Friend

Mary T. Brownell and Chriss Walther-Thomas, Dept. Editors

Dr. Marilyn Friend is a leading expert in the areas of professional collaboration, coteaching, and inclusive education for students with disabilities. She began her educational career with a dual degree in special education and general education. Her first teaching job was as a fifth-grade teacher in a large urban school district where many tensions existed within the school among the teachers and between the teachers and principal. The disagreements extended to the community, and several lawsuits had been filed by parents naming the principal and the school district. Because of the problems, teachers tended to keep to themselves. It was a hostile environment for a beginning teacher, and Dr. Friend felt very isolated there, reluctant to ask colleagues for much-needed advice.

In contrast, she spent her last year of public school teaching working as a special education teacher in a highly collaborative, small urban school. The teachers worked well together in both formal (e.g., curriculum committee) and informal (e.g., problem solving about students at risk for failure) situations to maximize their limited resources. At this school, Dr. Friend collaborated in a variety of instructional activities, including coteaching with a sixth-grade teacher at a time when such an arrangement was not even considered an option for delivering services to students with disabilities. Students with disabilities and typical learners succeeded in this setting, and the teachers supported and learned from each other. Because of these dramatically different experiences, Dr. Friend recognized the critical importance of collaboration in public school environments.

She decided to pursue the study of collaboration as a doctoral student at Indiana University, and in addition to special education, she included study in psychology because of its rich history of theory, literature, and practice related to collaboration. After graduating, she served as a faculty member at the University of Oklahoma, Northern Illinois University, and Indiana University–Purdue University at Indianapolis. Currently, she is the chairperson of the Department of Specialized Education Services at the University of North Carolina at Greensboro. Throughout her academic career, Dr. Friend has focused on effective collaboration, inclusive practices, and related areas such as teaming and consultation. She has written numerous articles and produced several videotapes on these topics that are widely used by teachers, teacher educators, and staff developers. She is the co-author of two best-selling texts on these topics, Including Students with Special Needs: A Practical Guide for Classroom Teachers (2002, authored with Dr. William Bursuck) and Interactions: Collaboration Skills for School Professionals (2000, authored with Dr. Lynne Cook). Additionally, Dr. Friend has been active in teacher education efforts, serving in a variety of national leadership positions in

the Council for Exceptional Children (CEC), including president of the Teacher Education Division (TED). Through her writing, research, teaching, staff development, and advocacy efforts, Dr. Friend has been a leading voice on the importance of preparing preservice and inservice teachers as well as administrators and related services personnel for roles as effective collaborators.

Q: Why is collaboration important in schools?

At the broadest level, collaboration is important in schools because it has become a defining characteristic of society in the 21st century. If you examine publications in business, health, social services, technology, and other major disciplines, you will find that collaboration is a unifying theme. In fact, Bennis and Biederman (1997) proposed that all the most societally defining inventions of the 20th century were the result of collaboration. Lisbeth Schorr's (1997) book about creating healthy communities and overcoming poverty is another example: The overriding theme is collaboration. Collaboration has become the primary contemporary strategy to foster innovation, create effective programs, and sustain them over time. Since schools reflect the society in which they exist, it is becoming a tenet that they must, too, rely on collaboration.

The importance of collaboration for schools is also a pragmatic matter: In this day and age there is simply too much for any one educator to know in order to effectively meet the needs of all his or her students. If in schools we would act in the understanding that some professionals should be experts in instructional strategies, some in the use of cooperative learning approaches, some in responding to troubling student behavior, some in assessment practices, and some in building students' self-esteem and social skills, we could draw on each others' knowledge and skills and collectively create more effective schools for our students. Too often, though, educators seem uncomfortable with this type of culture of sharing expertise. While we talk a lot about collaboration in education, in many schools each teacher seems to feel responsible for addressing academic and behavior concerns until the problems are so serious that the teacher is convinced that someone else should assume responsibility for solving them. We use the word *collaboration*, and some shared efforts do occur, but the culture of schools still fosters isolated, individual professional problem solving.

One other reason that collaboration is important for today's schools comes from a legislative and legal impetus. The expectation in the Individuals with Disabilities Education Act of 1997 concerning the least restrictive environment and the assumption that the general education classroom is that environment for many students with disabilities leads almost inevitably to increased attention on collaboration. Likewise, the law's provision for participation by parents in their children's education and by general education teachers sets the stage for the growing centrality of collaboration in schools.

But even beyond law concerning special education services, collaboration is being recommended as a way for schools to operate—in middle school teams, in site-based leadership teams, in collegial staff development, and so on. Collaboration is a means to accomplish the complex goals of schools, a way to build community while responding to the many pressures of the contemporary education system. We need collaboration to ensure that schools are positive, supportive, and effective places for students to learn and teachers to teach. Classroom teachers and other educators (e.g., special education teachers, reading specialists, Title I teachers) are working with increasingly diverse students; all school personnel are under tremendous pressure to ensure that all students achieve higher academic standards. In this context, collaboration is not a luxury; it is a necessity.

Q: What does it take to make collaboration work effectively in schools?

Although I could make many recommendations about specific ideas and strategies for promoting collaborative practices in schools, the very first and most fundamental one would be to raise teachers' and administrators' understanding of and commitment to collaboration as a critical part of school functioning, and then to extend that understanding to the general community. A disposition for collegiality is essential because of the elusive nature of collaboration: Unlike some trends in education, collaboration is a sum of subtleties and thus more difficult to build support for and give attention to. Maybe an example would help. If you asked any group of citizens about important trends in schools, technology would probably be mentioned. Many initiatives exist to ensure that all schools have adequate computer resources and that access to the Internet is available. Significant funding is committed to technology goals, and the private sector is helping schools become technologically up-to-date. However, if you asked that same group of citizens about collaboration in schools, it is likely that you would receive little response or support or possibly an assertion that teachers certainly should learn to work together. Without the concrete evidence of hardware and software and with the dilemma that collaboration requires time away from students for educators to interact, it is more difficult for collaboration to become a prominent issue in terms of public support, funding, or private sector attention. How common is it for a business to offer schools funding to build teams or opportunities to participate in staff development to become more effective at interpersonal communication skills? Collaboration is unlikely to receive the attention it deserves without increased understanding.

After that general notion of a commitment to collaboration, I would say that the most important factor in making collaboration a reality in schools is the principal. An expectation set at the district level certainly is helpful, but it seems that collaboration can be accomplished without such a central mandate if the principal not only desires a collaborative culture but also is willing to express that expectation and devote resources to reaching it. This moves collaboration far beyond a laudable approach that some teachers use informally because they see its value as a standard for a school. One outstanding principal I know worked in a school in which teachers tended to stay in their classrooms, where small cliques existed but little collaboration occurred. He decided a change was in order, and he took specific steps to recreate the school culture. He created lunch-hour study groups where teachers read about and debated various issues related to collaboration. He created working committees assigned to make important decisions concerning the school, and he taught committee members strategies for working effectively during meetings and for group problem solving. He asked an external consultant to meet with staff to identify concerns and resolve them, including interpersonal issues. After 2 years, teachers and other professionals in the school worked closely together, and they saw collaboration as an essential element of all aspects of their jobs. This all happened because someone in the school set the standard and led staff to it; the someone who can do this is the principal.

Q: What do teachers need to learn about working with others?

After the disposition supportive of collaboration that I mentioned before, all preservice and inservice teachers should have knowledge and skills that contribute to effective collaboration. For example, preservice teachers should learn and experience in their initial training the concept that "effective teachers work together." Thus, they should work with partners and in small groups in their methods classes, and they should reflect on the advantages and potential problems of working with colleagues. In field experiences and student teaching, they should have opportunities to watch effective collaboration among experienced educators, and they should discuss what makes the interactions effective and how they could do the same. For example, they might observe planning meetings in which coteachers set priorities and make decisions for the upcoming week. They might also participate in intervention assistance meetings during which professionals problem solve for students experiencing persistent serious academic or behavior problems. A third example would be to observe teacher interactions with parents. Experiences such as these can assist preservice teachers in developing an appreciation for the value of collaboration and in building a knowledge base for successful professional interactions. This approach also recognizes the importance of identifying collaboration skills. Expecting preservice teachers to learn about collaboration simply by being together in schools is not enough; proximity is a necessary but insufficient condition for collaboration.

Both preservice and inservice teachers should also learn and practice specific skills, especially communication skills. Here is one small example: Sometimes I hear teachers interacting in ways that are not particularly respectful of others' perspectives. If a teacher says, "Don't you think it would be better if we...," that professional is actually expressing his or her own opinion but trying to assign it to the other person in the interaction. That type of comment doesn't encourage colleagues to voice their opinions and may be perceived as a tactic to avoid hearing anyone else's opinion. A better way to interact might be to say, "My preference is that we…. What do you think?" In this case the speaker has owned and offered an opinion, not assigned it to the other person, and has invited the other person to express an opinion, too. In addition to appropriate communication skills, educators need to understand how to complete a process of working together. Most importantly, they need skills for engaging in a problem-solving process with others to reach a shared goal.

Third, teachers need to demonstrate through their actions that collaboration is not about working with best friends or, necessarily, with like-minded people. Collaboration is about trust and respect. It's about working together to create better outcomes for all students. If teachers learn to like each other in the process, that is a bonus, but it is not a prerequisite. I mention this because in some schools, the professionals who collaborate are those who are most comfortable with each other; others are not part of the culture. Educators collaborate because doing so benefits students. They sometimes work together, even if they would not socialize and sometimes even if they have rather opposing views of teaching and learning. Collaboration is not a personal preference; it is a strategy to do what is best for students.

Finally, experienced teachers need to understand how to work effectively with new teachers and with new partners who may have less experience in collaboration. When veteran teachers have built a strong background of interacting with others in consultative, teaming, or co-teaching relationships, they sometimes, consciously or unconsciously, think that their own experiences comprise the best way to collaborate. When their partners change, they are tempted to keep doing things the old way without allowing the new partnership to develop a character of its own. In addition, they may not understand that inexperienced colleagues do not have the same level of skills, experience, or confidence in the process. Effective collaboration is always about lifelong learning. Successful collaborators believe that there is still more to know, and they are respectful of their colleagues' level of understanding and comfort in working together.

Q: What are the biggest challenges that collaborators face?

Principals and teachers must first address pragmatic barriers in order to make collaboration work. By far, the biggest such barrier is time, not just time to work together but time for constructive communication. Time is such a precious resource in school environments. Teachers need time for planning and preparation, they need time for joint teaching, they need time to share their perspectives on the success of their efforts. Given the amount of time that professionals typically are expected to work alone with students and to spend on preparing reports and completing other responsibilities, not much time is left for collaborating with colleagues unless collaboration is viewed as a priority. In both large and small schools, in urban, suburban, and rural schools, teachers often find it nearly impossible to arrange common planning

time. Overcoming this barrier requires creative thinking. In one high school where I recently worked, teachers regularly used technology to facilitate their collaboration. This school was so large that finding common planning time was not realistic. As a result, teachers used e-mail to share ideas, plan lessons, communicate concerns, and jointly problem solve. For them, e-mail is an efficient communication approach, and although the teachers would like more opportunities for face-to-face interactions, they decided to be constructive about the constraints instead of succumbing to the temptation to complain about it.

Some institutional barriers to collaboration also seem to be emerging, possibly because of reform and accountability initiatives. Some teachers fear that collaborating to meet the needs of a diverse group of students may result in slowing the progress of typical learners. Some also fear that students with disabilities will not achieve high enough outcomes and that teachers will unjustly be held accountable for this. Additionally, some principals are hesitant to support adults working together when it appears that such time is taken away from instruction. They mistakenly see collaboration as less important than direct teaching, forgetting that teaching could be significantly more effective as the result of the collaboration. It is interesting that in schools that overcome this kind of thinking, many students who struggle to learn are making significant educational progress, and other students are not being held back.

As I noted earlier, some teachers and principals also have mindsets that can work against collaboration. For example, some teachers are territorial about classroom space and teaching procedures. They resent any indication that alternatives to their practices could also be effective. I hear from special education teachers that their role in some classrooms is that of assistant; it is such a waste of valuable teaching resources. But I am also upset when classroom teachers describe special educators who are reluctant to do anything other than work with small groups. Again, so many teaching and learning options are being overlooked.

Another "mindset" challenge has to do with administrators and their understanding of collaboration. Administrators sometimes do not understand the complexities of collaboration, and consequently, they are not sure how to nurture it, assess it, and determine the type of professional development needed to make it happen. Even when administrators are well intentioned, they do things that create hurdles for collaboration. For instance, a set of coteachers recently explained with frustration that their principal told them that coteaching was a great idea but that each teacher was to teach only her "own" students in the shared classroom! Principals need to know how to create a vision for collaboration as well as how to create structures and processes for collaboration.

Q: In addition to the strategies we've already discussed, what else can effective school leaders do to facilitate collaboration in their schools?

Principals can help their faculty members develop technical skills involved in collaboration. They need to know what the skills are, model them appropriately, and provide professional development opportunities that will enable people to develop new skills and enhance existing ones. It is also important for school leaders to stay involved in collaborative efforts to ensure that participants have the support they need to address challenging issues that are bound to arise. As teachers become more comfortable working with one another, tensions often develop as they become aware of differences in their philosophies and approaches to instruction. Principals can point out commonalties that exist and help teachers keep thinking about the main goals for their students. Effective principals serve as facilitators and problem solvers by sending the message that they are not afraid of difficult issues and that they don't give up when conflicts arise. They work effectively to bring people together to problem solve and get past the rough spots. For example, on one intervention team, members agreed with a highly vocal reading specialist to complete an extensive assessment of a student's skills. Outside the specialist's presence, though, other team members expressed regret at the decision and grumbled that they had gone along with the specialist just so that she would quit repeating her preference for the assessment. The principal called the team to a meeting to discuss how members were participating in decision making, how disagreements were being addressed, and how to express dissatisfaction during team interactions. The somewhat painful but tremendously honest conversation resulted in a huge improvement in the team's functioning, and it was the principal's ability to facilitate the breakthrough to a new level of collaborative skill that made the difference. I believe that collaboration is not about how big the school budget is or the size of classrooms or the number of personnel. Once you have healthy safe schools, it is more about people, expectations, and ways to work together.

Q: What if an administrator is not a strong supporter of collaboration?

Teachers can help administrators understand the importance of collaboration by providing information, discussing its importance, undertaking collaborative initiatives that are a result of their own efforts. They also can participate in collaborative endeavors if they are personally satisfying. However, having said that, I also want to make it clear that individual teachers can only go so far. It is not realistic to think that an individual teacher can be expected to set the standard for the entire school. Teachers can be a strong positive influence and enthusiastic participants and spokespeople for collaboration; principals are the ones who have to create the standard for it. If a principal is not supportive or is actively opposed to collaborative efforts, teachers may have to adjust their own expectations, at least temporarily. I have a cartoon that explains it well: One character explains to the other, "They say the secret of success is to be in the right place at the right time... But since you never know when the right time is going to be... I figure the best strategy is to find the right place and just hang out!" For teachers anxious to collaborate in nonsupportive atmospheres, the advice seems apt.

Q: What are some resources that teachers, teacher educators, and administrators can use to improve their knowledge of collaboration?

Many authors are now addressing the topic of collaboration. Here are some of the materials that teachers and administrators may find useful:

Bennis, W., & Biederman, P. W. (1997). *Organizing genius: The secrets of creative collaboration.* Reading, MA: Addison-Wesley.

Brownell, M. T., Yeager, E., Rennells, M. S., & Riley, T. (1997). Teachers working together: What teacher educators and researchers should know. *Teacher Education and Special Education, 20,* 340-359.

Burrello, L. C., Lashley, C. L., & Beatty, E. E. (2001). *Educating all students together: How school leaders create unified systems.* Thousand Oaks, CA: Corwin.

Daane, C. J., Beirne-Smith, M., & Latham, D. (2001). Administrators' and teachers' perceptions of the collaborative efforts of inclusion in the elementary grades. *Education, 121,* 331-338.

Fishbaugh, M. S. E. (2000). *The collaboration guide for early career educators.* Baltimore: Brookes.

Friend, M. (2000). Perspectives: Collaboration in the twenty-first century. *Remedial and Special Education, 20,* 130-132, 160.

Friend, M., Burrello, L., & Burrello, J. (Co-Producers). (2001). *Leading a district to scale: Access to the general education curriculum for every student* [videotape]. Bloomington: Indiana University, Elephant Rock Productions.

Friend, M., Burrello, L., & Burrello, J. (Co-Producers). (2001). *Successful high school inclusion: Making access a reality for all students* [videotape]. Bloomington: Indiana University, Elephant Rock Productions.

Friend, M., Burrello, L., & Burrello, J. (2000). *Complexities of collaboration* [videotape]. Bloomington: Indiana University, Elephant Rock Productions.

Friend, M., & Bursuck, W. (2002). *Including students with special needs: A practical guide for classroom teachers* (3rd ed.). Needham Heights, MA: Allyn & Bacon.

Friend, M., & Cook, L. (2000). *Interactions: Collaboration skills for school professionals* (3rd ed.). White Plains, NY: Longman.

Friend, M. (Co-Producer with L. Burrello & J. Burrello). (1995). *The power of two: Including students through coteaching* [videotape]. Bloomington, IN: Elephant Rock Productions. (Distributed by the Council for Exceptional Children, Reston, VA)

Martin, A. K., & Hutchinson, N. L. (1999). *Two communities of practice: Learning the limits to collaboration.* Paper presented at the annual meeting of the Educational Research Association (Montreal, Quebec, Canada). (ERIC Document Reproduction No. ED 435 732)

Schorr, L. B. (1997). *Common purpose: Strengthening families and neighborhoods to rebuild America.* New York: Anchor Books/Random House.

Walther-Thomas, C., Korinek, L., & McLaughlin, V. L. (2000). Collaboration to support students' success. *Focus on Exceptional Children, 32*(3), 1-18.

Walther-Thomas, C., Korinek, L., McLaughlin, V. L., & Williams, B. T. (2000). *Collaboration for inclusive education: Developing successful programs.* Boston: Allyn & Bacon.

From *Intervention in School and Clinic*, March 2002, pp. 223-228. © 2002 by Pro-Ed Inc. Reprinted by permission.

UNIT 2
Early Childhood

Unit Selections

5. **Music in the Inclusive Environment**, Marcia Earl Humpal and Jan Wolf
6. **Building Relationships With Challenging Children**, Philip S. Hall and Nancy D. Hall
7. **The Itinerant Teacher Hits the Road: A Map for Instruction in Young Children's Social Skills**, Faith Haertig Sadler

Key Points to Consider

- How does music benefit preschoolers with special needs in inclusive settings?

- Can teachers bond with sullen, angry, aggressive young children without punishing them? How?

- Describe the requirements which must be met by teachers who perform special educational services.

 **Links: www.dushkin.com/online/**
These sites are annotated in the World Wide Web pages.

Division for Early Childhood
http://www.dec-sped.org
Institute on Community Integration Projects
http://ici.umn.edu/projectscenters/
National Academy for Child Development (NACD)
http://www.nacd.org
Special Education Resources on the Internet (SERI)
http://seriweb.com

Public law 99-457 has been called one of the most important educational decisions of the U.S. It was a 1986 amendment (Part H) to PL94-142 (the Education for All Handicapped Children Act), which the U.S. Congress established as a grant incentive aimed at providing services for young children at risk of disability beginning at the age of 3. By 1991 this amendment to the now-renamed Individuals with Disabilities Education Act (IDEA) was reauthorized. It operates through "Child Find," which are organizational groups that look for babies, toddlers, and preschoolers with conditions of obvious disability (such as blindness, deafness, or orthopedic handicap). These young children can receive special educational services according to IDEA's mandate, "a free and appropriate education for all in the least restrictive environment." Many infants and young children are being found who are at "high risk" of developing educational disabilities (for example, low vision, hearing impairments, developmental delays) unless education begins before the age of 6. This outreach is having a profound impact on the care of families and children.

The United States is faced with multiple questions about the education of its future citizens—its young children. Many American babies are born preterm, small for gestational age, or with extremely low birth weight. This is a direct result of the United States' high rate of teenage pregnancy (nearly double that of most European countries and Canada) and its low rate of providing adequate prenatal care, especially for the young, the poor, or recent immigrant mothers. These infants are at high risk for developing disabilities and conditions of educational exceptionality. Early intervention can help these babies.

All services to be provided for any infant, toddler, or pre-schooler with a disability, and for his or her family, are to be articulated in an individualized family service plan (IFSP). The IFSP is to be written and implemented as soon as the infant or young child is determined to be at risk. IFSPs specify what services will be provided for the parents, for the diagnosed child, for siblings, and for all significant caregivers. Children with pervasive disabilities (such as autism, traumatic brain injuries, blindness, deafness, orthopedic impairments, severe health impairments, or multiple disabilities) may require extensive and very expensive early childhood interventions.

IFSPs are written in collaboration with parents, experts in the area of the child's exceptional condition, teachers, home-service providers, and other significant providers. They are updated every 6 months until the child turns 3 and receives an individualized education plan (IEP). A case manager is assigned to oversee each individual child with an IFSP to ensure high-quality and continuous intervention services.

In the United States, Child Find locates and identifies infants, toddlers, and young children who qualify for early childhood special education and family services. An actual diagnosis, or label of condition of exceptionality, is not required. Assessment is usually accomplished in a multidisciplinary fashion. It can be very difficult, but as much as possible, it is conducted in the child's home in a nonthreatening fashion. Diagnosis of exceptionalities in children who cannot yet answer questions is complicated. Personal observations are used as well as parent reports. Most of the experts involved in the multidisciplinary assessment want to see the child more than once to help compensate for the fact that all children have good days and bad days. In cases where the parents are non-English speakers and a translator is required, assessment may take several days.

Despite the care taken, many children who qualify for, and would benefit from, early intervention services are missed. Child Find associations are not well funded. There are constant shortages of time, materials, and multidisciplinary professionals to do assessments. Finding translators for parents who speak uncommon foreign languages adds to the problems. Occasionally the availability of funds for early childhood interventions encourages the over diagnosis of risk factors in infants from low-income, minority, immigrant, or rural families.

A challenge to all professionals providing early childhood special services is how to work with diverse parents. Some parents welcome any and all intervention, even if it is not merited. Other parents resist any labeling of their child as "disabled" and refuse services. Professionals must make allowances for cultural, economic, and educational diversity, multiple caregivers, and single parents. Regardless of the situation, parental participation is the "sine qua non" of early childhood intervention.

At-home services may include instruction in the educational goals of the IFSP, and in skills such as discipline, behavior management, nutrition, and health maintenance. At-home services also include counseling for parents, siblings, and significant others to help them deal with their fears and to help them accept, love, and challenge their special child to become all he or she is capable of being. A case manager helps ensure that there is cooperation and coordination of services by all team members.

Most children receiving early childhood services have some center-based or combined center- and home-based special education. Center care introduces children to peers and introduces the family to other families with similar concerns. It is easier to ensure quality education and evaluate progress when a child spends at least a part of his or her time in a well-equipped educational center.

The first article in this unit addresses the importance of rhythm and music in early childhood. New research suggests that music and math stimulate development of neurons in the same brain areas. Music not only helps organize and promote neuronal growth, it also enhances socialization between children and stimulates language and creative production.

The second article, "Building Relationships With Challenging Children" presents positive ways to help at-risk students. The authors, Philip and Nancy Hall eschew punishment. They recommend gentle intervention and bonding. They describe the components of these practices which help ensure that the student will become a good learner and achieve educational success.

The last article in unit 2 discusses the benefits of early intervention using teachers who travel from place to place to perform their special educational services. The extension of services from birth to the age of 3 in homes and local communities has given impetus to indirect service delivery models. A teacher can collaborate, consult, and provide technical assistance in many ways.

Music in the Inclusive Environment

Five-year-old Sam uses a wheelchair. Due to a difficult birth, he has little motor development or control and no spoken language. He understands but can't speak.

Twice a week, I [Jan] am the music teacher for 22 kindergartners, including Sam. His level of participation is that of an observer, and at times I am not sure what he feels about our time together. The children accept his level of ability and when we put his wheelchair in the center of the circle for "Ring around the Rosy," his squeals of delight give it all away. He laughs and bobs his head back and forth, eyes sparkling all the while as we circle his chair, fall down, and bounce back up only to play the game one more time.

Marcia Earl Humpal and Jan Wolf

What did Sam gain from this musical experience? Pure joy! At first I felt I was slighting him. Wasn't there a way to make his experience more active and inclusive? We tried pushing the wheelchair in the circle, but Sam's response was not the same. He became withdrawn. The experience of sharing the joy from his pivotal center position evoked the most expression.

Music in the early childhood environment offers varying levels of engagement ranging from simply listening or observing to joining in as an active participant.

To onlookers Sam may appear passive, but all of us who know him well are aware of his participation. The music reaches him, as it does all of us, in his way and at his time and place. His squeals and screeches, sparkling eyes, and smiling face communicate his delight to everyone in the room.

Music in the early childhood environment does not depend on specific skills or competence. It offers varying levels of engagement ranging from simply listening or observing to joining in as an active participant. Music stimulates the senses and involves children at many levels, reaching them aesthetically and appealing to their emotional sense. It is playful, soothing, and joyful! It promotes literacy growth by engaging children in experiences involving language; new vocabulary in an engaging context; print; and rhymes, chants, and songs that may inspire higher-level thinking concepts. It con-

Music lets everyone participate

Six-year-old Anthony has a diagnosis of autism. He has little tolerance for musical sounds. Every time we sing, he moans as though in pain from the sound. I [Jan] try to remember that maybe for Anthony our music is too loud.

One day the other children and I gather in the front of the room with drums, triangles, shakers, and sand blocks. I play my guitar. Anthony crawls under his desk and makes every effort to stay there. At the end of each repetition of our song, we switch instruments so everyone can have a chance to play something new.

As we near the end of the song, I nod to Emily, the teaching assistant. Emily understands my unspoken suggestion. She gets up and quietly offers Anthony her drum. As we continue singing and playing, Emily and I peek over to see Anthony playing the drum. He is still under the desk and perhaps is still somewhat bothered by the sounds, but he has found his own sense of pleasure in playing the instrument with us.

Anthony has found a way to join us, on his own time and his own terms. The music that so upset him has become an ally. He is now willing to play with the class, just from a distance.

tributes to a feeling of community as children come together through shared songs, rhymes, chants, and singing games.

Music enhances an inclusive classroom by leveling the playing field so everyone can be a participant. Whether a

Music calms and focuses the mind

I hurry into the school to get to my assigned first grade classroom. The children love music, and I [Jan] look forward to working with them. I crash nose-to-nose with a teaching assistant who works with the youngest children in the school district who have severe behavioral disabilities—the children in my assigned class. Many of them come to school with concerns that would make most of us stagger.

This is a particularly difficult Monday. The assistant quickly summarizes the turmoil. George has had a horrible weekend at home. Alexis has not taken her medication. Justin has spent the weekend away from the consistency of home with Mom and is in a spin as a result. Perhaps, I think, I can find a way to help.

In the classroom I find the teacher sitting in the rocking chair humming, rocking, and holding a child. Two other children are listening through headsets to Baroque music. Soft music comes from the CD player on the shelf. The music's power of relaxation fills the room. The teacher has found solutions on her own. It had been an overwhelming 90-minute beginning to the day, but now, with understanding and change of mood, the atmosphere is calm. The music speaks to the children's emotions. They can now leave their homeroom, go to their inclusive environments, and learn and play with their friends. Music has met the children's need for peace. It has elicited a sense of calm in all of them.

child is a listener or a player, music is accessible and partial participation does not detract from its positive effects.

The essence of music is joyful, nonjudgmental, noncompetitive, and predictable.

For all aspects of music making, children can respond in a range of ways. Some children may be able to sing complete songs with the group or make up their own songs while playing. For others, imitating vocal sounds or playing with their voices is "singing" (Johnson 1996). As an aesthetic expression, the essence of music is joyful, nonjudgmental, noncompetitive, and predictable. Everyone joins in at his or her own level of comfort.

Music activities can encourage interaction among all children in nonthreatening and enjoyable ways.

Musical activities can include all children in meaningful ways when they are designed to offer varied levels of participation. Music can engage all children as collaborators, participants, and community members in activities ranging from group singing and instrument playing to movement games. Individually, music allows children to personalize experiences through listening and bonding with recorded music, moving in expressive ways, entering into song dialogues with a friend, or creating sound segments on drums.

Music teaches social skills

Ariel has difficulty adjusting to the social demands of the classroom. She screams when her mother leaves in the morning and refuses to sit with the group during circle time. Sometimes she throws instruments against the wall or hits children who approach her. Because of this behavior, the children no longer try to be her friend. She plays and works alone. Within her established routine, she seems to be happy.

I [Marcia] come to Ariel's preschool class for 30 minutes each week to conduct music sessions. As a music specialist who is also a music therapist, I not only teach music concepts, but also help the classroom staff and specialists adapt activities and use music to reinforce goals such as sharing, learning concepts, and refining fine and gross motor movements. Often I suggest songs and strategies staff can use throughout the day to meet a variety of needs.

The classroom teachers and I have noticed that Ariel stops and looks when anyone sings a cleanup song. We discover that if we keep the song going and guide her to the toy shelves, Ariel will help with the cleanup. Barney's ditty, "Clean up, clean up, everybody everywhere, clean up, clean up, everybody do your share" really works if we keep singing it over and over until all the children complete the task.

Because music works to encourage Ariel to put toys away, we decide to try it for other tasks. I write simple messages to accompany familiar tunes. The teachers post these throughout the classroom and use them regularly during transitions. After cleaning up, it is time for snacks. "Mmmmm, good, mmmmm, good. Now it's time to have our snack, mmmmm good." When sung to the Campbell's Soup theme, these words round up the children, including Ariel.

As time passes Ariel learns to say good-bye to her mother and join the group for a short time when she hears specific songs. Near the end of the year, she begins to share instruments with a friend when the instructions are given in the context of music: "I'll pass the sticks from me to you; I'll pass the sticks, and you can do it too." Music helps Ariel be an involved member of the class.

Research supports the value of music in learning. Music releases endorphins that provide feelings of happiness and energy. It helps to organize the firing patterns in the cerebral cortex, strengthening creativity and spatial-temporal reasoning (Campbell 1997). A study by Colwell (1994) indicates that using music with a whole language approach to reading facilitates greater text accuracy. Music can also enhance print concepts and prewriting skills (Standley & Hughes 1997) as well as receptive and expressive language (Harding & Ballard 1983; Hoskins 1988; Birkenshaw-Fleming 1997). Music acts as a catalyst to calm listeners, improve special perceptions, and encourage focused, clear thinking (Campbell 1997).

Music can open doors and allow children to join in classroom routines with their friends. Music activities can encourage interaction among all children in nonthreaten-

Start the Music

In 2000 the National Association for Music Education (MENC), Texaco Foundation, NAEYC, and the U.S. Department of Education developed Start the Music, a series of projects and events designed to help bring age-appropriate music education to every child in America. These organizations solicited the expertise of early childhood music educators, music therapists, education association administrators, early childhood educators, and health care providers to identify best practices for early childhood music education and to develop strategies to implement those practices.

Developmentally and individually appropriate musical experiences are guided by these beliefs (MENC 1995):

- All children have music potential. They
  —bring their own unique interests and abilities to the music learning environment;
  —can develop critical thinking skills through musical ideas;
  —come to early childhood music experiences from diverse backgrounds;
  —should experience exemplary musical sounds, activities, and materials.
- Young children should not be expected to meet *performance* goals.
  —Their play is their work.

—They learn best in pleasant physical and social environments.
—They need diverse learning environments.
—They need effective adult models.

Start the Music recognizes the role adults play in assisting young children in their musical development. Families, caregivers, and teachers can all help children grow musically (Neelly, Kenney, & Wolf 2000, 1) by

- **immersing children in musical conversations** while singing, speaking rhythmically, moving expressively, and playing musical instruments. By doing these things, we stimulate children's initial awareness of the beauty and the structure of musical sound.

- **encouraging children's musical responses** by smiling, nodding, and responding with expressive sounds and movements. We thus show children that music making is valuable and important.

- **finding ways to encourage and motivate children's playful exploration,** interpretation, and understanding of musical sound.

Start the Music recognizes that all children are individuals and that music experiences should be a part of *every* child's world.

---

ing and enjoyable ways. In fact, music can actually teach social skills.

Inclusion has become the norm in preschool classrooms throughout the United States, and in some cases has been facilitated by early childhood inclusive music pilot programs (Davis 1990; Hughes et al. 1990; Humpal 1991; Furman & Furman 1996; Humpal & Dimmick 1996). Hughes and colleagues (1990) note that peer acceptance is often viewed as the most serious obstacle to successful inclusive programming and that acceptance can be successfully reached through structured musical interactions. Further, since the brain processes music in both hemispheres, music can stimulate cognitive functioning and may allow for understanding when the spoken word fails (Campbell 1997). Music may provide a cue for an upcoming event or may act as a gentle reminder of what is expected in a group situation.

Conclusion

Music should be a part of *every* young child's day (see "Start the Music"). Music's power to reach *all* children is driven by the sense of community originating from shared songs, rhymes, chants, singing games, and musical books. These activities serve as gateways to involving

individuals and groups of young children. Music creates joy through aesthetics. Music creates inspirational moments and opportunities to make sense out of chaos. Music *belongs* in the inclusive classroom.

References

Birkenshaw-Fleming, L. 1997. Music for young children: Teaching for the fullest development of every child. *Early Childhood Connections* 3 (2): 6–13.

Campbell, D. 1997. *The Mozart effect.* New York: Avon.

Colwell, C. 1994. Therapeutic application of music in the whole language kindergarten. *Journal of Music Therapy* 31 (4): 238–47.

Davis, R. 1990. A model for the integration of music therapy within the preschool classrooms for children with physical disabilities or language delays. *Music Therapy Perspectives* 8: 82–84.

Furman, A., & C. Furman. 1996. Music therapy for learners in a public school early education center. In *Models of music therapy interventions in school settings: From institution to inclusion,* ed. B. Wilson, 258–76. Silver Spring, MD: American Music Therapy Association. [Monograph]

Harding, C., & K. Ballard. 1983. The effectiveness of music as a stimulus and as a contingent reward in promoting the spontaneous speech of three physically handicapped preschoolers. *Journal of Music Therapy* 20 (2): 86–101.

Hoskins, C. 1988. Use of music to increase verbal response and improve expressive language abilities of preschool language-delayed children. *Journal of Music Therapy* 25 (2): 73–83.

Hughes, J., B. Robbins, B. MacKenzie, & S. Robb. 1990. Integrating exceptional and nonexceptional young children through music play: A pilot program. *Music Therapy Perspectives* 8: 52–56.

Humpal, M. 1991. The effects of an integrated early childhood program on social interaction among children with handicaps and their typical peers. *Journal of Music Therapy* 28 (3): 161–77.

Humpal, M., & J. Dimmick. 1996. Music therapy for learners in an early childhood community interagency setting. In *Models of music therapy interventions in school settings: From institution to inclusion*, ed. B. Wilson, 271–311. Silver Spring, MD: American Music Therapy Association. [Monograph]

Johnson, F. 1996. Models of service delivery. In *Models of music therapy interventions in school settings: From institution to inclusion*, ed. B. Wilson, 48–77. Silver Spring, MD: American Music Therapy Association.

MENC (National Association for Music Education). 1995. *Prekindergarten music education standards*. Reston, VA: MENC.

Neelly, L., S. Kenney, & J. Wolf. 2000. *Start the Music strategies*. Reston, VA: MENC.

Standley, J., & J. Hughes. 1997. Evaluation of an early intervention music curriculum for enhancing prereading/writing skills. *Music Therapy Perspectives* 15 (2): 79–86.

For further reading

American Music Therapy Association. 1999. Music therapy and the young child fact sheet. Silver Spring, MD: AMTA.

Boston, B.O. 2000. Start the Music: A report from the Early Childhood Music Summit. Online: http://www.menc.org/guides/startmusic/stmreport.htm

Campbell, D. 2000. *The Mozart effect for children*. New York: HarperCollins.

Miranda, L., A. Arthur, T. Milan, O. Mahoney, & B. Perry. 1998. The art of healing: The CIVITAS Healing Arts Project. *Early Childhood Connections* 4 (4): 35–39.

A Special Book for Children Ages 4–8

Millman, I. 1998. *Moses goes to a concert.* New York: Frances Foster.

Moses and his school friends are deaf. They communicate through American Sign Language (ASL). Today Moses and his classmates are going to a concert. Their teacher, Mr. Samuels, has two surprises in store for them to make this particular concert a special event. At the end of the book are two full conversations in sign language and a page showing the hand alphabet.

Marcia Earl Humpal, M.Ed., MT-BC, is a music therapist in the early childhood division of the Cuyahoga County Board of Mental Retardation and Developmental Disabilities in Cleveland, Ohio. Her model for early childhood inclusive music programs has been the topic of published research and numerous conference presentations.

Jan Wolf, M.S.Ed., is an adjunct instructor in early childhood education at Kent State University and music teacher at The Kindergarten Center, Medina City Schools, Ohio. Jan is a frequent presenter at conferences and is the author of articles on music and young children and the book *Teaching Music.*

From *Young Children*, March 2003, pp. 103-107. Reprinted with permission from the National Association for the Education of Young Children.

Building Relationships with Challenging Children

Teachers who intervene gently, forego punishment, work at bonding, and ensure student success can help at-risk students make positive changes in their lives and in the classroom.

Philip S. Hall and Nancy D. Hall

In their classic study, *400 Losers*, Ahlstrom and Havighurst (1971) were chagrined to discover that their six-year-long, intensive intervention program did not help a group of at-risk youth find success. But, to their surprise, a handful of the participants did turn their lives around. The adolescents who "made it" all had one experience in common: Each had developed a special relationship with either a teacher or a work supervisor during the treatment program. These adults valued the students, treated them as individuals, and expressed faith in their ability to succeed.

A strong relationship with an adult enables an at-risk youth to make life-altering changes. Educators can use specific strategies to develop these nurturing relationships, as one teacher's story demonstrates.

The Chocolate Milk Incident

When the 1st graders came into Ms. Hubble's room from recess, they were rambunctious and hard to settle. "Take your seats," Ms. Hubble told them, "and my two helpers for the week will come by with milk." That helped. At least, it helped everyone except Andreen. As the other students finished their milk and the helpers collected the empty cartons, Andreen got up from her desk. Taking her milk with her, she went to the salamander cage at the back of the room. She peered into the cage and began poking at the salamanders with her straw.

"Please take your seat, Andreen," Ms. Hubble said quietly, walking up to the girl and gently putting a hand on her shoulder. Lurching away, Andreen threw her milk carton into the air. The carton hit Ms. Hubble on the

chest, and chocolate milk gushed out, staining the teacher's white blouse.

Andreen was a new student in Ms. Hubble's class. A week ago, her mother had brought her to school but stayed only long enough to complete the necessary paperwork. Officially, Ms. Hubble knew little about Andreen, but the girl's appearance and behavior told the big picture. The facts that emerged when Andreen's records arrived from her previous school only filled in the blanks.

On her first day, Andreen came into the classroom disheveled and unkempt. Her long auburn hair, tangled and unwashed, coursed down her back over her faded brown dress. Seeing Andreen's appearance and downcast demeanor, the other 1st graders instantly shunned the little girl as if her plight were contagious.

But Andreen's appearance was not her only problem. Andreen had an attitude, and that attitude was not endearing. She was a sullen, angry little girl, hypersensitive about her space and possessions. She pushed or kicked students who walked close to her desk. At recess, her classmates quickly learned to exclude her because she played to win, even if it meant bullying and inventing new rules. In the classroom, Andreen seldom complied with Ms. Hubble's requests. Just that morning, Ms. Hubble had asked Andreen to put her math paper away and finish it later, and the girl had ripped up her paper and defiantly thrown it into her desk.

For a week, Ms. Hubble had been hoping that Andreen's attitude would improve with her adjustment to the new school. But now Ms. Hubble realized that if the little girl was ever going to be successful in school, she, as her teacher, needed to immediately put time and energy into building a relationship with her.

Gentle Intervention

As chocolate milk seeped into her blouse, Ms. Hubble reminded herself that her response to this incident would set the tone for their relationship. She must let Andreen know that she was physically and emotionally safe in her teacher's presence despite this behavior. The situation required a gentle intervention.

The principle of this key relationship-building technique is that when a child engages in behavior that threatens health, safety, property, and basic rights, educators do only what is necessary to protect themselves and others (Hall, 1989). This approach reduces the number of behaviors requiring intervention, so the educator can ignore a lot of students' inappropriate behaviors for the moment and deal with them later if necessary. A gentle intervention defuses rather than detonates the situation and allows the student to maintain a sense of dignity.

After Andreen threw the milk, she turned her back on Ms. Hubble and walked quickly toward another learning center, looking as if she were about to shove the first available thing off the table. "Students," the teacher announced to the class, "it's time for reading. Everyone take out your reading book." Andreen stopped. Turning, she looked at Ms. Hubble. Stepping to her left, so as to give Andreen an unobstructed path to her desk, Ms. Hubble whispered to Andreen, "We're on page 80." For a moment, Andreen thought about what to do. Then she abruptly went to her desk and got out her reading book. As Ms. Hubble walked to the front of the room, she caught Andreen's eye and nodded her approval.

Ms. Hubble's gentle intervention had five important components:

- She unobtrusively interrupted behavior that might have resulted in property destruction.
- She preserved Andreen's dignity.
- She directed Andreen toward a positive response.
- Her directive led Andreen to an appropriate response that could be praised.
- Her directive was, at that moment, the easiest response for Andreen to make. After all, the other students were getting out their reading books, and the most unobstructed path was to her desk.

What Ms. Hubble didn't do as the chocolate milk ran down her blouse was as important as what she did. To her credit, the teacher resisted the emotion-driven impulse to reprimand Andreen. At the very least, Ms. Hubble might have said, "Look at what you've done! You've stained my blouse. You should be ashamed of yourself." That would have felt good! Certainly Andreen had it coming. And the teacher might have added, "And for that little shenanigan, Andreen, you'll stay in from recess for the rest of the week!"

In the heat of the moment, any or all of those actions would have been understandable. But what would have been their effect? In all likelihood, either the admonition or the consequence would have spurred Andreen to sweep her arm across the table, knocking something to the floor. In response, Ms. Hubble would have had to move quickly to restrain Andreen before she broke more things; and if Andreen resisted, Ms. Hubble might have had to drag her down to the principal's office where, by golly, she would have learned her lesson!

Or would she have? Actually, all Andreen would have learned is that Ms. Hubble is, in her opinion, a mean person. An hour later, Andreen would have returned to the classroom temporarily subdued but full of resentment and mistrust.

No Punishment

Had Ms. Hubble made those comments to Andreen or restricted her recess, the teacher would have punished Andreen. Punishment, we believe, is anything an educator says or does to make a student feel guilty, humiliated, or remorseful so that the student will never behave that way again (Hall & Braun, 1988).

A key to building a relationship, however, is not punishing the student—ever. Why not? Because punishment strains or even breaks the bond between teacher and student. Punishment may temporarily control behavior, but it does nothing to teach the student an appropriate response. Worse, punishing a student often instills a desire for revenge. An effective response to behavior that threatens health, safety, property, or basic rights does not include doling out punishment.

That evening, Ms. Hubble phoned Andreen's mother. She did not phone to report the chocolate milk incident. Instead, she asked permission to spend some special time with Andreen. Ms. Hubble said,

> Many of the girls in class are coming to school with their hair in braids. It's the in thing. I would love to help Andreen put her hair in braids, if she wants. Would the two of us have your permission to do that?

The mother, of course, granted permission. "Please share our conversation with Andreen," Ms. Hubble concluded.

Bonding

The next day, Ms. Hubble devoted time to another key principle of relationship building—some call it *bonding* (McGee, Menolascino, Hobbs, & Menousek, 1987). To bond, we value the student for the socially appropriate behaviors that the student can demonstrate and then provide the structure, support, and recognition that the student needs to demonstrate these behaviors. During this bonding time, the adult does not place any expectations on the student for doing the activity the "right" way.

The activity provides opportunities for the adult to value the student, which enhances the student's sense of self-worth and encourages the development of internal standards for behavior. Moreover, when a teacher values a student, the student seems to be biologically inhibited from acting aggressively against that teacher. While the student is in this zone of positive regard, she is disposed to attend to the teacher. Expanding the zone of positive regard mitigates noncompliance and defiance.

That morning, Ms. Hubble talked privately to Andreen:

We can wash and comb your hair during the lunch break and then braid it during afternoon recess. Is that something you'd like to do?

And that is what they did. As they ate lunch privately in the classroom, the two of them chatted up a storm. They talked about anything that the little girl had on her mind, even for a fleeting instant. Ms. Hubble used the conversation not to pry, but rather to enter, by invitation only, into Andreen's world of interests, experiences, and thoughts. Some might call their student-driven conversation trite and meaningless. It wasn't. The conversation and the hair washing were a vehicle for Ms. Hubble to bond with Andreen.

The relationship that Ms. Hubble and Andreen developed that day had immediate results. When the other students saw that Ms. Hubble valued the new girl, they shifted their attitude. Several girls complimented Andreen on her braids and slowly began to take the new girl into their fold.

Ensuring Success

Ensuring success means providing the student with the structure and support for becoming a good learner. When students, especially those with difficult temperaments, fall at learning tasks, they often explode into defiant behaviors. On the day of the chocolate milk incident, Ms. Hubble retrieved the math assignment that Andreen had torn to pieces, carefully taped the paper together, identified the specific math skill that Andreen was missing, and began to address the problem with targeted instruction.

The New Paradigm

By implementing these relationship-building principles, Ms. Hubble enabled Andreen to change her behavior and attitude. When Andreen came into the classroom each morning, she no longer hung her head and scowled. She did not push or kick students who passed by her desk; rather, she smiled at them. When Ms. Hubble made a request, Andreen usually complied. Rather than tearing up her papers, Andreen took them home to show her mother. In Ms. Hubble's classroom, the relationship building with Andreen paid dividends.

Building relationships with students who have challenging behaviors is consistent with an emerging paradigm in education. In the old paradigm, educators developed behavior programs designed to squelch students' inappropriate behaviors, a process that focused on what the student was doing wrong. Educators assumed that when they had brought the inappropriate behaviors under control, the student would automatically demonstrate socially appropriate behaviors. Behavior programming typically contained objectives like "Andrew will decrease (or increase) this behavior," an approach that put most of the responsibility for behavior change on the student—the least capable person in the classroom.

The relationship-building approach more often leads to success.

In contrast, a relationship-building approach helps the student develop positive, socially appropriate behaviors by focusing on what the student is doing right. In the new paradigm, behavior programming puts the initial responsibility for behavior change on the teacher, the most capable and only professionally trained person in the classroom. The relationship-building approach more often leads to success.

References

Ahlstrom, W. M., & Havighurst, R. J. (1971). *400 losers*. San Francisco: Jossey-Bass.

Hall, P. S. (1989, Fall). Teaching for behavior change. *Counterpoint*, 3.

Hall, P. S., & Braun, V. R. (1988, June). Punishment: A consumer's perspective. *TASH Newsletter*, 9.

McGee, J. J., Menolascino, F. J., Hobbs, D. C., & Menousek, P. E. (1987). *Gentle teaching: A nonaversive approach for helping persons with mental retardation*. New York: Human Science Press.

Philip S. Hall (hallps@minotstateu.edu) is a professor in the school psychology program at Minot State University.

Nancy D. Hall (halln@minotstateu.edu), a former elementary school principal, is Vice President for Academic Affairs at Minot State University, 500 University Ave. West, Minot, ND 58707. Their most recent book is *Educating Oppositional and Defiant Children* (ASCD, 2003).

The Itinerant Teacher Hits the Road

A Map for Instruction in Young Children's Social Skills

Faith Haertig Sadler

Early childhood special educators will be expected to adopt new roles with resect to indirect service delivery models (e.g., collaboration, consultation, technical assistance, and training).... The impetus for new professional roles comes primarily from legislation supporting community inclusion of infants and preschoolers with disabilities and their families. (Buysse & Wesley, 1993, p. 418–420.)

The approaching identity crisis is here. For many teachers, "the former teaching role—working and interacting with individual children and their parents—takes a back seat to the themes of logistics, consulting, and relationship issues" (Gallagher, 1997, p. 384). This article is written by one of these new itinerant special education teachers.

What Do Itinerant Teachers Do?

In many large metropolitan school districts, families of young children are offered a continuum of inclusion options, ranging from classes with a few peer models; to blended team-taught classes; and, finally, to full inclusion in community early childhood programs. Frequently children with milder delays receive their early intervention services at the most inclusive end of this continuum. They remain in the general preschools or day-care settings that their parents have chosen for them.

"The former teaching role— working and interacting with individual children and their parents—[now] takes a back seat to the themes of logistics, consulting, and relationship issues"

The diversity of these settings reflects the diversity of families in the community, thus providing intervention settings likely to be culturally and linguistically appropriate. Members of an early childhood itinerant team typically travel weekly to these settings to facilitate the delivery of appropriate special education services. Itinerant staff might provide direct services; consultation; or, in most cases, a combination of the two.

What Do Itinerant Teachers Need?

One of the biggest frustrations for many itinerant teachers has been the lack of resources available to guide them in this new role. Not only do itinerant teachers need an actual map of the city; they also need a theoretical "map" to provide a framework for stepping into this new job description. Many materials are being developed for training child care personnel to include children with disabilities in their programs, as well as materials for training new special education teachers to function in

consulting roles. The latter typically focus on relating issues such as active listening, team building, and problem-solving at meetings (see box, "Online Resources" for examples of the materials available).

Little is available, however, in the way of practical tools to help itinerant teachers organize and implement their job. These materials could provide insight into the nuts and bolts of choosing and embedding interventions into natural environments or could provide tips for dealing with the logistics of scheduling both time to consult and time to provide direct services.

What Do Itinerant Teachers Need to Know and Do to Provide Social-Skills Instruction?

When addressing delays in students' social skills, itinerant teachers need to
- Understand the continuum of social-skills interventions identified in the literature.
- Have a collection of resources reflecting this continuum.
- Match types of interventions to children, given their social settings, and organize these into a schedule.
- Understand the special challenges of this model.

Gallagher's (1997) findings support this. Gallagher followed a group of teachers during their first year in the itinerant role and noted: "Although the importance of the consulting role for teachers moving into new roles is often addressed, the specifics needed for day-to-day implementation of the lofty goals of inclusion are seldom discussed in the literature" (p. 384).

Not only do itinerant teachers need an actual map of the city; they also need a theoretical "map" to provide a framework for stepping into this new job description.

School staff often call on itinerant teachers to address one important area of child development—social skills. It is disconcerting to note, however, that many teachers report discomfort with this new consulting role, especially in supporting children displaying poor social skills (Wesley, Buysse, & Keyes, 2000). The purpose of this article is to suggest a nuts-and-bolts type of framework for addressing social skills instruction within the itinerant model. This article discusses in less detail the relationship issues of this model and instead provides practical information that is currently missing from the literature. I hope these ideas will help teachers who are uncomfortable in this new role and spark a trend in the development of resource materials addressing the day-to-day implementation of this model. The first thing itinerant teachers need to do is build their understanding (see box, "What Do Itinerant Teachers Need to Know and Do?").

Understand the Continuum of Social-Skills Interventions

First, as the itinerant teacher, you need to have a knowledge base of the continuum of interventions identified within the research literature for addressing delays in social skills. One book that provides a concise summary of this is *Integrating Young Children with Disabilities into Community Programs*. In the chapter "Social Interaction Skills Interventions for Young Children with Disabilities in Integrated Settings," Odom and Brown (1993) ranked interventions from low intensity (which usually require low consultation time) to high intensity (which usually require high consultation time). Following is a discussion of four levels of their continuum as each might apply to the itinerant model.

Look for naturally occurring social situations where the child's objectives can be purposely taught and practiced.

Level A: Activity-Based Intervention. This is a naturalistic approach and the least intensive level of instruction. It also requires the least amount of preparation time for the itinerant teacher. Bricker (1998) noted: "Activity-based intervention is a child-directed, transactional approach that embeds children's individual goals and objectives in routine, planned, or child-initiated activities and uses logically occurring antecedents and consequences to develop functional and generative skills" (p. 11). When using this model to teach social skills, look for naturally occurring social situations where the child's objectives can be purposely taught and practiced. When this strategy is applied only to situations that are child initiated, it is referred to as "incidental teaching." According to Brown, McEvoy, and Bishop (1991), "Incidental teaching is different from more structured instruction in that it is conducted during unstructured activities for brief periods of time and typically when children show an interest in or are involved with materials, activities or other children" (p. 36).

When providing direct services at this level, you should remain in the vicinity of the student as he or she moves through classroom activities. This way, you can spontaneously embed instruction on social skills into the natural course of the child's participation. "During an incidental teaching episode, a teacher can provide an adult model or encourage a peer to model appropriate social behavior, as well as prompt and shape appropriate social responding" (Brown et al., 1991, p. 36). When acting in a consulting role, you help the classroom staff examine a typical schedule, looking for opportunities to coach social interactions and then train staff in a few prompting techniques.

Cooperative learning games could include "pairs of children playing different roles: blower and popper with bubbles, hider and seeker in the sand with hidden toys, filler and dumper with buckets and assorted materials, and chooser and gluer with art supplies and glue."

Because this intervention is so natural and easy to implement, it is likely to be embraced positively by classroom staff. This is a good intervention to start with while you get better acquainted with the child and the preschool program. It also works well in combination with other more intensive approaches. When using this intervention, you should schedule weekly sessions during free-choice time. The disadvantage to this approach is that instruction may be too sparse and indirect for some children.

Social skills for young children might include signs of affection, such as giving a high-five, hugging, or shaking hands—which can be incorporated in traditional childhood songs or games,

Level B: Affection Training. This approach provides mildly intensive instruction and does not require much preparation time. It involves collecting or creating songs and games for opening "circle time" that require children to interact affectionately (usually nonverbally) with one another. These signs of affection might include giving a high-five, hugging, or shaking hands and are included as part of traditional childhood songs or games, such as the song "If You're Happy and You Know It" or the game "Duck, Duck, Goose" (Cooper & McEvoy, 1996).

When providing direct services, you lead the "affection" activities at opening circle time. Cooper and McEvoy (1996) recommended:

Before the activities begin, discuss the importance of being friends.... Then ask the children to demonstrate ways to show friendship, such as shaking hands, smiling, or telling people that you like them. Explain to the children that they are giving each other signs of friendship. (p. 67)

When consulting with staff, you support site staff in creating and leading affection activities themselves. Because this type of intervention is fairly simple and introduces only minor changes into the classroom, classroom staff will probably welcome it. The interactions are basic and thus work well when classmates vary greatly in their developmental skills. These activities raise the comfort level among classmates and thus facilitate an increased number of peer interactions during the rest of the school day.

Level C: Structured Social-Skills Groups.

DeKlyen and Odom (1989) found that rates of peer interaction between preschool children with and without disabilities were related to the level of activity structure employed by teachers. In structured social-skills groups, you manipulate the social environment of the classroom by providing specially designed social integration activities for brief periods of time during the day (Odom & Brown, 1993). These

activities are structured in ways that require either social interaction (on a more complex level than the affection activities) or social cooperation. These activities could include simple board games, dramatic play themes with specific interactive roles, group art projects, assembly line cooking, or cooperative games.

Activities that apply concepts and structures from cooperative learning (Curran, 1990; Johnson, Johnson, & Holubec, 1988) would fall into this category. As Fad, Ross, and Boston, (1995) stated:

Cooperative learning has been proven to be an effective way to bring children with disabilities and their peers into an inclusive classroom structure.... Even very young children can learn social skills through cooperative learning—beginning with pairs of children playing different roles: blower and popper with bubbles, hider and seeker in the sand with hidden toys, filler and dumper with buckets and assorted materials, and chooser and gluer with art supplies and glue. (p. 28)

Adding a structured, peer-interaction play center as an option during free play is another way to apply this level of intervention. For example, a classroom may have a block center, home center, book center, art center, and the P.A.L.S. center. In the P.A.L.S. center, the staff "**P**air children, **A**rrange adult behavior, **L**imit materials, and **S**tructure the activity" (Chandler, 1998, p. 15).

This type of intervention is particularly useful for students who are fairly verbal and of normal intelligence but are outcasts from the group. These children may be affected by attention deficit disorder, a learning disability, Asperger's syndrome, or sensory integration disorder. They may be withdrawn, socially clumsy, or aggressive. If the preschool already has some structured instructional times in their program, then this type of intervention is usually accepted by the daily teaching staff. There are quite a few activity books on the market for this type of intervention. Searching

an online bookstore with search words such as "preschool" plus "friendship," "social skills," and "cooperation" will lead teachers to current titles.

This type of intervention involves a fair amount of time sifting through materials and hand picking those that match the child's needs and the program's styles. When using a direct-service approach, you lead these activities. When in a consulting role, you encourage and train site staff to plan and lead the activities themselves. When using this approach, you should schedule the weekly visit during free-choice, small-group, or circle time, depending on the nature of the activities chosen.

Level D: Direct Social-Interaction Interventions.

These activities are the most direct type of instructional approach to teaching social skills. They are also the least naturalistic requiring more direct changes to the typical early childhood classroom. They usually come as kits or instructional manuals and outline a step-by-step format for teaching play skills or problem-solving skills (conflict resolution). In addition to the costs of purchasing the curriculum, there is usually training required. As the itinerant teacher, you should implement this level of intervention directly. Because the instruction is systematic, it involves a lot of preparation time—at least during the first year while learning to use the curriculum. Once learned, however, it can be a great resource for many years.

This type of intervention can be lengthy or, if necessary, shortened to a few lessons on specific target skills. One way to do this is outlined in "Come and Play: Developing Children's Social Skills in an Inclusive Preschool" by Collins, Ault, Hemmeter, and Doyle (1996). They recommend collecting a baseline, targeting specific skills, and teaching the skills using role-plays during group instruction. Following group instruction, the teacher observes skills and prompts the children in the skills during free play. This is followed

Resources for Social Skills Interventions

Activity-Based Intervention

Bricker, D. (1998). *An activity-based approach to early intervention.* Baltimore: Paul H. Brookes.

Brown, W., McEvoy, M., & Bishop, N. (1991). Incidental teaching of social behavior. *TEACHING Exceptional Children, (24)* 1, 35–38.

Segal, M., & Adcock, D. (1993). *Play together grow together: A cooperative curriculum for teachers of young children, New edition.* Ft. Lauderdale, FL: Family Center of Nova Southeastern University.

Affection Training

Cooper, C. S., & McEvoy, M., (1996). Group friendship activities. *TEACHING Exceptional Children, (28)* 3, 67–69.

McEvoy, M. A., Twardosz, S., & Bishop, N. (1990, May). Affection activities: Procedures for encouraging young children with handicaps to interact with their peers. *Education and Treatment of Children, 13*(2), 159–167.

Structured Social Integration Groups

Chandler, L. (1998). Promoting positive interaction between preschool-age children during free play: The PALS center. *Young Exceptional Children (1)* 3, 14–19.

Fad, K. S., Ross, M., & Boston, J. (1995). We're better together: Using cooperative learning to teach social skills to young children. *TEACHING Exceptional Children (27)* 4, 28–34.

Orlick, T. (1978). *The cooperative sports & games book.* New York: Pantheon Books.

Sher, B. (1998). *Self-esteem games: 300 fun activities that make children feel good about themselves.* New York: Wiley.

Smith, C. A. (1993). *The peaceful classroom: 162 easy activities to teach preschoolers compassion and cooperation.* Beltsville, MD: Gryphon House, Inc.

Direct Social Interaction Interventions

Collins, B. C., Ault, M. J., Hemmete, M. L., & Doyle, P. M. (1996, September/October). Come and play: Developing children's social skills in an inclusive preschool. *TEACHING Exceptional Children, (29)*, 1, 16–21.

Committee for Children. (1991). *Second Step: A violence prevention curriculum, level pre-K.* Seattle, WA: Author. (ERIC Document Reproduction Service No. ED 365 739)

McGinnis, E., & Goldstein, A. P. (1990). *Skills streaming in early childhood: Teaching prosocial skills to the preschool and kindergarten child.* Champaign, IL: Research Press.

Odom, S. L., & McConnell, S. R. (1997). *Play time/social time: Organizing your classroom to build interaction skills.* Minneapolis: University of Minnesota, Institute on Community Integration. (ERIC Document Reproduction Service No. ED 412 705/EC 305 924)

Rosenthal-Malek, A. (1997, January/February). Stop and think! Using metacognitive strategies to teach students social skills. *TEACHING Exceptional Children, (29)* 3, 29–31.

then by collecting more data, evaluating, and making modifications. Skills that might be taught this way include inviting a friend to play, sharing toys, asking for a turn, and responding to friends.

Curriculum kits that teach problem-solving may be designed to cover an entire school year. Many preschools do not want to take this much time away from their general curriculum. In this situation it is helpful to teach just the basic problem-solving steps. These self-interrogation strategies are also referred to as "metacognitive strategies." In the article "Stop and Think!" Rosenthal-Malek (1997) described

one way to do this. The self-interrogation strategies are taught in a group format just before free play. Then, the strategies taught at group are immediately promoted and practiced in free-play situations. *The Second Step Curriculum* (Committee for Children, 1991) teaches children to ask themselves: "What's the problem?" "What can I do?" "What would happen if… ?" "What should I try first?" and "Is it working?"

For this intervention, you should schedule the weekly visit during either a large- or small-group instructional time. This type of intervention works best if the classroom teacher remains with the group during the

lessons and reinforces the concepts during the rest of the week.

Gather Resources

The second thing an itinerant teacher must do is collect resources reflecting this continuum. Because you will have little time to spend preparing or hunting down materials, the resources must be kept right at hand. A typical day could include visiting three or four students at different schools, with the time in between spent in your car: driving or doing paperwork, making calls on a cell phone, and eating lunch to avoid an additional drive to the office.

One good resource would be professional books that review and summarize the research literature. These can be helpful because the itinerant teacher must be able to articulate what he or she does and, in most cases, train others to do it. If you have been in the self-contained classroom for a long time, much of your decision making has become intuitive. Sometimes terminology or the rationale behind certain techniques has gotten buried, along with the class notes from graduate school. Professional books can help you review the language of current best practices. One book that provides a brief overview of the research is: *Including Children with Special Needs in Early Childhood Programs* edited by Mark Wolery and Jan S. Wilbers (1994). This book is published by NAEYC and is very reasonably priced.

Activity books are also helpful for generating ideas for lessons, especially because planning time is so limited. Kits are another good resource; however, they are expensive and usually lengthy to implement. Teacher-made handouts are nice because they can be tailored to each situation; but they are time-consuming to create.

Articles from back issues of *TEACHING Exceptional Children* are a great resource. These articles were created for teachers; they are concise, easy to locate by topic, and inexpensive to obtain. It is particularly helpful that these articles may be copied up to 100 times for non-profit use. Articles such as these can be used to help you quickly organize ideas before meetings; when appropriate, they can be left behind for classroom staff to read (for helpful materials, see box, "Resources for Social Skills Interventions").

Match Types of Interventions to Children and Settings

Third, as the itinerant teacher, you must know how to match interventions to children, given their individual situations. This is where you need strong skills in observing and relating to others. Start by asking the parents what they value about this setting and what their expectations and hopes are for how their child will do here socially. Next, you observe the child in the natural environment, study the child's assessment results, and ask the classroom staff about their concerns. As an itinerant teacher, you must

- Become familiar with the program's philosophy and curriculum.
- Notice the program's cultural and linguistic characteristics.
- Look at the daily schedule, the number of students in the class, and the number of teachers and their skill level.

This information gathering helps you get a feel for this particular social "climate." You need to understand how the child is currently functioning within this environment, how peers and teachers feel about him or her, and how the staff feel about the presence of a special education itinerant teacher.

Obviously, you can't just assess all these things and then tell the parents plus site staff what you have "decided" to do. At this point, you must draw on your knowledge of collaboration and teaming models. One resource on this topic is *Partnership in Family-Centered Care: A Guide to Collaborative Early Intervention* (Rosin et al., 1996).

To meet legal timelines, you need to move fairly quickly to facilitate a meeting where the individualized education program (IEP) can be developed with the classroom staff and parents. At the end of the IEP meeting, you can propose that you could come and "float" during several weekly visits, after which a meeting can be held to plan how the team will teach the IEP objectives. This keeps you within the legal timelines for conducting the meeting but allows more time for assessing the situation and building rapport before recommending any specific level or type of intervention.

To prepare for the second meeting, consider one more piece of information: your weekly schedule. In some systems a full-time itinerant special education teacher sees each student 1 hour per week (plus often additional time spent meeting with staff) and 16–20 students in a week. That means some students are seen during circle time, some during free-choice time, some during small-group time, and so on. Teachers must implement some interventions, however, within certain types of activities. Thus, before recommending a particular type of intervention, ask yourself these questions:

- What level of intervention will meet the child's objectives as described on the IEP?
- Will this level be embraced by parents and by classroom staff?
- How can I fit this type of intervention into my schedule?

Understand the Special Challenges of This Model

Finally, as the itinerant teacher, you must understand the challenges you will face. You will be working in someone else's classroom, a classroom most likely chosen by the parents. That classroom's teaching staff, plus the parents, have much more contact time with the student than you do. For interventions to be really effective, classroom staff and parents must embrace them.

How can you motivate staff and parents to work with you?

- Start your work with the student at the low end of the continuum by modeling the incidental teaching techniques in the classroom. Odom, McConnell, and Chandler (1994) found that teachers are more inclined to use naturalistic interventions to teach social interaction, instead of intensive individual interventions. You can also suggest that parents use these incidental teaching techniques at home during play-dates with classmates or relatives. Starting on the lowest level of the continuum shows the classroom teachers and parents that specialized instruction doesn't have to severely change the way they interact with the child. This can help establish trust.

- Be familiar with the continuum of interventions and be able to articulate it in everyday terms. This capability will help parents and classroom staff view you as a useful resource.

- Encourage families and site staff to plan activities that reflect their own character at any level of intervention.

- Keep in mind that this model is primarily an indirect one when planning ways to monitor progress. Even if you are providing direct services once a week, you are also hoping to facilitate change in the daily behavior of classroom staff and parents.

- Measure student progress by collecting data on IEP objectives; but also be watching for signs that the classroom staff and parents are addressing the objectives. One tool for such communication is a traveling notebook that goes everywhere with the child in a backpack. Classroom teachers, parents, therapists, and the itinerant teacher all use this notebook to jot down their anecdotal notes about the child's activities; and they read one another's entries.

Final Thoughts

Because weekly instruction by the itinerant teacher is sparse and because it takes time to effect change in classroom staff and parents, the impact of this service delivery model is slow at first. The continuous modeling provided by a classroom of peers without disabilities, however, can be powerful for many children. It is also an enabling experience to have early childhood teachers and special education teachers working side by side. This coteaching experience slowly increases the capacity of the community to meet the needs of children with disabilities.

This article has provided a map to assist the itinerant teacher in addressing student delays in social skills. As more teachers become familiar with this new role, they may draw even more maps providing practical information for the itinerant teacher. Some day we will no longer be in an identity crisis, but be confidently navigating our way in early childhood settings everywhere.

References

Bricker, D. (1998). *An activity-based approach to early intervention* (2nd ed.). Baltimore: Paul H. Brookes.

Brown, W., McEvoy, M., & Bishop, N. (1991). Incidental teaching of social behavior. *TEACHING Exceptional Children, (24)* 1, 35–38.

Buysse, V., & Wesley, P. W. (1993). The identity crisis in early childhood special education: A call for professional role clarification. *Topics in Early Childhood Special Education, 13* (4), 418–429.

Chandler, L. (1998). Promoting positive interaction between preschool-age children during free play: The PALS center. *Young Exceptional Children, (1)* 3, 14–19.

Collins, B. C., Ault, M. J., Hemmeter, M. L., & Doyle, P. M. (1996, September/October). Come and play: Developing children's social skills in an inclusive preschool. *TEACHING Exceptional Children, (29)* 1, 16–21.

Committee for Children. (1991). *Second Step: A violence prevention curriculum, level pre-K.* Seattle, WA: Author.

Cooper, C. S., & McEvoy (1996). Group friendship activities. *TEACHING Exceptional Children, (28)* 3, 67–69.

Curran, L. (1990). *Cooperative learning lessons for little ones: Literature-based language arts and social skills.* San Juan Capistrano, CA: Resources for Teachers.

DeKlyen, M., & Odom, S. L. (1989). Activity structure and social interaction with peers in developmentally integrated play groups. *Journal of Early Intervention, 13,* 342–351.

Fad, K. S., Ross, M., & Boston, J.(1995). We're better together: Using cooperative learning to teach social skills to young children. *TEACHING Exceptional Children, (27)* 4, 28–34.

Gallagher, P. A. (1997). Teachers and inclusion: Perspectives on changing roles. *Topics in Early Childhood Special Education, 17,* 363–386.

Johnson, D. W., Johnson, R., & Holubec, E. (1988). *Cooperation in the classroom* (Rev. ed.). Edina, MN: Interaction Book Company.

Odom, S. L., & Brown, W. H. (1993). Social interaction skills interventions for young children with disabilities in integrated settings. In C. A. Peck, A. L. Odom, & D. D. Bricker (Eds.), *Integrating young children with disabilities into community programs* (pp. 39–64). Baltimore: Paul H. Brookes.

Odom, S. L., McConnell, S. R., & Chandler, L. K. (1994). Acceptability and feasibility of classroom-based social interaction interventions for young children with disabilities. *Exceptional Children, 60,* 226–236.

Rosenthal-Malek, A. (1997, January/February). Stop and think! Using metacognitive strategies to teach students social skills. *TEACHING Exceptional Children, (29)* 3, 29–31.

Rosin, P., Whitehead, A., Tuchman, L., Jensien, F., Begun, A. & Irwin, L. (1996). *Partnership in family-centered care: A guide to collaborative early intervention.* Baltimore: Paul H. Brookes.

Wesley, P. W., Buysse, V., & Keyes, L. (2000). Comfort zone revisited: Child characteristics and professional comfort with consultation. *Journal of Early Intervention, 23* (2), 106–115.

Wolery, M., & Wilbers, J. S. (Eds.). (1994) *Including children with special needs in early childhood programs.* Washington DC: National Association for the Education of Young Children.

Faith Haertig Sadler *(CEC Chapter #28), Team Leader and Teacher, Early Childhood Itinerant Team, Seattle Public Schools, Washington.*

Address correspondence to the author at Seattle Public Schools, Wilson Room 104, 1130 N. 90th, Seattle, WA 98103 (e-mail: fsadler@at@;uswest.net).

From *Teaching Exceptional Children,* September/October 2001, pp. 60–66. © 2001 by The Council for Exceptional Ithildren. Reprinted by permission.

UNIT 3
Learning Disabilities

Unit Selections

Key Points to Consider

- Describe scaffolded instruction. What is the goal of scaffolding for students with LDs?

- How has neuroscience mapped dyslexia? What reading methods work best for students with dyslexia?

- How has the high school program called LEAD helped students with LDs? How does it work?

- What can be done to reduce the social isolation of students with learning disabilities?

 **Links: www.dushkin.com/online/**
These sites are annotated in the World Wide Web pages.

Children and Adults With Attention Deficit/Hyperactivity Disorder (CHADD)
http://www.chadd.org
The Instant Access Treasure Chest
http://www.fln.vcu.edu/ld/ld.html
Learning Disabilities Association of America (LDA)
http://www.ldanatl.org
Learning Disabilities Online
http://www.ldonline.org
OHSU Center on Self Determination
http://cdrc.ohsu.edu/selfdetermination/education/moving/communitysolutions.html
Teaching Children With Attention Deficit Disorder
http://www.kidsource.com/kidsource/content2/add.html

Learning how to learn is one of life's most important tasks. For students with disabilities of learning it is a most critical lesson. Today general education teachers and special educators must seriously attend to the growing numbers of students who have a wide range of different learning disabilities (LDs). LD enrollments in inclusive, regular education classes have skyrocketed. They are the fastest growing and largest category of exceptionalities in elementary, middle, and high schools. Children with LDs now make up over 50 percent of those receiving special educational services.

The ways in which students with LDs are identified and served have been radically transformed with the reauthorization of PL94-142 in 1997 as PL105-17, or IDEA (Individuals with Disabilities Education Act). New assessment methods have made the identification of students with LDs easier and far more common. Many law makers and educators, however, feel that students who have other problems (for example, behavior disorders, poor learning histories, or dysfunctional families) are erroneously being diagnosed with LDs. IDEA requires states to place students with disabilities in regular classrooms as much as possible or lose their federal funding. A landmark U.S. Supreme Court case in November of 1993 (*Carter v. Florence Co., S.C.*) ruled that public schools must give appropriate educational services to students with LDs or pay the tuition for private schools to do so. This ruling opened a floodgate of new litigation by parents. IDEA has turned out to be much more expensive than Congress envisioned when it enacted this celebrated (and defiled) education bill 25 years ago.

Is the rapid increase in students assessed to have learning disabilities really an artifact of misdiagnoses, exaggeration, and a duping of the system that makes funding available for special needs? Neonatal medical technology and achievements in preventive medicine and health maintenance have greatly reduced

the numbers of children who are born deaf, blind, severely physically disabled, or with multiple exceptional conditions. The very same medical technology has greatly increased the numbers of children kept alive who are born prematurely, small for gestational age, with low birth weight, and "at-risk" for less severe disabilities such as LDs.

A learning disability is usually defined by the lay public as difficulty reading or calculating. IDEA defines it as a disorder in the processes involved in understanding or in using language, spoken or written, that may manifest itself in an imperfect ability to listen, speak, read, write, spell, or do mathematical calculations. Learning disabilities are identified differently outside of education. *The Diagnostic and Statistical Manual of Mental Disorders* (4th edition) divides LDs into academic skills disorders (reading, mathematics, written expression) and attention deficit hyperactive disorder (ADHD). The National Joint Committee for Learning Disabilities (NJCLD) separates LDs into specific problems related to the acquisition and use of listening, speaking, reading, writing, reasoning, or mathematical abilities. Attention deficit hyperactive disorder, if not accompanied by any specific learning problem or any specific behavioral/emotional disorder, can be assessed as a health disability by both IDEA and NJCLD especially if it can be ameliorated with medication. Due to parental pressures, the IDEA definition of LDs has been amended administratively to include ADHD if the deficit in attention leads to difficulty in learning. In this compendium, ADHD is treated as a health disability.

The rest of the definition of an LD is an exclusionary definition. It helps clarify the nature of LDs. They are not developmental disabilities. They are not deficiencies in any of the sensory systems (vision, hearing, taste, touch, smell, kinesthetics, vestibular sensation). They are not problems associated with health or physical mobility. They are not emotional or behavioral disorders. They are not disabilities of speech or language. They can be assessed as true LDs only if there is a discrepancy between the child's ability to learn and his or her actual learning.

IDEA's strong emphasis on a free and appropriate educational placement for every child with a disability has forced schools to be more cautious about all assessments and labeling. Increasing numbers of children are now being assessed as LD who once might have been labeled developmentally disabled or disabled by speech, language, emotions, behavior, or one of the senses. A child with an LD may concurrently have a disability in any of these other areas, but if this occurs, both the LD and any other disabilities must be addressed in an individualized education plan (IEP) designed especially for that unique child.

Recent research suggests that reading disabilities may affect about 15 percent of elementary school-aged children. If this is accurate, many LD children are not yet being identified and serviced. The causes of LDs are unknown. Usually some central nervous system glitches are believed to underlie the disabilities, even if their existence cannot be demonstrated. Other suspected causes include genetic inheritance, poor nutrition, or exposure to toxic agents. The NJCLD definition of LD presumes biological causation and lifetime chronicity.

This unit on learning disabilities addresses both the successes and the frustrations of educating children with LDs. The first article in the section discusses the importance of a supportive environment. It describes scaffolded instruction, the systematic sequencing of prompted content, materials, tasks, and teacher and peer support to optimize learning. The goal of scaffolding is to support students until they can carry out tasks or skills independently. The careful sequencing helps control frustration and assists students to clear their minds of the word "can't." Guidelines for effective scaffolding are given by Martha Larkin.

In the second article Sally and Bennett Shaywitz review the latest research on dyslexia. Functional magnetic resonance imaging studies are demonstrating the glitches between recognizing sounds and recognizing words in the brains of students with dyslexia. Early intervention can correct or compensate for these glitches.

The third article describes methods used by one school's LEAD (Learning and Education About Disabilities) group. It has multiple components that help students with LDs gain confidence and self-esteem. The LEAD group helps prepare them for all of life.

The last selection depicts the problems of social skills in students with LDs. Deborah Court and Sarah Givon suggest ways to improve these skills.

Providing Support for Student Independence Through Scaffolded Instruction

Martha J. Larkin

Students with learning disabilities need a supportive environment to function successfully in school—and later in the workplace. A supportive environment enables them to capitalize on their strengths and minimize or cope effectively with their weaknesses. Gerber, Ginsberg, and Reiff (1992) noted characteristics of successful adults with learning disabilities:

- Having the desire to excel.
- Reframing their disability in a positive manner.
- Setting explicit personal goals.
- Being willing to take risks.
- Taking advantage of strengths.

If students with learning and other disabilities are to exhibit characteristics of successful adults, they need appropriate support in school. Such support includes "scaffolding," or providing steps that lead to achievement (see box, "What Is Scaffolded Instruction?").

In this article, we visit a special education teacher who practiced effective scaffolding. This teacher shares her thoughts about the challenges she faced in assisting a student to achieve independence. Several other teachers provide guidelines for effective scaffolding.

Breaking the Failure Cycle

Many students who receive special education services as early as second and third grades already have become well immersed in a "failure cycle." These students are not identified to receive special educational services until the number of their failures well exceeds the number of their successful experiences. Melanie (not her real name), a third grader identified with a learning disability, lost all hope that she could be successful in school until Anna Davis (again, not her real name), a special education teacher, provided her a supportive environment (see box, "Meet Melanie").

Through scaffolded instruction, Anna Davis provided Melanie with the support she needed to become a successful reader and to begin developing confidence in her abilities. As Anna's comments indicated, ensuring a supportive environment for Melanie and her peers with disabilities is a substantial challenge. It is labor intensive and time consuming, and success is measured in small increments. As Melanie performs tasks with less teacher assistance, she gains more self-confidence and is more likely to take risks (e.g., attempting to perform a portion or even entire tasks independently). A measure of success for Melanie and many of her peers with learning disabilities is achieving the independence in at least some academic areas.

Educators can learn much from teachers like Anna who facilitate a caring, supportive environment for their students—to help them strive for independence.

How Can Teachers Provide Effective Scaffolded Instruction?

In a summary of the literature, Hogan and Pressley (1997) listed eight essential elements of scaffolded instruction: pre-engagement; establishing a shared goal; actively diagnosing the understandings and needs of the learners; providing tailored assistance; maintaining pursuit of the goal; giving feedback; controlling for frustration and risk; and assisting internationalization, independence, and generalization to other contexts. Teachers need not follow these elements in lockstep succession, but use them as general guidelines for dynamic, flexible scaffolding. Let's examine each, as it applies to the example of Melanie.

Pre-engagement with the Learner and Curriculum. During pre-engagement, the teacher considers curriculum goals and student needs to select an appropriate task (Hogan & Pressley, 1997). Anna Davis selected appropri-

What Is Scaffolded Instruction?

Scaffolded instruction is "the systematic sequencing of prompted content, materials, tasks, and teacher and peer support to optimize learning" (Dickson, Chard, & Simmons, 1993, p. 12). Scaffolding provides students with the help they need and allows them to complete a task with assistance before they are able to complete it independently (Pearson, 1996). The goal of scaffolding is to support students until they can apply the new skills and strategies independently. This means a gradual decrease in supports and a gradual increase in student responsibility with the responsibility for learning shifting from the teacher to the student (Rosenshine & Meister, 1992). In other words, scaffolded instruction means that teachers make sure that their students have the necessary support to complete a task successfully. When learning something new or difficult, students may need more assistance; and as they begin to demonstrate task mastery, the support is removed gradually. Through appropriately scaffolded instruction, students accept more responsibility for their learning and become more independent learners.

Dixon (1994) provided an example of scaffolded instruction as it might be used to teach a child with physical disabilities or a young child how to use a playground slide. An adult might begin by carrying the child up the steps to the slide and holding the child while both adult and child slide together. After a few times of sliding together, some of the scaffolding or adult support may be removed by placing the child low on the slide, allowing him or her to slide independently for a short distance. Gradually the scaffolding would be removed as the child assumed more responsibility toward sliding the entire distance independently.

Dixon (1994) cautioned against removing the scaffolding all at once or prematurely. Doing so— on a playground slide—could cause serious physical injury to the child. Likewise, removing scaffolding prematurely or never providing students with any supports in academic subjects could result in "serious intellectual injury." Physical injuries can heal, but achievement injuries may be difficult to rehabilitate (Dixon).

Ensuring a supportive environment for students with disabilities is a substantial challenge.

Establishing a Shared Goal. Mutual goal setting for Melanie and Anna was not difficult. Unlike some students who say that they don't want to learn to read, Melanie did want to read. Like many teachers of third-grade students with disabilities, Anna devoted a large portion of the day to teaching her students to read. As noted by Hogan and Pressley (1997), motivating students toward establishing a shared goal is providing a delicate balance between allowing the student to lead and following the traditional path of teacher-directed instruction.

Actively Diagnosing the Understandings and Needs of the Learners. The teacher must be sensitive to the learner and be knowledgeable of content matter to compare student performance to external standards for growth (Hogan & Pressley, 1997). Anna was sensitive to Melanie's need to feel successful and comfortable with the reading process. Anna reminded Melanie of her recent successful reading experiences when Melanie was convinced that she could not perform a similar reading task. In addition, Anna frequently questioned her students to determine their understanding of a task.

Providing Tailored Assistance. Hogan and Pressley (1997) suggested that assistance could take the form of cueing or prompting, questioning, modeling, telling, or discussing. Although Anna used all these forms of assistance, most of the examples provided will focus on cueing. The following illustrates how she used cueing to help Melanie with letter reversals.

> In reading, we used the rabbits [small plastic counters] for phonemic awareness. We were practicing spelling words. When you have *b* and *d*, if you turn the rabbits in that direction [the stomach of one rabbit counter points in the direction of the round part of the letter *b*, and another points in the opposite direction for the letter *d*], they're getting a pictorial cue again of which way [the letter should be turned]. I noticed that when Melanie wrote *bud*, she reversed her *b*s and *d*s. I said to her, "Remember the rabbits." She looked down and said, "Oh yeah," erased it, and put it the correct way. I think it's better to use little clues rather than saying, "Oh, you reversed that letter, or that letter is wrong." All I had to do is say, "Remember the rabbits," because I think that is a far more positive way of saying it.

Maintaining Pursuit of the Goal. Students who have been immersed in the "failure cycle" may have trouble maintaining pursuit of the goal. Particularly for compli-

ate reading tasks for Melanie, as guided by Melanie's individualized education program (IEP) goals. Anna was aware of the difficulties that Melanie had with reading and her lack of self-confidence in her reading ability.

Meet Melanie

Melanie said she wanted to be able to read. She didn't realize that she could read and that was a goal she desired. She said, "If I can only read like everyone else."

Then I said, "Well, you can."

She said, "No, I can't. I don't know how."

I said, "Yes, you do; but you don't know you do." I basically showed her that she could read. She is one of the stronger readers of the group.

I showed her that she knew how to do word-attack skills because she didn't think that she did. I showed her how to look for the small word in the big word and how to leave out a word she didn't know by reading the whole sentence and then figuring out the word. She learned to understand what she read just by asking the *who, what, where,* and *why* questions. She never asked herself those questions before because she never knew that was something you did. So she feels pretty good about herself.

Melanie attempts to pass over areas in which she is uncertain, rather than shut down and say she can't do it. I say, "Now, look how well you did there. Look how well you read and understood what you read. Now, let's try this. It is a little bit harder, but let's try it."

I will keep saying, "Look, remember what you did before? Think about how you used the techniques that you were using at that time to read that passage. Now let's try this one." If you don't make her feel that she has succeeded in one place, Melanie would tend to shut down and not want to try.

—*Anna Davis*

cated tasks, teachers may need to provide more support for students to be persistent and focused (Hogan & Pressley, 1997). Anna gave Melanie extra praise and encouragement to increase her level of motivation. Notice how Anna bolstered Melanie's confidence at the slightest indication that Melanie was slipping into failure.

Giving Feedback. Hogan and Pressley (1997) noted that the teacher who uses scaffolding summarizes student progress and highlights behaviors that lead to success in anticipation that students eventually will self-monitor their own learning. Anna provided feedback appropriately to Melanie by summarizing the progress that she had made in reading; Anna mentioned particular behaviors (i.e., Anna called them "techniques") that led to Melanie's success. Anna was keen on giving immediate feedback (i.e., as soon as possible following a behavior or task completion, usually within the same class period) to

her students and giving feedback in a way that students could have opportunities to correct their errors.

As a student performs tasks with less and less teacher assistance, she gains more self-confidence and is more likely to take risks.

Controlling for Frustration and Risk. The teacher needs to create an environment in which students are free to try alternatives without being penalized and in which mistakes are considered part of learning (Hogan & Pressley, 1997). Anna's classroom environment was one in which students could feel safe in taking risks with their learning. Students like Melanie knew that errors were part of the learning process. Anna described her classroom as

> easy-going, relaxed, a place where learning is fun, where success if far more important than failure. Feedback is positive, so that there is no negativism. These kids have come from classes where they've been put down all of their life, three years of school.... They have been just miserable, and they hurt. They think they are dumb and can never learn. My job is to tell them, "Yes, you can learn, and you will, and this is how we are going to do it. It's easy. It's fun. Let's get on with it." I teach to make them succeed.

Assisting Internalization, Independence, and Generalization to Other Contexts. This means helping students to become less dependent on the teacher's extrinsic signals for what to do next and providing students with the opportunity to practice the skills in different contexts (Hogan & Pressley, 1997). Successful instruction is defined by the degree to which the student uses the information learned to meet the demands of natural settings (Ellis & Larkin, 1998). Anna wanted her students to become independent learners; she recognized that once the students left her classroom and the elementary school, there would be fewer opportunities for teacher assistance. Students would have to become more independent, or run the risk of failure. Anna valued student independence but realized that it would have to occur gradually for some:

> I'm hoping I can find some small tiles where I can put letters on the tiles instead of using the rabbits. We are going to start moving the tiles so that I can see where there's awareness of the vowel sounds. Now we have done vowels for two years and [mastery] is still not there. I'll have to use the tiles where they [the students] place them. They're going to get a visual as well as a kinesthetic [cue], so when they write the word, I'm hoping it transfers.

Guidelines for Effective Scaffolding

- *Identify what students know.* Effective scaffolding requires that teachers are cognizant of what a student already knows (background or prior knowledge), the student's misconceptions, and the student's current zone of proximal development (i.e., which competencies are developing and which are beyond the student's current level of functioning; Pressley, Hogan, Wharton-McDonald, Mistretta, & Ettenberger, 1996). For example, Anna was aware that some of her students "think in terms of money." When she taught "rounding" to those students, Anna used the familiar concept of money.

- *Begin with what students can do.* Laura (not her real name), another special education teacher, was aware of individual student ability levels. When Laura began reading lessons, she gave the students with learning disabilities an opportunity to read something that could be read independently or with little teacher assistance. This enabled students to begin the reading lesson successfully.

- *Help students achieve success quickly.* Laura found that writing and penmanship tasks were laborious for some of her students with written expression disabilities. When she assisted her special education students in the general education classroom for a lesson on storytelling, Laura asked the students to dictate their ideas while she wrote them on paper. This accommodation enabled the students who had difficulty with written expression to generate ideas without worrying how to convey them on paper. Also, Laura served as an adult listener to reinforce the notion that storytelling and written expression is an act of communication and shared experience.

- *Help students to "be" like everyone else.* Miller and Fritz (1998) interviewed a successful adult with learning disabilities about his school history and found that a major theme was the individual's desire to be regarded like other students. These researchers suggested that as much as possible, teachers orient classroom tasks for students' work to be perceived as being like that of their peers. For example, Anna suggested that Mark (not his real name), a struggling student, be moved into a third-grade text like that of his peers. She informed Mark of his responsibility to work hard, but also let him know that she would be there to give him the assistance he needed. Anna noted that when Mark was placed in the third-grade math book with her assistance, he was still struggling with math, but was holding his own. She was confident that she made the right decision to place him in a more difficult math book, with assistance, because Mark felt good about using the same book as his third-grade peers.

- *Know when it's time to stop.* Anna learned from experience that continued drill and practice may not always be effective. She stated, "Overkill erases." Anna found that once her students had demonstrated mastery of a skill, continued practice may result in the students' refusing to work or students' producing work with numerous errors. For example, when some of Anna's students with learning disabilities were asked to complete a general education math assignment with 50 problems, she noticed that the students completed the first three rows of problems without an error. Students began making numerous errors on the final three rows. Anna found that employing systematic review and purposeful practice with a limited number of math problems was effective. She also noted that a just a few written or spoken questions regarding reading or language arts assignments provided needed review without overkill.

- *Help students be independent when they have command of the activity.* Effective scaffolding means that teachers need to listen and watch for clues from their students as to when teacher assistance is or is not needed. Obviously, teachers do not want students to fail, but they should not allow students to become too dependent on the teacher. As special education teacher Beverly (not her real name) noted, achieving independence is different for individual students. Some students may be at identical skill levels, but emotionally may be at different levels regarding the amount of frustration they can tolerate. Students may not be able "to be weaned" from teacher assistance at the same time. In other words, some students will need more teacher support while learning to perform a task; others will demonstrate task mastery more quickly. Like the mother bird that helps her chicks leave the nest to become independent birds, teachers need to help their students gradually move from teacher assistance to student independence as students demonstrate command of the task or activity.

By expressing that she hopes the visual and kinesthetic cues from the use of the tiles will aid transfer, Anna recognized how difficult the generalization of learned skills may be for some students with learning disabilities. Students first must acquire and maintain skills at a proficient level before they can be generalized to other contexts. Although much of her instructional time was spent helping students with skill acquisition and maintenance, Anna fostered independence and generalization in the area of student self-monitoring for errors. Just like she cued her students when they made letter reversals in reading, Anna also used cues to call students' attention to number reversals in math

> For number reversals like 5, 3, 6, and 7, I usually will say something like, "You really have to discipline your 3. It keeps jumping around on you." The kids laugh and they go, "Oh, yeah!"

Students who have been immersed in the "failure cycle" may have trouble maintaining pursuit of the goal.

Anna's sense of humor not only made the students feel at ease with error monitoring and correction, but also gave them opportunities to practice these skills when the teacher made a error.

> I usually tell them it is safe to make mistakes in here, because your teacher makes them every day.... I allow them to catch me on mistakes.... Yesterday, I couldn't get that word spelling right, *s-c-r-a-t-c-h*. The students were laughing and having a wonderful time, but I turned that into learning. "You tell me how to spell it, because I'm having a terrible time with this word."

Anna tried to provide cues only when students needed them (e.g., struggling with a familiar task in a new context, or making an error). To lessen teacher dependence gradually, Anna cued students to use "error monitoring" strategies when she gave the directions for an assignment. "When you do your sentences on page 86, please read them to yourself. Sometimes, when you read them to yourself, you find what you left out." Another way Anna used cues was to help students to verbalize how they recognized their own errors (e.g., "How did you recognize your mistake, Randy?"). Anna seized this opportunity to help Randy (not his real name) identify the naturally occurring events that alerted him to his error. Although Anna's students needed more assistance with generalization of skills, they were making progress on the road to independence.

In addition to the eight essential elements of scaffolded instruction, teachers like Anna have developed their own guidelines for effective scaffolding (see box, "Guidelines").

Final Thoughts

Students with learning disabilities need a supportive classroom environment that can help them recognize their strengths and feel confident about their abilities in order to achieve at least some degree of independent functioning. Through carefully scaffolded instruction, special education and general education teachers can take proactive paths of moving their students towards independence and achieving success. This path will be challenging for teachers and students. To provide effective scaffolding for some or all students in the classroom across several content areas may require an enormous amount of time and energy from the teacher (Pressley et al., 1996). Teachers must tailor scaffolding to meet individual student needs. Also, effective scaffolding requires the provision of "calibrated assistance" (Wong, 1998). Teachers must be cognizant of the kinds and degrees of assistance provided to individual students (for more about scaffolded instruction, see box, "Resources"). Support or assistance must be removed gradually (Rosenshine & Meister, 1992).

Finally, teachers need to pay attention to clues from their students as to when teacher support is or is not needed. As noted by Beed, Hawkins, and Roller (1991). "Independence must somehow be achieved through the daily interaction between teachers and children" (p. 648).

Although the examples in this article have focused on elementary school students and teachers, scaffolding principles and techniques can guide teachers to assist students on any grade level to become more independent learners.

References

Beed, P. L., Hawkins, E. M., & Roller, C. M. (1991). Moving learners toward independence: The power of scaffolded instruction. *The Reading Teacher, 44*, 648–655.

Dickson, S. V., Chard, D. J., & Simmons, D. C. (1993). An integrated reading/writing curriculum: A focus on scaffolding. *LD Forum, 18* (4), 12–16.

Dixon, R. (1994). Research-based guidelines for selecting a mathematics curriculum. *Effective School Practices, 13* (2), 47–61.

Ellis, E. S., & Larkin, M. J. (1998). Strategic instruction for adolescents with learning disabilities. In B. Y. L. Wong (Ed.), *Learning about learning disabilities* (2nd ed.; pp. 585–656). San Diego, CA: Academic Press.

Gerber, P. J., Ginsberg, R., & Reiff, H. B. (1992). Identifying alterable patterns in employment success for highly successful adults with learning disabilities. *Journal of Learning Disabilities, 25*, 474–487.

Hogan, K., & Pressley, M. (1997). Scaffolding scientific competencies within classroom communities of inquiry. In K. Hogan & M. Pressley (Eds.), *Scaffolding student learning: Instructional approaches & issues* (pp. 74–107). Cambridge, MA: Brookline Books.

Miller, M., & Fritz, M. F. (1998). A demonstration of resilience. *Intervention in School and Clinic, 35*, 265–271.

Pearson, P. D. (1996). Reclaiming the center, *The first R: Every child's right to read* (pp. 259–274). New York: Teachers College Columbia University.

Pressley, M., Hogan, K., Wharton-McDonald, R., Mistretta, J., & Ettenberger, S. (1996). The challenges of instructional scaffolding: The challenges of instruction that supports student

Resources for Scaffolded Instruction

Beed, P. L., Hawkins, E. M., & Roller, C. M. (1991). Moving learners toward independence: The power of scaffolded instruction. *The Reading Teacher, 44*, 648–655.

Dickson, S. V., Chard, D. J., & Simmons, D. C. (1993). An integrated reading/writing curriculum: A focus on scaffolding. *LD Forum, 18* (4), 12–16.

Dixon, R. C., & Carnine, D. (1993). Using scaffolding to teach writing. *Educational Leadership, 51* (3), 100–102.

Gambrell, L. B., Morrow, L. M., Neuman, S. B., & Pressley, M. (Eds.). (1999). *Best practices in literacy instruction.* New York: The Guilford Press.

Graves, M. F., & Braaten, S. (1996). Scaffolded reading experiences: Bridges to success. *Preventing School Failure, 40* (4), 169–173.

Graves, M. F., Graves, B. B., & Braaten, S. (1996). Scaffolded reading experiences for inclusive classes. *Educational Leadership, 53* (5), 14–16.

Hiebert, E. H., & Raphael, T. E. (1998). *Early literacy instruction.* Fort Worth, TX: Harcourt Brace College Publishers.

Hogan, K., & Pressley, M. (Eds). (1997). *Scaffolding student learning: Instructional approaches & issues.* Cambridge, MA: Brookline Books.

Kameenui, E. J., & Carnine, D. W. (1998). *Effective teaching strategies that accommodate diverse learners.* Upper Saddle River, NJ: Merrill.

Meichenbaum, D., & Biemiller, A. (1998). *Nurturing independent learners: Helping students take charge of their learning.* Cambridge, MA: Brookline Books.

Palincsar, A. S. (1991). Scaffolded instruction of listening comprehension with first graders at risk for academic difficulty. In A. McKeough & J. L. Lupart (Eds.), *Toward the practice of theory-based instruction* (pp. 50–65). Hillsdale, NJ: Erlbaum.

Pressley, M., Hogan, K., Wharton-McDonald, R., Mistretta, J., & Ettenberger, S. (1996). The challenges of instructional scaffolding: The challenges of instruction that supports student thinking. *Learning Disabilities Research & Practice, 11* (3), 138–146.

Rosenshine, B., & Meister, C. (1992). The use of scaffolds for teaching higher-level cognitive strategies. *Educational Leadership, 49* (7), 26–33.

Soderman, A. K., Gregory, K. M., & O'Neill, L. T. (1999). *Scaffolding emergent literacy: A child-centered approach for preschool through grade 5.* Boston: Allyn & Bacon.

Wollman-Bonilla, J. E., & Werchadlo, B. (199). Teacher and peer roles in scaffolding first graders' responses to literature. *Reading Teacher, 52*, 598–608.

Wong, B. Y. L. (Ed.). (1998). Scaffolding. (Special issue). *Journal of Learning Disabilities, 31* (4).

thinking. *Learning Disabilities Research & Practice, 11* (3), 138–146.

Rosenshine, B., & Meister, C. (1992). The use of scaffolds for teaching higher-level cognitive strategies. *Educational Leadership, 49* (7), 26–33.

Wong, B. Y. L. (1998). Analyses of intrinsic and extrinsic problems in the use of the scaffolding metaphor in learning disabilities intervention research: An introduction. *Journal of Learning Disabilities, 31*, 340–343.

Martha J. Larkin *(CEC Chapter #356), Assistant Professor of Special Education, State University of West Georgia, Carrollton, Georgia.*

Address correspondence to the author at Department of Special Education and Speech Language Pathology, 1600 Maple Street, State University of West Georgia, Carrollton, GA 30118 (e-mail: mlarkin@westga.edu).

This research was supported by a grant from the Donald D. Hammill Foundation. The author would like to thank the special education teachers in Alabama and Virginia who opened the doors to their classrooms and gave so willingly of their time, expertise, and perspectives.

Reading Disability and the Brain

Neurological science and reading research provide the scientific knowledge we need to ensure that almost every child becomes a successful reader.

Sally E. Shaywitz and Bennett A. Shaywitz

The past decade has witnessed extraordinary progress in our understanding of the nature of reading and reading difficulties. Never before have rigorous science (including neuroscience) and classroom instruction in reading been so closely linked. For the first time, educators can turn to well-designed, scientific studies to determine the most effective ways to teach reading to beginning readers, including those with reading disability (National Reading Panel, 2000).

What does the evidence tell us? Several lines of investigation have found that reading originates in and relies on the brain systems used for spoken language. In addition, accumulating evidence sheds light on the nature of reading disability, including its definition, prevalence, longitudinal course, and probable causes. Although the work is relatively new, we have already made great progress in identifying the neural systems used for reading, identifying a disruption in these systems in struggling readers, and understanding the neural mechanisms associated with the development of fluent reading.

Reading and Spoken Language

Spoken language is instinctive . . . built into our genes and hard-wired in our brains. Learning to read requires us to take advantage of what nature has provided: a biological module for language.

For the object of the reader's attention (print) to gain entry into the language module, a truly extraordinary transformation must occur. The reader must convert the print on the page into a linguistic code: the phonetic code, the only code recognized and accepted by the language system. Unless the reader-to-be can convert the printed characters on the page into the phonetic code, these letters remain just a bunch of lines and circles, totally devoid of meaning. The written symbols have no inherent meaning of their own but stand, rather, as surrogates for the sounds of speech (Shaywitz, 2003).

To break the code, the first step beginning readers must take involves spoken language. Readers must develop *phonemic awareness*. They must discover that the words they hear come apart into smaller pieces of sound (Shaywitz, 2003).

On the basis of highly reliable scientific evidence, investigators in the field have now reached a strong consensus: Reading reflects language, and reading disability reflects a deficit within the language system. Results from large and well-studied populations with reading disability confirm that in young school-age children (Fletcher et al., 1994; Stanovich & Siegel, 1994) and in adolescents (Shaywitz et al., 1999), a weakness in accessing the sounds of spoken language represents the most robust and specific correlate of reading disability (Morris et al., 1998). Such findings form the foundation for the most successful, evidence-based interventions designed to improve reading (National Reading Panel, 2000).

Understanding Reading Disability

Reading disability, or *developmental dyslexia*, is characterized by an unexpected difficulty in reading in children and adults who otherwise possess the intelligence, motivation, and education necessary for developing accurate and fluent reading (Lyon, 1995; Lyon, Shaywitz, & Shaywitz, 2003). Dyslexia is the most common and most carefully studied of the learning disabilities, affecting 80 percent of all individuals identified as learning disabled and an estimated 5-17 percent of all children and adults in the United States (Shaywitz, 2003).

Incidence and Distribution of Dyslexia

Recent epidemiological data indicate that like hypertension and obesity, reading ability occurs along a continuum. Reading disability falls on the left side of the bell-shaped curve representing the normal distribution of reading ability (Shaywitz, Escobar, Shaywitz, Fletcher, & Makuch, 1992).

Dyslexia runs in families: One-fourth to one-half of all children who have a parent with dyslexia also have the disorder (Scarborough, 1990), and if dyslexia affects one child in the family, it is likely to affect half of his or her siblings. Recent studies have identified a number of genes involved in dyslexia (Fisher & DeFries, 2002).

Good evidence, based on surveys of randomly selected populations of children, now indicates that dyslexia affects boys and girls equally (Flynn & Rahbar, 1994; Shaywitz, Shaywitz, Fletcher, & Escobar, 1990; Wadsworth, DeFries, Stevenson, Gilger, & Pennington, 1992). Apparently, the long-held belief that only boys suffer from dyslexia reflected bias in school-identified samples: The more disruptive behavior of boys results in their being referred for evaluation more often, whereas girls who struggle to read are more likely to sit quietly in their seats and thus be overlooked.

Longitudinal studies (Bruck, 1992; Fletcher, 1996; Francis, Shaywitz, Stuebing, Shaywitz, & Scarborough, 1984; Shaywitz et al., 1995) indicate that dyslexia is a persistent, chronic condition rather than a transient "developmental lag." Children do not outgrow reading difficulties. The evidence-based interventions now available, however, can result in improved reading in virtually all children.

Neurobiological Origins of Dyslexia

For more than a century, physicians and scientists have suspected that dyslexia has neurobiological origins. Until recently, however, they had no way to examine the brain systems that we use while reading. Within the last decade, the dream of scientists, educators, and struggling readers has come true: New advances in technology enable us to view the working brain as it attempts to read.

Reading reflects language, and reading disability reflects a deficit within the language system.

Perhaps the most convincing evidence for a neurobiological basis of dyslexia comes from the rapidly accumulating and converging data from functional brain imaging investigations. The process of functional brain imaging is quite simple. When we ask an individual to perform a discrete cognitive task, that task places processing demands on specific neural systems in the brain. Through such techniques as functional magnetic resonance imaging (fMRI), we can measure the changes that take place in neural activity in particular brain regions as the brain meets those demands. Because fMRI uses no ionizing radiation and requires no injections, it is noninvasive and safe. We can use it to examine children or adults on multiple occasions.

Using functional brain imaging, scientists around the world have discovered not only the brain basis of reading but also a glitch in the neural circuitry for reading in children and adults who struggle to read. Our studies and those of other investigators have identified three regions involved in reading, all located on the left side of the brain. In the front of the brain, Broca's area (technically the inferior frontal gyrus) is involved in articulation and word analysis. Two areas located in the back of the brain are involved in word analysis (the parieto-temporal region) and in fluent reading (the occipito-temporal region, also referred to as the word form area).

Studies of dyslexic readers document an underactivation of the two systems in the back of the brain together with an overactivation of Broca's area in the front of the brain. The struggling readers appear to be turning to the frontal region, which is responsible for articulating spoken words, to compensate for the fault in the systems in the back of the brain.

Researchers have observed this neurobiological signature of dyslexic readers across cultures and across different languages (Paulesu et al., 2001). The observation of this same pattern in both children and adults supports the view that reading difficulties, including the neural disruption, do not go away with maturity. To prevent failure for students with reading disability, we must identify the disability early and provide effective reading programs to address the students' needs.

The Importance of Fluency

In addition to identifying the neural systems used for reading, research has now revealed which systems the brain uses in two important phases in the acquisition of literacy.

Beginning reading—breaking the code by slowly, analytically sounding out words—calls on areas in the front of the brain (Broca's area) and in the back of the brain (the parieto-temporal region).

But an equally important phase in reading is fluency—rapid, automatic reading that does not require attention or effort. A fluent reader looks at a printed word and instantly knows all the important information about that word. Fluent reading develops as the reader builds brain connections that eventually represent an exact replica of the word—a replica that has integrated the word's pronunciation, spelling, and meaning.

Fluency occurs step-by-step. After systematically learning letters and their sounds, children go on to apply this knowledge to sound out words slowly and analytically. For example, for the word "back," a child may initially represent the word by its initial and final consonants: "b—k." As the child progresses, he begins to fill in the interior vowels, first making some errors—reading "back" as "bock" or "beak," for example—and eventually sounding out the word correctly. Part of the process of becoming a skilled reader is forming successively more detailed and complete representations of familiar words (Shaywitz, 2003).

After the child has read the word "back" correctly over and over again, his brain has built and reinforced an exact model of the word. He now reads that word fluently—accurately, rapidly, and effortlessly. Fluency pulls us into reading. A student who reads fluently reads for pleasure and for information; a student who is not fluent will probably avoid reading.

In a study involving 144 children, we identified the brain region that makes it possible for skilled readers to read automatically (Shaywitz et al., 2002). We found that the more proficiently a child read, the more he or she activated the occipito-temporal region (or word form area) in the back of the brain. Other investigators have observed that this brain region responds to words that are presented rapidly (Price, Moore, & Frackowiak, 1996). Once a word is represented in the word form area, the reader recognizes that word instantly and effortlessly. This word form system appears to predominate when a reader has become fluent. As a result of this finding, we now know that development of the word form area in the left side of the brain is a key component in becoming a skilled, fluent reader.

Helping Struggling Readers Become More Fluent

Our study of 144 children also revealed that struggling readers compensate as they get older, developing alternate reading systems in the front of the brain and in the *right* side of the brain—a functioning system, but, alas, not an automatic one (Shaywitz, 2003). These readers do not develop the critical left-side word form region necessary for rapid, automatic reading. Instead, they call on the alternate secondary pathways. This strategy enables them to read, but much more slowly and with greater effort than their classmates.

This research evidence of a disruption in the normal reading pathways provides a neurobiological target for reading interventions. In a new study (Shaywitz et al., 2003), we hypothesized that an evidence-based, phonologically mediated reading intervention would help dyslexic readers develop the fast-paced word form systems serving skilled reading, thus improving their reading accuracy and fluency. Under the supervision of Syracuse University professor Benita Blachman, we provided 2nd and 3rd grade struggling readers daily with 50 minutes of individual tutoring that was systematic and explicit, focusing on helping the students understand the *alphabetic principle*, or how letters and combinations of letters represent the sounds of speech.

Students received eight months (105 hours) of intervention during the school year in addition to their regular classroom reading instruction. The experimental intervention replaced any additional reading help that the students might have received in school. Certified teachers who had taken part in an intensive training program provided the tutoring.

Immediately after the yearlong intervention, students in the experiment made significant gains in reading fluency and demonstrated increased activation in left hemisphere regions, including the inferior frontal gyrus and the parieto-temporal region. One year after the experimental intervention ended, these students were reading accurately and fluently and were activating all three left-side brain regions used by good readers. A control group of struggling readers receiving school-based, primarily nonphonological reading instruction had not activated these reading systems.

These data demonstrate that an intensive, evidence-based reading intervention brings about significant and durable changes in brain organization so that struggling readers' brain activation patterns come to resemble those of typical readers. If we provide intervention at an early age, then we can improve reading fluency and facilitate the development of the neural systems that underlie skilled reading.

Evidence-Based Effective Reading Instruction

In addition to new neurological research on the nature of reading, educators can draw on a body of rigorous, well-designed, scientific studies to guide reading instruction. In 1998, the U.S. Congress mandated the National Reading Panel to develop rigorous scientific criteria for evaluating reading research, apply these criteria to existing reading research, identify the most effective teaching methods, and then make findings accessible for parents and teachers. As a member of the Panel, I can attest to its diligence. After two years of work, the Panel issued its report (2000).

The major findings of the report indicate that in order to read, all children must be taught alphabetics, comprising phonemic awareness and phonics; reading fluency; vocabulary; and strategies for reading comprehension. These elements must be taught systematically, comprehensively, and explicitly; it is inadequate to present the foundational skills of phonemic awareness and phonics incidentally, casually, or fragmentally. Children do not learn how letters represent sounds by osmosis; we must teach them this skill explicitly. Once a child has mastered these foundational skills, he or she must be taught how to read words fluently.

Good evidence now indicates that we can teach reading fluency by means of repeated oral reading with feedback and guidance. Using these methods (described in detail in Shaywitz, 2003, pp. 176-246), we can teach almost every child to read. It is crucial to align all components of a program with one another—for example, to provide so-called decodable booklets that give the student practice in the specific letter-sound linkages we are teaching. The use of decodable booklets enables the repeated practice necessary to build the automatic systems in the word form region that lead to fluent reading.

Neuroscience and Reading Research Agree

We are now in an era of evidence-based education. Objective scientific evidence—provided by brain imaging studies and by the National Reading Panel's rigorous scientific review of the literature—has replaced reliance on philosophy or opinion.

In considering a reading program, educators should ask several key questions:

- Is there scientific evidence that the program is effective?
- Was the program or its methodology reviewed by the National Reading Panel?
- In reading instruction, are phonemic awareness and phonics taught systematically and explicitly?
- How are students taught to approach an unfamiliar word? Do they feel empowered to try to analyze and sound out an unknown word first rather than guess the word from the pictures or context?
- Does the program also include plenty of opportunities for students to practice reading, develop fluency, build vocabulary, develop reading comprehension strategies, write, and listen to and discuss stories (Shaywitz, 2003)?

Children do not learn how letters represent sounds by osmosis; we must teach them this skill explicitly.

Children are only 7 or 8 years old once in their lifetime. We cannot risk teaching students with unproven programs. We now have the scientific knowledge to ensure that almost every child can become a successful reader. Awareness of the new scientific knowledge about reading should encourage educators to insist that reading programs used in their schools reflect what we know about the science of reading and about effective reading instruction.

References

Bruck, M. (1992). Persistence of dyslexics' phonological awareness deficits. *Developmental Psychology, 28*(5), 874-886.

Fisher, S., & DeFries, J. C. (2002). Developmental dyslexia: Genetic dissection of a complex cognitive trait. *Nature Reviews Neuroscience, 3*, 767-780.

Fletcher, J., Shaywitz, S., Shankweiler, D., Katz, L., Liberman, I., Stuebing, K., et al. (1994). Cognitive profiles of reading disability: Comparisons of discrepancy and low achievement definitions. *Journal of Educational Psychology, 86*(1), 6-23.

Flynn, J., & Rahbar, M. (1994). Prevalence of reading failure in boys compared with girls. *Psychology in the Schools, 31*, 66-71.

Francis, D. J., Shaywitz, S. E., Stuebing, K. K., Shaywitz, B. A., & Fletcher, J. M. (1996). Developmental lag versus deficit models of reading disability: A longitudinal, individual growth curves analysis. *Journal of Educational Psychology, 88*(1), 3-17.

Lyon, G. R. (1995). Toward a definition of dyslexia. *Annals of Dyslexia, 45*, 3-27.

Lyon, G. R., Shaywitz, S. E., & Shaywitz, B. A. (2003). A definition of dyslexia. *Annals of Dyslexia, 53*, 1-14.

Morris, R. D., Stuebing, K. K., Fletcher, J. M., Shaywitz, S. E., Lyon, G. R., Shankweiler, D. P., et al. (1998). Subtypes of reading disability: Variability around a phonological core. *Journal of Educational Psychology, 90*, 347-373.

National Reading Panel. (2000). *Teaching children to read: An evidence-based assessment of the scientific research literature on reading and its implications for reading instruction.* Washington, DC: National Institute of Child Health and Human Development.

Paulesu, E., Demonet, J. F., Fazio, F., McCrory, E., Chanoine, V., Brunswick, N., et al. (2001). Dyslexia-cultural diversity and biological unity. *Science, 291*, 2165-2167.

Price, C., Moore, C., & Frackowiak, R. S. J. (1996). The effect of varying stimulus rate and duration on brain activity during reading. *Neuroimage, 3*(1), 40-52.

Scarborough, H. S. (1984). Continuity between childhood dyslexia and adult reading. *British Journal of Psychology, 75*, 329-348.

Scarborough, H. S. (1990). Very early language deficits in dyslexic children. *Child Development, 61*, 1728-1743.

Shaywitz, B. A., Holford, T. R., Holahan, J. M., Fletcher, J. M., Stuebing, K. K., Francis, D. J., et al. (1995). A Matthew effect for IQ but not for reading: Results from a longitudinal study. *Reading Research Quarterly, 30*(4), 894-906.

Shaywitz, B. A., Shaywitz, S., Blachman, B., Pugh, K., Fullbright, R., Skudlarski, P., et al. (2003). *Development of left occipito-temporal systems for skilled reading following a phonologically-based intervention in children.* Paper presented at the Organization for Human Brain Mapping, New York.

Shaywitz, B. A., Shaywitz, S. E., Pugh, K. R., Mencl, W. E., Fullbright, R. K., Skudlarski, P., et al. (2002). Disruption of posterior brain systems for reading in children with developmental dyslexia. *Biological Psychiatry, 52*, 101-110.

Shaywitz, S. (2003). *Overcoming dyslexia: A new and complete science-based program for reading problems at any level.* New York: Knopf.

Shaywitz, S. E., Escobar, M. D., Shaywitz, B. A., Fletcher, J. M., & Makuch, R. (1992). Evidence that dyslexia may represent the lower tail of a normal distribution of reading ability. *New England Journal of Medicine, 326*(3), 145-150.

Shaywitz, S. E., Fletcher, J. M., Holahan, J. M., Schneider, A. E., Marchione, K. E., Stuebing, K. K., et al. (1999). Persistence of dyslexia: The Connecticut Longitudinal Study at adolescence. *Pediatrics, 104*, 1351-1359.

Shaywitz, S. E., Shaywitz, B. A., Fletcher, J. M., & Escobar, M. D. (1990). Prevalence of reading disability in boys and girls: Results of the Connecticut Longitudinal Study. *Journal of the American Medical Association, 264*(8), 998-1002.

Stanovich, K. E., & Siegel, L. S. (1994). Phenotypic performance profile of children with reading disabilities: A regression-based test of the phonological-core variable-difference model. *Journal of Educational Psychology, 86*(1), 24-53.

Wadsworth, S. J., DeFries, J. C., Stevenson, J., Gilger, J. W., & Pennington, B. F. (1992). Gender ratios among reading-disabled children and their siblings as a function of parental impairment. *Journal of Child Psychology and Psychiatry, 33*(7), 1229-1239.

Sally E. Shaywitz (sally.shaywitz@yale.edu) is Professor of Pediatrics and **Bennett A. Shaywitz** (bennett.shaywitz@yale.edu) is Professor of Pediatrics and Neurology at the Yale University School of Medicine. They are Codirectors of the National Institute of Child Health and Human Development—Yale Center for the Study of Learning and Attention.

Reading Disability and the Brain, an article based upon the book Overcoming Dyslexia, by Sally E. Shaywitz (NY:Knopf, 2003). Grateful acknowledgement is made to Sally Shatwitz c/o Writers' Representatives LLC. (to whom all rights inquiries should be directed) for permission to reprint "Dyslexia and the Brain".

Successful Strategies for Promoting Self-Advocacy Among Students with LD: The LEAD Group

Students with learning disabilities (LD) often need to be taught self-determination skills to be better prepared for life after high school. This article describes the methods used by one school district to promote self-advocacy and self-awareness skills for students with LD. Through multicomponent group activities, students learned about their strengths and disabilities and how to advocate for their educational needs and rights. Advocacy skills were also applied to leadership roles, monitoring, and community education activities. Important features that contributed to the success of the program are described.

Al Pocock, Stan Lambros, Meagan Karvonen, David W. Test, Bob Algozzine, Wendy Wood, and James E. Martin

Self-determination has been increasingly recognized as a critical outcome for students with disabilities as they prepare to transition to the adult world (Field, Martin, Miller, Ward, & Wehmeyer, 1998b). The U.S. Department of Education, Office of Special Education Programs, has funded numerous projects to develop self-determination conceptual models, assessments, and interventions (Ward & Kohler, 1996). Research demonstrates that self-determination is associated with greater quality of life (Wehmeyer & Schwartz, 1998) and more positive adult outcomes (Wehmeyer & Schwartz, 1997). Field, Martin, Miller, Ward, and Wehmeyer (1998a) conceptualized self-determination as follows:

> a combination of skills, knowledge, and beliefs that enable a person to engage in goal directed, self-regulated, autonomous behavior. An understanding of one's strengths and limitations together with a belief in oneself as capable and effective are essential to self-determination. When acting on the basis of these skills and attitudes, individuals have greater ability to take control of their lives and assume the role of successful adults.

A recent review of research literature shows that self-advocacy skills and self-awareness are the subsets of self-determination most often taught to individuals with learning disabilities (LD; Algozzine, Browder, Karvonen, Test, & Wood, 2001). Techniques used to promote self-awareness in students with LD often include the use of interest inventories, learning style assessments, and experiential activities designed to allow students to "try out" different activities (e.g., careers), as well as gain knowledge about LD.

Self-advocacy instruction for high school students often focuses on knowledge about rights and responsibilities, effective communication and negotiation skills, identifying and requesting accommodations and modifications, and instruction on participating in and even directing one's own Individualized Education Program (IEP) meeting. Some programs help students generalize their self-advocacy skills and knowledge to other environments, such as college or the workplace.

The next level of self-advocacy for individuals with disabilities is learning to apply those skills to a larger, systemic level: ensuring that society honors the rights of *all* individuals with disabilities. Creating a society that is responsive to the needs and rights of individuals with disabilities requires that self-advocates develop leadership skills, as well as other self-advocacy skills (Field et al., 1998b).

Many resources exist that teachers can use to help students with disabilities develop self-advocacy skills. In a literature review on self-advocacy instruction, Merchant and Gajar (1997) determined that self-advocacy is most often taught through the use of

- role play (Durlack, Rose, & Bursuck, 1994);
- strategies such as I-PLAN (*I*nventory strengths and areas of improvement, *P*rovide information, *L*isten and respond, *A*sk questions, *N*ame your goals; Van Reusen, Deschler, & Schumaker, 1989); or
- Direct instruction, including a description of the target behavior, demonstration, rehearsal, practice, feedback, and practice in a natural environment.

Numerous published curricula also include lessons that target self-advocacy skills:

- *Self-Directed IEP* (Martin, Marshall, Maxson, & Jerman, 1996);
- *Choicemaker Self-Determination Curriculum Series* (Martin & Marshall, 1995);
- *Next S.T.E.P.* (Halpern, Herr, Wolf, Doren, Johnson, & Lawson, 1997); *Steps to Self-Determination* (Field & Hoffman, 1996);
- *Take Charge for the Future* (Powers et al., 1996); and
- *Whose Future is it Anyway?* (Wehmeyer & Kelchner, 1995).

This article describes a program called Learning and Education About Disabilities (LEAD) implemented in one school district that uses a number of research-supported practices to successfully promote self-advocacy and other self-determination skills for students with LD. LEAD was selected as one of six exemplar sites as part of the Self-Determination Synthesis Project, a comprehensive research synthesis project funded by the Office of Special Education Programs, Department of Education. (More information about the exemplary sites and the entire project is available on the project Web site at http://www.uncc.edu/sdsp)

LEAD

Background

LEAD began in 1996 in response to concerns expressed by high school students with LD. Students and parents had reported that some general education teachers were re-luctant to provide accommodations and modifications. Some students were having difficulty coping with their disability, and a guidance counselor who worked with several students with LD noticed that they lacked the self-awareness and disability awareness necessary to effectively explain their needs to teachers. The guidance counselor formed a support group with the intent of helping students better understand their learning disabilities and more effectively advocate for their academic needs. Since its inception, the group has grown from 4 to include as many as 17 students each academic year. LEAD participants meet during a class period and receive course credit that counts toward graduation. The group is co-led by the guidance counselor and a special education teacher. While the majority of LEAD students are diagnosed with LD, students with attention deficit disorder and hearing impairments have also been members.

Philosophy and Content

The primary tenet of the LEAD group is that of student ownership. Students determined the group's mission statement, which includes "increasing the level of understanding and awareness of the social, academic, and emotional aspects of learning disabilities.... We focus on not allowing disabilities to become liabilities." The group includes four elected officers who meet weekly to determine the group's upcoming activities. The group's coleaders share the philosophy of student ownership of the educational process and believe in promoting leadership opportunities.

To accommodate the needs of a growing group with varied backgrounds, LEAD now consists of two separate groups: one for ninth graders and one for an advanced group. Both groups have a weekly schedule that includes two days devoted to educational activities, one day for mentoring, and a fourth day for a support group meeting (see Figure 1). All members of both groups participate in community presentations. There is some flexibility in the schedule in order to plan for community presentations and address unexpected issues that arise. Each of the main content areas of LEAD is described in the following sections.

SELF-AWARENESS AND DISABILITY KNOWLEDGE. The LEAD group discovered early that although students had developed an awareness of their feelings about having a learning disability, they did not know themselves educationally. Because self-awareness is a critical foundation for being able to advocate effectively for oneself, the coleaders decided to focus on helping students first become more aware of themselves academically. In order to help students understand themselves better, students' cumulative folders, with IEPs, test results, and other data, became the class's textbook, for use in discussing academic strengths and weaknesses. A psychologist taught

Ninth-grade group				
Monday	**Tuesday**	**Wednesday**	**Thursday**	**Friday**
No class	Education day • The referral process	Support day • Informal discussion led by counselor	Education day • Begin new unit: Evaluation and interpretation of testing	Mentoring • Mentor pairs at other schools
Advanced group				
Monday	**Tuesday**	**Wednesday**	**Thursday**	**Friday**
Officers meet • Plan for next academic year • Plan mentoring activities	Education day • Review video of previous presentation, evaluate performance • Discuss classroom accomodations that can prevent students from needing to go to the resource room	Support day • Informal discussion led by counselor	Education day • Revise community presentation to include more about what LEAD membership entails	Mentoring • Mentor pairs at other schools

Figure 1. Sample week of LEAD activities.

the students about intelligence and achievement testing and how to understand their own IQ test results. Students not only benefited from learning that they were highly intelligent, but they also learned how their learning strengths and weaknesses were reflected in the IQ subtest scores. Students who had also taken personality inventories learned to interpret their information as a means of better understanding their strengths and areas in which they needed support. The unit on the evaluation and interpretation of test data (see sidebar, Sample LEAD Lesson Plan Outline), which spans six class sessions, has been extremely well received by LEAD students and their parents.

Equipped with knowledge about their strengths and needs, LEAD participants decide which additional topics they wish to cover; the coleaders determine how best to deliver the information and promote the related skills. Using a combination of personal knowledge and published resources (e.g., Sousa, 2000), the coleaders have created their own curriculum to include topics such as brain differences, the definition and diagnosis of different types of learning disabilities, accommodations and modification, legal rights under the Individuals with Disabilities Education Act and the Americans with Disabilities Act legislation, facilitating IEP and 504 meetings, learning styles, multiple intelligences, and other similar topics. Adults with LD serve as guest speakers, providing students with information about how they have learned to navigate the adult world.

The disability-related knowledge and self-awareness that LEAD students develop is then used as a basis for their self-advocacy. By knowing what accommodations

or modifications they require, students can brainstorm as a group how to best approach specific teachers with a request for an accommodation. Group members often talk through an entire scenario or use role-playing to practice their self-advocacy skills. One of the group's coleaders often accompanies freshmen on their first visit with a teacher to discuss accommodations. If a request is not successful, the coleaders and group members will help the student develop other ideas for negotiating with the teacher. As students gain experience in negotiating with their teachers, the coleaders remove themselves from those conversations, and the group members serve as a sounding board for problematic requests. The special education teacher who coleads the group works individually with teachers to develop the supports necessary for students' accommodations; however, the students are responsible for negotiating accommodations that do not significantly increase teachers' responsibilities.

LEAD students further refine their communication skills using an exercise in which one of the group's coleaders plays the role of a "non-believer," often a skeptical teacher or community member who claims not to believe in LD or the need for accommodations. In this "devil's advocate" role, the coleaders offer objections, stereotypes, misinterpretations, and other challenges to the students as they develop counterpoints and enhance their ability to articulate their disability. For example, a statement about the students looking "normal, not handicapped" might prompt a response about students' specific learning problems and how they impact the quality of their academic work. The coleader might then make further objections based on the quality of students' responses that then require the students to explain themselves more effectively or add details that they omitted from their previous responses.

SUPPORT GROUP. Through support group meetings, LEAD students discuss the challenges they face in coping with their disabilities. The support group component of LEAD has many of the common characteristics of effective group therapy (Corey & Corey, 1997). Group members provide a level of empathy that they believe individuals without disabilities are incapable of providing. They help each other cope with feelings such as shame and anxiety and build the confidence they need to approach teachers about accommodations. Group members also challenge each other at times when individuals try to hide their disability or do not take opportunities to self-advocate. The group relies less on the coleaders as facilitators for support group discussions compared with educational activities.

COMMUNITY PRESENTATIONS. The LEAD group frequently makes presentations to parents, students, preservice special education teachers, and teachers in nearby school districts. The group has also presented at state and national learning disabilities conferences and to their own high school faculty. The purpose of the presentations is to educate others about learning disabilities, but the scope of each presentation varies according to the audience. For example, group members can respond to questions from teachers about what teachers can do if they suspect a student has a learning disability, or how teachers can help their students become better self-advocates. The sidebar Sample Format of LEAD Group contains a sample format for a presentation to teachers.

Presentations to the business community include general information about young adults with LD and a panel discussion in which business leaders ask students about issues such as disclosure and confidentiality. LEAD participants also ask business representatives about how they compensate for weaknesses and accentuate their strengths in the workplace.

The disability-related knowledge and self-awareness that LEAD students develop is ... used as a basis for their self-advocacy.

One particularly dramatic element of most LEAD presentations is a poem written by one of the LEAD group students (see Figure 2). Audience members are given a handwritten copy [of] the student's first draft of a poem, followed by a later version of that poem after accommodations (e.g., use of computer spelling and grammar check features) were provided. This exercise helps audience members understand how a student with LD views the world; the poem's author speaks about how he real-

izes his mistakes but is unable to correct them. Students typically spend a few minutes during LEAD class prior to each presentation determining the schedule and priorities for that presentation. Continuing the philosophy of student ownership, the group's coleaders do not participate in the planning session, nor do they participate in the presentation itself.

Sample LEAD Lesson Plan Outline: Evaluation and Interpretation of Test Data

Testing background

1. Reliability
2. Validity
3. Percentiles

WJ

1. Subtests
2. What do they measure?
3. How would it apply to school subjects?
4. What do the scores mean?

WISC-III/WAIS-R

1. Full scale score
2. Performance subtests
   • Discussion of each subtest
   • How do the performance subtests indicate strengths and weaknesses?
3. Verbal subtests
4. Discussion of each subtest
5. How do the verbal subtests indicate strengths and weaknesses?

Review of what testing means

1. How important are the tests?
2. Do the tests determine your success or failure?
3. How is eligibility determined?
4. Is it worth the time?
5. Appropriate accommodations based on test data (lead-in to next unit)

Note. WJ = Woodcock-Johnson Psycho-Educational Battery (1977); WISC-III = Wechsler Intelligence Scale for Children–Third Edition (1991); WAIS-R = Wechsler Adult Intelligence Scale–Revised (1981).

Community presentations also serve as teaching opportunities as each presentation is videotaped and reviewed in subsequent LEAD class meetings. Students have an opportunity to critique their performance by identifying the strengths of the presentation, brainstorming ways to more effectively communicate answers to unexpected or complex questions from the audience, and reflecting on things that they wished they had said. Even in those cases where students believe they have answered well, the group reviews segments of the videotape and discusses ways in which they might have made their point more effectively.

MENTORING. Beginning in LEAD's third year, students decided they wanted to help elementary and middle school students benefit from their own experiences in navigating the educational system. LEAD members worked with coleaders to develop ideas for building rapport with younger students and age-appropriate methods for delivering materials and messages. In the current mentoring approach, two LEAD members, a ninth grader and an upperclassman, are paired with small groups of students with LD in two elementary schools and one middle school.

While mentoring activities initially emphasized structured educational activities about disabilities, LEAD students discovered that a "big sibling" approach was a more effective way to informally educate younger students. Increased emphasis has been placed on building rapport and enhancing younger students' self-esteem. The LEAD mentors meet with younger students for an hour each week at the younger students' assigned schools for conversations about issues raised by the younger students. Mentors take opportunities to normalize the younger children's experiences and point out their strengths in the course of discussion. For example, if an elementary student says he is embarrassed about needing extra help in reading, the mentor might say that she also needed extra help when she was in elementary school, that she was still a "normal" person, and that she was glad she had received help because now she relied on those reading skills in high school. Middle school mentors start talking about the LEAD group in the second semester so that ninth graders can decide whether they want to join the group the next year.

Implementation Issues

Although the LEAD group has enjoyed strong administrative support from the beginning, a few barriers were encountered in the process of starting the LEAD group. The primary difficulty was student scheduling; numerous conflicts made it difficult to find time for the group to meet. Instead of being structured as a club or part-time seminar, the class was turned into a full-time elective course that students could choose as an alternative to other electives often chosen by students with LD.

Another roadblock encountered by LEAD early in the process was the disbelief among some general education teachers that learning disabilities even exist and that LEAD would be a beneficial class. As teachers have retired from the school, students from LEAD have met with the new teachers to help them understand the group's purpose. The emphasis placed on student responsibility for accommodations has also minimized the impact of accommodations on general education teachers' workload, dispelling one of the myths held by some teachers.

Sample Format of LEAD Group Presentation to Teachers

Introduce agenda

Read LEAD mission statement

Definition of learning disability

Individual introductions: name, type of problem or deficit, and a specific area of strength or a skill

Poem (see Figure 2): handout and discussion

Example accommodations

Question and answer session, with group president or leader acting as moderator

---

Original poem

Aloene loste wakling down the steert of this urben jungele. Whatein fore the love of my life not whet nowen too call me from behinded
It's not no colldnot sher if it day or night just whored wher I an going Alon and lost walking in the erbine jungle on to a road off inlitamet
An intlitament of sperit to become more than it is nowe too grwe past the brondres that logec has in slaved it in. I her the bet of the stepe as my feet shelf me along the street of the jungle 1, 2, 3 the Bat of the hert as it is awankend with now relization of the futer and the past. What Ive inconted and hop to incotedr on joner of lefe not wheat past it forst mark of trumph.

Poem with accommodations provided

Alone, lost walking down the streets of this urban jungle
Waiting for the love of my life not yet known
To call me from behind.
It's hot, not cold, and not sure if it's day or night
Just worried where I am going alone and lost.
Walking in the urban jungle on a road to enlightenment.

An enlightenment of the spirit
To become more than it is now.
To grow past the boundaries that logic has enslaved it in.
I hear the beat of the steps as my feet shuffle me along
The streets of the jungle.

One, two, three, the beat of the heart
As it is awakened with new realizations
Of the future and the past.
What I have encountered and hope to encounter on a
    journey of life not yet past its first marker of triumph.

Figure 2. Poem used to illustrate the impact of accommodations on a student's writing.
Used with permission.

Effective Practices

LEAD students, parents, and teachers all agree that LEAD has helped students become effective advocates, both for themselves, as well as all individuals with LD. Some of the critical factors that have helped LEAD be successful follow:

• **INTRODUCING SELF-DETERMINATION COMPONENT SKILLS IN AN EFFECTIVE SEQUENCE.** LEAD students first need to understand their strengths, challenges, learning styles, and interests before explaining them to others. As students become more self-aware, self-advocacy skills such as communication and negotiation are introduced. The additional skills of communicating to large groups and mentoring younger students build upon the LEAD students' earlier self-awareness and self-advocacy skills.

• **MAINTAINING A PHILOSOPHY OF STUDENT OWNERSHIP, WITH AN APPROPRIATE BALANCE OF SUPPORT, GUIDANCE, AND INDEPENDENCE.** Student ownership of the LEAD group's tasks and objectives has been of primary importance since day one. The coleaders help students enhance their self-awareness and self-advocacy skills within the context of the students' interests. At the same time, younger students are not expected to immediately grasp the concepts and develop effective advocacy skills without some guidance and coaching. One of the group's coleaders described the process of transferring ownership to students in the following way:

> For ninth graders, we hold both their hands while they're here. By the time they're in tenth grade we have released one [hand]. By the time they're in eleventh grade we're not holding them anymore. By the time they're in the twelfth grade we're patting them on the back and telling them, 'good luck'.

The LEAD group members have adopted a similar philosophy as they help students in nearby districts develop their own groups. LEAD students do not give the other students the "answers" about what accommodations they can ask for because they believe each student has to determine that for himself or herself.

• **EFFECTIVE MODELING OF SELF-ADVOCACY SKILLS.** Modeling functions in several different ways for LEAD. The group's coleaders, each of whom has a disability, are models for the LEAD students. Within the group, upperclassmen with better-developed self-awareness, leadership, and self-advocacy skills serve as models for the underclassmen. All of the LEAD group members serve as models for the elementary and middle school students that they mentor, as well as for students with LD in their high school who do not participate in LEAD.

• **OPPORTUNITIES FOR IMPROVING SELF-ADVOCACY SKILLS EMBEDDED IN ACTIVITIES OUTSIDE THE CLASSROOM.** When invited to present to the National Learning Disability Association Conference in Washington DC, LEAD participants had to present their plan to the local Board of Education in order to receive approval for the trip. Graduating seniors who expressed interest in attending college visited campuses and talked with representatives from the Disability Services offices. The group's coleaders observed and videotaped these interactions in order to help the students improve their ability to assess the availability of necessary supports at the colleges they were considering. Creativity is required of the group's coleaders as they identify these teachable moments for a group that determines their own curriculum.

• **CREATING A SCHOOL CULTURE THAT SUPPORTS SELF-ADVOCACY.** School and district administrators have become increasingly supportive of LEAD as they have visited with the students during class and observed their presentations to community groups and teachers. The district superintendent became a strong advocate for the group after accompanying them to the conference in Washington DC; now he helps them form relationships with the local business community. The principal's support of the group led him to allow the students to make a presentation to the high school's entire faculty during an inservice day. The group's coleaders also work one-on-one with general education teachers to explore how to support students' self-advocacy and respond to students' requests for accommodations. The special education teacher who coleads the group also coteaches mainstream English classes. The coleader models methods that promote students' self-advocacy within the classroom, and the two teachers have also collaborated to develop instructional methods that benefit students with and without LD. For example, they simultaneously deliver instruction differently based on students' learning styles and allow all students in the class to choose which method they prefer.

Implications for Practitioners

The LEAD group has successfully improved self-awareness, self-advocacy, and leadership skills among high school students with LD and other disabilities. While developing their own skills, they have also had a significant impact on others.

> What I've gotten out of LEAD, out of the kids...is that self-examination, that self-assessment, and it's forced me at 55 years old, I'm sitting down re-looking at my strengths and weaknesses through the eyes that they look at themselves with—through tough eyes. (School District Superintendent)

The students in LEAD have raised the community's consciousness about individuals with LD and helped younger students understand their own disabilities and how they can affect their educational experiences.

Implementing this innovative program has required ambition and creativity on the part of the students and coleaders, and support from administrators and parents. Students who participate in LEAD must have some degree of willingness to be open and acknowledge that they have a disability for the supportive and educational parts of the program to be effective. Even without all of these successful elements in place, certain parts of LEAD could apply to any program designed to enhance students' self-advocacy skills. Changes to the LEAD group structure and content could be modified depending on the students who participate. The LEAD group students expressed a definite bias against using prepared lesson plans and published curricula, but students at other schools may be more comfortable with the use of formal instructional materials. LEAD students have decided to write one participant's 504 Plan as a group; the same exercise could be used to help members develop their IEPs. Younger students who enter LEAD with less knowledge about learning disabilities could participate in a semester-long, intensive education component before integrating fully with the older students. The leadership structure of the LEAD group could also be adapted from a traditional four-officer structure to one based on the group's functions to allow students the opportunity to assume leadership roles within the group.

Although it may be challenging for educators to allow students to have control over the curriculum, student-directed work on self-awareness, leadership, and self-advocacy will ultimately be more effective in promoting those skills than will teachers providing instruction in what they *presume* to be students' needs. Teachers can still determine how to deliver instruction based on students' self-identified needs and preferences. Ultimately, LEAD has succeeded in helping students develop not only the critical skills of self-advocacy and self-awareness, but also fostering an altruistic philosophy that, when combined with leadership skills, can be effective in changing society's views of individuals with LD.

ABOUT THE AUTHORS

Al Pocock, MA, has been a special education teacher at Cheyenne Mountain High School for 19 years. **Stan Lambros**, MEd, is a counselor at Cheyenne Mountain High School in Colorado Springs, Colorado. He has been counseling students for 15 years, including 7 years in the school setting. **Meagan Karvonen**, MA, is the coordinator of the Self-Determination Synthesis Project. Her research interests include school-based health and mental health intervention, and self-determination. **David W. Test**, PhD, is a professor and graduate coordinator for the Special Education Program at UNC Charlotte. His research interests include transition, promoting self-determination, and applied behavior analysis. **Bob Algozzine**, PhD, is a professor in the Department of Educational Administration, Research, and Technology at UNC Charlotte. His recent research has been published in the *High School Journal*, the *Journal of Educational Research*, and *Teacher Education and Special Educa-tion*. **Wendy Wood**, PhD, is an assistant professor of special education at UNC Charlotte. Her interests include self-determination, supported employment, and transition. **James E. Martin**, PhD, is the Zarrow Endowed Professor in Special Education and director of the Zarrow Center for Learning Enrichment at the University of Oklahoma. He is a co-developer of the *ChoiceMaker Self-Determination Curriculum Series* and author of many articles on self-determination. Address: David W. Test, Special Education Program, UNC Charlotte, 9201 University City Blvd., Charlotte, NC 28223-0001; e-mail: dwtest@email.uncc.edu

AUTHORS' NOTES

1. The LEAD Group at Cheyenne Mountain High School was one of six exemplar sites nationwide identified and studied as part of the Self-Determination Synthesis Project (SDSP). The SDSP is a research synthesis project conducted with support from the U.S. Department of Education, Office of Special Education Programs (Grant No. H324D980069), awarded to the University of North Carolina at Charlotte. The opinions expressed do not necessarily reflect the position or policy of the Department of Education, and no official endorsement should be inferred.

2. For more information about LEAD, contact Cheyenne Mountain High School at 719/475-6110.

3. The authors wish to thank Diane Browder for her comments on an earlier version of this manuscript.

REFERENCES

Algozzine, R. F., Browder, D. B., Karvonen, M., Test, D. W., & Wood, W. M. (2001). Effects of self-determination interventions on individuals with disabilities. *Review of Educational Research, 71*(2), 49–108.

Corey, M. S., & Corey, G. (1997). *Groups: Process and practice* (5th ed.). Pacific Grove, CA: Brooks/Cole.

Durlak, C. M., Rose, E., & Bursuck, W. D. (1994). Preparing high school students with learning disabilities for the transition to post-secondary education: Teaching the skills of self-determination. *Journal of Learning Disabilities, 27*, 51–59.

Field, S., & Hoffman, A. (1996). *Steps to self-determination*. Austin: PRO-ED.

Field, S., Martin, J., Miller, R., Ward, M., & Wehmeyer, M. (1998a). *A practical guide to teaching self-determination*. Reston, VA: Council for Exceptional Children.

Field, S., Martin, J., Miller, R., Ward, M., & Wehmeyer, M. (1998b). Self-determination for persons with disabilities: A position statement of the division on career development and transition. *Career Development for Exceptional Individuals, 21*, 113–128.

Halpern, A. S., Herr, C. M., Wolf, N. K., Doren, B., Johnson, M. D., & Lawson, J. D. (1997). *Next S.T.E.P.: Student transition and educational planning*. Austin: PRO-ED.

Martin, J. E., & Marshall, L. H. (1995). Choicemaker: A comprehensive self-determination transition program. *Intervention in School and Clinic, 30*, 147–156.

Martin, J. E., Marshall, L. H., Maxson, L., & Jerman, P. (1996). *Self-directed IEP*. Longmont, CO: Sopris West.

Merchant, D. J., & Gajar, A. (1997). A review of literature on self-advocacy components in transition programs for students with learning disabilities. *Journal of Vocational Rehabilitation, 8*, 223–231.

Powers, L. E., Sowers, J., Turner, A., Nesbitt, M., Knowles, A., & Ellison, R. (1996). TAKE CHARGE: A model for promoting self-determination among adolescents with challenges. In L. E. Powers, G. H. S. Singer, & J. Sowers (Eds.), *On the road* to autonomy: *Promoting self-competence for children and youth with disabilities* (pp. 291–322). Baltimore: Brookes.

Sousa, D. A. (2000). *How the brain learns: A classroom teacher's guide* (2nd ed.). Thousand Oaks, CA: Corwin.

Van Reusen, A. K., Deshler, D. D., & Schumaker, J. B. (1989). Effects of a student participation strategy in facilitating the involvement of adolescents with learning disabilities in the Individualized Education Program planning process. *Learning Disabilities, 1*(2), 23–34.

Ward, M. J., & Kohler, P. D. (1996). Teaching self-determination: Content and process. In L. E. Powers, G. H. S. Singer, & J. Sowers (Eds.), *On the road to autonomy: Promoting self-competence for children and youth with disabilities* (pp. 275–290). Baltimore: Brookes.

Wechsler, D. (1981). *Wechsler adult intelligence scale—Revised.* San Antonio, TX: Psychological Corp.

Wechsler, D. (1991). *Wechsler intelligence scale for children—Third edition.* San Antonio, TX: Psychological Corp.

Wehmeyer, M. L., & Kelchner, K. (1995). *Whose future is it anyway?* Arlington, TX: The Arc of the United States.

Wehmeyer, M. L., & Schwartz, M. (1997). Self-determination and positive adult outcomes: A follow up study of youth with mental retardation or learning disabilities. *Exceptional Children, 63,* 245–255.

Wehmeyer, M. L., & Schwartz, M. (1998). The relationship between self-determination and quality of life for adults with mental retardation. *Education and Training in Mental Retardation and Developmental Disabilities, 33,* 3–12.

Woodcock, R. W., & Johnson, W. B. (1977). *Woodcock-Johnson psycho-educational battery.* Allen, TX: DLM Teaching Resources.

From *Intervention in School and Clinic,* March 2002, pp. 209-216. © 2002 by Pro-Ed Publishers. Reprinted by permission.

Group Intervention
Improving Social Skills of Adolescents With Learning Disabilities

Deborah Court • Sarah Givon

The move to integrate students with learning disabilities into the general education system calls for assistance in helping them in adjusting socially. Children and adolescents with learning disabilities have social difficulties in comparison with their peers (Asher, Parker, & Walker, 1996; Elliot, 1988; Margalit & Levin-Alyagon, 1994). They report feelings of loneliness, isolation, and lack of fulfillment in social situations. This social isolation deepens over time, contributing to negative self-image and difficulty in social functioning at maturity (Elliot, 1988).

One Israeli middle school developed a social skills intervention program as part of the general support framework that was offered to students with learning disabilities. Twelve students, ages 13 and 14, participated in a case study of this program. This article describes the program, discusses the results and their implications for other educators, and provides practical suggestions for teachers.

Social Skills Deficits and Friendship Groups

Adolescence is a critical time in the social world in terms of self-evaluation and self-confidence. Healthy social interaction is important and helps to prepare youth for normal adult functioning, including independence and fitting in to a work environment. (Bauminger, 1990).

> **STUDENTS WHO HAVE CHALLENGES IN SOCIAL SKILLS OFTEN DEVELOP SOCIAL ISOLATION THAT DEEPENS OVER TIME, CONTRIBUTING TO NEGATIVE SELF-IMAGE.**

According to Smilansky (1988), during a child's process of maturing, friendship groups fulfill essential functions in terms of socialization: support, social comparison, models to imitate, conscience, the giving of status and authority, support in separating from parents, and a basis for future connections. The group offers training in social connections and different kinds of social interactions.

For these reasons, social skills training in a group setting can be especially helpful to youngsters with social difficulties. Group treatment is built on three elements that have been shown to be effective: (a) creation of a social situation, (b) active participation in discussion, and (c) the use of group support (Shectman, 1993). Group counseling has been shown to be an important element of a treatment program for adolescents with learning disabilities (Margalit, 1991). In such a group, the adolescent is equal with the other members and can cope with social skills in an active way. This is an important factor in improving social skills.

The present case study involved two groups, one with six boys and one with six girls, all 13 or 14 years in age. Interviews with the students, observations in various settings, and a loneliness questionnaire (Margalit, 1995) determined students' feelings. Six of the students had nonverbal disabilities (four of these were extroverted and socially rejected, and two were introverted and socially rejected), and six had verbal learning disabilities (four were introverted and socially neglected, and two were more extroverted and somewhat more accepted by classmates).

The Nature of the Life Skills Program

Each group met once a week during a 5-month period. Meetings were built into students' regular class timetables so as not to be disruptive. This was a multifaceted, modular treatment program. The model includes practice in problemsolving strategies, as well as emotional development and self-awareness that are affectively based (expressing feelings and imagining the feelings of others; see Figure 1).

Students participated in 20 hour-long meetings during which they discussed a variety of topics concerning social skills. Topics included making friends, getting to know people, assertiveness, dealing with anger, small talk, and listening. Each lesson presented one particular skill.

Each lesson included visual, verbal, and written media so that each participant could grasp the material, no matter what his or her learning disability was. The students examined different methods of solving imagined problems, and the students related problems they had experienced or seen in real life. The tools and rationale presented by the group leader (the researcher) helped students to advance in social (and self) understanding. They learned

new skills, practiced during the week, and talked about what happened at the next meeting. They also tried to observe other people using these skills in social situations.

Results

Though these results were unanticipated, we did find marked differences in self-evaluation and self-image between boys and girls. Boys saw the treatment groups as a place to solve problems in a legitimate way, as they would in a lesson offering extra academic assistance, for example, and perhaps because of this they felt no stigma or social embarrassment about attending the sessions.

Despite their willingness to attend, however, they had more difficulty than girls in discussing and developing awareness of their problems. The extroverted boys, especially, expressed a need to "fix" the environment and their friends rather than confronting their own problems.

In contrast, it was difficult to convince the girls to come to the room where the sessions took place. They worried about the opinions of their peers, trying to arrive stealthily and unseen by others. Despite this behavior, all the girls were very aware of their own social difficulties. They were open and, even in the pretreatment interviews, spoke with pain about their social situations.

Identification and Expression of Social Feelings—The Emotional Realm

Almost all the participants showed great improvement in identifying and expressing their feelings and understanding their social situation. Only two boys did not, and their inconsistent results were likely caused by interruptions in the Ritalin they were taking. These boys passed through stages of denial, blaming the environment, demanding change in others, and lacking understanding of their social situations.

The other 10 students, those with verbal and those with nonverbal disabilities, reached the stage where they were able to check and evaluate their standing and their social situations, to discuss them clearly and with good communication, to express feelings, and to correctly identify their own feelings. Not everyone succeeded in identifying *others'* feelings. This was most prominent among those with nonverbal disabilities who found it difficult to "read" social situations and the feelings of others. They were absorbed in their own situation and had difficulty explaining others. One of these boys said during treatment, "I feel that I understand what I need to do, but I don't yet understand how to do it." One of the girls said, "I understand the words that you're saying, but with my friends it doesn't happen."

Figure 1. The Life Skills Program

Topics	Activities
• Self-development	• Role playing and simulations of real and hypothetical situations
• Friendship	
• Communication skills and behavior	• Group analysis of hypothetical events
• Problem-solving and decision making	
• Coping with situations of stress and change	• Discussions of problems seen on TV and read about in stories
• Assertiveness	
• Self- and program evaluation	• Discussions of personal problems and success in the social realm

Note: While the authors would be happy to supply the entire life skills program upon request, at present it exists only in Hebrew.

Social Skills—The Cognitive and Executive Realm

Most of the participants advanced in the area of social skills, though in some cases the advancement was slight, probably because of the relatively short duration (5 months) of the treatment. Two of the boys regressed. These were the two with attention deficit disorder who took Ritalin inconsistently.

The most significant changes in social skills were found among students with verbal learning disabilities. There was an especially dramatic change among four participants with verbal learning disorders who, before treatment, were neglected by their classmates; were introverted, shy, and taciturn; and did not take part in conversations or discussions in their home classes or peer groups. The greatest change among these four was in problem-solving.

It appears that the model of problem-solving presented during treatment strongly influenced all participants and was helpful to those with both verbal and nonverbal disabilities. Those with verbal disabilities improved in terms of communication and identification and expression of feelings.

One girl from this group said at the end of the treatment, "Using the things I learned here really helped me... Now I have more confidence to speak and to express my opinion because usually I'm quiet. But in the small group, I felt that I did speak enough, and I said what I had to say."

All students had difficulty in initiating social contacts, and no improvement was seen in this area. All agreed that the treatment time was too short and that more time was needed.

Interpersonal Relations and Social Interactions—The Social Realm

Most of the participants felt that there was a slight change in their social standing after the treatment. Four participants who were socially neglected, introverted, and had a verbal learning disability changed their social standing, not only according to their own assessment, but according to the before-and-after treatment sociometric questionnaires in their classrooms and their teachers' assessments. This was especially true if they had a particular friend in the home classroom (even if the classroom teacher assisted the friendship).

Improved social skills made it easier to find a friend, and having a friend seemed in itself to make classmates view participants more favorably. Improved social standing, however, did not affect participants' feelings of loneliness, and, in some cases, feelings of loneliness increased.

Four participants with nonverbal disabilities who were socially rejected, extroverted, and aggressive—especially the two boys who stopped taking their Ritalin—reported increased loneliness. Two participants with nonverbal disabilities who were introverted and had a tendency to blame themselves, experienced greater feelings of loneliness as their awareness and understanding of their social situations increased. They became depressed and experienced feelings of failure because, despite their improved personal skills and strong efforts to participate more socially, their peer group was not responsive, seeming unable to grasp that changes had taken place in these students.

One of the girls said, "I really want to change my standing in the classroom. It's hard for me to get into a popular group in the class. The kids still relate to my old image. ... There are closed groups in the class. No one understands that I am starting to change, and they won't give me a chance to get into a group."

Feedback from parents indicated that in most cases, they saw significant improvement in their children's afterschool connections with friends. Many reported that their children started to go to afterschool activities at school and that the atmosphere at home surrounding interactions within the family (i.e., with siblings and parents) improved. Some participants started to attend youth groups, and some found new friends in their neighborhoods and had more confidence when playing outside. This was more pronounced among boys, except for the two boys who experienced interruptions in their Ritalin schedule. All the participants expressed the feeling that they had advanced in terms of social connections and interaction; but, again, they felt that others in the environment were not responsive.

One of the introverted boys said, "I feel that I have advanced. I am more assertive and don't always give in." One of the boys who was extroverted and aggressive said, "Now I am trying to 'think positively.'"

Some of the participants expressed their desire to use some of the techniques they had learned to improve the atmosphere at home. One of the girls said, "I have to help more at home, so Dad will understand us and not yell so much... He denies that he's a 'hothead.'"

Parents made similar comments: "She is trying to teach us... She tells us to 'think positively.'" The parents confirmed that their children's attempts to be a positive influence at home gave them a "push" and that the atmosphere was indeed improved.

Friendship Connections and Feelings of Loneliness—The Interpersonal Realm

One of the interesting findings was that most of the participants had increased feelings of loneliness after treatment. Before treatment, most had difficulty defining friendship. The need for an intimate friend increased with treatment. Two girls and two boys who felt they had undergone real change after treatment stated that others in the environment were not aware of their changes and that their classmates related to them as if they had not changed. Thus, it was still hard for them to find friends. Four of the participants, whose classroom teachers helped to match them with a friend, felt more confident and expressed less loneliness, even though the friendships were not of the same quality as those naturally formed.

As far as the kind of connections participants had with these teacher-orchestrated friends, it appeared that they were of lower quality, less concrete, and less intimate than naturally formed friendships. All participants expressed their desire for naturally formed, equal friendships, and most hoped a friend would help them, spend time with them, understand them, and do things together that they liked to do.

The girls showed more signs of intimacy and emotional connection in their descriptions of a good friend. At the end of treatment, girls said things like the following:

- "[A friend is] someone who won't forget me and will always help me."
- "We would have interesting and personal conversations."
- "We would play together outside and at home."
- "Always together."
  Boys said things like these:
- "[A friend is] someone who always does what I want, like my servant."
- "A friend [is someone] that likes what I like, like soccer and basketball."

Implications for Educators

There seem to be connections among several factors in the lives of the students in our study: (a) the kind of learning disability, (b) the nature of the adolescent's behavior, and (c) his or her social standing and social skills. In our study, students with verbal learning disabilities made greater social advancements than did those with nonverbal learning disabilities. This correlates with findings from other studies that children with nonverbal learning disabilities are at high risk for social difficulties and are the least socially adaptive (Gross-Tsur et al., 1995). We found that social skills prac-

tice did not greatly influence these participants or change their situation, in spite of their desire for change and their good verbal ability. Those with nonverbal disabilities may have a defective ability to acquire communication skills. Those with verbal disabilities can acquire these skills because of their better ability to understand gestures, read facial features, and speak with normal intonation.

THE TEACHER HAS A CRUCIAL ROLE IN DIRECTING STUDENTS, FINDING POTENTIAL FRIENDSHIP PAIRS, AND CREATING SITUATIONS THAT REQUIRE COOPERATION.

Given these factors, it may be that students with nonverbal disabilities would prosper under a different kind of treatment that teaches them in a specific way how to substitute socially positive behaviors for problem behaviors. To design such a program that includes this tailor-made dimension, educators would first need to identify problem behaviors through a functional behavior assessment of the kind suggested in the Individuals with Disabilities Education Act (IDEA; Fitzsimmons, 1998). Part of the rationale for such assessments is that problem behaviors fulfill social needs, such as the need for attention. If new social skills and positive behaviors can fulfill these same needs, there is a good chance that students with nonverbal disabilities can learn to replace old behaviors with new. In future development of the Life Skills program, we will introduce functional behavior assessments for students with nonverbal learning disabilities as part of the pretreatment assessment.

One of the surprises in our findings was that most of the participants' feelings of loneliness increased after treatment. With advancement in social skills and in the students' expectations

for change, understanding of their situations increased, as well as their feelings of loneliness. Students whose teachers matched them with a friend felt less lonely. We agree with Bergen (1993) and Margalit (1991) that the teacher has a crucial role in directing students, finding potential friendship pairs, and creating situations that require cooperation, as well as helping and encouraging parents to nurture these friendships outside of school.

The relatively slight improvement in social standing achieved by all participants may have been affected by the short, 5-month duration of the treatment. Their peer group did not have enough time to sense the changes. Social stigmas that are sometimes attached to those with learning disabilities can be hard to change, and it may be that some kind of directed intervention is needed in the home classrooms. If teachers and counselors worked consistently toward the goal of changing classroom culture, it might be possible to create an environment that is more flexible and more accepting of differences.

WITH ADVANCEMENT IN SOCIAL SKILLS AND IN THE STUDENTS' EXPECTATIONS FOR CHANGE, UNDERSTANDING OF THEIR SITUATIONS INCREASED AS WELL AS THEIR FEELINGS OF LONELINESS.

More research is needed on the relationship between verbal and nonverbal learning disabilities and adolescents' social skills. Research should also investigate the effects of different kinds of intervention, including group and individual treatment and the role of the teacher in encouraging friendships. Our study suggests the importance of detailed diagnosis of each student to design appropriate intervention. On the basis of our results, we propose several ideas for teachers and counselors in the areas of diagnosis, social skills intervention design, friendships, and classroom culture. The goal is to help adolescents with learning disabilities have fuller, happier social lives.

Suggestions for Teachers

Diagnosis

- Special education teachers and classroom teachers should utilize all diagnostic and anecdotal evidence available to determine whether a student's disability is verbal or nonverbal in nature.

- Students with nonverbal disabilities could also benefit from a functional behavior assessment.

- Evidence should be collected as to whether the student is socially neglected or rejected, introverted or extroverted, and whether he or she has friends at school and at home.

Intervention Design

- Analysis of these areas should be done to decide what kind of social skills treatment program is likely to be most beneficial and whether group or individual treatment is preferable. Possibly, those with nonverbal learning disabilities are more in need of learning how to replace specific problem behaviors with new behaviors, strengthening their sense of self, and one-on-one counseling and emotional support to improve their ability to cope with characteristics that they cannot change. Those with verbal learning disabilities may respond better to group counseling.

- The topics covered in our Life Skills program and the various discussion and simulation methods employed were helpful to students. We would add a section on initiating social contacts.

Friendships and Classroom Culture

- Assistance by the classroom teacher in helping students form friendships is important, even if these friendships are not of the same quality as naturally formed friendships. Students with any kind of friendship may feel less lonely and may experience increased self-esteem that will lead to greater overall social ease.

- The classroom teacher should engage in teaching *all* students in the home classroom in a structured, systematic way how to help support those with learning disabilities. This could increase the success of intervention programs and improve the integration of those with learning disabilities into general education classrooms. The goal is to help these adolescents become independent adults able to fully integrate into the activities of society.

References

Asher, S. R., Parker, J. G., & Walker D. L. (1996). Distinguishing friendship from acceptance: Implications for intervention and assessment. In W. M. Bukowski, A. F. Newcomb, & W. W. Hatup (Eds.), *The company they make: Friendships in childhood and adolescence.* Cambridge: Cambridge University Press.

Bauminger, N. (1990). *Main characteristics of social skills in adolescents with learning disabilities.* Unpublished master's thesis, The Hebrew University of Jerusalem, Israel (in Hebrew).

Bergen, D. (1993). Teaching strategies: Facilitating friendship development in inclusion classrooms. *Childhood Education, 69*(4), 234–236.

Dimitrovsky, L., Spector, H., Levy-Shiff, R., & Vakil, E. (1998) Interpretation of facial expressions of affect in children with learning disabilities with verbal or nonverbal deficits. *Journal of Learning Disabilities, 31*(3), 286–292.

Elliot, S. N. (1988, April). *Children's social skill deficits: A review of assessment methods and measurement issues.* Paper presented at the annual convention of the American Educational Research Association, New Orleans, LA.

Fitzsimmons, M. (1998). *Functional behavior assessment and behavior intervention plans.* Reston, VA: ERIC Clearinghouse on Disabilities and Gifted Education. ERIC/OSEP Digest E571.

Gross-Tsur, V., Shalev, R. S., Manor, O., & Amir, N. (1995). Developmental right-hemisphere syndrome: Clinical spectrum of the nonverbal learning disability. *Journal of Learning Disabilities, 28*(2), 80–86.

Levin, G. (1997). *Emotional style and emotional problems of learning disabled children.* Unpublished master's thesis, The Hebrew University of Jerusalem, Israel (in Hebrew).

Margalit, M., & Levin-Alyagon, M. (1994). Learning disability subtyping, loneliness, and classroom adjustment. *Learning Disability Quarterly, 17*(4), 297–310.

Margalit, M. (1991). Understanding loneliness among students with learning disabilities. *Behaviour Change, 8*(4), 167–173.

Margalit, M. (1995). Development trends in special education: Advancement in coping with loneliness, social connections and feelings of coherence. In *Education for the 21st century* (pp. 489–510). Tel-Aviv, Israel: Ramot Publishers (in Hebrew).

Rourke, B. P. (1988). Socioemotional disturbances of learning disabled children. *Journal of Consulting and Clinical Psychology, 56*(6), 801–810.

Rourke, B. P. (1989). *Nonverbal learning disabilities: The syndrome and the model.* New York: Guilford.

Shectman, Z. (1993). Group counseling in school in order to improve social skills among students with adaptation problems. *The Educational Counselor, 3*(1) (pp. 47–67) (in Hebrew).

Smilansky, S. (1988). *The challenge of adolescence.* Tel Aviv, Israel: Ramot Publishers (in Hebrew).

Deborah Court, *Lecturer, School of Education, Bar-Ilan University, Ramat-Gan, Israel.* **Sarah Givon,** *Doctoral Candidate, Bar-Ilan University, Ramat-Gan, Israel, and Lecturer, Jerusalem College, Israel. Address correspondence to Deborah Court, School of Education, Bar-Ilan University, Ramat-Gan, Israel 52900. (e-mail: d_court@inter.net.il).*

UNIT 4
Speech and Language Impairments

Unit Selections

12. **Language Differences or Learning Difficulties**, Spencer J. Salend and AltaGracia Salinas
13. **Young African American Children With Disabilities and Augmentative and Alternative Communication Issues**, Phil Parette, Mary Blake Huer, and Toya A. Wyatt

Key Points to Consider

- How can a multidisciplinary team help prevent the over assignment of linguistically diverse children to communication disordered placements? How can assessment tools be selected and adapted for sensitivity to cross-cultural perspectives?

- Why is cultural sensitivity important to speech/language clinicians who work with clients from diverse backgrounds? What is the importance of family involvement to the success of augmentative and alternative communication?

 **Links: www.dushkin.com/online/**
These sites are annotated in the World Wide Web pages.

Issues in Emergent Literacy for Children With Language Impairments
http://www.ciera.org/library/reports/inquiry-2/2-002/2-002.html

Speech and Language Disorders Fact Sheet
http://www.nichcy.org/pubs/factshe/fs11txt.htm

Speech Disorders WWW Sites
http://www.socialnet.lu/handitel/wwwlinks/dumb.html

Speech and language impairments, although grouped together as a category of disability by IDEA (Individuals with Disabilities Education Act), are not synonymous. Language refers to multiple ways to communicate (for example by writing, signing, body, or voice), whereas speech refers to vocal articulation.

Many children have difficulty learning to read because of speech and/or language impairments. If they cannot receive language and/or express speech sounds correctly, the total lexicon makes less sense. Likewise, some children assessed as dyslexic (difficulty with the lexicon) are reading disabled primarily because of their disorders with speech and/or language. Telling these disorders apart can be challenging. Learning to communicate may also be difficult for children with hearing impairments, developmental disorders, some physical disorders (e.g. Cerebral palsy), and some emotional disorders (e.g. Elective mutism).

Speech is the vocal utterance of language. It is considered disordered in three underlying ways: voice, articulation, and fluency. Voice involves coordinated efforts by the lungs, larynx, vocal cords, and nasal passages to produce recognizable sounds. Voice can be considered disordered if it is incorrectly phonated (breathy, strained, husky, hoarse) or if it is incorrectly resonated through the nose (hyper-nasality, hypo-nasality). Articulation involves the use of the tongue, lips, teeth, and mouth to produce recognizable sounds. Articulation can be considered disordered if sounds are mispronounced or if sounds are added, omitted, or substituted for other sounds, such as using the *z* sound for the *s* sound or *w* for *l*.

Fluency involves appropriate pauses and hesitations to keep speech sounds recognizable. Fluency can be considered disordered if sounds are very rapid with extra sounds (cluttered) or if sounds are blocked or repeated, especially at the beginning of words. Stuttering is an example of a fluency disorder of speech.

Language is the rule-based use of voice sounds, symbols, gestures, or signs to communicate. Language problems refer to the use of such devises in combinations and patterns that fail to communicate, fail to follow the arbitrary rules for that language, or lead to a delay in the use of communication devices relative to normal development in other areas (physical, cognitive, social).

The prevalence rates of speech and language disorders are higher than the rates for any other condition of disability in primary school. The exact extent of the problem, however, has been questioned because assessment of communication takes a variety of forms. Shy children may be diagnosed with delayed language. Bilingual or multilingual children are often mislabeled as having a language disorder because they come from linguistically and culturally diverse backgrounds. Many bilingual children do not need the special services provided by speech-language clinicians but do benefit from instruction in English as a second language.

All children with language or speech disorders are entitled to assessment and remediation as early in life as the problem is realized. Because children's speech is not well developed between birth and age 3, most disorders are not assessed until preschool. Students with speech-language disorders are entitled to a free and appropriate education in the least restrictive environment possible and to transitional help into the world of work, if needed, after their education is completed.

Disordered language is usually more difficult to remedy than delayed language. Disordered language may be due to a receptive problem (difficulty understanding voice sounds), an expressive problem (difficulty producing the voice sounds that follow the arbitrary rules for that language), or both. Language disorders include aphasia (no language) and dysphasia (difficulty producing language). Many language disorders are the result of a difficulty in understanding the syntactical rules and structural principles of the language (form), or they are the result of a difficulty in perceiving the semantic meanings of the words of the language (content). Many language disorders are also due to a difficulty in using the language pragmatically, in a practical context (function).

Most speech and language impairments are remediated between elementary school and high school. An exception to this is speech problems that persist due to physical impairments such as damage or dysfunction of lungs, larynx, vocal cords, or nasal passages. Another exception is language problems that persist due to concurrent disabilities such as deafness, autism, compromised mentation, traumatic brain injuries, or some emotional and behavioral disorders.

Speech-language clinicians usually provide special services to children with speech and language impairments in pull-out sessions in resource rooms. Computer technology is also frequently used to assist these children in both their regular education classes and in pull-out therapy sessions.

The first article addresses the confusion that exists over whether a child has a cultural/linguistic difference in speech/language or whether the child is, in fact, disabled in the area of communication. Students with limited English proficiency should not be labeled communication disordered unless they are significantly disabled in their mother tongue as well.

The second article discusses the use of augmentative and alternate communication (AAC) systems. Many users of AAC are children from culturally/linguistically diverse backgrounds. It is important for speech/language clinicians to heed alternate assessment procedures. If a minority child has a significant communication disorder, the clinician must be especially attentive to family and community social values, cultural mistrust, and communication needs. Family involvement is crucial to the success of AAC systems.

Language Differences or Learning Difficulties

The Work of the Multidisciplinary Team

Spencer J. Salend and AltaGracia Salinas

Maria moved to the United States from Mexico and was placed in Ms. Shannon's fourth-grade class where she sat quietly at her desk and kept to herself. Whenever directions were given, she seemed lost and later had difficulty completing tasks and participating in class discussions. During teacher-directed activities, Maria often either looked around to see what her classmates were doing and then mimicked them, or played with materials at her desk.

Ms. Shannon was concerned about Maria's lack of progress in developing English proficiency and her inability to pay attention and complete her work. Ms. Shannon thought Maria might have a learning disability and referred her to the multidisciplinary team to determine if she needed special education. The team organized the assessment process for Maria by considering the following questions:

- Who can assist the team in making decisions about Maria's educational program?
- What factors should the team consider in determining Maria's educational strengths and needs?
- What strategies should the team employ to assess Maria's educational strengths and needs?
- Should the team recommend a special education placement for Maria?

Educators often refer students like Maria for placement in special education (Ortiz, 1997). As Ortiz indicated, students learning a second language and students with learning disabilities often exhibit similar difficulties with learning, attention, social skills, and behavioral and emotional balance. As a result, multidisciplinary teams are increasingly working with educators like Ms. Shan-

non to conduct meaningful assessments and determine appropriate educational programs for a growing number of students whose primary language is not English.

Recommendations for Multidisciplinary Teams

Using the experiences of Maria and her teachers, this article provides recommendations for helping multidisciplinary teams accurately and fairly assess second-language learners and differentiate language differences from learning difficulties. The article includes six recommendations, as follows:

- Diversify the composition of the multidisciplinary teams and offer training.
- Compare student performance in both the native and secondary languages.
- Consider the processes and factors associated with second-language acquisition.
- Employ alternatives to traditional standardized testing.
- Identify diverse life experiences that may affect learning.
- Analyze the data and develop an appropriate educational plan.

These recommendations also can assist multidisciplinary teams in developing educational programs for second-language learners and in complying with the Individuals with Disabilities Education Act (IDEA), which states that students should not be identified as having a disability if their eligibility and school related difficulties are based on their proficiency in English, or their lack of opportunity to receive instruction in reading or mathematics.

Diversify the Composition of the Multidisciplinary Teams and Offer Training

IDEA requires that a multidisciplinary team of professionals and family members, with the student when appropriate, make important decisions concerning the education of students referred for special education. Initially, the team determines if students are in need of and eligible for special education services. When teachers refer second-language learners to the multidisciplinary team, the team frequently faces many challenges, such as differentiating linguistic and cultural differences from learning difficulties, and developing an appropriate educational program that addresses students' linguistic, cultural, and experiential backgrounds.

The composition and training of the multidisciplinary team are critical factors in determining the educational needs of second-language learners (Ochoa, Robles-Pina, Garcia, & Breunig 1999). Therefore, the team should include family and community members, as well as professionals who are fluent in the student's native language, understand the student and the family's culture, and can help collect and interpret the data in culturally and linguistically appropriate ways. The inclusion of these people allows the team to learn about the family's and the student's cultural perspective and experiential and linguistic background, and to assist in the determination of the origins of the student's learning difficulties. Team members can help determine what students' learning difficulties can be explained by sociocultural perspectives, experiential factors, and sociolinguistic variables.

The composition of multidisciplinary teams for second-language learners should include educators who are trained in assessing second-language learners and designing educational programs to meet their varied needs. Such membership may include English as a Second Language (ESL) teachers, bilingual educators, and migrant educators. Whereas ESL teachers offer instruction in English to help students build on their existing English language skills, bilingual educators teach students in both their native language and in English. Because bilingual educators are fluent in the family's native language, they can be instrumental in involving family and community members in the team process and in assessing students' skills in their native language. In the case of migrant students like Maria, the team also can benefit from the input of migrant educators, who provide individualized instruction to migrant students and serve as a liaison between the family, the school and the community (Salend, 2001).

For example, the multidisciplinary team assembled for Maria was expanded to include Ms. Garcia, a bilingual migrant educator who worked with Maria and her family in their home and had training and experience with the second language acquisition process, as well as in working with students from culturally and linguistically diverse backgrounds. Ms. Garcia worked with other members of the team to gather information about Maria's school, home-life and experiential background, to interact with and collect information from Maria, her mother, and other family members, to assess Maria's skills in Spanish, and to identify strategies to support Maria's learning.

The multidisciplinary team can foster the success of the process by working as a collaborative and interactive team (Chase Thomas, Correa, & Morsink, 2001; Salend, 2001). The collaborative and interactive nature of the team can be enhanced by agreeing upon goals, learning about each other's beliefs, experiences and expertise, understanding and coordinating each other's roles, being sensitive to cross-cultural perspectives and communication styles, establishing equal status relationships, and addressing differences directly and immediately. Successful teams adopt a problem solving approach and employ effective interpersonal and communication skills so that all team members feel comfortable identifying issues to be considered by the team, collecting and sharing information, seeking clarification from others, participating in discussions, and making decisions via consensus.

Multidisciplinary teams work with educators to conduct meaningful assessments and determine appropriate educational programs for a growing number of students whose primary language is not English.

Teams can enhance the effectiveness of the process for second-language learners by offering training to team members. Teams should provide this training to all school personnel, and it can help the team members be aware of the effect of sociocultural perspectives, experiential backgrounds, and linguistic variables on students' behavior and school performance. Team members also will benefit from training in employing culturally responsive instructional, behavior management and mental health interventions, understanding the second language acquisition process and the problems associated with the assessment of students from culturally and linguistically diverse backgrounds, and selecting and adapting assessment instruments (Salend, Dorney, & Mazo, 1997).

Teams often face mismatches between members of the team and second-language learners in terms of their different cultural, linguistic, and socioeconomic backgrounds (Gay, 2002).

- What is my definition of diversity?

- What are my perceptions of students from different racial and ethnic groups? With language or dialects different from mine?
- What are the sources of these perceptions?
- How do I respond to my students based on these perceptions?
- What kinds of information, skills, and resources do I need to acquire to effectively teach from a multicultural perspective?
- In what ways do I collaborate with other educators, family members and community groups to address the needs of all my students? (p. 4).

Thus, team members may find it helpful to engage in activities to examine their own cultural perspectives and consider how their cultural beliefs affect their expectations, beliefs, and behaviors and may differ from those held by students and their families (Cartledge, Kea, & Ida, 2000; Hyun & Fowler, 1995; Obiakor, 1999). Montgomery (2001) offered a self-assessment tool that team members can use to reflect upon their understanding of diversity. The tool includes the following questions:

Compare Student Performance in Both the Native and Secondary Languages

After multidisciplinary team members meet, they need to make a plan for assessment. The assessment plan for second-language learners should collect data to compare student performance in both the native and secondary languages. Team members can collect data relating to students' performance in both languages through the use of informal and standardized tests, language samples, observations, questionnaires, and interviews. These methods can be employed to examine students' language proficiency, language dominance, language preference, and code switching. Language proficiency relates to the degree of skill in speaking the language(s) and includes receptive and expressive language skills. Although proficiency in one language does not necessarily mean lack of proficiency in another language, language dominance refers to the language in which the student is most fluent and implies a comparison of the student's abilities in two or more languages. Language preference identifies the language in which the student prefers to communicate, which can vary depending on the setting. Code switching relates to using words, phrases, expressions and sentences from one language while speaking another language.

Collect data relating to students' performance in both languages through the use of informal and standardized tests, language samples, observations, questionnaires, and interviews.

Through observations, informal assessment, and interviews with Maria and her family members, the multidisciplinary team found out that Maria was proficient in Spanish but lacked proficiency in English. It was observed that when Maria spoke Spanish, she was expressive, used the correct tense and age-appropriate vocabulary, and understood all the communications directed to her. Whereas Maria used Spanish to initiate and maintain interactions with others in an organized and coherent manner, her English was characterized by the use of gestures and short, basic sentences to communicate. In addition, observations and interviews revealed that Maria preferred to speak Spanish in all settings, and that Spanish was the dominant language spoken at home, since Maria's mother did not speak English.

Consider the Processes and Factors Associated with Second Language Acquisition

The assessment process for second-language learners like Maria should recognize that learning a second language is a long-term, complex, and dynamic process that involves different types of language skills and various stages of development (Collier, 1995). Therefore, when assessing second-language learners, the multidisciplinary team needs to consider the factors that affect second-language acquisition and understand the stages students go through in learning a second language.

Because proficiency in a second language involves the acquisition of two distinct types of language skills, the team needs to assess students' basic interpersonal communication skills and cognitive/academic language proficiency. The former, the interpersonal skills are the social language skills that guide the development of social relationships (e.g., "Good morning. How are you?"). Even though they are relatively repetitive, occur within a specific and clearly defined context, and are not cognitively demanding, research indicates that they typically take up to 2 years to develop in a second language (Cummins, 1984).

Cognitive proficiency, on the other hand, refers to the language skills that relate to literacy, cognitive development, and academic development in the classroom. It includes understanding such complex academic terms as photosynthesis, onomatopoeia, and least common denominator. Because this proficiency does not have an easily understood context, and tends to be cognitively demanding, it often takes up to 7 years for children to develop and use these language skills. Since cognitive skills developed in one's first language foster the development of cognitive proficiency in one's second language, we must gather information on students' proficiency and educational training in their native language.

An analysis of Maria's English language skills indicated that she was starting to develop a mastery of interpersonal language skills and struggling in terms of her cognitive language proficiency. For example, Ms. Shannon reported that when Maria was given directions to perform a classroom activity in English, she had difficulty completing it. However, when the directions were explained in Spanish, she was able to complete the task.

In learning a second language, students go through developmental stages that team members should consider when evaluating students' learning.

In learning a second language, students also go through developmental stages (see Figure 1) that team members should consider when evaluating students' learning (Maldonado-Colon, 1995). Initially, second-language learners' understanding of the new language is usually greater than their production. Many second-language learners go through a silent period in which they process what they hear but refrain from verbalizing. This is often misinterpreted as indicating a lack of cognitive abilities, disinterest in school, or shyness. Once students are ready to speak their new language, their verbalizations gradually increase in terms of their semantic and syntactic complexity.

Observations of Maria in her class indicated that she was focusing on understanding via mimicking others and using visual and context clues, and that she communicated via pointing, physical gestures and the occasional use of one to three-word phrases. Therefore, the multidisciplinary team felt that she was functioning at the preproduction and early production stages of learning English.

The team should also be aware of other factors that may affect students and their developmental progress in maintaining their native language and learning their new language such as age, educational background, and language exposure. Students who have been educated in their native language often progress faster in learning a new language that those who have not had a formal education (Thomas & Collier, 1997). In addition, students may attempt to apply the rules of their first language to their second language, which can affect their pronunciation, syntax, and spelling (Tiedt & Tiedt, 2001). And as some students learn a second language, they may experience language loss in their native language. Similarly, children who simultaneously learn two languages from birth may initially experience some temporary language delays in achieving developmental language milestones and some language mixing. These tend to disappear over time (Fierro-Cobas & Chan, 2001).

Figure 1. Stages of Second-Language Learning

1. **Preproduction or Silent period.** Students focus on processing and comprehending what they hear but avoid verbal responses. They often rely on modeling, visual stimuli, context clues, key words and use listening strategies to understand meaning, and often communicate through pointing and physical gestures. They may benefit from classroom activities that allow them to respond by imitating, drawing, pointing, and matching.

2. **Telegraphic or Early Production period.** Students begin to use two- or three-word sentences, and show limited comprehension. They have a receptive vocabulary level of approximately 1,000 words and an expressive level that typically includes approximately 100 words. They may benefit from classroom activities that employ language they can understand, require them to name and group objects, and call for responses to simple questions.

3. **Interlanguage and Intermediate Fluency period.** Students speak in longer phrases and start to use complete sentences. They often mix basic phrases and sentences in both languages. They may benefit from classroom activities that encourage them to experiment with language and develop and expand their vocabulary.

4. **Extension and Expansion period.** Students expand on their basic sentences and extend their language abilities to employ synonyms and synonymous expressions. They are developing good comprehension skills, employing more complex sentence structures, and making fewer errors when speaking. They may benefit from classroom literacy activities and instruction in vocabulary and grammar.

5. **Enrichment period.** Students are taught learning strategies to assist them in making the transition to the new language.

6. **Independent Learning period.** Students begin to work on activities at various levels of difficulty with heterogeneous groups.

SOURCE: *Creating Inclusive Classrooms: Effective and Reflective Practices* (4th ed., p. 91) by S. J. Salend, 2001, Columbus, OH: Merrill/Prentice Hall. Reprinted by permission of Pearson Education, Inc.

Employ Alternatives to Traditional Standardized Testing

As mandated by the latest reauthorization of IDEA, rather than relying solely on potentially biased, standardized tests, the multidisciplinary team should employ a variety of student-centered, alternative assessment procedures to assess the educational needs of students from culturally and linguistically diverse backgrounds accurately. Such assessment alternatives include performance-based and portfolio assessment, curriculum-based measurements, instructional rubrics, dynamic assessment, student journals and learning logs, and self-evaluation techniques (Salend, 2001). These assessment alternatives can provide the Multidisciplinary Team with more complete profiles of students like Maria including their academic strengths and needs, learning styles and the impact of the school environment on their learning.

In the case of Maria, the multidisciplinary team worked with Maria and Ms. Shannon to create a portfolio that showed that Maria's decoding and reading comprehension skills in Spanish were age appropriate. It also revealed that she reads phonetically, engages in self-correction, and uses context and semantic cues. These results were also confirmed by Maria's performance on a standardized Spanish reading test.

Identify Diverse Life Experiences That May Affect Learning

Many second-language learners have diverse life experiences that can have a significant effect on their learning. These experiences may include being separated from family members for extended periods of time (Abrams, Ferguson, & Laud, 2001). Identifying these experiences can help the team determine if students' learning difficulties are related to the existence of a disability or other experiential factors. Therefore, the team can use the guidelines in Figure 2 to collect information to determine if a student's difficulties in learning result from language, cultural, and experiential factors, acculturation, psychological and family traumas, economic hardships, racism, or lack of exposure to effective instruction.

Learning a second language is a long-term, complex, and dynamic process that involves different types of language skills and various stages of development.

Ms. Garcia was able to obtain information about Maria by speaking with Maria and her mother. Ms. Garcia reported that Maria had not had an easy life. She lived in a rural village in Mexico and sporadically attended a school that had limited resources. Maria traveled to the United States with her mother and her three siblings a year ago to join her father and two older brothers who had been working in the United States. Two other siblings remained in Mexico with the hope of joining the family when enough money could be saved to bring them to the United States. Two other siblings remained in Mexico with the hope of joining the family when enough money could be saved to bring them to the United States. However, within 6 months of living in the

United States, Maria's parents separated; and her father returned to Mexico. Maria reported that she misses her life in Mexico and her siblings who are still living there.

Upon arriving in the United States, Maria's mother found a job working as a migrant farmworker. Because she doesn't speak English, did not attend school, and works long hours to make ends meet, Maria's mother finds it difficult to help Maria with her schoolwork and relies on Maria to help take care of the younger children, and to cook and clean. Maria's mother also said that although her children watch cartoons in English, the interactions in the home are in Spanish. Interactions with the family also revealed that the family has few links to and interactions with the community, and that their lifestyle parallels the traditions of Mexico.

Code switching relates to using words, phrases, expressions and sentences from one language while speaking another language.

This information was helpful to the multidisciplinary team in providing information regarding Maria's learning abilities. First, it revealed that Maria's learning ability may be related to the fact that she has not regularly attended school and that the school she attended in Mexico is very different form her current school. Second, Maria's mother relies on her to help around the house; and Maria has quickly learned to perform these roles, which shows that she learns by active participation and is viewed by her mother as responsible and independent. Third, Maria has had limited exposure to English, which affects her progress in learning English and performing in school.

Analyze the Data and Develop an Appropriate Educational Plan

After the team has collected the data, team members meet to analyze the data and make decisions about students' educational programs. For second-language learners, the analysis should focus on examining the factors that affect learning and language development, determining if learning and language difficulties occur in both languages, and developing an educational plan to promote learning and language acquisition. Damico (1991) offered questions that can guide the team in examining the data to assess the extent to which students' diverse life experiences and cultural and linguistic backgrounds serve as

Figure 2. Life Experience Factors and Questions

Length of Residence in the United States

- How long and for what periods of time has the student resided in the United States?
- What were the conditions and events associated with the student's migration?
- If the student was born in the United States, what has been the student's exposure to English?

Students may have limited or interrupted exposure to English and the U.S. culture, resulting in poor vocabulary and slow naming speed, and affecting their cultural adjustment. Trauma experienced during migration or family separations as a result of migration can be psychological barriers that affect learning. Being born and raised in the United States does not guarantee that students have developed English skills and have had significant exposure to English and the U.S. culture.

School Attendance Patterns

- How long has the student been in school?
- What is the student's attendance pattern? Have there been any disruptions in school?

Students may fail to acquire language skills because of failure to attend school on a regular basis.

School Instructional History

- How many years of schooling did the student complete in the native country?
- What language(s) were used to guide instruction in the native country?
- What types of classrooms has the student attended (bilingual education, English as a second language, general education, speech/language therapy services, special education)?
- What has been the language of instruction in these classes?
- What is the student's level of proficiency in reading, writing, and speaking in the native language?
- What strategies and instructional materials have been successful?
- What were the outcomes of these educational placements?
- What language does the student prefer to use in informal situations with adults? In formal situations with adults?

Students may not have had access to appropriate instruction and curricula, resulting in problems in language acquisition, reading, and mathematics.

Cultural Background

- How does the student's cultural background affect second language acquisition?
- Has the student had sufficient time to adjust to the new culture?
- What is the student's acculturation level?
- What is the student's attitude toward school?

Since culture and language are inextricably linked, lack of progress in learning a second language can be due to cultural and communication differences and/or lack of exposure to the new culture. For example, some culturesrely on the use of body language in communication as a substitute for verbal communication. Various cultures also have different perspectives on color, time, gender, distance, and space that affect language.

Performance in Comparison to Peers

- Does the student's language skill, learning rate, and learning style differ from those of other students from similar experiential, cultural, and linguistic backgrounds?
- Does the student interact with peers in the primary language and/or English?
- Does the student experience difficulty following directions, understanding language, and expressing thoughts in the primary language? In the second language?

The student's performance can be compared to that of students who have similar traits rather than to that of students whose experiences in learning a second language are very different.

Home Life

- What language(s) or dialect(s) are spoken at home by each of the family members?
- When did the student start to speak?
- Is the student's performance at home different from that of siblings?
- What language(s) or dialect(s) are spoken in the family's community?
- Is a distinction made among the uses of the primary language or dialect and English? If so, how is that distinction made? (For example, the non-English language is used at home, but children speak English when playing with peers.)
- What are the attitudes of the family and the community toward English and bilingual education?
- In what language(s) does the family watch television, listen to the radio, and read newspapers, books, and magazines?
- What is the student's language preference in the home and community?
- To what extent does the family interact with the dominant culture and in what ways?

Important information concerning the student's language proficiency, dominance, and preference can be obtained by soliciting information from family members. Similarly, the student's acquisition of language can be enhanced by involving family members.

Health and Developmental History

- What health, medical, sensory, and developmental factors have affected the student's learning and language development?

A student's difficulty in learning and acquiring language may be related to various health and developmental variables.

Source: Creating Inclusive Classrooms: Effective and Reflective Practices (4th ed.; p. 94–95) by S. J. Salend, 2001, Columbus, OH: Merrill/Prentice Hall. Reprinted by permission of Pearson Education, Inc.

Figure 3. Differentiating Instruction for Second-Language Learners

- Establish a relaxed learning environment that encourages students to use both languages.
- Label objects in the classroom in several languages.
- Encourage and show students how to use bilingual dictionaries and Pictionaries.
- Use repetition to help students acquire the rhythm, pitch, volume, and tone of the new language.
- Use simple vocabulary and shorter sentences, and limit the use of idiomatic expressions, slang, and pronouns.
- Highlight key words through reiteration, increased volume and slight exaggeration, and writing them on the chalkboard.
- Use gestures, facial expressions, voice changes, pantomimes, demonstrations, rephrasing, visuals, props, manipulatives, and other cues to communicate and convey the meaning of new terms and concepts.

- Preview and teach new vocabulary, phrases, idioms, structures and concepts through use of modeling, and hands-on experiences.
- Supplement oral instruction and descriptions with visuals such as pictures, charts, maps, graphs, and graphic organizers.
- Offer regular summaries of important concepts and check students' understanding frequently.
- Emphasize communication rather than form.
- Correct students indirectly by restating their incorrect comments in correct form.

Sources: Choice of Languages in Instruction: One Language or Two?, by A. Brice and C. Roseberry-MeKibbin, 2001, *TEACHING Exceptional Children, 33*(4), pp. 10–16.
The Changing Face of Bilingual Education, by R. Gersten, 1999, *Educational Leadership, 56*(7), pp. 41–45.
Below the Tip of the Iceberg: Teaching Language Minority Students, by V. Fueyo, 1997, *TEACHING Exceptional Children, 30*(1), pp. 61–65.

explanations for the difficulties they may be experiencing in schools. These questions include the following:

- What factors and conditions may explain the student's learning and/or language difficulties (e.g., stressful life events, lack of opportunity to learn, racism, acculturation, and experiential background)?
- To what extent does the student demonstrate the same learning and/or language difficulties in community settings as in school and/or in the primary language?
- To what extent are the student's learning and/ or language difficulties due to normal second language acquisition, dialectical differences, or cultural factors?
- Did bias occur prior to, during, and after assessment such as in the reliability, validity, and standardization of the test as well as with the skills and learning styles assessed?
- To what extent were the student's cultural, linguistic, dialectic and experiential backgrounds considered in collecting and analyzing the assessment data (e.g., selection, administration, and interpretation of the test's results, prereferral strategies, learning styles, family involvement)?

These questions also can guide the team in differentiating between two types of second-language learners (Rice & Ortiz, 1994), and planning appropriate educational programs for these students. One type of second-language learner demonstrates some proficiency in the native language but experiences difficulties in learning a new language that are consistent with the typical difficulties individuals encounter in learning a second language. Although these kinds of behavior are similar to those shown by students with learning difficulties, these students' educational needs can best be addressed through participation in a bilingual education or an English as a Second Language (ESL) program.

The other type of second-language learner exhibits language, academic, and social behavior in the first and second languages that are significantly below those of peers who have similar linguistic, cultural, and experiential backgrounds (Ortiz, 1997). These students may benefit from a special education program and individualized educational programs (IEPs) that address their own linguistic, cultural, and experiential needs (Garcia & Malkin, 1993; Ortiz, 1997). Both types of second-language learners would benefit from the use of strategies for differentiating instruction presented in Figure 3.

Team members will benefit from training in employing culturally responsive instructional, behavior management and mental health interventions.

In the case of Maria, the multidisciplinary team determined that she did not have a disability. The assessment data led the team to conclude that Maria had age-appropriate decoding, reading comprehension, and speaking skills in Spanish and that her difficulties in learning English appeared to be related to the normal process of second-language acquisition and cultural and experiential factors. They also decided that Maria didn't qualify for special education services under the IDEA because her school-related difficulties were based on her lack of proficiency in English and the limited opportunities she has had to receive instruction.

The multidisciplinary team determined that Maria would benefit from the services of a bilingual educator because she needed to strengthen her native language skills to learn academic content and to provide a better foundation for learning English. They also recommended strategies for establishing home-school partnerships and communications, and encouraged her teachers to use cooperative learning strategies and the strategies in Figure 3. The team also developed a plan to collect data to examine the effectiveness of these intervention strategies on Maria's learning, language development, socialization, and her success in school.

Final Thoughts

The ability to acquire and use language has a great effect on students' learning behavior and educational performance. As a result, many second-language learners like Maria exhibit types of behavior that resemble students with learning difficulties and are referred to the multidisciplinary team. Because the team process may vary across school districts, educators need to consider how the recommendations can be incorporated into their assessment process to differentiate between language differences from learning difficulties, and to provide second-language learners with appropriate educational programs.

References

Abrams, J., Ferguson, J., & Laud, L. (2001). Assessing ESOL students. *Educational Leadership, 59*(3), 62–65.

Brice, A., & Roseberry-MeKibbin, C. (2001). Choice of languages in instruction: One language or two? *TEACHING Exceptional Children, 33*(4), 10–16.

Cartledge, G., Kea, C. D., & Ida, D. J. (2000). Anticipating differences—Celebrating strengths: Providing culturally competent services for students with serious emotional disturbance. *TEACHING Exceptional Children, 32*(3), 30–37.

Chase Thomas, C., Correa, V., & Morsink, C. (2001). *Interactive teaming: Enhancing programs for students with special needs* (3rd ed.). Columbus, OH: Merrill/Prentice-Hall.*

Collier, V. (1995). Acquiring a second language for school. *Directions in Language and Education, 1*(4), 1–12.

Cummins, J. (1984). *Bilingualism and special education: Issues in assessment and pedagogy.* San Diego, CA: College-Hill.

Damico, J. S. (1991). Descriptive assessment of communicative ability in Limited English Proficient students. In E. Hamayan & J. S. Damico (Eds.), *Limiting bias in the assessment of bilingual students* (pp. 157–218). Austin, TX: PRO-ED.*

Fierro-Cobas, V., & Chan, E. (2001). Language development in bilingual children: A primer for pediatricians. *Contemporary Pediatrics, 18*(7), 79–98.

Fueyo, V. (1997). Below the tip of the iceberg: Teaching language minority students. *TEACHING Exceptional Children, 30*(1), 61–65.

Gay, G. (2002). Preparing for culturally responsive teaching. *Journal of Teacher Education, 53*(2), 106–116.

Gersten, R. (1999). The changing face of bilingual education. *Educational Leadership, 56*(7), 41–45.

Langdon, H. W. (1989). Language disorder or difference? Assessing the language skills of Hispanic students. *Exceptional Children, 56*, 160–167.

Maldonado-Colon, E. (1995, April). *Second language learners in special education: Language framework for inclusive classrooms.* Paper presented at the international meeting of the Council for Exceptional Children, Indianapolis.

Montgomery, W. (2001). Creating culturally responsive, inclusive classrooms. *TEACHING Exceptional Children, 33*(4), 4–9.

Obiakor, F. E. (1999). Teacher expectations of minority exceptional learners: Impact on accuracy of self-concepts. *Exceptional Children, 66*, 39–53.

Ochoa, S. H., Robles-Pina, R., Garcia, S. B., & Breunig, N. (1999). School psychologists' perspectives on referrals of language minority students. *Multiple Voices, 3*(1), 1–13.

Ortiz, A. A. (1997). Learning disabilities occurring concomitantly with linguistic differences. *Journal of Learning Disabilities, 30*, 321–332.

Rice, L. S., & Ortiz, A. A. (1994). Second language difference or learning disability? *LD Forum, 19*(2), 11–13.

Salend, S. J. (2001). *Creating inclusive classrooms: Effective and reflective practices* (4th ed.). Columbus, OH: Merrill/Prentice-Hall.*

Salend, S. J., Dorney, J. A., & Mazo, M. (1997). The roles of bilingual special educators in creating inclusive classrooms. *Remedial and Special Education, 18*, 54–64.

Thomas, W. P., & Collier, V. P. (1997). *School effectiveness for language minority students.* Washington, DC: National Clearinghouse for Bilingual Education.

Tiedt, P. L., & Tiedt, I. (2001). *Multicultural teaching: A handbook of activities, information, and resources* (6th ed.). Boston: Allyn & Bacon.*

Spencer J. Salend (CEC Chapter #615), Professor, Department of Educational Studies, State University of New York at New Paltz.
AltaGracia Salinas, Special Education Teacher, Alexandria City Public Schools, Virginia.

Address correspondence to Spencer J. Salend, Department of Educational Studies, OMB 112, SUNY New Paltz, 75 South Manheim Blvd., New Paltz, NY 12561 (e-mail: salends@ newpaltz.edu).

From *Teaching Exceptional Children*, March/April 2003, pp. 36-43. © 2003 by The Council for Exceptional Children. Reprinted by permission.

Early Childhood Special Education

Young African American Children with Disabilities and Augmentative and Alternative Communication Issues

Phil Parette, Mary Blake Huer, and Toya A. Wyatt

INTRODUCTION

Increasing emphasis has been placed on providing augmentative and alternative communication (AAC) systems to young children with disabilities to assist them in receiving a free and appropriate public education (see e.g., Huer, 1994; Soto, Huer, & Taylor, 1997). As defined by the American Speech-Language-Hearing Association (1991), an AAC system is an "integrated group of components, including the symbols, aids, strategies, and techniques used by individuals to enhance communication" (p. 10). AAC devices that are frequently used by young children include low-tech (e.g., communication boards and notebooks) and high-tech (electronic) devices.

A growing population of potential users of AAC devices in early childhood settings are from African American backgrounds. Although such students comprise about 16% of the school-age population (Meese, 2001), they make up a disproportionate number of students among the special education enrollment (van Keulen, Weddington, & DeBose, 1998). By the year 2020, African Americans are expected to be the third largest non-European American population of AAC consumers in the United States (Soto et al., 1997). This represents a 46.7% increase in growth in two decades. Earlier projections reported by Cole (1989) suggested that one-third of the caseload of speech/language pathologists after the run of the century would be children from culturally/linguistically diverse backgrounds, supporting the position taken by the Council for Educational Diagnostic Services (1995) that cultural sensitivity will be a key issue.

The remainder of this article focuses on AAC issues relevant to young African American children with disabilities and their families. Specific areas addressed include family issues and assessment.

ROLE OF THE AFRICAN AMERICAN FAMILY IN AAC SERVICE DELIVERY

Any decision making pertaining to the selection and provision of appropriate AAC devices for young African American children with disabilities should involve families to the greatest extent possible. Numerous professionals have noted the importance of the family in AAC service delivery (see e.g., Angelo, 1996; Beukelman & Mirenda, 1998; Light & McNaughton, 1993; Parette, Brotherson, & Huer, 2000). When family members are not involved in AAC decision-making, important family issues may not be addressed, resulting in the prescription of inappropriate devices (Parette & Angelo, 1996). For example, if family routines and stressors are not considered, abandonment of the AAC device may result (Batavia, Dillard, & Phillips, n.d.; Dillard, 1989).

More recently, Huer, Parette, and Saenz (2001) have discussed the importance of multicultural family issues in the AAC profession, noting that perceptions of AAC service delivery held by children with disabilities and their families from various cultural/linguistic groups perceive the roles of professionals and families in AAC decision making differently (see, e.g., Angelo, 1996; Parette, VanBiervliet, Reyna, & Heisserer, 1999). Ultimately, as noted by Huer et al. (2000), the success of any AAC system will be influenced by family perceptions and understanding of (a) education systems and the professionals serving their children with disabilities, (b) the nature of disabilities, and (c) communication barriers encountered prior to and subsequent to AAC intervention.

Professionals who typically specialize in AAC service delivery for young children and their families are individuals from the mainstream, or Euro American culture (Blackstone, 1993;

Hetzroni & Harris, 1996). As a result, misunderstandings regarding family values, needs, priorities, and resources may sometimes occur during AAC decision making (Kemp & Parette, 2000). Such misunderstandings may affect the efficiency of the decision-making process and resulting appropriateness of AAC recommendations made for a particular child and family who are from African American backgrounds. Specific family issues are described in the following sections.

Stress

Introducing an AAC system into a family setting may often by a stressful event (Parette, Stuart, Huer, Hostetler, & Wommack, 1996), given that such systems require additional caregiving responsibilities beyond daily routines (Angelo, Jones, & Kokoska, 1995; Angelo, Kokoska, & Jones, 1996). Professionals should clearly communicate the expectations and demands that will be placed on family members to learn to use the AAC system and maintain it over time. Once such information is provided to families, alternative AAC systems may be explored to minimize stress.

Communication Partners

When working with families to identify a child's AAC needs, attention must always be given to *communication partners* (e.g., parent[s], grandparent[s], aunts/uncles, siblings, cousins, friends, teachers, therapists, neighbors; Beukelman & Mirenda, 1998; Huer & Wyatt, 1999). For African American children, extended family networks are likely to play a significant role in defining key communication partners and providing sources of support. Willis (1998) noted that in traditional African American communities, there is an emphasis on (a) extended *family networks;* (b) group effort for the common good of all; and (c) family as the primary source of strength, resilience, and survival. In many African American communities, the responsibility for child rearing may be shared by multiple adult members (who may or may not be "kin") as well as older siblings (Harrison & Alvy, 1982; Huer & Wyatt, 1999). The increased likelihood of multiple caregivers becomes an important consideration in designing appropriate AAC intervention systems. As with any young child, it is important for team decision-makers to identify at least two or three communication partners who can provide information about the communication skills of the child. However, early childhood practitioners must recognize that these partners may not always be members of the traditional nuclear family unit and may often be members of the community at large or churches. Within African American communities, churches have historically fulfilled the function of teaching social values and leadership skills, and providing educational and community outreach programs to those in need (Harrison & Alvy, 1982; Willis, 1998). Churches also provide a range of social services to support families and "promote childhood and youth development" (Willis, 1998, p. 188). Given the important supportive role of churches, practitioners should consider how church members and programs may support training

and other AAC services being considered by the team (Huer & Wyatt, 1999).

Another issue relevant to communication partners is the tendency of many African Americans to speak simultaneously with one another (Huer, 1999). This may be an important consideration for some families, as AAC systems may not allow such simultaneous conversation. For example, some AAC systems may require the communication partner to listen and watch the young child with a disability during his or her communication efforts, versus engaging in multiple conversation simultaneously.

Cultural Mistrust

When working with families to obtain information relevant to the AAC decision-making process, early childhood practitioners must consider that numerous factors may negatively impact the type and amount of information disclosed by African American family members. Terrell, Battle, and Grantham (1998) documented the historical experience of African American individuals with institutional racism and discrimination, contributing to a high level of cultural mistrust toward non-African American individuals. As noted by Harris (1996), personal disclosure may be viewed as an open invitation to trouble. It can also affect the overall formation of rapport, acceptance of final recommendations, and/or decisions to seek continued services (Huer & Wyatt, 1999). When working with families, practitioners should provide (a) a rationale for certain questions being asked (e.g., those that are most likely to be viewed with suspicion or as prying and private), and (b) explanations regarding how information will be used during and following the course of intervention (Wyatt, 1998).

Communication Needs and Values

Communication need varies within and between families (Beukelman & Mirenda, 1998). As noted by Huer and Wyatt (1999), the role of the early childhood practitioner is to facilitate improved communication *wherever there is a communication need.* This is achieved by examining the range of alternative forms of communication that augment the student's residual communication skills. With regard to African American young children, the alternative forms of communication chosen should reflect the preferred communication forms and styles used by the family and the community in which the student and family reside. Presented in Table I are communication style issues that may potentially influence AAC decision making.

Language Use Patterns and Communication Style

Much has been written about the linguistic system used by African American individuals (see e.g., Dillard, 1972; Terrell et al., 1998; van Keulen et al., 1998; Wyatt, 1998). Descriptors have been prevalent in the professional literature when discussing characteristics of African American language patterns, including *Black English* (Covington, 1976) and *Ebonics* (Sey-

Table I. Implications for Providing Information and Meeting with Families During AAC Decision-Making

Communication Style Issue Area	Implications
Providing Information	• Eye contact with a conversation partner may be viewed as a sign of disrespect • Family members may prefer to observe a person and read their nonverbal cues during a conversation to understand intent • Family members may tend to be forthright or direct in stating their opinions, and do not restrict emotions • Active participation in discussions may be encouraged, and turn-taking may be viewed as being too restrictive • Extended family system may serve as a supportive and therapeutic base
Meetings	• Factors which may contribute to lack of participation in assessment processes include problems with scheduling, transportation, and knowledge of the service plan development process • Families may be more oriented to situations than to time

Source: Adapted from "Family, vendor, and related service personnel perceptions of culturally sensitive augmentative and alternative communication service delivery," by H. P. Parette, paper presented to the Symposium on Culturally and Linguistically Diverse Exceptional Learners, New Orleans, LA. © Howard P. Parette, 1997. Adapted with permission.

mour, Champion, & Jackson, 1995). While viewed by non-Euro Americans as being different, to typical African Americans their language is simply considered English (van Keulen et al., 1998). Many young children who have needs for AAC systems will have grown up in communities where African American English is used consistently and is a preferred linguistic style. Even for the nonspeaking African American child, this may be an important factor to consider when designing an AAC system and training program. As much as possible, practitioners should attempt to design systems and training programs that take these potential language differences into account. Such differences are likely to have some impact on decisions about symbols used in the AAC system, vocabulary selected, speech output (in the case of electronic devices), and the use of augmentative nonverbal communication strategies (e.g., eye gaze, gestures) within the communication process (Huer & Wyatt, 1999).

Of particular importance to many families when considering electronic AAC devices is the issue of dialect (Huer, 1999). African American children and their families may want the speech generated by AAC devices to reflect their cultural settings and not sound like Euro American voices—a characteristic of many current electronic speech devices.

Family and Community Social Values

Central to many African American communities is an emphasis on family, community, and group effort (Parette et al., 1999; Roseberry-McKibbin, 1995; Willis, 1998). Children and families may prefer to blend into social and community settings and not be viewed as being different from others. When AAC devices are selected for families, there is often an expectation by the child care facility and school that the family use the device in community settings. Families have reported reluctance to use AAC systems if the device draws unnecessary attention to the child and family in social settings (see e.g., Huer, 1999; Smith-Lewis, 1992). The device may also exacerbate the stigma associated with the child's racial background (i.e., not only does the child have a disability, but he or she is African American; Huer, 1999).

However, there is also strong value placed on *independence*, or "the ability to stand on one's own feet" (Willis, 1998, p. 183). As Huer and Wyatt (1999) have noted, the family is seen as key to the attainment of this goal. Consequently many families will express particular interest in the degree to which an AAC system will promote the young child's independence in the community.

Many families will also value strongly the importance of *interdependence* and *cooperation* (King, 1993; van Keulen et al., 1998). Hence, early childhood practitioners must clearly communicate to the family and child how the AAC device will be used in cooperative settings; similarly, family members and other communication partners may have to be taught cooperative strategies that enable the child who uses to AAC system to most effectively participate in social and other communication settings.

Willis (1998) reported the perceived importance of a *good education* as an important value in the African American community because "it is something that no one can take away" (p. 185). This value is particularly important in light of the historical struggles endured by African Americans in attaining certain educational rights (Billingsley, 1974; van Keulen et al., 1998; Willis, 1998). For practitioners, this emphasis on educational attainment and independence are important considerations when trying to select the most appropriate AAC device, that is, one that provides a young child with the best opportunity to become an independent communicator and to gain access to a quality education (Huer & Wyatt, 1999).

ASSESSMENT MODELS AND AFRICAN AMERICANS

Numerous individuals have described approaches for determining the AAC needs of children with disabilities (Beukelman & Mirenda, 1992; Beukelman, Yorkston, & Dowden, 1985; Blackstone, 1986; Huer, 1987; Huer, 1988; Huer, 1997; Light, 1989). Presented in Table II is an overview of each of these models. Unfortunately, with the early exception of Light's Communication Competence model, which emphasized the im-

Table II. AAC Assessment Models

Model	Key Components
Candidacy Models	• Targets individuals with chronic expressive communication disorders, and strong cognitive/linguistic capabilities • Individuals with potential to develop speech and lower cognitive functioning were excluded
Competence Model Light (1989)	• Targets the assessment of adequacy of communication based on sufficient knowledge, judgment and skills needed to communicate within one's culture • Emphasizes four areas of communicative competence: linguistic (both disability and indigenous cultures); operational (technical skills to operate AAC system); social (for communication within and outside the person's cultural group); and strategic (communication strategies that may vary from traditional means within the cultural group)
Communication Needs Model Beukelman, Yorkston, & Dowden (1985)	• Targets literate and nonliterate individuals • Documents the communication needs of individuals • Determines how many needs are met using current communication strategies • Reduces the number of unmet communication needs using AAC interventions
Participation Model Beukelman & Mirenda (1988)	• Based on the functional participation requirements of peers without disabilities of same chronological age as potential AAC user • Identifies participation patterns and communication needs • Assesses opportunity barriers • Assesses access barriers • Plans and implements interventions for present and future • Evaluates intervention effectiveness
Communicative Competence and Culture Model (Hetzroni & Harris, 1996)	• Emphasizes assessment of potential AAC user within context of six interrelated domains: extended family, nuclear family, school, community, clinicians and other professionals, and other cultural influences • Evaluators must develop greater awareness of their own microcultures • Uses an inventory based on Competence Model (linguistic, social, operational, strategic)
Cultural Family-Centered Model (Parette, 1998)	• Views family as backdrop against which six interrelated influences are examined: ethnicity; acculturation, culture, service system issues, technology features, child characteristics • External influences (social, life experiences, developmental expectations, dominant/mainstream culture) are evaluated within content of potential impact on family
Culturally Inclusive Assessment of AAC (Huer, 1997)	• Inclusive protocol, emphasizing the need to address cultural features directly *Includes a practitioner self-assessment before engaging in delivery of services to children within cultural communities which may differ from their own • Examines child's communication partners, needs, and capabilities

portance of examining competence within one's culture, many of these approaches advocated in the 1970s and 1980s have typically failed to address cultural factors. More recently, efforts have been described to include cultural issues in AAC decision-making models. For example, Parette (1998) provided a model for decision making that included six issue areas (i.e., acculturation, culture, service system concerns, technology features, child characteristics, and ethnicity) that must be viewed against the backdrop of the family. The family, in turn, is viewed as being affected by a variety of external factors including the dominant/mainstream culture, developmental expectations, social influences, and life experiences.

Hetzroni and Harris (1996) described a model in which a "thin layer" (p. 54) representing the first interactions with the potential AAC user provides the early childhood practitioner with an understanding of (a) the culture learned to a particular point in time, (b) the values and rules learned, and (c) the behaviors resulting from the knowledge. This understanding cuts across six interrelated spheres of influence: (a) community, (b) extended family, (c) nuclear family, (d) school setting, (e) clinicians and other professionals and (f) other cultural influences (Hetroni & Harris, 1996).

One particularly promising culturally sensitive approach—the Culturally Inclusive Assessment of AAC Model—has been described by Huer (1997) and interpreted with regard to African American individuals (Huer & Wyatt, 1999). Generally, this model includes a protocol outlining strategies for self-assessment by practitioners and information-gathering strategies related to a young child's communication partners, needs, and capabilities. This model offered direction for practitioners providing services to African American children with disabilities who do not share similar life experiences with the clinician performing the assessment. As noted by Huer and Wyatt, the model integrates specific and appropriate questions into the evaluation process to ensure the collection of the most accurate and representative information in light of possible culturally based differences.

Asking Appropriate Questions

Using the model proposed by Huer (1997), three basic questions must be asked by early childhood practitioners working with young African American children with disabilities and their families:

1. With whom does the African American child using AAC communicate on a regular basis?
2. What are the needs of the African American child for communication during everyday activities?
3. What specific capabilities, knowledge, and skills, does the African American child demonstrate?

Additional questions that may be useful to ask when working with these individuals include:

4. What are some of the potential barriers to meeting the communication needs of the African American child?
5. What are some of the strategies useful for practitioners when working around potential barriers and enhancing the African American child's current communication abilities?

Huer and Wyatt (1999) noted that to answer these questions, early childhood practitioners should consider the various cultural issues that may influence (a) the type of responses received from the child, as well as (b) the actual information-gathering process. Differing cultural views, beliefs, and attitudes of African American individuals can influence the frequency and nature of communication interactions with others (Huer & Wyatt, 1999). The structural makeup of the child's family and demographic makeup of his/her community can also affect social practices, attitudes, and values as they pertain to communication use patterns. The cultural orientation and language use patterns within the family and community can also lead to culturally based communication style differences.

Each of the above factors is likely to affect the communication assessment and service delivery process when working with young African American children with disabilities and their families. Specifically, they can influence the nature of information gathered and observations made. They can also influence the manner in which information is obtained and observations are made. Differing cultural views toward communication and other disabilities can impact whether final practitioner suggestions and recommendations are accepted. Language code and style preferences can impact on decisions about the type of vocabulary, symbols and AAC systems selected. Family and community resources can also either limit or enhance the delivery of quality services.

CONCLUSIONS

Descriptions of African American culture, lifestyles, family values, and communication styles and patterns are readily available to professionals (see e.g., Roseberry-McKibbin, 1995; Willis, 1998). However, information regarding the practice of AAC within African American communities has only recently begun to emerge, with efforts being made to more effectively educate professionals about the cultural systems of these individuals and their influence on AAC decision making (VanBiervliet & Parette, 1999). It seems reasonable to suggest that if practitioners learn about the lifestyles of persons from various cultures (Barrera, 1993; Hanson, Lynch, & Wayman, 1990;

Harry et al., 1995; Roseberry-McKibbin, 1995) they will plan more appropriate services for young children from various ethnic and cultural backgrounds (Hetzroni & Harris, 1996; Huer, 1997b). Issues explored in this article may potentially assist early childhood professionals to more effectively work with African American families and their children with disabilities during the process of making decisions about AAC devices.

ACKNOWLEDGMENTS

This manuscript is supported in part by Grant No. H029K50072 from the U.S. Department of Education to the first author. Opinions expressed herein are those of the authors alone and should not be interpreted to have agency endorsement.

REFERENCES

American Speech-Language-Hearing Association. (1991). Report: Augmentative and alternative communication. *Asha, 33* (Suppl. 5), 9–12.

Angelo, D. H. (1996). AAC in the family and home. In S. L. Glennen & D. C. Decoste (Eds.), *Handbook of augmentative and alternative communication* (pp. 523–541). San Diego, CA: Singular.

Angelo, D. H., Jones, S. D., & Kokoska, S. M. (1995). Family perspective on augmentative and alternative communication: Families of young children. *Augmentative and Alternative Communication, 11*, 193–201.

Angelo, D. H., Kokoska, S. M., & Jones S. D. (1996). Family perspective on augmentative and alternative communications: Families of adolescents and young adults. *Augmentative and Alternative Communication, 12*, 13–20.

Barrera, I. (1993). Effective and appropriate instruction for all children: The challenge of cultural/linguistic diversity and young children with special needs. *Topics in Early Childhood Special Education, 13*, 461–487.

Batavia, A. I., Dillard, D., & Phillips, B. (n.d.) *How to avoid technology abandonment*. Washington, DC: Request Rehabilitation Engineering Center, National Rehabilitation Hospital.

Beukelman, D., & Mirenda, P. (1992). *Augmentative and alternative communication: Management of severe communication disorders in children and adults*. Baltimore: Brookes.

Beukelman, D. R., & Mirenda, P. (1998). *Augmentative and alternative communication. Management of severe communication disorders in children and adults*. (2nd ed.). Baltimore: Brookes.

Beukelman, D., Yorkston, K., & Dowden, P. (1985). *Communication augmentation: A casebook of clinical management*. Austin, TX: Pro-ed.

Billingsley, A. (1974). *Black families and the struggle for survival: Teaching our children to walk tall*. New York: Friendship Press.

Blackstone, S. W. (Ed.). (1986). *Augmentative communication: an introduction*. Rockville, MD: American Speech-Language-Hearing Association.

Blackstone, S. W. (1993). For consumers. Cultures in the community. *Augmentative Communication News, 6*(2), 1–10.

Cole, L. (1989, September). E pluribus pluribus: Multicultural imperatives for the 1990s and beyond. *American Speech, Language, Hearing Association Newsletter*, 65–70.

Council for Educational Diagnostic Services. (1995, Summer). Assessment issues: A mini-interview with Don Hammill. *CECS Communique, 22*(4), 4.

Covington, A. (1976). Black people and Black English: Attitudes and deeducation in a biased macroculture. In D. S. Harrison & T. Trabasso (Eds.), *Black English: A seminar* (pp. 255–264). Hillsdale, NJ: Erlbaum.

Dillard, D. (1989). *National study on abandonment of technology. 1989 Annual Report on the National Rehabilitation Hospital's Rehabilitation Engineering Center's Evaluation of Assistive Technology* (Cooperative Agreement No. H133E0016). Washington, DC: National Institute on Disability and Rehabilitation Research.

Dillard, J. L. (1972). *Black English: Its history and usage in the United States*. New York: Random House.

Hanson, M. J., Lynch, E. W., & Wayman, K. I. (1990). Honoring the cultural diversity of families when gathering data. *Topics in Early Childhood Special Education, 10*, 112–131.

Harris, J. L. (1996). Issues in recruiting African American participants for research. In A. G. Kamhi, K. E. Pollock, & J. L. Harris (Eds.), *Communication development and disorders in African American children* (pp. 19–34). Baltimore: Brookes.

Harrison, D. S., & Alvy, K. T. (1982). *The context of black parenting*. Studio City, CA: Center for the Improvement of Child Caring.

Harry, B., Grenot-Scheyer, M., Smith-Lewis, M., Park, Hyun-Sook, Xin, F., & Schwartz, I. (1995). Developing culturally inclusive services for individuals with severe disabilities. *Journal of the Association for Persons with Severe Handicaps, 20*, 99–109.

Hetzroni, O. E., & Harris, O. L. (1996). Cultural aspects in the development of AAC users. *Augmentative and Alternative Communication, 12*, 52–58.

Huer, M. B. (1987). 1986 ISAAC Round Table Discussion—Formal assessment tools: What we have, what we need. *The ISAAC Bulletin, 10*, 14–17.

Huer, M. B. (1988). *The nonspeech test for receptive and expressive language*. Wauconda, IL: Don Johnston.

Huer, M. B. (1994, November). *Diversity now: Multicultural issues in AAC*. A miniseminar presented at the National Annual Meeting for the American Speech-Language-Hearing Association, New Orleans, LA.

Huer, M. B. (1997). Culturally inclusive assessments for children using augmentative and alternative communication (AAC). *Journal of Children's Communication Development, 19* (1), 23–34.

Huer, M. B. (1999). Focus group with parents with AAC devices. In H. P. Parette & A. VanBiervliet (Eds.), *Families, cultures, and AAC* (CD-ROM; pp. 194–228). Little Rock, AR: Southeast Missouri State University and University of Arkansas for Medical Sciences.

Huer, M. B., Parette, H. P., & Saenz, T. I. (2001). Conversations with Mexican-Americans regarding children with disabilities and augmentative and alternative communication. *Communication Disorders Quarterly, 22*, 197–206.

Huer, M. B., & Wyatt, T. (1999). Cultural factors in the delivery of AAC services to the African American community. *ASHA Special Division 14 Newsletter, 5* (1), 5–9.

Kemp, C., & Parette, H. P. (2000). Barriers to minority parent involvement in assistive technology (AT) decision-making processes. *Education and Training in Mental Retardation and Developmental Disabilities, 35* (4), 385–393.

King, S. H. (1993). The limited presence of African American teachers. *Review of Educational Research, 63*, 115–149.

Light, J. (1989). Toward a definition of communication competence for individuals using augmentative and alternative communication systems. *Augmentative and Alternative Communication, 5*, 137–144.

Light, J., & McNaughton, D. (1993). Literacy and augmentative and alternative communication (AAC): The expectations and priorities of parents and teachers. *Topics in Language Disorders, 13* (2), 33–46.

Meese, R. L. (2001). *Teaching students with mild disabilities* (2nd ed.). Belmont, CA: Wadsworth Thomson Learning.

Parette, H. P. (1998). Cultural issues and family-centered assistive technology decision-making. In S. L. Judge, & H. P. Parette (Eds.), *Assistive technology for young children with disabilities: A guide to providing family-centered services* (pp. 184–210). Cambridge, MA: Brookline.

Parette, H. P., & Angelo, D. H. (1996). Augmentative and alternative communication impact on families: Trends and future directions. *The Journal of Special Education, 30*, 77–98.

Parette, H. P., Brotherson, M. J., & Huer, M. B. (2000). Giving families a voice in augmentative and alternative communication decision-making. *Education and Training in Mental Retardation and Developmental Disabilities, 35*, 177–190.

Parette, H. P., Stuart, S., Huer, M. B., Hostetler, S., & Wommack, J. D. (1996, November). *Qualitative methodology and AAC decision-making with families across cultures*. Paper presented to the American Speech-Language-Hearing Association 1996 Annual Convention, Seattle, WA.

Parette, P., VanBiervliet, A., Reyna, J. W., & Heisserer, D. (Eds.). (1999). *Families, culture, and augmentative and alternative communication (AAC). A multimedia instructional program for related service personnel and family members*. [On-line]. Source: http://cstl.semo.edu/parette/homepage/database.pdf

Roseberry-McKibbin, C. (1995). *Multicultural students with special language needs*. Oceanside, CA: Academic Communication Associates.

Seymour, H. N., Champion, T., & Jackson, J. (1995). The language of African American learners: Effective assessment and instructional programming for children with special needs. In B. A. Ford, F. E. Obiakor, & J. M. Patton (Eds.), *Effective education of African American exceptional learners. New perspectives* (pp. 89–121). Austin, TX: Pro-ed.

Smith-Lewis, M. (1992). *What is mental retardation? Perceptions from the African American community*. Unpublished manuscript. Hunter College, New York.

Soto, G., Huer, M. B., & Taylor, O. (1997). Multicultural issues. In L. L. Lloyd, D, H. Fuller, & H. H. Arvidson (Eds.), *Augmentative and alternative communication* (pp. 406–413). Boston: Allyn and Bacon.

Terrell, S. L., Battle, D. E., & Grantham, R. B. (1998). African American cultures. In D. E. Battle (Ed.), *Communication disorders in multicultural populations* (2nd ed., pp. 31–71). Boston: Butterworth-Heinemann.

van Keulen, J. E., Weddington, G. T., & DeBose, C. E. (1998). *Speech, language, and the African American child*. Boston: Allyn and Bacon.

VanBiervliet, A., & Parette, H. P. (1999). *Families, cultures, and AAC* [CD-ROM]. Little Rock, AR: Southeast Missouri State University and University of Arkansas for Medical Sciences.

Willis, W. (1998). Families with African American roots. In E. W. Lynch & M. J. Hanson (Eds.), *Developing cross-cultural competence. A guide for working with young children and their families* (2nd ed. pp. 165–207). Baltimore: Brookes.

Wyatt, T. A. (1998). Assessment issues with multicultural populations. In D. E. Battle (Ed.), *Communication disorders in multicultural populations* (2nd ed., pp. 379–425). Boston: Butterworth-Heinemann.

Phil Parette, Southeast Missouri University.

Mary Blake Huer, California State University–Fullerton.

Toya A. Wyatt, California State University–Fullerton.

Correspondence should be directed to Phil Parette, e-mail: pparette @semovm.semo.edu.

From *Early Childhood Education Journal*, Spring 2002, pp. 201-207. © 2002 by Kluwer Academic/Plenum Publishers. Reprinted by permission.

UNIT 5
Developmental Disabilities

Unit Selections

14. **The Secrets of Autism**, J. Madeleine Nash
15. **Citizenship and Disability**, Michael Bérubé
16. **Inscrutable or Meaningful? Understanding and Supporting Your Inarticulate Students**, Robin M. Smith

Key Points to Consider

- How would you explain the surge in autistic disorders? What are social scientists discovering through brain imaging techniques?

- What do we lose as a society if we revoke and/or reinterpret the moral and legal rights of our citizens with developmental disabilities? Do they, in fact, enrich our lives?

- Students with developmental disabilities may have atypical facial expressions and speech. Are these inscrutable or meaningful? How can teachers and others interpret and use these messages?

 **Links: www.dushkin.com/online/**
These sites are annotated in the World Wide Web pages.

Arc of the United States
http://www.thearc.org

Disability-Related Sources on the Web
http://www.arcarizona.org/dislnkin.html

Gentle Teaching
http://www.gentleteaching.nl

In our efforts to be more "politically correct" and to not inflict pain, we now avoid labels such as "mentally retarded." We always put the individual first and add the condition of disability second (when and if it is necessary). Students and adults who have cognitive skills falling two standard deviations below the norm for their age are now considered cognitively developmentally disabled. Children who have sustained brain damage through traumatic brain injury, even if they score two standard deviations below the intellectual norm for age, are traumatically brain injured, not developmentally disabled. Children and adults with autism or variants of autism (such as Asperger's syndrome) are subsumed under a separate disability category by the U.S. Individuals with Disabilities Education Act (IDEA) as well. Three out of four individuals with classic autism do score two standard deviations below the IQ mean. Nevertheless, cognitive developmental disorders, traumatic brain injuries, and autism are each recognized as separate disability categories by IDEA.

Children with significantly subnormal intelligence were once classified as "educable," "trainable," or "custodial" for purposes of placement. These terms are strongly discouraged today. Even severely developmentally disabled children are educable and can benefit from some schooling. They must leave where they are, to be where we hope they can be. The current preferred categorical terms for children who are developmentally challenged are "intermittent," "limited," "extensive," and "pervasive." These terms refer to how much support the individuals need to function and to succeed as much as possible.

IDEA mandates free and appropriate public school education for every child, regardless of mentation. While the legal windows on education are from ages 6 to 16 in the United States, individuals with developmental disabilities are entitled to a free and appropriate education from age of assessment (birth, early childhood) to age 21. This encompasses parent-child education programs and preschool programs early in life and transitional services into the community and world of work after the public school education is completed.

The inclusion of children with disabilities in regular education classes has been controversial (see Unit 1) throughout the time span since 1975. Some school systems have succeeded brilliantly in integrating students with cognitive developmental disabilities into their regular classes. Other schools have fought the law every step of the way. Their dark histories are full of lawsuits brought by parents to try to obtain the services to which the law entitles them. The less-than-stellar school systems, and some U.S. states that have been notorious laggards, complain that the law is too cumbersome. There have been few negative consequences for school systems or whole state education departments who have resisted placing cognitively disabled students in regular classrooms. Therefore some parents still invoke formal complaint procedures against schools to get their children out of full-time special classes or special schools.

A child with cognitive developmental disabilities who is in the mildest "intermittent" classification needs support at school at times when special needs arise and at times of life transitions. This terminology is generally used for children whose disabilities do not create an obvious and continual problem. These children have slower mentation but also have many abilities.

The next level of support, classified as "limited," is usually used for children whose disabilities create daily limitations on their abilities but who can achieve a degree of self-sufficiency after an appropriate education in the least restrictive environment. Limited refers to the period of time from diagnosis until adulthood (age 21). The "extensive" support classification extends the support throughout the lifespan for individuals whose developmental disabilities prohibit them from living independently. The "pervasive" support classification is used infrequently. It is only for those individuals whose disabilities prevent them from most activities of self-help. Pervasive support is intensive and life-sustaining in nature.

The majority of children with developmental disabilities can be placed in the intermittent support classification. To casual observers, they often do not appear to have any disabilities. However, their ability to process, store, and retrieve information is limited. In the past, this group of children was given IQ measurements between two and three standard deviations below the mean (usually an IQ below 70 but above 55). Intelligence testing is an inexact science with problems of both validity and reliability. The current definition of developmental disability endorsed by the American Association on Mental Deficiency (AAMD) does not include any IQ scoring results other than to use the phrase "subaverage intellectual functioning." It emphasizes the problems that individuals with developmental disabilities have with adaptive skills such as communication, self-care, home living, social skills, community use, self-direction, health and safety, functional academics, leisure, and work.

The causes of developmental disabilities (DD) are unclear. About one-half of all individuals with DD are suspected of having sustained some brain damage prenatally, neonatally, or in childhood. Among the better-known factors that damage brain tissue are early birth or low birth weight, anoxia, malnutrition, drugs, viruses, radiation, trauma, and tumors.

The first article in this unit depicts a boy with Asperger's syndrome, a developmental disability that is related to autism. More than a million people in the United States suffer from one of the autistic disorders, five times more than that have Down's syndrome. The surge in autistic disorders is not well understood. J. Madeleine Nash reviews some of the new research on autism and its related conditions. Advanced brain imaging techniques are revealing neurological factors. Social scientists are exploring the role of the environment.

The second article, "Citizenship and Disability" addresses the question of disability rights. Legal rights granted by IDEA and the Americans with Disability Act (ADA) can be reinterpreted and/or revoked. The author gives cogent reasons for not allowing this to happen, whatever our political and economic straits. Persons with developmental disabilities, non-disabled peers, and democracy (all of us) benefit from moral equality.

The third article, "Inscrutable or Meaningful?" discusses the importance of deciphering the emotions, behaviors, and atypical speech and language processes of students with developmental disabilities. Understanding and supporting inarticulate students is critical to their education.

SCIENCE

THE SECRETS OF AUTISM

THE NUMBER OF CHILDREN DIAGNOSED WITH AUTISM AND ASPERGER'S IN THE U.S. IS EXPLODING. WHY?

By J. MADELEINE NASH

TOMMY BARRETT IS A DREAMY-EYED FIFTH-GRADER WHO lives with his parents, twin brothers, two cats and a turtle in San Jose, Calif., the heart of Silicon Valley. He's an honor-roll student who likes math and science and video games. He's also a world-class expert on Animorph and Transformer toys. "They're like cars and trains and animals that transform into robots or humans—I love them!" he shouts exuberantly.

And that is sometimes a problem. For a time, in fact, Tommy's fascination with his toys was so strong that when they weren't around he would pretend to *be* the toys, transforming from a truck into a robot or morphing into a kitten. He would do this in the mall, in the school playground and even in the classroom. His teachers found this repetitive pantomime delightful but disturbing, as did his mother Pam.

Autistic disorders may afflict nearly 300,000 kids in the U.S. alone

By that point, there were other worrisome signs. Pam Barrett recalls that as a 3-year-old, Tommy was a fluent, even voluble talker, yet he could not seem to grasp that conversation had reciprocal rules, and, curiously, he avoided looking into other people's eyes. And although Tommy was obviously smart—he had learned to read by the time he was 4—he was so fidgety and unfocused that he was unable to participate in his kindergarten reading group.

When Tommy turned 8, his parents finally learned what was wrong. Their bright little boy, a psychiatrist informed them, had a mild form of autism known as Asperger syndrome. Despite the fact that children with

Asperger's often respond well to therapy, the Barretts, at that moment, found the news almost unbearable.

That's because just two years earlier Pam and her husband Chris, operations manager of a software-design company, had learned that Tommy's twin brothers Jason and Danny were profoundly autistic. Seemingly normal at birth, the twins learned to say a few words before they spiraled into their secret world, quickly losing the abilities they had just started to gain. Instead of playing with toys, they broke them; instead of speaking, they emitted an eerie, high-pitched keening.

Up to 20 genes may be involved in autism, but they're not the only factors

First Jason and Danny, now Tommy. Pam and Chris started to wonder about their children's possible exposure to toxic substances. They started scanning a lengthening roster of relatives, wondering how long autism had shadowed their family.

The anguish endured by Pam and Chris Barrett is all too familiar to tens of thousands of families across North America and other parts of the world. With a seeming suddenness, cases of autism and closely related disorders like Asperger's are exploding in number, and no one has a good explanation for it. While many experts believe the increase is a by-product of a recent broadening of diagnostic criteria, others are convinced that the surge is at least in part real and thereby cause for grave concern.

In the Barretts' home state of California, for instance, the number of autistic children seeking social services has more than quadrupled in the past 15 years, from fewer than 4,000 in 1987 to nearly 18,000 today. So common are

The Geek Syndrome

At Michelle Winner's social-skills clinic in San Jose, Calif., business is booming. Every week dozens of youngsters with Asperger syndrome file in and out of therapy sessions while their anxious mothers run errands or chat quietly in the waiting room. In one session, a rosy-cheeked 12-year-old struggles to describe the emotional reactions of a cartoon character in a video clip; in another, four little boys (like most forms of autism, Asperger's overwhelmingly affects boys) grapple with the elusive concept of teamwork while playing a game of 20 Questions. Unless prompted to do so, they seldom look at one another, directing their eyes to the wall or ceiling or simply staring off into space.

Yet outside the sessions the same children become chatty and animated, displaying an astonishing grasp of the most arcane subjects. Transformer toys, video games, airplane schedules, star charts, dinosaurs. It sounds charming, and indeed would be, except that their interest is all consuming. After about five minutes, children with Asperger's, a.k.a. the "little professor" or "geek" syndrome, tend to sound like CDs on autoplay. "Did you ask her if she's interested in astrophysics?" a mother gently chides her son, who has launched into an excruciatingly detailed description of what goes on when a star explodes into a supernova.

Although Hans Asperger described the condition in 1944, it wasn't until 1994 that the American Psychiatric Association officially recognized Asperger syndrome as a form of autism with its own diagnostic criteria. It is this recognition, expanding the definition of autism to include everything from the severely retarded to the mildest cases, that is partly responsible for the recent explosion in autism diagnoses.

There are differences between Asperger's and high-functioning autism. Among other things, Asperger's appears to be even more strongly genetic than classic autism, says Dr. Fred Volkmar, a child psychiatrist at Yale. About a third of the fathers or brothers of children with Asperger's show signs of the disorder. There appear to be maternal roots as well. The wife of one Silicon Valley software engineer believes that her Asperger's son represents the fourth generation in just such a lineage.

It was the Silicon Valley connection that led *Wired* magazine to run its geek-syndrome feature last December. The story was basically a bit of armchair theorizing about a social phenomenon known as assortative mating. In university towns and R.-and-D. corridors, it is argued, smart but not particularly well-socialized men today are meeting and marrying women very like themselves, leading to an overload of genes that predispose their children to autism, Asperger's and related disorders.

Is there anything to this idea? Perhaps. There is no question that many successful people—not just scientists and engineers but writers and lawyers as well—possess a suite of traits that seem to be, for lack of a better word, Aspergery. The ability to focus intensely and screen out other distractions, for example, is a geeky trait that can be extremely useful to computer programmers. On the other hand, concentration that is too intense—focusing on cracks in the pavement while a taxi is bearing down on you—is clearly, in Darwinian terms, maladaptive.

But it may be a mistake to dwell exclusively on the genetics of Asperger's; there must be other factors involved. Experts suspect that such variables as prenatal positioning in the womb, trauma experienced at birth or random variation in the process of brain development may also play a role.

Even if you could identify the genes involved in Asperger's, it's not clear what you would do about them. It's not as if they are lethal genetic defects, like the ones that cause Huntington's disease or cystic fibrosis. "Let's say that a decade from now we know all the genes for autism," suggests Bryna Siegel, a psychologist at the University of California, San Francisco. "And let's say your unborn child has four of these genes. We may be able to tell you that 80% of the people with those four genes will be fully autistic but that the other 20% will perform in the gifted mathematical range."

Filtering the geeky genes out of the high-tech breeding grounds like Silicon Valley, in other words, might remove the very DNA that made these places what they are today.

—By J. Madeleine Nash.
With reporting by Amy Bonesteel/Atlanta

cases of Asperger's in Silicon Valley, in fact, that *Wired* magazine coined a cyber-age term for the disorder, referring to its striking combination of intellectual ability and social cluelessness as the "geek syndrome." *Wired* went on to make a provocative if anecdotal case that autism and Asperger's were rising in Silicon Valley at a particularly alarming rate—and asked whether "math-and-tech genes" might be to blame (*see box*).

Yet the rise in autism and Asperger's is hardly confined to high-tech enclaves or to the children of computer programmers and software engineers. It occurs in every job category and socioeconomic class and in every state. "We're getting calls from school systems in rural Georgia," observes Sheila Wagner, director of the Autism Resource Center at Atlanta's Emory University. "People are saying, 'We never had any kids with autism before, and now we have 10! What's going on?'"

It's a good question. Not long ago, autism was assumed to be comparatively rare, affecting as few as 1 in 10,000 people. The latest studies, however, suggest that as many as 1 in 150 kids age 10 and younger may be affected by autism or a related disorder—a total of nearly 300,000 children in the U.S. alone. If you include adults, according to the Autism Society of America, more than a million people in the U.S. suffer from one of the autistic disorders (also known as pervasive developmental disorders or PDDs). The problem is five times as common as Down syndrome and three times as common as juvenile diabetes.

No wonder parents are besieging the offices of psychologists and psychiatrists in their search for remedies. No wonder school systems are adding special aides to help teachers cope. And no wonder public and private research institutions have launched collaborative initiatives aimed at deciphering the complex biology that produces such a dazzling range of disability.

In their urgent quest for answers, parents like the Barretts are provoking what promises to be a scientific revolution. In response to the concerns they are raising, money is finally flowing into autism research, a field that five years ago appeared to be stuck in the stagnant backwaters of neuroscience. Today dozens of scientists are racing to identify the genes linked to autism. Just last month, in a series of articles published by *Molecular Psychiatry*, scientists from the U.S., Britain, Italy and France reported that they are beginning to make significant progress.

Meanwhile, research teams are scrambling to create animal models for autism in the form of mutant mice. They are beginning to examine environmental factors that might contribute to the development of autism and using advanced brain-imaging technology to probe the deep interior of autistic minds. In the process, scientists are gaining rich new insights into this baffling spectrum of disorders and are beginning to float intriguing new hypotheses about why people affected by it develop minds that are strangely different from our own and yet, in some important respects, hauntingly similar.

AUTISM'S GENETIC ROOTS

AUTISM WAS FIRST DESCRIBED IN 1943 BY JOHNS HOPKINS psychiatrist Leo Kanner, and again in 1944 by Austrian pediatrician Hans Asperger. Kanner applied the term to children who were socially withdrawn and preoccupied with routine, who struggled to acquire spoken language

GUIDE FOR PARENTS
How do you tell if your child is autistic? And what should you do if he or she is?

WHAT TO LOOK FOR

SIGNS OF AUTISM

(Usually apparent in toddlers; watch for cluster of symptoms)
- No pointing by 1 year
- No babbling by 1 year; no single words by 16 months; no two-word phrases by 24 months
- Any loss of language skills at any time
- No pretend playing
- Little interest in making friends
- Extremely short attention span
- No response when called by name; indifference to others
- Little or no eye contact
- Repetitive body movements, such as hand flapping, rocking
- Intense tantrums
- Fixations on a single object, such as a spinning fan
- Unusually strong resistance to changes in routines
- Oversensitivity to certain sounds, textures or smells

SIGNS OF ASPERGER'S

(Usually diagnosed at 6 or older)
- Difficulty making friends
- Difficulty reading or communicating through nonverbal social cues, such as facial expressions
- No understanding that others may have thoughts or feelings different from his or her own
- Obsessive focus on a narrow interest, such as reciting train schedules
- Awkward motor skills
- Inflexibility about routines, especially when changes occur spontaneously
- Mechanical, almost robotic patterns of speech

(Even "normal" children exhibit some of these behaviors from time to time. The symptoms of autism and Asperger's, by contrast, are persistent and debilitating.)

—By Amy Lennard Goehner

yet often possessed intellectual gifts that ruled out a diagnosis of mental retardation. Asperger applied the term to children who were socially maladroit, developed bizarre obsessions and yet were highly verbal and seemingly

GUIDE FOR PARENTS *continued*

Snapshots from the Autistic Brain

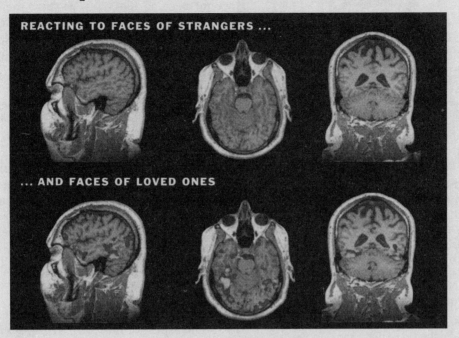

REACTING TO FACES OF STRANGERS ...

... AND FACES OF LOVED ONES

Neuroimaging studies confirm what scientists long suspected: autistic brains don't react to facial cues the way normal brains do. But in one regard the conventional wisdom was wrong. In a breakthrough study, Karen Pierce at the University of California at San Diego has shown that when faces of strangers are replaced by faces of loved ones, the autistic brain lights up like an explosion of Roman candles.

WHERE TO START

GET AN EVALUATION: Take your child to a developmental pediatrician with expertise in autism or Asperger syndrome. The pediatrician will evaluate your child with a team of specialists (speech therapists, occupational therapists, behavior therapists) to determine the areas in which your child needs help.

EARLY INTERVENTION: Every state is mandated to provide a free evaluation and early-intervention services for children. To find out whom to contact in your state, consult the National Information Center for Children and Youth with Disabilities (funded by the Department of Education) at 800-695-0285 or *nichcy.org/ index.html*. Ask about support groups in your area.

HOW TO TREAT IT

There is no cure for autism, but there are many treatments that can make a difference:
SPEECH THERAPY: Can help overcome communication and language barriers
OCCUPATIONAL THERAPY: Helps with sensory integration and motor skills
BEHAVIORAL THERAPY: Improves cognitive skills and reduces inappropriate behavior
EDUCATIONAL THERAPY: A highly structured approach works best
MEDICATION: Can reduce some symptoms
SPECIAL DIETS: Eliminating certain food groups, such as dairy, helps some children

HELPFUL WEBSITES

ONLINE ASPERGER SYNDROME INFORMATION AND SUPPORT *www.aspergersyndrome.org*
AUTISM SOCIETY OF AMERICA *autism-society.org*
FAMILIES FOR EARLY AUTISM TREATMENT *www.feat.org*
AUTISM RESOURCES *autism-info.com*
YALE CHILD STUDY CENTER *info.med.yale.edu/ chldstdy/autism*

Network: Other parents can be great sources in finding the right treatments.

quite bright. There was a striking tendency, Asperger noted, for the disorder to run in families, sometimes passing directly from father to son. Clues that genes might be central to autism appeared in Kanner's work as well.

VACCINES
Are the Shots Safe?

Ask the parents of autistic children whether they believe childhood vaccines can cause autism, and the answer will probably be yes. They have heard of too many cases of babies who were perfectly normal until they got their measles, mumps and rubella (MMR) shot and then, within weeks—if not days—started throwing tantrums, losing language skills and generally tuning out.

Ask doctors the same question, and they are likely to cite the panel of experts convened by the Institute of Medicine last year. They studied the evidence but found no explanation for how vaccines might possibly cause autism. Included in the review were studies that showed no significant difference in the incidence of autism disorders before and after MMR immunization became routine in 1988 in Britain. "We bent over backward to look for the biological mechanisms that would support a link," says the panel's chairwoman, Dr. Marie McCormick of the Harvard School of Public Health.

But failing to prove that something can happen is not the same as proving it doesn't, and the issue is still a matter of furious debate. The only scientific evidence against childhood vaccines comes from Dr. Andrew Wakefield, formerly at the Royal Free Hospital in London. His theory is that autism stems from a severe immune reaction to something in the vaccine. In February he published a paper showing that immunized children with autism and bowel disorders have higher levels of measles particles in their intestinal tissue than normal children do. The evidence is not entirely persuasive, however; measles particles in the tissues do not necessarily mean that the virus—or the vaccine—causes autism.

What about all the children whose symptoms appeared shortly after their MMR? The association may be purely coincidental. The shots are given at 15 months, which is when behavior and speech patterns in babies usually become sufficiently pronounced for parents to start noticing that something is wrong. Most of the evidence suggests that autism is primarily a genetic disorder. It may be that some symptoms appear immediately after birth but are too subtle to be spotted in the first year or so of life.

To get more definitive answers, the National Institutes of Health and the Centers for Disease control have each launched their own investigations. Karyn Seroussi of Poughkeepsie, N.Y., for one, supports this research. "If it's the shots, I want to know," says Seroussi, an autism advocate and parent of an autistic son. "If it's not, I want to know what the heck it is that's causing autism." On that, both parents and doctors can agree.

—By Alice Park

But then autism research took a badly wrong turn. Asperger's keen insights languished in Europe's postwar turmoil, and Kanner's were overrun by the Freudian juggernaut. Children were not born autistic, experts insisted, but became that way because their parents, especially mothers, were cold and unnurturing.

In 1981, however, British psychiatrist Dr. Lorna Wing published an influential paper that revived interest in Asperger's work. The disorder Asperger identified, Wing observed, appeared in many ways to be a variant of Kanner's autism, so that the commonalities seemed as important as the differences. As a result, researchers now believe that Asperger and Kanner were describing two faces of a highly complicated and variable disorder, one that has its source in the kaleidoscope of traits encoded in the human genome. Researchers also recognize that severe autism is not always accompanied by compensatory intellectual gifts and is, in fact, far likelier to be characterized by heartbreaking deficits and mental retardation.

Perhaps the most provocative finding scientists have made to date is that the components of autism, far more than autism itself, tend to run in families. Thus even though profoundly autistic people rarely have children, researchers often find that a close relative is affected by some aspect of the disorder. A sister may engage in odd repetitive behavior or be excessively shy; a brother may have difficulties with language or be socially inept to a noticeable degree. In similar fashion, if one identical twin has autism, there is a 60% chance that the other will too and a better than 75% chance that the twin without autism will exhibit one or more autistic traits.

How many genes contribute to susceptibility to autism? Present estimates run from as few as three to more than 20. Coming under intensifying scrutiny, as the papers published by *Molecular Psychiatry* indicate, are genes that regulate the action of three powerful neurotransmitters: glutamate, which is intimately involved in learning and memory, and serotonin and gamma-aminobutiric acid (GABA), which have been implicated in obsessive-compulsive behavior, anxiety and depression.

Those genes hardly exhaust the list of possibilities. Among the suspects are virtually all the genes that control brain development and perhaps cholesterol and immune-system function as well. Christopher Stodgell, a developmental toxicologist at New York's University of Rochester, observes that the process that sets up the brain resembles an amazingly intricate musical score, and there are tens of thousands of genes in the orchestra. If these genes do what they're supposed to do, says Stodgell, "then you have a Mozart's *Concerto for Clarinet*. If not, you have cacophony."

A DIFFERENCE OF MIND

AUTISTIC PEOPLE OFTEN SUFFER FROM A BEWILDERING ARRAY of problems—sensory disturbances, food allergies, gas-

My Brother

KARL TARO GREENFELD

My autistic brother Noah and I once played to-gether. He was two, and I was a year older. We wres-tled, and I tickled him. He responded in a high-pitched giggle, halfway between a baby's gurgle and a child's laughter. I can't remember ever playing with him again. Noah stayed forever a baby, profoundly re-tarded, always dependent, never very communicative. And my role changed, much too early, from playmate to steward. There was barely any sibling rivalry. There were no battles to be fought. He would always be the center of attention.

I was treated as a sort of supporting player. Because my father had written a trilogy of books about our fam-ily with Noah as the title character (starting with *A Child Called Noah*; 1972), I would often be asked what it was like having an autistic brother. I never figured out how to respond. The answer I always gave—that I had never known any other life or any other brother— seemed cryptic and somehow unsatisfactory.

But that remains the only answer I can give. Noah, who can't speak, dress or go to the bathroom com-pletely unassisted, will always be the center of our family. He never earned that role; his needs dictated it. I wasn't consciously resentful of this as a child. There was no more reason to be angry about this than there was about the rigid laws of basic arithmetic.

I accepted the fact that Noah and his problems could fill a battleship of parental duty and obligation, leaving my mother and father too spent to worry about the more banal problems of their normal son. But at some point in my early teens, in the confusing years of adolescence, I stopped having friends over. Noah's condition dictated what we ate and when we slept and to a great degree how we lived. We never had fancy furniture because he chewed on the couch cushions and spit on the carpets. He would pull apart anything more complicated than a pencil. I was ashamed of our home and family. Already marked as different by virtue of being Asian American in a pre-dominantly white community, I came to see Noah as an additional stigmatizing mark.

My father used to say every family has a skeleton in its closet. Only ours was out in the open. I don't even remember if I talked about Noah in school. My friends knew about him, but after the first few questions, there wasn't much to say. Noah didn't change. Autism is a condition, I knew from close up, for which there are no miraculous cures. So he always stayed Noah. This kid who shared the same black hair and brown eyes as I had but couldn't talk and wanted to be left alone. So what was there to say about Noah? He was my brother who was never going to grow up.

Noah is 35 now and has been living in institutions since he was 18. My parents visit him every weekend at the state-run Fairview Developmental Center in Costa Mesa, Calif. I go whenever I am in town. (Cur-rently I live in Hong Kong.) We bring Noah his favorite foods: sushi, fresh fruit and Japanese crackers and take him for a walk or a ride. Sometimes he lashes out at me. Spitting. Scratching. Pulling hair. but he knows me; I can tell by the wary squint he gives me. We're brothers, after all.

My parents are now in their 70s. My father under-went open-heart surgery a few years ago. Eventually, the responsibility for Noah will fall solely upon me. I imagine I may have to move my own family back to California to visit him every weekend, so that those caring for him will know that despite Noah's temper tantrums and violent outbursts, he is loved; he is a brother and part of a family. He is still the center of my life. My travels, from Los Angeles to New York City to Paris to Tokyo to Hong Kong, will always bring me back to him. I don't know any other life. I have no other brother.

Greenfeld is the editor of TIME ASIA.

---

trointestinal problems, depression, obsessive compulsive-ness, subclinical epilepsy, attention-deficit hyperactivity disorder. But there is, researchers believe, a central defect, and that is the difficulty people across the autistic spec-trum have in developing a theory of mind. That's psycho-logese for the realization, which most children come to by the age of 4, that other people have thoughts, wishes and desires that are not mirror images of their own. As Univer-sity of Washington child psychologist Andrew Meltzoff sees it, the developmental stage known as the terrible twos occurs because children—normal children, anyway—make the hypothesis that their parents have independent minds and then, like proper scientists, set out to test it.

Children on the autistic spectrum, however, are "mind blind"; they appear to think that what is in their mind is identical to what is in everyone else's mind and that how they feel is how everyone else feels. The notion that other people—parents, playmates, teachers—may take a differ-ent view of things, that they may harbor concealed mo-tives or duplicitous thoughts, does not readily occur. "It took the longest time for Tommy to tell a lie," recalls Pam Barrett, and when he finally did, she inwardly cheered.

FIRST PERSON

My Son

AMY LENNARD GOEHNER

I didn't know the world that my friends with normal—or, as we call them, typically developing—kids live in until recently. Two and a half years ago, my husband and I adopted our second child, Joey. And as he has grown to be a toddler, every milestone he has reached has been bittersweet—a celebration but also a painful reminder of all the milestones our 8-year-old son Nate has never reached.

Before Joey could talk, he pointed—as if to say, "Hey, Mom, look at that dog over there"—the way kids do to engage you. I flashed back to the evaluation forms we filled out for Nate when we were taking him to specialists. One question that appeared on every form was "Does your child point?" It's a major developmental step, a gesture that communicates a child's desire to share something outside himself. Nate never pointed.

When Nate was 2 and not talking, we took him to a big New York City hospital to get him evaluated. The neurologist gave us his diagnosis almost apologetically, in a very quiet voice. I remember just two words: "Maybe autistic."

When I stopped crying, I went to my office and called everyone I had ever met who was in any way connected to the world of special-needs kids. We made a lot of mistakes before finding the perfect match for Nate (and us)—a wonderful speech therapist whom we later dubbed our captain. When she met Nate, he was nonverbal and running around her office like a self-propelled buzz saw. She looked at us calmly and said, "Let's get busy. We've got work to do."

We've been working ever since. In addition to continual speech, behavior and occupational therapy, we have dabbled in what one of our doctors called "the flavor of the week"—vitamins and supplements and other "can't miss" cures. We shelled out a small fortune for every must-have tool that Lori, Nate's occupational therapist, mentioned even casually, including weighted vests (to help "ground" Nate) and special CDs (to help desensitize him to loud sounds). "Every time Lori opens her mouth, it costs me a hundred bucks," my husband once said.

Recently I read Joey a picture book that contained illustrations of fruit. Joey pretended to pick the fruit off the page and eat it, offering me a bit. Again I flashed back to those evaluation forms: "Does your child engage in pretend/imaginative play?" Nate's idea of play is to drop sticks and small stones into a drain at the playground. He could do this for hours if we let him. Last week Joey took a long noodle from his bowl of soup, dragged it across the table and said, "Look, it's a train. There's the freight car." Then Nate took a noodle from his soup. He tossed it onto the ceiling.

Yet maybe because I entered motherhood through the special-needs world, I somehow feel more a part of it than I do the "normal" one. The challenges in this world are greater, but the accomplishments—those firsts—are that much sweeter.

The other day I heard Joey singing a song about trains, and I realized that I couldn't remember the first time I heard my second son sing. I just took it for granted. With Nate, I never take anything for granted.

When Nate was 6, I was invited to hear his class put on a concert. I had no idea what to expect, as Nate doesn't sing. What he does do is make loud, repetitive noises, occasionally while rocking back and forth. But I went anyway. And when the music teacher approached Nate and began to sing a song Nate loved to listen to, Nate looked down, stared at his hands and very quietly chimed in, "A ram sam sam, a ram sam, gooly, gooly, gooly… " The other moms rushed to hand me tissues as tears streamed town my face. I was listening to Nate sing. For the first time.

Goehner is head arts reporter at TIME

Meltzoff believes that this lack can be traced to the problem that autistic children have in imitating the adults in their lives. If an adult sits down with a normal 18-month-old and engages in some interesting behavior—pounding a pair of blocks on the floor, perhaps, or making faces—the child usually responds by doing the same. Young children with autism, however, do not, as Meltzoff and his colleague Geraldine Dawson have shown in a series of playroom experiments.

The consequences of this failure can be serious. In the early years of life, imitation is one of a child's most powerful tools for learning. It is through imitation that children learn to mouth their first words and master the rich nonverbal language of body posture and facial expression. In this way, Meltzoff says, children learn that drooping shoulders equal sadness or physical exhaustion and that twinkling eyes mean happiness or perhaps mischievousness.

For autistic people—even high-functioning autistic people—the ability to read the internal state of another person comes only after long struggle, and even then most of them fail to detect the subtle signals that normal individuals unconsciously broadcast. "I had no idea that other

FIRST PERSON

Myself

TEMPLE GRANDIN

I was 2 ½ years old when I began to show symptoms of autism: not talking, repetitious behavior and tantrums. Not being able to communicate in words was a great frustration, so I screamed. Loud, high-pitched noises hurt my ears like a dentist's drill hitting a nerve. I would shut out the hurtful stimuli by rocking or staring at sand dribbling through my fingers.

As a child, I was like an animal with no instincts to guide me. I was always observing, trying to work out the best ways to behave, yet I never fit in. When other students swooned over the Beatles, I called their reaction an ISP—interesting social phenomenon. I wanted to participate but did not know how. I had a few friends who were interested in the same things I was, such as skiing and riding horses. But friendship always revolved around what I did rather than who I was.

Even today personal relationships are something I don't really understand. I still consider sex to be the biggest, most important "sin of the system," to use my old high school term. From reading books and talking to people at conventions, I have learned that autistic people who adapt most successfully in personal relationships either choose celibacy or marry someone with similar disabilities.

Early education and speech therapy pulled me out of the autistic world: Like many autistics, I think in pictures. My artistic abilities became evident when I was in first and second grade, and they were encouraged. I had a good eye for color and painted watercolors of the beach.

But words are like a foreign language to me. I translate them into full-color movies, complete with sound, which run like a videotape in my head. When I was a child, I believed that everybody thought in pictures. Not until I went to college did I realize that some people are completely verbal and think only in words. On one of my earliest jobs I thought the other engineer was stupid because he could not "see" his mistakes on his drawings. Now I understand his problem was a lack of visual thinking and not stupidity.

Autistics have trouble learning things that cannot be thought about in pictures. The easiest words for an autistic child to learn are nouns because they relate directly to pictures. Spatial words such as *over* and *under* had no meaning for me until I had a visual image to fix them in my memory. Even now, when I hear the word under by itself, I automatically picture myself getting under the cafeteria tables at school during an air-raid drill, a common occurrence on the East Coast in the early 1950s.

Teachers who work with autistic children need to understand associative thought patterns. But visual thinking is more than just associations. Concepts can also be formed visually. When I was little, I had to figure out that small dogs were not cats. After looking at both large and small dogs, I realized that they all had the same nose. This was a common visual feature of all the dogs but none of the cats.

I credit my visualization abilities with helping me understand the animals I work with. One of my early livestock design projects was to create a dip-vat and cattle-handling facility for a feed yard in Arizona. A dip vat is a long, narrow, 7-ft.-deep swimming pool through which cattle move in single file. It is filled with pesticide to rid the animals of ticks, lice and other external parasites. In 1978 dip-vat designs were very poor. The animals often panicked because they were forced into the vat down a steep, slick decline. They would refuse to jump into the vat and would sometimes flip over backward and drown.

The first thing I did when I arrived at the feedlot was put myself inside a cow's head and see with its eyes. Because their eyes are on the sides of their head, cattle have wide-angle vision. Those cattle must have felt as if they were being forced to jump down an airplane escape slide into the ocean.

One of the first steps was to convert the ramp from steel to concrete. If I had a calf's body and hooves, I would be very scared to step on a slippery metal ramp. The final design had a concrete ramp at a 25° downward angle. Deep grooves in the concrete provided secure footing. The ramp appeared to enter the water gradually, but in reality it abruptly dropped away below the water's surface. The animals could not see the drop-off because the dip chemicals colored the water. When they stepped out over the water, they quietly fell in because their center of gravity had passed the point of no return.

Owners and managers of feedlots sometimes have a hard time comprehending that if devices such as dip vats and restraint chutes are properly designed, cattle will voluntarily enter them. Because I think in pictures, I assume cattle do too. I can imagine the sensations the animals feel. Today half the cattle in the U.S. are handled in equipment I have designed.

Grandin is an assistant professor of animal sciences at Colorado State University.

people communicated through subtle eye movements," says autistic engineer Temple Grandin, "until I read it in a magazine five years ago" (*see box*).

At the same time, it is incorrect to say autistic people are cold and indifferent to those around them or, as conventional wisdom once had it, lack the high-level trait known as empathy. Last December, when Pam Barrett felt overwhelmed and dissolved into tears, it was Danny, the most deeply autistic of her children, who rushed to her side and rocked her back and forth in his arms.

Another misperception about people with autism, says Karen Pierce, a neuroscientist at the University of California at San Diego, is the notion that they do not register faces of loved ones as special—that, in the words of a prominent brain expert, they view their own mother's face as the equivalent of a paper cup. Quite the contrary, says Pierce, who has results from a neuroimaging study to back up her contention. Moreover, the center of activity in the autistic mind, she reported at a conference held in San Diego last November, turns out to be the fusiform gyrus, an area of the brain that in normal people specializes in the recognition of human faces.

In a neuroimaging study, Pierce observed, the fusiform gyrus in autistic people did not react when they were presented with photographs of strangers, but when photographs of parents were substituted, the area lit up like an explosion of Roman candles. Furthermore, this burst of activity was not confined to the fusiform gyrus but, as in normal subjects, extended into areas of the brain that respond to emotionally loaded events. To Pierce, this suggests that as babies, autistic people are able to form strong emotional attachments, so their social aloofness later on appears to be the consequence of a brain disorganization that worsens as development continues.

In so many ways, study after study has found, autistic people do not parse information as others do. University of Illinois psychologist John Sweeney, for example, has found that activity in the prefrontal and parietal cortex is far below normal in autistic adults asked to perform a simple task involving spatial memory. These areas of the brain, he notes, are essential to planning and problem solving, and among their jobs is keeping a dynamically changing spatial map in a cache of working memory. As Sweeney sees it, the poor performance of his autistic subjects of the task he set for them—keeping tabs on the location of a blinking light—suggests that they may have trouble updating that cache or accessing it in real time.

To Sweeney's collaborator, University of Pittsburgh neurologist Dr. Nancy Minshew, the images Sweeney has produced of autistic minds in action are endlessly evocative. They suggest that essential connections between key areas of the brain either were never made or do not function at an optimal level. "When you look at these images, you can see what's not there," she says, conjuring up an experience eerily akin to looking at side-by-side photographs of Manhattan with and without the Twin Towers.

A MATTER OF MISCONNECTIONS

DOES AUTISM START AS A GLITCH IN ONE AREA OF THE brain—the brainstem, perhaps—and then radiate out to affect others? Or is it a widespread problem that becomes more pronounced as the brain is called upon to set up and utilize increasingly complex circuitry? Either scenario is plausible, and experts disagree as to which is more probable. But one thing is clear: very early on, children with autism have brains that are anatomically different on both microscopic and macroscopic scales.

For example, Dr. Margaret Bauman, a pediatric neurologist at Harvard Medical School, has examined postmortem tissue from the brains of nearly 30 autistic individuals who died between the ages of 5 and 74. Among other things, she has found striking abnormalities in the limbic system, an area that includes the amygdala (the brain's primitive emotional center) and the hippocampus (a seahorse-shaped structure critical to memory). The cells in the limbic system of autistic individuals, Bauman's work shows, are atypically small and tightly packed together, compared with the cells in the limbic system of their normal counterparts. They look unusually immature, comments University of Chicago psychiatrist Dr. Edwin Cook, "as if waiting for a signal to grow up."

An intriguing abnormality has also been found in the cerebellum of both autistic children and adults. An important class of cells known as Purkinje cells (after the Czech physiologist who discovered them) is far smaller in number. And this, believes neuroscientist Eric Courchesne, of the University of California at San Diego, offers a critical clue to what goes so badly awry in autism. The cerebellum, he notes, is one of the brain's busiest computational centers, and the Purkinje cells are critical elements in its data-integration system. Without these cells, the cerebellum is unable to do its job, which is to receive torrents of information about the outside world, compute their meaning and prepare other areas of the brain to respond appropriately.

Several months ago, Courchesne unveiled results from a brain-imaging study that led him to propose a provocative new hypothesis. At birth, he notes, the brain of an autistic child is normal in size. But by the time these children reach 2 to 3 years of age, their brains are much larger than normal. This abnormal growth is not uniformly distributed. Using MRI-imaging technology, Courchesne and his colleagues were able to identify two types of tissue where this mushrooming in size is most pronounced.

These are the neuron-packed gray matter of the cerebral cortex and white matter, which contains the fibrous connections projecting to and from the cerebral cortex and other areas of the brain, including the cerebellum. Perhaps, Courchesne speculates, it is the signal overload caused by this proliferation of connections that injures the Purkinje cells and ultimately kills them. "So now," says Courchesne, "a very interesting question is, What's driving this abnormal brain growth? If we could understand that, then we might be able to slow or stop it."

A proliferation of connections between billions of neurons occurs in all children, of course. A child's brain, unlike a computer, does not come into the world with its circuitry hard-wired. It must set up its circuits in response to a sequence of experiences and then solder them together through repeated neurological activity. So if Courchesne is right, what leads to autism may be an otherwise normal process that switches on too early or too strongly and shuts off too late—and that process would be controlled by genes.

Currently Courchesne and his colleagues are looking very closely at specific genes that might be involved. Of particular interest are the genes encoding four brain-growth regulators that have been found in newborns who go on to develop mental retardation or autism. Among these compounds, as National Institutes of Health researcher Dr. Karin Nelson and her colleagues reported last year, is a potent molecule known as vasoactive intestinal peptide. VIP plays a role not only in brain development but in the immune system and gastrointestinal tract as well, a hint that other disorders that so frequently accompany autism may not be coincidental.

The idea that there might be early biomarkers for autism has intrigued many researchers, and the reason is simple. If one could identify infants at high risk, then it might become possible to monitor the neurological changes that presage the onset of behavioral symptoms, and someday perhaps even intervene in the process. "Right now," notes Michael Merzenich, a neuroscientist at the University of California, San Francisco, "we study autism after the catastrophe occurs, and then we see this bewildering array of things that these kids can't do. What we need to know is how it all happened."

The genes that set the stage for autistic disorders could derail developing brains in a number of ways. They could encode harmful mutations like those responsible for single-gene disorders—cystic fibrosis, for instance, or Huntington's disease. They could equally well be garden-variety variants of normal genes that cause problems only when they combine with certain other genes. Or they could be genes that set up vulnerabilities to any number of stresses encountered by a child.

A popular but still unsubstantiated theory blames autism on the MMR (measles, mumps and rubella) vaccine, which is typically given to children at around 15 months (*see box*). But there are many other conceivable culprits. Researchers at the University of California at Davis have just launched a major epidemiological study that will test the tissues of both autistic and nonautistic children for residues of not only mercury but also PCBs, benzene and other heavy metals. The premise is that some children may be genetically more susceptible than others to damage by these agents, and so the study will also measure a number of other genetic variables, like how well these children metabolize cholesterol and other lipids.

Drugs taken by some pregnant women are also coming under scrutiny. At the University of Rochester, embryologist Patricia Rodier and her colleagues are exploring how certain teratogens (substances that cause birth defects) could lead to autism. They are focusing on the teratogens' impact on a gene called HOXA1, which is supposed to flick on very briefly in the first trimester of pregnancy and remain silent ever after. Embryonic mice in which the rodent equivalent of this gene has been knocked out go on to develop brainstems that are missing an entire layer of cells.

In the end, it is not merely possible but likely that scientists will discover multiple routes—some rare, some common; some purely genetic, some not—that lead to similar end points. And when they do, new ideas for how to prevent or correct autism may quickly materialize. A decade from now, there will almost certainly be more effective forms of therapeutic intervention, perhaps even antiautism drugs. "Genes," as the University of Chicago's Cook observes, "give you targets, and we're pretty good at designing drugs if we know the targets."

Paradoxically, the very thing that is so terrible about autistic disorders—that they affect the very young—also suggests reason for hope. Since the neural connections of a child's brain are established through experience, well-targeted mental exercises have the potential to make a difference. One of the big unanswered questions, in fact, is why 25% of children with seemingly full-blown autism benefit enormously from intensive speech- and social-skills therapy—and why the other 75% do not. Is it because the brains of the latter are irreversibly damaged, wonders Geraldine Dawson, director of the University of Washington's autism center, or is it because the fundamental problem is not being adequately addressed?

The more scientists ponder such questions, the more it seems they are holding pieces of a puzzle that resemble the interlocking segments of Tommy Barrett's Transformer toys. Put the pieces together one way, and you end up with a normal child. Put them together another way, and you end up with a child with autism. And as one watches Tommy's fingers rhythmically turning a train into a robot, a robot into a train, an unbidden thought occurs. Could it be that some dexterous sleight of hand could coax even profoundly autistic brains back on track? Could it be that some kid who's mesmerized by the process of transformation will mature into a scientist who figures out the trick?

—With reporting by Amy Bonesteel/Atlanta

Citizenship and Disability

Michael Bérubé

IN THE SIX YEARS since I published a book about my son Jamie, *Life As We Know It*, a great deal has changed in Jamie's life—starting with his realization that there is a book about him. When I completed the book Jamie was only four, and had not yet entered the public K–12 system. But I did not stop serving as Jamie's recorder and public representative when I finished that book: I still represent him all the time, to school officials, camp counselors, babysitters and friends, to academic audiences, and to Down Syndrome Associations. I take it as one of my tasks to watch for important things he's never done before, as a way of charting and understanding the irreplaceable and irreducible little person he is, especially as he gets less and less little, and more and more capable of representing himself.

Jamie is now in his sixth year of school, having entered kindergarten in 1997–1998. In the intervening years he has not continued to perform at grade level (he is repeating fourth grade, at age eleven), and he has occasionally presented his schoolmates with some eccentric behavior. On the other hand, he has learned to read, to do two- and three-digit addition and subtraction, to multiply two-digit numbers, and most recently to do division by single numbers, with and without remainders. My wife, Janet, and I did not teach him these things, but the minute it became clear that he could do them in school, we picked up the ball and ran with it. We've tried to make every available use of his startlingly prodigious memory, and we've learned that when he tells us that such and such bird is not a parrot but is instead a scarlet macaw, he's usually right. He has some idiosyncrasies that do not serve him well in school or in testing situations: at one point he memorized the numbers on the wrong side of his flash cards, the serial numbers that indicate each card's place in the deck. He likes to pretend that he does not know left from right, referring instead (with perverse delight) to his "left foot" and his "other foot." He is a stubborn ignatz, as people find whenever they try to get him to do something he has no interest in, or whenever his teachers or aides try to make him move from one task to another. For a while he tried to put off unpleasant tasks by telling his teachers or therapists, "Let's do that tomorrow"; before long he realized that this didn't work, and began

saying instead, "We did that yesterday"—a ruse with which he has had some success.

His conversational skills are steadily improving, but unless you're talking to him about one of the movies he's seen or one of the routines he's developed at school or at home, you'll find that his sense of the world is sometimes unintelligible, sometimes merely a bit awry. He recently received an invitation to a classmate's birthday party (his third such invitation since we moved to central Pennsylvania sixteen months ago: we count and cherish each one), and Janet asked him what the birthday boy looked like: "he's a small boy," said Jamie, holding his hand around his shoulder level.

"What color is his hair?" she asked.

"Black," Jamie replied.

"What color are his eyes?"

"Blue."

"Does he wear glasses?" (Jamie has worn glasses for about five years.)

"No," Jamie said, "just eyes."

But then, Janet and I did not expect him to be able to describe his classmates at all. Nor did we expect him to be so talented a mimic; he can imitate both of us, just as he can imitate break dancers and gymnasts and snakes and lemurs. We did not expect him to be able to do multiplication or division; we did not expect him to open books and ask us to "read and tell all the things"; we did not expect him to be able to ask us "why" questions, as when he asked me why I could not leave him alone in a hotel room while I went to park the car. We did not expect him to win a spelling award in second grade for maintaining an average above 90 on his spelling tests for the year. We did not expect him to be designated by his classmates in third grade as the kid with the best sense of humor.

Over eleven years, then, we've come to expect that Jamie will defeat or exceed our expectations when we least expect him to. And from this I draw two points. One, he's a child. Two, and this is a somewhat more elaborate conclusion, although it can be derived from point one: it might be a good idea for all of us to treat other humans as if we do not know their potential, as if they just might in fact surprise us, as if they might defeat or exceed our expectations. It might be a good idea for us to check the history of the past two centuries whenever we think we know what "normal"

human standards of behavior and achievement might be. And it might be a very good idea for us to expand the possibilities of democracy precisely because democracy offers us unfinished and infinitely revisable forms of political organization that stand the best chance, in the long run, of responding adequately to the human rights of the unpredictable creatures we humans are. That might be one way of recognizing and respecting something you might want to call our human dignity.

JAMIE IS, of course, one reason why I am drawn to the question of disability rights and their relation to democracy: every morning I take him to school, I know how very fortunate he is to be living under a social dispensation that entitles him to a public education alongside his nondisabled peers. But beyond my immediate interest in forwarding Jamie's interests, I want to argue that disability issues are—or should be—central to theories of social justice in a much broader sense. Nancy Fraser's account of the "politics of recognition" and the "politics of redistribution" (*Adding Insult to Injury: Social Justice and the Politics of Recognition*), for example, offers a theory that tries to accommodate what were the two major strands of American progressive-left thought in the 1990s, multiculturalism and democratic socialism (in all their varieties)—or what Richard Rorty, in *Achieving Our Country*, termed the "cultural left" and the "reformist left," the former concerned primarily with combating social stigma and the latter concerned primarily with combating greed. Fraser has shown convincingly that the politics of recognition and redistribution offer a productive way to think about feminism: cultural politics with regard to body images or sexual harassment, for example, are not to be understood as distractions from "real" politics that address comparative worth or the minimum wage. Rather, recognition politics have consequences for the redistribution of social goods and resources even though they cannot be reduced to their redistributive effects. And since many left intellectuals in the 1990s were all too willing to think of politics as a zero-sum game in which any attention paid to multiculturalism had to come at the expense of democratic socialism and vice versa, Fraser's work seems to offer a way for the left to champion a progressive tax code and an end to racial profiling at the same time.

It is striking, nonetheless, that so few leftists have understood disability in these terms. Disability is not the only area of social life in which the politics of recognition are inseparable from the politics of redistribution; other matters central to citizenship, such as immigration, reproductive rights, and criminal justice, are every bit as complex. Nonetheless, our society's representations of disability are intricately tied to, and sometimes the very basis for, our public policies for "administering" disability. And when we contemplate, in these terms, the history of people with cognitive and developmental disabilities, we find a history in which "representation" takes on a double valence: first, in that people who were deemed incapable of representing themselves were therefore represented by a socio-medical apparatus that defined—or, in a social-constructionist sense, created-the category of "feeblemindedness"; and second, in the sense that the visual and rhetorical representations of "feebleminded" persons then set the terms for public policy. One cannot plausibly narrate a comprehensive history of ideas and practices of national citizenship in the post–Civil War United States without examining public policy regarding disability, especially mental disability, all the more especially when mental disability was then mapped onto certain immigrant populations who scored poorly on intelligence tests and were thereby pseudo-scientifically linked to criminality. And what of reproductive rights? By 1927, the spurious but powerful linkages among disability, immigration, poverty, and criminality provided the Supreme Court with sufficient justification for declaring involuntary sterilization legal under the Constitution.

THERE IS AN obvious reason why disability rights are so rarely thought of in terms of civil rights: disability was not covered in the Civil Rights Act of 1964. And as Anita Silvers points out, over the next twenty-five years, groups covered by civil rights law sometimes saw disability rights as a dilution of civil rights, on the grounds that people with disabilities were constitutively incompetent, whereas women and minorities faced discrimination merely on the basis of social prejudice. Silvers writes, "[t]o make disability a category that activates a heightened legal shield against exclusion, it was objected, would alter the purpose of legal protection for civil rights by transforming the goal from protecting opportunity for socially exploited people to providing assistance for naturally unfit people." The passage of the Americans with Disabilities Act (ADA) in 1990 did add disability to the list of stigmatized identities covered by antidiscrimination law,

but thus far the ADA has been interpreted so narrowly, and by such a business-friendly judiciary, that employers have won over 95 percent of the suits brought under the act.

Perhaps if plaintiffs with disabilities had won a greater number of cases over the past thirteen years, the conservative backlash against the ADA—currently confined to a few cranks complaining about handicapped parking spaces and a wheelchair ramp at a Florida nude beach—would be sufficiently strong as to spark a movement to repeal the law altogether. But then again, perhaps if the law were read more broadly, more Americans would realize their potential stake in it. In 1999, for instance, the Supreme Court ruled on three lower-court cases in which people with "easily correctable" disabilities—high blood pressure, nearsightedness—were denied employment. In three identical 7–2 decisions, the Court found that the plaintiffs had no basis for a suit under the ADA precisely *because* their disabilities were easily correctable. As disability activists and legal analysts quickly pointed out, this decision left these plaintiffs in the ridiculous situation of being too disabled to be hired but somehow not disabled enough to be covered by the ADA; or, to put this another way, plaintiffs' "easily correctable" disabilities were not so easily correctable as to allow them access to employment. One case involved twin sisters who were denied the opportunity to test as pilots for United Airlines on the grounds that their eyesight did not meet United's minimum vision requirement (uncorrected visual acuity of 20/100 or better without glasses or contacts) even though each sister had 20/20 vision with corrective lenses (*Sutton v. United Airlines, Inc.*); another involved a driver/mechanic with high blood pressure (*Murphy v. United Parcel Service*); the third involved a truck driver with monocular vision (20/200 in one eye) who in 1992 had received a Department of Transportation waiver of the requirement that truck drivers have distant visual acuity of 20/40 in each eye as well as distant binocular acuity of 20/40 (*Albertson's, Inc. v. Kirkingburg*). Because, as Silvers argues, "litigation under the ADA commonly turns on questions of classification rather than access," all three plaintiffs were determined to have no standing under the law. The question of whether any of them was justly denied employment was simply not addressed by the Court. Indeed, in writing her opinion for the majority, Justice Sandra Day O'Connor explicitly refused to consider the wider question of "access," noting that 160 million Americans would be covered by the ADA if it were construed to include people with "easily correctible" disabilities (under a "health conditions approach"), and since Congress had cited the number 43 million in enacting the law, Congress clearly

could not have intended the law to be applied more widely. "Had Congress intended to include all persons with corrected physical limitations among those covered by the Act, it undoubtedly would have cited a much higher number of disabled persons in the findings," wrote O'Connor. "That it did not is evidence that the ADA's coverage is restricted to only those whose impairments are not mitigated by corrective measures."

It is possible to object that O'Connor's decision was excessively literalist, and that the potential number of Americans covered by the ADA is, in any case, quite irrelevant to the question of whether a woman can fly a plane when she's got her glasses on. But I've since come to believe that the literalism of the decision is an indirect acknowledgment of how broad the issues at stake here really are. If the ADA were understood as a broad civil rights law, and if it were understood as a law that potentially pertains to the entire population of the country, then maybe disability law would be understood not as a fringe addition to civil rights law but as its very fulfillment.

RIGHTS CAN BE created, reinterpreted, extended, and revoked. The passage of the ADA should therefore be seen as an extension of the promise of democracy, but only as a promise: any realization of the potential of the law depends on its continual reinterpretation. For the meaning of the word, just as Wittgenstein wanted us to believe (in order that we might be undeceived about how our words work), lies in its use in the language. Similarly, the Individuals with Disabilities Education Act of 1975 (originally the Education for All Handicapped Children Act) was not some kind of breakthrough discovery whereby children with disabilities were found to be rights-bearing citizens of the United States after all, and who knew that we'd had it all wrong for 199 years? On the contrary, the IDEA *invented* a new right for children with disabilities, the right to a "free and appropriate public education in the least restrictive environment." And yet the IDEA did not wish that right into being overnight; the key terms "appropriate" and "least restrictive" had to be interpreted time and again, over the course of fifteen years, before they were understood to authorize "full inclusion" of children with disabilities in "regular" classrooms. Nothing about the law is set in stone. The only philosophical "foundation" underlying the IDEA and its various realizations is our own collective political will, a will that is tested and tested again every time the Act comes up for reauthorization. Jamie Bérubé currently has a right to an inclusive public education, but that right is neither intrinsic nor innate. Rather, Jamie's rights were invented, and implemented slowly and with great difficulty.

The recognition of his human dignity, enshrined in those rights, was invented. And by the same token, those rights, and that recognition, can be taken away. While I live, I promise myself that I will not let that happen, but I live with the knowledge that it may: to live any other way, to live as if Jamie's rights were somehow intrinsic, would be irresponsible.

Of course, many of us would prefer to believe that our children have intrinsic human rights and human dignity no matter what; irrespective of any form of human social organization; regardless of whether they were born in twentieth-century Illinois or second-century Rome or seventh-century central Asia. But this is just a parent's—or a philosophical foundationalist's—wishful thinking. For what would it mean for Jamie to "possess" rights that no one on earth recognized? A fat lot of good it would do him. My argument may sound either monstrous or all too obvious: if, in fact, no one on earth recognized Jamie's human dignity, then there would in fact be no human perspective from which he would be understood to possess "intrinsic" human dignity. And then he wouldn't have it, and so much the worse for the human race.

In one respect, the promise of the IDEA, like the promise of the ADA, is clear: greater inclusion of people with disabilities in the social worlds of school and work. But in another sense the promise is unspecifiable; its content is something we actually cannot know in advance. For the IDEA does not merely guarantee all children with disabilities a free appropriate public education in the least restrictive environment. Even more than this, it grants the right to education in order that persons with disabilities might make the greatest possible use of their other rights—the ones having to do with voting, or employment discrimination, or with life, liberty, and the pursuit of happiness.

IDEA is thus designed to enhance the capabilities of all American children with disabilities regardless of their actual abilities—and this is why it is so profound a democratic idea. Here again I'm drawing on Nancy Fraser, whose theory of democracy involves the idea of "participatory parity," and the imperative that a democratic state should actively foster the abilities of its citizens to participate in the life of the polity as equals. Fraser's work to date has not addressed disability, but as I noted above, it should be easy to see how disability is relevant to Fraser's account of the politics of recognition and the politics of redistribution. This time, however, I want to press the point a bit harder. Fraser writes as if the promise of democracy entails the promise to enhance participatory parity among citizens, which it does, and she writes as if we knew what "participatory parity" itself means, which we don't. (This is why the promise of disability rights is unspecifiable.)

L ET ME EXPLAIN. First, the idea of participatory parity does double duty in Fraser's work, in the sense that it names both the state we would like to achieve and the device by which we can gauge whether we're getting there. For in order to maintain a meaningful democracy in which all citizens participate as legal and moral equals, the state needs to judge whether its policies enhance equal participation in democratic processes. Yet at the same time, the state needs to enhance equal participation among its citizens simply in order to determine what its democratic processes will be. This is not a metatheoretical quibble. On the contrary, the point is central to the practical workings of any democratic polity. One of the tasks required of democrats is precisely this: to extend the promise of democracy to previously excluded individuals and groups some of whom might have a substantially different understanding of "participatory parity" than that held by previously dominant groups and individuals.

Could anything make this clearer than the politics of disability? Imagine a building in which political philosophers are debating, in the wake of the attacks of September 11, 2001, the value and the purpose of participatory parity over against forms of authoritarianism or theocracy. Now imagine that this building has no access ramps, no Braille or large-print publications, no American Sign Language interpreters, no elevators, no special-needs paraprofessionals, no in-class aides. Contradictory as such a state of affairs may sound, it's a reasonably accurate picture of what contemporary debate over the meaning of democracy actually looks like. How can we remedy this? Only when we have fostered equal participation in debates over the ends and means of democracy can we have a truly participatory debate over what "participatory parity" itself means. That debate will be interminable in principle, since our understandings of democracy and parity are infinitely revisable, but lest we think of deliberative democracy as a forensic society dedicated to empyreal reaches of abstraction, we should remember that debates over the meaning of participatory parity set the terms for more specific debates about the varieties of human embodiment. These include debates about prenatal screening, genetic discrimination, stem-cell research, euthanasia, and, with regard to physical access, ramps, curb cuts, kneeling buses, and buildings employing what is now known as universal design.

Leftists and liberals, particularly those associated with university humanities departments, are commonly charged with being moral relativists, unable or unwilling to say (even after September 11) why one society might be "better" than another. So let me be especially clear on this final point. I think there's a very good reason to extend the franchise, to widen the conversation, to democratize our debates, and to make disability central to our theories of egalitarian social justice. The reason is this: a capacious and supple sense of what it is to be human is better than a narrow and partial sense of what it is to be human, and the more participants we as a society can incorporate into the deliberation of what it means to be human, the greater the chances that that deliberation will in fact be transformative in such a way as to enhance our collective capacities to recognize each other as humans entitled to human dignity. As Jamie reminds me daily, both deliberately and unwittingly, most Americans had no idea what people with Down syndrome could achieve until we'd passed and implemented and interpreted and reinterpreted a law entitling them all to a free appropriate public education in the least restrictive environment. I can say all this without appealing to any innate justification for human dignity and human rights, and I can also say this: Without a sufficient theoretical and practical account of disability, we can have no account of democracy worthy of the name.

Perhaps some of our fellow citizens with developmental disabilities would not put the argument quite this way; even though Jamie has led me to think this way, he doesn't talk the way I do. But those of us who do participate in political debates, whether about school funding in a specific district or about the theory and practice of democracy at its most abstract, have the obligation to enhance the abilities of our children and our fellow citizens with disabilities to participate in the life of the United States as political and moral equals with their nondisabled peers—both for their own good, and for the good of democracy, which is to say, for the good of all of us.

MICHAEL BÉRUBÉ is the Paterno Family Professor in Literature at Pennsylvania State University. This article is adapted from a talk given at the 2002 convention of the Arc of the United States (formerly the Association of Retarded Citizens of the United States).

From *Dissent*, Spring 2003. © 2003 by Dissent Magazine.

Inscrutable or Meaningful?

Understanding and Supporting Your Inarticulate Students

Robin M. Smith

Interpreting movement.
Time.
Assistive technology.
Choice.
Audiotapes.
Sticky notes.

What do these dissimilar items or concepts have in common? Teachers can use them all in adapting lessons for students who have difficulties in communicating with others.

This article explores ways teachers can build competence in such students, rather than focus on their deficits. Along the way, you can learn how to observe your students to discover their strengths and weaknesses, translate body language, unravel the ways they process language, appreciate indications of humor, and interpret different kinds of behavior and its intent. Tips include ways to encourage group membership and participation, ways to influence student behavior, and ways to encourage communication and independent decision making by students.

Understanding Teaching Approaches

All three students described in this article (see box, "What Does It Mean to be Nonverbal?") studied with two kinds of teachers—which we will refer to as deficit-oriented and competence-oriented (Smith, 2000). How these teachers perceive their students affected how they taught and evaluated them. Their students often responded according to how they were treated and perceived in class (Smith, Ryan, & Salend, 2001). How teachers perceive their students will influence how they instruct, evaluate, and affect their students (Biklen & Duchan, 1994; Rosenthal, 1997; Smith, 1999).

Focusing on Deficits

Deficit-oriented teachers often perceive their students with developmental disabilities as inscrutable—that is, because the students are difficult to understand, they think the students must therefore be lacking basic understanding of the things going on around them. Those students who also have cognitive disabilities may not have typical speech or facial expression; and the students may also experience language-processing disabilities, such as problems with word retrieval, delayed understanding of complex speech, or need for a longer response time in conversation.

Deficit-oriented teachers tend to teach to a medial model of repairing the (often) irreparable individual. Their descriptions of students foster ranking, sorting, and diagnosing. Such medical-model descriptions obscure the individual abilities of students who may have unusual approaches to communicating their understanding, wants, and needs. For example, teachers may consider a nonverbal student who is labeled with severe mental retardation to be unable to participate in class discussions, and therefore may have the student doing something different elsewhere in the classroom or even in another room.

Deficit-oriented teachers who think their students are inscrutable and uncomprehending may miss student communications and key skills and strengths or fail to see their relevance. In the example of Tyrone (see box), his deficit-oriented teacher had no idea Tyrone understood the class discussion and therefore made few requests that he respond. Tyrone's teacher accepted his homework assignments but did not ask about missing assignments.

Focusing on Competence

Competence-oriented teachers, on the other hand, perceive students as whole persons and teach with the students' strengths in mind. Instead of questioning if students can participate in a class activity, these teachers think about *how* students can be involved in the activity. Such teachers acquire the skill of "reading" students who communicate in ways that greatly differ from their peers. They learn how students show engagement, boredom, contentment, and dissatisfaction. They are aware of their students' strengths and how these strengths might be used to support learning and achievement.

Competence-oriented teachers' descriptions of students tend to foster understanding and communication with students. For example, in Teresa's case (see box), whereas her competence-oriented teacher assisted her with exams, essays, and had meaningful typed conversations with her, her deficit-oriented teacher frequently encountered passive and active resistance from Teresa and experienced little or no meaningful communication with her.

Understanding Student Communication

You might compare students like Teresa, Tyrone, or Gerard—who differ from peers in the way they move, process information, and communicate—to a foreign visitor who does not speak your language very well but is likely to understand it. As the "native speaker," you as teacher can take on the role of interpreter as you learn the student's own language.

The following guidelines, summarized in Table 1, are designed to help you

What Does It Mean to be Nonverbal? Three Students

Many of us tend to focus on the student's disability, not the person, and thus see students who are nonverbal or inarticulate as simply "difficult to understand." Students who are labeled mentally retarded or who have impaired communication, especially, are the victims of such first impressions (Goode, 1989).

The three students described here have studied with two kinds of teachers, which will become evident as you read. The first type of teachers regarded their students as inscrutable or incompetent, rather than as sources of meaningful activity and communication. They had difficulty seeing intelligence and using the strengths of their students. The second category of teachers not only saw the students' intelligence and competencies, but also helped them engage academically.

Gerard was a high school student labeled mentally retarded who spoke in short phrases. When asked a direct question, he often responded, "I don't know." Several of his teachers, both general and special education, said that he understood little of what was going on in class. A paraprofessional who did feel Gerard understood his schoolwork was working with him on some questions in a textbook about managing money. She asked him what he should do with his paycheck. Gerard shook his head and said, "I don't know." She said,

"Let me put this another way. When you work at [your job], what do you do with your check? Does your mom put it in the bank or do you spend it?" He said, "Bank."

Tyrone, a student with autism, spoke in short phrases and often repeated favorite expressions and topics in his conversation. Two teachers described him as "a mystery" and had no idea if he understood what was happening in class. One day, one of these teachers was questioning the students about a history worksheet they had done on the early 1900s, asking them about historic people and events. "John Jacob Astor?" A student replied, "American Fur Company." The teacher mentioned the Broadway musical about the Astor family, asking for the title. Tyrone called out, "Scrooge." The teacher laughed, "Good guess."

Teresa was nonverbal and communicated inconsistently by pointing and making sounds. Teachers supported her pointing to answer choices written on Post-It notes. With gentle physical support, she could sustain pointing to letters in a large keyboard for a short time. She took quizzes and typed short conversations with a teacher assigned to help her with communication skills. Her other teacher assigned for the same purpose, however, was unable to engage Teresa in typed conversations and said, in her presence, "I don't think she knows her letters."

learn about your students and become an effective interpreter.

Get to Know Your Students' Communication Strengths and Needs

Your ability to engage students depends on your knowledge of their communication strengths and needs. If you spend some time getting to know your students, you can identify these strengths and needs by doing the following:

- Sharing with the students that you are trying to get to know them, their communication styles and patterns, and their interests, and thus explaining why you are asking some questions that might seem obvious to them. Let them know you want to learn about what they have invented as strategies to communicate.

- Drawing on the knowledge of others who know the student—for example, paraprofessionals, family members, and friends.

- Observing students and asking yourself questions like these:

   —How does this student typically show interest?

   —How does this student show understanding?

   —Are there atypical or meaningful body movements that are special to this student?

   —Is this student following the conversation even when looking around or pacing? How do I know?

Understand Movement Differences

Some students have movement differences associated with their disability. We must not misinterpret movement differences as discipline problems, resistance, boredom, or incomprehension. For example, although Tyrone often walks around the room during a discussion, he is a full participant, understanding others' communication and making relevant contributions on request.

When Tyrone is seated in class, however, he has a different way of being in motion. Although he often writes a list of five names over and over, apparently engrossed in his notebook, he will answer a question when asked. Though some teachers may consider him disengaged, his repetitive writing helps him concentrate by blocking out other distractions. You can learn about and examine your students' movement differences by observing them and asking yourself:

- Does this student have trouble starting, executing, stopping, combining, continuing, or switching activities? These are some common movement differences identified by Donnellan and Leary (1995, p. 80) in people with autism and mental retardation. These behaviors reflect neither intention nor intelligence. They reflect the need for understanding and accommodation.

- Do the movements have particular meaning? Sometimes the movements have no meaning. Students with Tourette's syndrome, for example, cannot control certain words, shouts, or twitches.

Understand Language-Processing Differences

Some students can speak, but are inarticulate. Whereas students may be capable of one- or two-word sentences or short phrases, their teachers may think they are intellectually limited or lazy.

Some common indications that students have difficulty with processing language are as follows:

- Difficulty with word retrieval when answering a direct question. Gerard (see box) was inarticulate and also had difficulty finding the words he

Table 1. Understanding Students' Communication

Get to know communication strengths/needs	Let them know you want to learn about their communication strategies. Draw on the knowledge of others: family, friends, paraprofessionals. Observe how students show interest and understanding. Learn how unique body movements can be interpreted as meaningful.
Understand movement differences	Identify problems with starting, executing, stopping, combining, continuing, or switching activities. Identify meanings of recurring movements or intensity of movements.
Understand processing differences such as:	Difficulty with word retrieval Limited response repertoire Longer wait time to respond Difficulty responding to someone else's initiated conversation
Look for signs of sophisticated thinking	Humor Insight
Understand refusal or resistance relating to:	Personal considerations or preferences Academic considerations such as needs for modifications; appropriateness of the task; need for coaching; ability to physically carry out the task.
Understand unintentional behaviors	Abrupt behaviors may not be related to noncompliance, nonunderstanding, or lack of interest. Student may be "stuck" in a repetitive thought or feeling. Less participation may be fatigue rather than disinterest.

needed to communicate with others. Sometimes, when he replied, "I don't know," his conversation partner repeated the question in a different way that also gave him extra time to come up with an answer. Sometimes Gerard could immediately answer a question if his attention were already on the topic, such as during a class discussion. In the previous example, Gerard selected the correct answer from choices presented to him.

- Some students may have a limited response repertoire. As a result, they rely on consistent alternative responses. When asked a direct question, Gerard responded "Yes," "No," or "I don't know." In health class, he responded appropriately to every question the teacher asked, including rhetorical ones. ("Would you get on a plane if the pilot were high?" "No.")
- Some students need a longer wait time to prepare and articulate their responses. Therefore, teachers need to provide students with a sufficient amount of time in which to respond.
- Some students have difficulty responding in conversations that someone else has initiated. Regarding Gerard's social conversation skills, his special education teacher said he was lazy because he answered, "I don't know" so often.

Yet, he initiated a conversation with a teacher about plans for the weekend; and when asked what he was going to do, said that his parents were taking him to a concert.

You can change the way you communicate with students once you realize they process language differently. You can speak slower or with longer wait time in between thoughts. You also can ask more "yes/no" questions or phrase questions to include the words students need to respond appropriately. When students appear to be restless, you can ask them if they are bored or need a break.

Look for Signs of Sophisticated Thinking, Such as Humor or Insight

Students who are nonverbal or inarticulate may show sophistication with a few choice words, a joke, a comeback, or the timing of a behavior.

For example, Tyrone's naming the Astor play, "Scrooge," was an obvious sign of sophistication. Tyrone's jokes and his correct one-word answers in other classes were also a sign of sophisticated thinking. One time his paraprofessional yawned when helping with a worksheet and said, "Excuse me." Tyrone responded, "You need a blanket."

Understand Refusal and Resistance

Although teachers generally consider refusal and resistance unproductive and inappropriate, for some students these strategies may be their most effective method of communication. This is particularly true of students who lack the motor coordination to write or type and who do not speak.

For example, one day a teacher was absent; and the students had a period of reading, resting, and chatting. Gerard's paraprofessional tried in vain to get him to work on yesterday's assignment. Gerard looked around and leafed through a magazine.

After a few minutes, the paraprofessional asked, "Are you being this way because all the other kids don't have to work today and you don't want to, either?"

He responded, "Yes."

Like Gerard's paraprofessional, you can attempt to understand your students' refusal and resistance by examining the following:

- Are there personal considerations and preferences? Ask students questions to find out if they are tired, sick, thirsty, bored, dislike this topic, or want to do the same thing as other students.
- Are there academic considerations? Does the task need to be modified in any way? Does the expected task

Table 2. Competence-Oriented Supports	
Plan ahead for student participation	Pre-arrange a time to call on students Call on students for yes/no or choice answers Assign a task the student can do to contribute to the whole class Prepare choices students can point to during group discussions Prepare prerecorded choices and answers the student can activate with a switching device
Maximize student decision making	Support decisions at each step of a project Use sticky notes to write exam choices Use augmentative communication systems: communication, picture/symbol/word books; pointing, recording devices, keyboard devices, etc. Use alternative forms of written communication (e.g., arranging sentence cards for essays) Ask student to confirm answers or meaning of their communication.
Minimize effect of unintentional behaviors	Study consistency of certain behaviors Discover appropriate prompts to help students through problematic movements

make sense to the student? Does the student need coaching to stay focused and on task? Can the student physically carry out the task?

Understand When Students' Behaviors Are Unintentional

Sometimes students have unusual verbal responses and utterances, as well as nonverbal actions they cannot control. Understanding such behavior will help you to carefully interpret unusual and unexpected verbal responses and nonverbal behavior.

Because students' processing delays and unintentional verbal and physical types of behavior may be misinterpreted, based on the responses of typical students, you can inquire into such differences by considering the following:

- Is unintentional behavior misinterpreted as noncompliance, nonunderstanding, or lack of interest? Some students with developmental disabilities have unintentional types of behavior, appearing as abrupt behavior changes. Students may have tics, use inappropriate language, call out irrelevant phrases, pace, strike or challenge others, or walk out of the room or building. An event, a feeling, or a physical response to the environment, such as the sound of fluorescent lights or computer hard drives, may trigger some of this behavior.
- Are repetitive words or phrases signs that student is "stuck" in an emotion? A student may be involuntarily involved in a repetitive thought or feeling, particularly when nervous. Some coaching or prompting may help a student move

on. It may help to ask the student if he or she is "stuck."

- Is less-than-usual participation or speech misinterpreted as lack of interest? For some students, this lack of participation may be a sign of the effort it takes to suppress an involuntary behavior, such as a movement, sound, or tic.

Competence-Oriented Supports to Involve Inarticulate or Nonspeaking Students

As you get to know your students, you do not have to wait until you are expert in "their language." The use of competence-oriented strategies, summarized in Table 2, can cause you to see how your students demonstrate engagement and understanding.

In addition, you will be providing more opportunity for participation. Eugene Marcus (personal communication, 1994), a man with autism who communicates by typing said, "Treat every individual who you meet as a dignitary from another country who does not speak your language very well." The following are some suggestions for implementing Marcus's mandate in your classes.

Plan Ahead for Participation During Group Discussions

Pre-arrange a time to call on students. For example, Teresa's special education teacher met with the health teacher and arranged with him to call on Teresa for a particular question from the homework assignment. Then, she prerecorded the answer into Teresa's speaking device. Teresa pushed a button on her speaking

device when called on in class to answer the question.

Call on students for yes/no or choice answers. For example, a student named Nick could not speak but nodded his head when the teacher asked him if he agreed with what another student said.

Assign a task students can do to contribute to a small group or the whole class. For example, Gerard's social studies teacher asked him to find a picture of the Great Wall in the school library. With the help of his paraprofessional, he found the picture while the class was doing a written assignment; and then he showed the photo to his social studies class during a discussion about China.

Arrange choices for students to point to when answering questions during whole-group and small-group lessons and during exams. Teachers, paraeducators, or peers can prepare these choices in advance or spontaneously use Post-it notes or an erasable white board.

Use recording devices with switches students can operate. For example, with the help of teachers and peers, students can answer questions with prerecorded responses, give reports, turn on background sounds for others' reports, and even prepare small-talk conversations in advance using a cassette recorder.

Maximize Students' Decision Making

Support students to decide during each step of a project they cannot physically do alone. For example, Tyrone did not have the fine-motor coordination to cut and paste pictures for a collage in his health class. His paraeducator asked him to decide on a topic for a collage. Tyrone chose the materials, the color scheme, which pictures to cut out, and where to glue them.

Use Post-it notes to record possible choices during exams or spontaneous conversations and ask students to select their responses. For example, during an exam, the teacher wrote the choices for fill-in-the-blank questions on Post-it notes; and Teresa then pointed to her choice. Because Teresa was not always consistent in her movements, the teacher then confirmed the choice by changing the order of the three choices—and Teresa would point to the same one.

Use communication books (pictures with words, phrases, or sentences on laminated cards) for the common conversations. Communication books work well in role-plays, pairs, and small groups, as peers or teachers support students to participate and contribute.

Use alternative forms of written communication. Teachers can help students write drafts using Post-it notes or cards, and then make sure the students approve of the order. For an essay on health careers, Teresa chose sentences from texts that her paraprofessional wrote on cards. She later put them in order, along with transitional sentences suggested by her paraeducator.

Use augmentative communication systems, such as typing, pointing to letters or pictures, or facilitated communication to facilitate independent choice making. Nick, who did not speak and lacked fine-motor coordination, was looking at menu choices that were in small type and close together. When the paraeducator wrote the prices larger and farther part, Nick was able to point to the correct choice through a type of facilitated communication: Paraeducator provided only slight resistance by pulling back on his sleeve (Biklen & Cardinal, 1997).

Seek confirmation when students are too concise, inconsistent, or are engaging in automatic and repetitive phrases. You can encourage detail by saying, "I don't understand what you meant; please type/ say it again," or "Please say more." If a

student is inconsistent when pointing and is taking an exam, you might ask after each choice, "Is that your answer?"

Minimize the Effect of Unintentional Behavior

Learn if there is consistency for particular unintentional behaviors. For example, teachers can learn if behaviors such as pacing or walking out of the room are related to anxiety and try to discover ways to ease students' anxiety.

Discover appropriate prompts and indirect means to overcome unintentional and problematic differences in movement. Some students have trouble initiating and need pre-arranged cues to begin a task, whereas others have problems completing several steps of a task and need a series of cues to complete the task. Still others will have difficulty stopping. Necessary accommodations will be different for each student, and these supports will help with such problems as difficulty in starting, continuing, and stopping an activity (see Donnellan & Leary, 1995).

For example, touching Teresa's elbow enabled her to begin pointing to her answers on a test. A picture schedule helped another student, Sally, go through the steps of a classroom activity that included getting out her supplies, using them correctly, and putting them away without prompting.

Both teachers and peers can incorporate all these suggestions. Peers can learn to draw out responses from each other and may even provide the educators with creative, fresh approaches.

Final Thoughts

We need to think of our roles not only as developers of social, academic, and functional skills in students, but also as interpreters and communication allies of inarticulate students. These are the same sensitivities we automatically use with students without disabilities in general education settings, with our peers, and often with young children—when we re-

member how much they really do understand.

References

Biklen, D., & Cardinal, D. (1997). *Contested words, contested science: Unraveling the FC controversy.* New York: Teachers College Press.

Biklen, D., & Duchan, J. (1994). I am intelligent: The social construction of mental retardation. *Journal of the Association for Persons with Severe Handicaps, 19*(3), 173–184.

Donnellan, A. M., & Leary, M. R. (1995). *Movement differences and diversity in autism/mental retardation: Appreciating and accommodating people with communication and behavior challenges* (4th ed.). Madison, WI: DRI Press.

Goode, D. A. (1989). Who's Bobby? Ideology and method in the discovery of a Down syndrome person's competence. In P. M. Ferguson, D. L. Ferguson, & S. J. Taylor (Eds.), *Interpreting disability: A qualitative reader* (pp. 197–212). New York: Teachers College Press.

Rosenthal, R. (1997). *Interpersonal expectancy effects: A forty-year perspective.* Paper presented at the American Psychological Association Convention, Chicago. (ERIC Document Reproduction Service No. ED 415 460)

Smith, R., Ryan, S., & Salend, S. (2001). Watch your language: Closing or opening the special education curtain. *TEACHING Exceptional Children, 33*(4), 18–23.

Smith, R. M. (1999). Academic engagement of students with significant disabilities and educators' perceptions of competence. *The Professional Educator, 22*(1), 17–31.

Smith, R. M. (2000). View from the ivory tower: How academics construct disability. In B. B. Swadner & L. Rogers (Eds.), *Semiotics and disability: Interrogating the categories of difference* (pp. 55–733). New York: State University of New York (SUNY) Press.

Robin M. Smith *(CEC Chapter #615), Assistant Professor of Special Education, Educational Studies, State University of New York at New Paltz, New York.*

Address correspondence to the author at Educational Studies Department, State University of New York–New Paltz, 75 S. Manheim Blvd., New Paltz, NY 12561 (e-mail: smithrm@newpaltz.edu)

UNIT 6

Emotional and Behavioral Disorders

Unit Selections

Key Points to Consider

- Which emotional and behavioral disorders should be referred for psychiatric treatment? How can teachers detect them?

- How have choice-making opportunities for students with emotional and behavioral problems helped break the cycle of negative responses that hinders their progression through the educational system?

- After reading the article by Brent Richardson and Margery Shupe, suggest why teachers need to be in touch with their own feelings and how they can increase self-awareness.

- How can chronic and intense behavioral difficulties be ameliorated in the classroom to allow learning to take place?

 **Links: www.dushkin.com/online/**
These sites are annotated in the World Wide Web pages.

Educating Students With Emotional/Behavioral Disorders
http://www.nichcy.org/pubs/bibliog/bib10txt.htm
Pacer Center: Emotional Behavioral Disorders
http://www.pacer.org/ebd/

The definition of a student with emotional behavioral disorder (EBD) usually conjures up visions of the violence perpetrated by a few students who have vented their frustrations by taking guns to school. One of the hot topics in special education today is whether or not students with emotional and behavioral disorders are too dangerous to be included in regular education classes. The statistics show that students with EBDs are as likely to be the victims of violence or bullying by nondisabled classmates as to be the troublemakers. The definition of EBDs broadly includes all emotionally disordered students with subjective feelings such as sadness, fear, anger, guilt, or anxiety that give rise to altered behaviors that are outside the range of normal.

Should children with chronic and severe anger, already convicted of problem behaviors such as violent acts or threats of violence, be re-enrolled in inclusive regular education classes with individualized education plans (IEPs)? Although teachers, other

pupils, and school staff may be greatly inconvenienced by the presence of one or more behaviorally disordered students in every classroom, the law is clear. The school must "show cause" if a child with EBD is to be permanently moved from the regular classroom to a more restrictive environment.

The 1994 Gun-Free Schools Act in the United States requires a one-year expulsion of a student who brings a firearm to school. The Individuals with Disabilities Education Act (IDEA) in its 1997 reauthorization made a compromise for students with EBDs or other conditions of disability. If bringing a gun to school is related to their disability (for example, as the result of being teased or bullied), they are exempt from the Gun-Free Schools Act legislation. They can be expelled, but only for 10 days while the school determines their degree of danger to others. If they are judged to really be dangerous, they can temporarily be given an alternate educational placement for 45 days, subject to reassessment. Their IEPs should not be rewritten to place them in a permanent restrictive setting unless their acts were clearly unrelated to their disabilities (hard to prove). This double standard is very controversial. Students without disabilities are expelled with no educational provisions for one full year.

For educational purposes, children with behavior disorders are usually divided into two main behavioral classifications: (1) withdrawn, shy, or anxious behaviors and (2) aggressive, acting-out behaviors. The debate about what constitutes a behavior disorder, or an emotional disorder, is not fully resolved. The Diagnostic and Statistical Manual of Mental Disorders (4th edition) (DSM-IV) sees serious behavioral disorders as a category first diagnosed in infancy, childhood, or adolescence. Among the DSM-IV disorders of childhood are, eating disorders, tic disorders, elimination disorders, separation anxiety disorders, reactive attachment disorders, oppositional defiant disorder, and conduct disorder .

An alliance of educators and psychologists proposed that IDEA remove the term "serious emotional disturbances" and instead focus on behaviors that adversely affect educational performance. Conduct is usually considered a sign of emotional disorder, such as anxiety, depression, or failure of attachment, can be seen as behaviorally disordered if it interferes with academic, social, vocational, and personal accomplishment. So also can eating, elimination, or tic disorders and any other responses outside the range of "acceptable" for school or other settings. Such a focus on behavior can link the individualized educational plan curriculum activities to children's behavioral response styles.

Inclusive education does not translate into acceptance of disordered behaviors in the regular education classroom. Two rules of thumb for the behavior of all children, however capable or incapable, are that they conform to minimum standards of acceptable conduct and that disruptive behaviors be subject to fair and consistent disciplinary action. In order to ensure more orderly, well-regulated classroom environments, many schools are instituting conflict management courses.

What causes students to act out with hostile, aggressive behaviors directed against school personnel or other students? An easy, often-cited reason is that they are barraged with images of violence on the news, in music, on videos, on television programs, and in movies. It is too facile: Media barrage is aimed at everyone, yet only a few decide that they want to become violent and harm others. Aggressive, bullying children commonly come from homes where they see real violence, anger, and insults. They often feel disconnected, rejected, and afraid. They do not know how to communicate their distress. They may appear to be narcissistic, even as they seek attention in negative, hurtful ways. They usually have fairly easy access to weapons, alcohol, and other substances of abuse. They usually do not know any techniques of conflict management other than acting out.

The first article describes the more common psychiatric disorders which contribute to students' symptoms of EBDs. Forness, Walker, and Kavale discuss the problems with both assessment and treatment of these disorders. Both behavioral therapy and drug therapy may be needed as well as good communication and collaboration between parents, students, and teachers.

The authors of "Making Choices—Improving Behavior—Engaging in Learning" suggest that allowing students to make choices and engage in their own education can help break the cycle of negative responses.

Brent Richardson and Margery Shupe, in the third selection, point out how self-awareness in educators can reduce conflicts with students with EBD. They identify strategies to increase teachers' self-awareness.

The fourth article, "Classroom Problems That Don't Go Away" gives suggestions for ameliorating and/or preventing conflicts and anti-social acts within the regularized education curriculum by teaching alternative behaviors.

Psychiatric Disorders and Treatments

A Primer for Teachers

Steven R. Forness • Hill M. Walker • Kenneth A. Kavale

Children who have social or emotional problems require understanding and support from teachers and family members and may occasionally require counseling to help the child deal with his or her feelings and explore ways of coping. Psychiatric disorders, on the other hand, are generally much more disabling, more difficult to diagnose correctly, and sometimes require very specific therapeutic or medical treatments, meaning treatment with psychopharmacology (medications used to help the child control his or her emotional or behavioral symptoms).

Child psychopharmacology is a controversial field that is often sensationalized in the popular media. Coverage in the media often suggests that large numbers of children are being prescribed medication for only minor problems. Studies suggest that only a small fraction of children with serious psychiatric disorders are actually receiving such medication (Jensen et al., 1999; Zito et al., 1998). In the hands of a competent pediatrician or child psychiatrist, moreover, these medications

are not only effective but an essential component of an overall treatment program for many, if not most, children with psychiatric disorders.

> ## Psychiatric disorders are likely to be prevalent in children or adolescents receiving special education.

Careful treatment with these medications has been shown not only to effect dramatic improvement in behavioral or emotional responses of these children, but also to improve their social and academic functioning. Specific behavioral and related therapies are also critical. These may be used alone, prior to, or concurrent with psychopharmacologic treatment; and combined behavioral and psychopharmacologic treatments are often better than either used alone (Forness & Kavale, 2001; Forness, Kavale, & Davanzo, 2002).

Psychiatric disorders are classified in the fourth edition of the American

Psychiatric Association's *Diagnostic and Statistical Manual (DSM IV; 1994)*. *DSM IV* is used primarily by psychiatrists and psychologists to diagnose mental health problems in both children and adolescents. The diagnostic information contained here is taken directly from *DSM IV*, and treatment issues are referenced separately. All of these disorders were diagnosed only after a thorough evaluation that included

1. Screening for health, vision, or hearing problems.
2. Review of the child's developmental history.
3. Interviews with the parents and the child.
4. Review of information from teachers or school records.
5. Careful consideration of context and occurrence of symptoms.

Psychiatric disorders are likely to be prevalent in children or adolescents receiving special education (Garland et al., 2001). Educators working with these children should be familiar enough with such disorders so they can readily detect and refer children to mental health professionals and collaborate with these professionals in ongoing treatment. These disorders are discussed in the following paragraphs in terms of definition or diagnosis and therapeutic and psychopharmacologic treatment.

Oppositional Defiant and Conduct Disorders

Diagnosis

Both oppositional defiant and conduct disorders involve disruptive behavior. Oppositional defiant disorder often seems developmentally to precede a later diagnosis of conduct disorder. Both disorders probably occur in at least 4% of children or adolescents (Forness, Kavale, & Walker, 1999). Children with oppositional defiant disorder are those who have persistent patterns of negativistic, hostile, or defiant behavior directed primarily toward adults. Children with conduct disorder show consistent patterns of behavior in which they violate the rights of others or transgress age-appropriate social norms.

In oppositional defiant disorder, symptoms may include

- Persistent temper tantrums.
- Arguing with adults.
- Refusing to comply with reasonable adult requests.
- Annoying others.
- Vindictiveness.

The symptoms of an oppositional defiant disorder bother adults but are not considered as troublesome as conduct disorder, in which symptoms usually cluster into more serious patterns of

- Overt aggression toward people or animals.
- Destruction of property.
- Deceitfulness or theft.
- Serious violations of rules such as staying out all night and truancy from school.

As is the case with all psychiatric disorders, oppositional defiant disorder and conduct disorder are diagnosed in *DSM IV* when the child meets a set number of symptoms

from among a list of several symptoms typical of the disorder. Children must have 4 from a list of 8 symptoms to be diagnosed with oppositional defiant disorder and at least 3 from a list of 15 symptoms to be diagnosed with conduct disorder. These symptoms must also meet the criteria of causing significant impairment in social, academic, or related functioning. In conduct disorder, presence of only 3 symptoms is termed *mild conduct disorder*, whereas moderate and severe conduct disorder are characterized by increasing numbers of symptoms and increasingly greater harm to others.

> The symptoms of an oppositional defiant disorder bother adults but are not considered as troublesome as conduct disorder.

Treatment

The primary treatment for both oppositional defiant disorder and conduct disorder is behavioral therapy (Kavale, Forness, & Walker, 1999). Usually this takes the form of a reward or a reinforcement system in which the child earns points for appropriate behavior and is ignored or even given time-outs for inappropriate behavior. Points are usually exchanged for privileges or tangible awards at home or school. A major part of such behavioral therapy is parent or teacher consultation, so that adults can learn how to praise or reward good behavior and ignore inappropriate behavior. Social skills training is also helpful for children who do not seem to know how to behave or interact appropriately.

Unlike most psychiatric disorders, medication is not usually used to control symptoms of oppositional defiant disorder or conduct disorder directly. Both disorders, however, are very likely to co-occur or be comorbid (more than one condition existing at the same time) with a wide range of other psychiatric disorders

(Forness, Kavale, & Walker, 1999). Psychopharmacology for these disorders (such as attention deficit hyperactivity disorder, depression, or anxiety disorders) may often improve symptoms of oppositional defiant disorder or conduct disorder, as well.

Attention Deficit/Hyperactivity Disorder

Diagnosis

This disorder is found in 3%-5% of children or adolescents (Forness & Kavale, 2002). It is diagnosed when a child has persistent problems in inattentive or in hyperactive-impulsive behavior. At least some of these symptoms must have appeared prior to 7 years of age. The symptoms must also persist to a degree that markedly impairs the child's functioning in two or more settings, such as home and school.

Symptoms of inattention include

- Failing to give close attention to details in school work or related activities.
- Difficulty in sustaining attention.
- Seeming not to listen.
- Difficulty in organization.
- Distractibility.

Symptoms of hyperactivity or impulsivity include

- Excessive fidgeting.
- Inability to sit still in the classroom or other situations when this is expected.
- Running about or even climbing things excessively.
- Extreme restlessness or talkativeness.
- Difficulty waiting for turn.
- Interrupting conversations.

The child must usually meet criteria in *DSM IV* for six of nine symptoms in inattention or six of nine symptoms of hyperactivity-impulsivity. Children can thus be diagnosed with three subtypes of attention deficit/hyperactivity disorder (ADHD): predominantly inattentive, predominantly hyperactive-impulsive, or combined. It is usually important to rule out other psychiat-

Titration

The process of determining the right dose of medication, called titration, requires close collaboration between child, parents, and teachers (Wilens, 2001). The goal of titration is to use the lowest effective dose of medication while avoiding unwanted side effects.

Side effects occur because these medications, while very helpful, are still imperfect. Although stimulants target certain areas of the brain, they sometimes also spill over into other areas for which they were not intended, thus causing side effects such as loss of appetite, insomnia, dizziness, or irritability. These side effects may occur only at higher doses for some children or may occur with some children for some stimulants and not for others. At other times, these side effects may diminish as time goes by or as the child gets used to the drug. For some children, they may persist to the point where another medication or treatment must be tried instead.

In recent medication studies, researchers present side effects that occur on the drug as well as side effects that occur on placebo pills that contain no active medication. Interestingly, many children with ADHD seemed to show problems with irritability, insomnia, and poor appetite even when not on medication. Medication side effects are usually only slightly more frequent than problems that, upon careful observation, existed previously in these children before they were placed on medication.

Titration is somewhat easier with stimulants because these medications usually act within an hour or so and generally wash out of the body within a few hours or by the end of the day. The process of finding the right dose or switching to another medication may be accomplished within a few days or weeks.

Antidepressant medications, on the other hand, may take at least 3 or more weeks to obtain a full therapeutic effect. Other medications such as antipsychotics or neuroleptics for schizophrenia or other treatment-resistant disorders may take weeks to establish the most effective regimen. Thus, effective titration for these medications may commonly take weeks or even months. The side effects of these medications are also likely to be more debilitating and may also include

- Sedation.
- Dizziness.
- Problems in heart rhythms, especially in children with a family history of heart disease.
- Tremors.
- Significant weight gain.

Prescribing physicians should warn patients and their families about what to look for in terms of both therapeutic effects and adverse side effects. Physicians should also schedule regular follow-up visits to assess and monitor both the effects and the side effects of each medication. Competent physicians do careful patient and family education to prepare the child and his or her family for the titration process. During titration, they will usually provide the family and the child's teachers with checklists of symptoms and side effects so that significant adults in the child's environment can also monitor and provide regular feedback to the physician on how the medication is working.

Certain medications require more careful screening and monitoring of health status or drug effects through blood work, electrocardiograms, and the like. Physicians should give families careful instructions for regular administration of these medications, as well as numbers to call in case of unexpected emergencies.

---

ric disorders (such as depression, anxiety disorder, schizophrenia, or autism) before diagnosing ADHD, since these diagnoses may be more serious and usually take precedence. In many cases, a child may have both ADHD and one or more of these other disorders.

Treatment

The most effective treatment for ADHD generally combines both psychopharmacologic and behavioral interventions (MTA Cooperative Group, 1999a,1999b). Stimulant medications such as Ritalin, Adderall, or Dexedrine are usually the first medications considered. While it often seems paradoxical to treat an overactive child with stimulants, these drugs stimulate brain chemi-

cals, called neurotransmitters, to work more effectively, thus allowing the child to slow down and concentrate. Children not responding to stimulant medications have sometimes been treated with other psychopharmacologic medications, such as antidepressants like Tofranil or Wellbutrin. There are other medications that can be used if the child does not respond to these drugs or when ADHD co-occurs or is comorbid with certain other psychiatric disorders.

Selecting the appropriate medication involves a process called titration (see box). Table 1 depicts some of the primary stimulants and the approximate length of time each drug lasts or has noticeable effects in the child being treated. Some of the primary side effects (see Table 1)

may occur only during the titration phase of treatment and may disappear in all but a few children.

Children with ADHD may also respond to psychosocial or behavioral treatments (Forness & Kavale, 2002). Behavioral interventions include establishing predictable routines and expectations for children, both at home and at school, and reinforcing the child for meeting these expectations. By increasing goals gradually, the child does not have to be "perfect" at the outset but can accomplish small steps over a period of days or weeks. Parent education and teacher consultation can help adults in the child's life to set reasonable expectations, reinforce effective behavior, ignore hyperactive or distractible behavior, use time-out effectively, and collaborate by developing consis-

Table 1. Stimulants	
Generic (and Trade) Name	**Duration**
Methylphenidate or MPH (Ritalin)	3-4 hours
Dextroamphetamine (Dexedrine)	6-8 hours
Amphetamine (Adderall)	7-10 hours
Sustained MPH (Concerta)	10-12 hours

Side effects: appetite loss, stomachache, headache, insomnia

tent expectations and reinforcers between home and school.

Research evidence on treatment of ADHDs comes both from a reanalysis of 115 recent medication studies (Forness, Kavale, Sweeney, & Crenshaw, 1999) and from a long-term nationwide study of nearly 600 children funded by the National Institute of Mental Health (NIMH; MTA Cooperative Group, 1999a, 1999b). This evidence suggests that psychopharmacologic treatment seems to be a critical factor in effective intervention for ADHD. The message from this research is also clear that best practice is a combination of medication and behavioral therapies (Swanson et al., 2001). In the NIMH study, combined treatment also tended to improve scores on reading tests and on ratings of social skills on long-term follow-up, if children remained on medication (Arnold et al., 2000).

Evidence suggests that the presence of co-occurring or comorbid psychiatric disorders in children with ADHD may influence treatment outcome (Jensen et al., 2001). Children with ADHD and no other disorders tend to respond best, sometimes with only medication. Children with ADHD and comorbid anxiety disorders seem to respond almost as well, either to medication or to behavioral therapy. Children with ADHD and comorbid oppositional defiant disorder or conduct disorder also respond relatively well

but only if combined psychopharmacologic and behavioral treatments are used.

Depression or Other Mood Disorders

Diagnosis

Although childhood onset of depressive or other mood disorders does not occur as frequently as ADHD, it is not uncommon and may affect more than 2% of children and at least twice that number of adolescents (Birmaher & Brent, 1998). There are essentially three major types of mood disorders: depression, dysthymia, and bipolar or manic depressive disorder. Depression is diagnosed in *DSM IV* when the child has a depressed or irritable mood or loss of interest or pleasure in most activities. Other symptoms may include

- Unexplained fluctuations in weight.
- Insomnia.
- Loss of energy.
- Diminished ability to think or concentrate.
- Feelings of excessive guilt or worthlessness.

Of nine different symptoms, at least five must occur nearly every day during a 2-week period for depression to be diagnosed.

Dysthymia is diagnosed by a depressed or irritable mood on most days for at least a year and must also be accompanied by at least two of six other symptoms. Including

- Insomnia.
- Low energy or fatigue.
- Low self-esteem.
- Poor concentration.
- Feelings of hopelessness.

The diagnosis of bipolar or manic depressive disorder depends on fluctuations in mood, from depressed episodes, as noted previously, to manic episodes. Manic episodes are characterized by distinct periods in which the child or adolescent has an abnormal and persistently elevated or expansive mood and in which three of seven other symptoms are present, such as

- Decreased need for sleep.
- Excessive talkativeness.
- Distractibility.
- Psychomotor agitation.

> The most effective treatment for attention deficit hyperactivity disorder generally combines both psychopharmacologic and behavioral interventions.

All of these disorders must cause significant distress or functional impairment and require that certain other disorders, such as schizophrenia or substance abuse, be ruled out before making the diagnosis. Bipolar disorders in children are relatively rare and may be difficult to diagnose because of less distinct patterns of cycling than occur in adults; however, they become more common during adolescence and early adulthood.

Treatment

Treatment for depression usually involves cognitive behavioral therapies and psychopharmacologic treatment. Psychopharmacology for dysthymia is less predictable because symptoms may not always be consistently present, but it may be used depending on the child's or adolescent's age and presentation of symptoms (Wagner & Ambrosini, 2001).

In medicating for depression, physicians usually begin with one of the drugs known as selective serotonin reuptake inhibitors (SSRIs), such as Zoloft, Prozac, or Paxil. If the child or adolescent fails to respond to two or more of these medications, tricyclic antidepressants such as Tofranil or atypical antidepressants, such as Wellbutrin, may be tried.

In bipolar or manic depressive disorder, physicians may begin with lithium and, in some cases, attempt a trial of other mood stabilizers such

Table 2. Antidepressants/Mood Stabilizers

Class (Examples)	Full Effects
SSRI (Zoloft, Paxil, Luvox, Prozac)	2 to 4 weeks
Tricyclics (Tofranil, Elavil)	2 to 4 weeks
Atypicals (Wellbutrin, Effexor, Serzone)	2 to 4 weeks
Stabilizers (Lithium, Depakote)	7 to 10 days

Side effects: stomachache, agitation, headache, dry mouth, dizziness.

as Depakote. Examples of these medications in each classification are provided in Table 2, along with the approximate time it may take to obtain a full therapeutic effect. Table 2 also lists some of the most frequently occurring side effects.

Psychopharmacologic treatment in each of these disorders, however, can be quite complex because large numbers of children or adolescents may not respond favorably enough to continue treatment or may suffer from side effects that tend to lead to discontinuation of the drug. In a significant number of cases, more than one medication may be required for effective treatment. Pediatricians usually do not have sufficient training to manage such treatment effectively, so most children with these disorders should be referred to board certified child or adolescent psychiatrists for the best outcome.

Cognitive behavioral therapies may also be effective for treatment of depressive disorders (Asarnow, Jaycox, & Tompson, 2001). Such treatment focuses on the child or adolescent monitoring his or her mood, involvement in activities, stress, or other symptomatic behaviors and is then taught to coach himself or herself through "self talk," which is designed to give a sense of control over the symptoms and negate feelings of despair, low self-esteem, helplessness, and the like. Supportive therapy and education about the nature of the child's partic-

ular disorder can help and may assist in better outcomes for psychopharmacologic treatment, if warranted.

Monitoring suicidal symptoms is especially critical in children or adolescents with these disorders. These disorders also sometimes tend to have a diagnostic progression, with dysthymia putting a child at higher risk for depression and depression putting a child at higher risk for bipolar or manic depressive disorder. Early detection and treatment is therefore very critical.

Anxiety Disorders

Diagnosis

Anxiety disorders occur in approximately 4% of children and in a slightly larger percentage of adolescents (Bernstein & Shaw, 1997). *DSM IV* lists several types of anxiety disorders, including obsessive-compulsive disorder, generalized anxiety disorder, separation anxiety disorder, and posttraumatic stress disorder. Obsessive-compulsive disorder is marked by obsessions or compulsions that cause marked distress, are excessively time consuming, or significantly interfere with the child's or adolescent's functioning or social relationships. Obsessions are recurrent and persistent thoughts or impulses that seem to have no relationship to real-life problems or that the child or adolescent seems unable to ignore or suppress, despite the fact that he or she recognizes these as merely a product of his or her own mind.

Compulsions are repetitive behaviors (such as hand washing, ordering of objects, checking on things) or mental acts (such as counting objects or repeating words silently) that, according to rigid rules, the child or adolescent feels driven to perform and are aimed at preventing or reducing some imagined distress. These behaviors or mental acts do not seem to be connected in a realistic way to this distress or are clearly excessive.

Children or adolescents may be diagnosed with generalized anxiety disorder when they demonstrate excessive worry about events or activities (such as social functioning or school performance) and find it difficult to control these responses. Worrying must cause clinically significant impairment in social or academic functioning and also be associated with at least three of six anxiety symptoms:

- Restlessness.
- Fatigue.
- Concentration problems.
- Irritability.
- Muscle tension.
- Sleep disturbance.

Separation anxiety disorder is diagnosed when a child has developmentally inappropriate and excessive anxiety concerning separation from home or family. This must cause clinically significant distress or impairment and be accompanied by at least three of eight symptoms, such as

- Excessive worrying about injury or loss of a major family member.
- Anxiety about separation from family through being kidnapped or getting lost.
- Persistent refusal or reluctance to attend school because of fear of separation.
- Sleep disturbance.
- Complaints of physical symptoms whenever separation from a major family member occurs or is anticipated.

The diagnosis of posttraumatic stress disorder is made when a child or adolescent has experienced or witnessed a traumatic event that involved intense fear, helplessness, or horror. Subsequently, following that actual event, other symptoms have to occur. The traumatic event has to be persistently re-experienced in terms of at least one of the following:

- Intrusive recollections.
- Recurrent dreams.
- Feeling that the event is actually recurring.

- Intense distress upon exposure to cues that remind the child of the event or a physiologic reaction to such cues, like shaking or sweating.

There must also be persistent avoidance of at least three things that remind the child or adolescent of the traumatic event, such as

- Avoiding thoughts or situations.
- Inability to recall important details of the trauma.
- Feeling detached from others.
- Restriction of emotional range.

Finally, the child must demonstrate at least two of five symptoms of increased arousal, such as

- Sleep disturbance.
- Irritability.
- Difficulty concentrating.
- Hypervigilance.
- Exaggerated startle response.

> Community agencies and regional centers often provide education for parents in using behavioral approaches to further develop social and functional skills at home.

Treatment

Treatment for each of these anxiety disorders varies, depending on the specific diagnosis, but generally involves cognitive or behavioral therapies and possible psychopharmacologic treatment (Ollendick & King, 1998). The cognitive therapies generally focus on providing the child both with ways to monitor his or her own internal anxieties and with a sense of control through "self talk." For example, a young child with an obsessive-compulsive disorder may be taught to pretend that his or her ob-

sessions or compulsions are like a "little monster" trying to trick him or her into performing these rituals. The child is then shown ways to make the monster less threatening or powerful.

Other cognitive or behavioral approaches focus, in similar ways, on the unreality of the anxiety and how to anticipate responding in a more adaptive way. Reinforcement schemes may also be employed to assist or motivate the child in establishing a sense of control and participating more gradually over a period of time in anxiety-provoking events.

Psychopharmacologic treatment may involve anxiolytic or antidepressant medications (Green, 2001). The anxiolytic or anxiety-breaking medications are drugs such as Klonopin, Ativan, or Buspar. These medications are relatively fast-acting and must often be taken two or three times per day. Their major side effects include sedation or drowsiness and, in a few children, may cause a sudden onset of agitation, silliness, talkativeness, or even increased anxiety, a response that usually wears off within a couple of hours.

Stopping these drugs abruptly may also lead to increased agitation or anxiety, so their use should be withdrawn gradually, as is the case with most other psychopharmacologic medications discussed. Usually anxiolytics are used in children on a short-term basis only. The antidepressants that have been found most helpful for anxiety disorders are SSRI medications (such as Paxil or Luvox) or atypical antidepressants (such as Effexor). For children and younger adolescents, SSRIs and atypical antidepressants have become the first choice for treatment of most anxiety disorders.

Schizophrenic or Other Psychotic Disorders

Diagnosis

These disorders are exceedingly rare, especially in children—the rate

is probably less than a tenth of a percent (McClellan & Werry, 2000). *DSM IV* diagnoses children or adolescents with schizophrenia when at least two of the following symptoms are present:

- Delusions (such as thinking one has special powers or feeling that people are out to do one harm).
- Hallucinations (such as hearing voices or seeing things that no one else experiences).
- Disorganized speech.
- Grossly disorganized behavior.
- Certain symptoms of social withdrawal.

These symptoms must generally be present over a period of at least 6 months and must markedly affect one or more areas of functioning, like school or interpersonal relationships. Separate diagnoses exist for brief or atypical psychotic disorders, which last less than a month or do not meet full criteria.

Treatment

Treatment is usually a combination of behavioral training (including social skills training) and psychopharmacology (Vitiello, Bhatara, & Jensen, 1999). Medications for schizophrenia are currently the new or atypical neuroleptic or antipsychotic drugs such as Risperdal, Zyprexa, and Seroquel. These medications may diminish agitation almost immediately but take days to diminish hallucinations. After several weeks, these medications will improve disorganized thinking and social withdrawal. Side effects, however, can be severe, including sedation or even abnormal facial or motor movements.

These side effects tend to limit their use especially in children but, in rare cases, are seen as unavoidable or preferable in the face of full-blown psychosis, which can be devastatingly frightening to children or adolescents with the disorder and to those around them. In some instances, these newer neuroleptic drugs are also being used for treatment resistant depression and anxiety disorders.

Autistic Spectrum Disorders

Diagnosis

These disorders also occur quite infrequently but may not be as rare as childhood- onset schizophrenia (Volkmar, Cook, Pomeroy, Realmuto, & Tanguay, 1999). Autistic spectrum disorder is diagnosed by at least six symptoms across three areas:
1. Social impairment, such as
- Lack of eye contact.
- Failure to develop peer relationships.
- Lack of sharing enjoyment or interests with others.
- Lack of social or emotional give and take.
2. Communicative impairment, such as
- Delays in spoken language.
- Inability to initiate or sustain conversations.
- Repetitive or odd use of phrases.
- Lack of make-believe or social-imitative play.
3. Restrictive or repetitive behavior, such as
- Intense preoccupations with restricted patterns of interest.
- Inflexible routines or rituals.
- Repetitive motor mannerisms such as hand-or finger-flapping.
- Preoccupation only with parts of objects.

At least some of these symptoms must have occurred prior to 3 years of age. About three of every four children with autism may also have severe cognitive delays as well.

Asperger's disorder is diagnosed if at least three symptoms are present from the social impairment and restricted or repetitive behavior lists above but there are no significant delays in language or cognitive development. Pervasive developmental disorder may be diagnosed if it is not clear that symptoms were present prior to 3 years of age or if sufficient symptoms are not clearly present.

Treatment for children with autistic spectrum disorders relies primarily on developing basic language and social skills using behavioral strategies and reinforcement systems. Academic skills are taught according to the child's cognitive or intellectual levels. Community agencies and regional centers often provide education for parents in using behavioral approaches to further develop social and functional skills at home. There are as yet no recognized psychopharmacologic medications to treat autism directly. Some children with autism may also be at risk for other psychiatric disorders or symptoms, however, and they might be responsive to psychopharmacologic medications for such disorders (Sweeney, Forness, & Levitt, 1998).

Other Diagnoses in *DSM IV*

DSM-IV includes learning disorders, mental retardation, and communication disorders. Although they are not strictly considered mental health disorders, they are sometimes closely associated with certain psychiatric disorders. Children with these disorders are also at significantly higher risk for comorbid or co-occurring psychiatric disorders (Beichtman, Cantwell, Forness, Kavale, & Kauffman, 1998; King, DeAntonio, McCracken, Forness, & Ackerman, 1994). Eating disorders such as anorexia nervosa are listed as psychiatric disorders in *DSM IV* and involve refusal to maintain normal weight for height and age (usually defined as less than 85% of expected weight), coupled with an intense fear of gaining weight and a disturbance of body image related to weight. This disorder affects primarily adolescent girls who are often apt to focus obsessively on academic achievement, in addition to their obsession with weight or diet (Lewis, 2002).

Tourettes disorder is also listed in *DSM IV* and involves chronic motor and sometimes vocal tics occurring many times a day, usually in bouts. This disorder is often treated by SSRI

or antihypertensive medications such as Clonidine (Sweeney et al., 1998).

Substance-related disorders, such as alcohol or drug abuse are listed in *DSM IV* as psychiatric disorders and involve recurrent substance use that results in poor work or school performance, hazardous behavior such as impaired driving, or recurrent social or personal problems.

Final Thoughts

This is neither an exhaustive list nor a comprehensive description of childhood psychiatric disorders but, rather, an introduction for teachers and other school professionals to some of the major diagnoses that can impair school learning or classroom behavior. Detection and treatment of these disorders may sometimes greatly improve academic progress and social adjustment of children with more serious school learning or behavior problems. A behavioral checklist for teachers and parents has therefore been developed that is based on *DSM IV* and provides both primary and possible comorbid psychiatric diagnoses (Gadow & Sprafkin, 1994). Introductory materials to further educate teachers and parents about psychopharmacology have also been developed for those interested in particular medications (Konopasek, 2002; Wilens, 2001).

References

American Psychiatric Association. (1994). *Diagnostic and statistical manual of mental disorders* (4th ed.). Washington, DC: Author.

Arnold, L. E., Jensen, P. S., Hechtman, L., Hoagwood, K., Greenhill, L., & MTA Cooperative Group. (2000, October). *Do MTA treatment effects persist? New followup at 2 years.* Paper presented at the annual meeting of the American Academy of Child and Adolescent Psychiatry, New York.

Asarnow, J. R., Jaycox, L. H., & Tompson, M. C. (2001). Depression in youth: Psychosocial interventions. *Journal of Clinical Child Psychology, 30,* 33–47.

Beichtman, J. H., Cantwell, D. P., Forness, S. R., Kavale, K. A., & Kauffman,

J. M. (1998). Practice parameters for the diagnostic assessment and treatment of children and adolescents with language and learning disorders. *Journal of the American Academy of Child and Adolescent Psychiatry, 37*(10 Supplement), 42S–62S.

Bernstein, G. A., & Shaw, K. (1997). Practice parameters for the assessment and treatment of children and adolescents with anxiety disorders. *Journal of the American Academy of Child and Adolescent Psychiatry, 36*(10 Supplement), 69–84.

Birmaher, B., & Brent, D. (1998). Practice parameters for the assessment and treatment of children and adolescents with depressive disorders. *Journal of the American Academy of Child and Adolescent Psychiatry, 37*(10 Supplement), 63–83.

Forness, S. R., & Kavale, K. A. (2001). Ignoring the odds: Hazards of not adding the medical model to special education decisions. *Behavioral Disorders, 26,* 269– 281.

Forness, S. R., & Kavale, K. A. (2002). Impact of ADHD on school systems. In P. S. Jensen & J. R. Cooper (Eds.), *Attention deficit hyperactivity disorder: State of the science best practices. (pp. 1–20, 24).* Kingston, NJ: Civic Research Institute.

Forness, S. R., & Kavale, K. A., & Davanzo, P. A. (2002). Interdisciplinary treatment and the limits of behaviorism. *Behavioral Disorders, 27,* 168–178.

Forness, S. R., Kavale, K. A., Sweeney, D. P., & Crenshaw, T. M. (1999). The future of research and practice in behavioral disorders: Psychopharmacology and its school treatment implications. *Behavioral Disorders, 24,* 305–318.

Forness, S. R., Kavale, K. A., & Walker, H. M. (1999). Identifying children at risk for antisocial behavior: The case for comorbidity. In R. G. Gallimore, C. Bernheimer, D. L. MacMillan, & D. Speece (Eds.), *Developmental perspectives on children with high incidence disabilities* (pp. 135– 155). Mahwah, NJ: Lawrence Erlbaum.

Gadow, K., & Sprafkin, J. (1994). Child Symptom Inventory manual. Stony Brook, NY: Checkmate Plus.

Garland, A. F., Hough, R. L., McCabe, K. M., Yeh, M., Wood, P. A., & Aarons, G. A. (2001). Prevalence of psychiatric disorders in youths across five sectors of care. *Journal of the American Academy of Child and Adolescent Psychiatry, 40,* 409–418.

Green, W. H. (2001). *Child and adolescent clinical psychopharmacology* (3rd ed.). New York: Guilford Press.

Jensen, P. S., Hinshaw, S. P., Kraemer, H. C., Lenora, N., Newcorn, J. H., Abikoff, H. B., March, J. S., Arnold, L. E., Cantwell, D. P., Conner, C. K., Elliott, G. R., Greenhill, L. L., Hechtman, L., Hoaz, B., Pelham, W. E., Severe, J. B., Swanson, J. M., Wells, K. C., Wigal, T., & Vitiello, B. (2001). ADHD comorbidity findings from the MTA study: Comparing comorbid subgroups. *Journal of the American Academy of Child and Adolescent Psychiatry, 40,* 147–158.

Jensen, P. S., Kettle, L., Roper, M. T., Sloan, M. T., Dulcan, M. K., Hoven, C., Bird, H. R., Bauermeister, J. J., & Payne, J. D. (1999). Are stimulants overprescribed? Treatment of ADHD in four U.S. communities. *Journal of the American Academy of Child and Adolescent Psychiatry, 38,* 797–804.

Kavale, K. A., Forness, S. R., & Walker, H. M. (1999). Interventions for ODD and CD in the schools. In H. Quay & A. Hogan (Eds.), *Handbook of disruptive behavior disorders* (pp. 441–454). New York: Plenum.

King, B. H., DeAntonio, C., McCracken, J. T., Forness, S. R., & Ackerman, V. (1994). Psychiatric consultation to persons with severe and profound mental retardation. *American Journal of Psychiatry, 151,* 1802– 1808.

Konopasek, D. E. (2002). *Medication "Fact Sheets": A medication reference guide for the non-medical professional.* Anchorage, AK: Arctic Tern.

Lewis, M. (Ed.). (2002). *Child and adolescent psychiatry: A comprehensive textbook* (3rd ed.). New York: Guilford Press.

McClellan, J., & Werry, J. (2000). Summary of the practice parameters for the assessment and treatment of children and adolescents with schizophrenia. *Journal of the American Academy of Child and Adolescent Psychiatry, 39,* 1580–1582.

MTA Cooperative Group, (1999a). A 14–month randomized clinical trial of treatment strategies for attention deficit/hyperactivity disorder. *Archives of General Psychiatry, 56,* 1073–1086.

MTA Cooperative Group. (1999b). Moderators and mediators of treatment response for children with attention deficit/hyperactivity disorder. *Archives of General Psychiatry, 56,* 1088–1095.

Ollendick, T., & King, N. (1998). Empirically supported treatments for children with phobic and anxiety disorders: Current status. *Journal of Clinical Child Psychology, 27,* 156–167.

Swanson, J. M., Kraemer, H. C., Hinshaw, S. P., Arnold, L. E., Conners, C. K., Abikoff, H. B., Clevenger, W., Davies, M., Elliot, G. R., Greenhill, L. L., Hechtman, L., Hoza, B., Jensen, P. S., March, J. S., Newcorn, J. H., Owns, E. B., Pelham, W., Schiller, E., Severe, J. B., Simpson, S., Vitiello, B., Wells, K., Wigal, T., & Wu, M. (2001). Clinical relevance of the primary findings of the MTA: Success rates based on severity of ADHD and ODD symptoms at the end of treatment. *Journal of the American Academy of Child and Adolescent Psychiatry, 40,* 168–179.

Sweeney, D. P., Forness, S. R., & Levitt, J. G. (1998). An overview of medications commonly used to treat behavioral disorders associated with autism, Tourette's disorder, and pervasive developmental disorders. *Focus on Autism and Other Developmental Disabilities, 13,* 144–150.

Vitiello, B., Bhatara, V. S., & Jensen, P. S. (1999). Special section: Current knowledge and unmet needs in pediatric psychopharmacology. *Journal of the American Academy of Child and Adolescent Psychiatry, 38,* 501–565.

Volkmar, F., Cook, E. H., Pomeroy, J., Realmuto, G., & Tanguay, P. (1999). Practice parameters for the assessment and treatment of children, adolescents, and adults with autism and other pervasive developmental disorders. *Journal of the American Academy of Child and Adolescent Psychiatry, 38*(12 Supplement), 32–54.

Wagner, K. D., & Ambrosini, P. J. (2001). Childhood depression: Pharmacological therapy/treatment (Pharmacotherapy of childhood depression). *Journal of Clinical Child Psychology, 30,* 88–97.

Wilens, T. E. (2001). *Straight talk about psychiatric medication for kids.* New York: Guilford Press.

Zito, J. M., Safer, D. J., Riddle, M. A., Johnson, R. E., Speedie, S. M., & Fox, M. (1998). Prevalence variations in psychotropic treatment of children. *Journal of Child and Adolescent Psychopharmacology, 8,* 99–105.

Steven R. Forness, *(CEC Chapter #520), Professor and Chief Educational Psychologist, UCLA Neuropsychiatric Hospital, Los Angeles, California.* **Hill M. Walker** *(CEC OR Federation), Professor and Director, Institute on Violence and Destructive Behavior, University of Oregon, Eugene.* **Kenneth A. Kavale,** *Professor, Division of Curriculum and Instruction, University of Iowa, Iowa City.*

Address correspondence to Steven R. Forness, UCLA Neuropsychiatric Hospital, 760 Westwood Plaza, Los Angeles, CA 90049.9.

Making Choices— Improving Behavior— Engaging in Learning

Kristine Jolivette, Janine Peck Stichter, and Katherine M. McCormick

Do you have students who display inappropriate types of behavior, or who seem depressed, or who lack friends? Perhaps these are students with emotional and behavioral disorders (EBD; see box), and maybe the students present challenges that you find difficult to deal with and that interfere with their educational progress.

This article highlights one strategy, providing opportunities to make choices, that is effective in increasing appropriate behaviors for students with EBD (Munk & Repp, 1994), most notably when used by classroom teachers during ongoing classroom routines (Jolivette, Wehby, Canale, & Massey, 2001b; see also the box, "What Does the Literature Say?" for a link between the research literature on choice and related behavioral characteristics of students with EBD.)

We present a hypothetical case example to show how a teacher might incorporate choice-making opportunities for a student with EBD who is failing math in school. In the course of this article, we suggest practical strategies that both special and general education teachers may use in their academic curricula to encourage students to make appropriate choices. These opportunities may have benefits that long outlast the particular task or situation, to enhance relationships within the classroom, engage students in learning, and promote a positive classroom environment.

Opportunities to Make Choices

Choice-making opportunities provide students the opportunity to make decisions that may affect their daily routines (e.g., choice of academic task). For example, a student may choose

- From a list of explorers which explorer to write a report on.
- To begin another game with a different peer during free time.
- To use colored markers while illustrating a picture as part of a book report.
- The type of medium (poster, costume, movie) to use for a presentation on a country in social studies.

These varied choice-making opportunities occur frequently in most classrooms. They may seem trivial at first glance, but such choices can have significant implications for the type and level of student participation (Jolivette, Stichter, Sibilsky, Scott, & Ridgely, 2001a).

Several recent classroom investigations into the use of "choice" for students with EBD have shown that this strategy is effective in increasing (or decreasing) specific behaviors in school (Cosden, Gannon, & Haring, 1995; Dunlap et al., 1994; Jolivette et al., 2001b). These results suggest that providing students with EBD the opportunity to make

What Are Characteristics of Students with Emotional and Behavioral Disorder?

Students with EBD often have these characteristics:

- An inability to learn that cannot be explained by intellectual, sensory, or health factors.
- An inability to build or maintain satisfactory interpersonal relationships with peers and teachers.
- Inappropriate types of behavior or feelings under normal circumstances.
- A general pervasive mood of unhappiness or depression.
- A tendency to develop physical symptoms or fears associated with personal or school problems (Individuals with Disabilities Education Act, IDEA, 1997, CFR 300.7 (a) 9).

In addition, students with EBD may display these characteristics during academic situations when teacher demands are consistently high and if they have a history of school failure (e.g., performing below grade level).

choices during academic situations can promote increased levels of functional and prosocial student behavior. Here are some findings:

- Cosden et al. (1995) found that student accuracy and completion of academic tasks increased when the students were provided with opportunities to choose the task or reinforcer.
- Dunlap et al. (1994) found that the levels of task engagement increased while levels of disruptive behavior decreased when students were provided with opportunities to choose the academic task to complete.
- Jolivette et al. (2001b) found that student task engagement increased, as did the number and accuracy of attempted problems, when students were provided with opportunities to choose the order in which to complete three tasks (same concept but variable formats).

Case Study: Isaac

Isaac is a 7-year-old first-grader with EBD who attends a combined first/second-grade special education class for students with EBD. He had a full-scale IQ of 79 (verbal = 85 and performance = 74), according to the WISC-III. Isaac's teacher reports that he performs below grade level in mathematics and that he is noncompliant and off task during independent math seatwork activities.

Isaac performs at the grade equivalence of beginning kindergarten (K.0) on the Woodcock-Johnson Calculation, Applied Problems, and General Math subtests (Woodcock & Johnson, 1989). In addition, Isaac is rated in the clinical range for the areas of hyperactivity, aggression, conduct problems, and somatization on the Behavior Assessment System for Children (BASC).

Isaac commonly displays the following behaviors during 15-minute regularly scheduled independent math activities:

- Ripping up or throwing the math worksheet to the floor when prompted to begin to work.
- Verbally disrupting the peer next to him.
- Making black pencil marks over the surface of the worksheet instead of solving the problems.
- Asking a peer for assistance on the first few problems.

- Asking the teacher for access to various manipulative items for use with the worksheet and if given a negative verbal response, verbally threatening the teacher.
- Walking around the classroom when the expectation was for him to be at his desk.
- Questioning the teacher as to what he was going to do after math.

The teacher also reports that because of Isaac's inappropriate behaviors during math, Isaac was experiencing academic failure in math and was not meeting his individualized education program (IEP) math objectives.

To address Isaac's inappropriate behavior, the teacher removed privileges (e.g., free time), moved Isaac's desk away from the other desk pods, and retaught basic math skills on a one-to-one basis during his free time. The teacher states, however, that Isaac's inappropriate behaviors have only escalated; and he continues to make little progress in math.

Strategies for Infusing Opportunities to Make Choices into Math

Given Isaac's behavior and lack of success in math, we suggest providing Isaac with opportunities to make choices during his regularly scheduled, independent math periods to increase his appropriate social and academic behaviors. Because the punitive consequences (loss of privileges and isolation) were ineffective, perhaps the teacher can try another approach: providing opportunities to make choices. This may be a more proactive plan in addressing Isaac's inappropriate behaviors and math failure, and perhaps it will encourage Isaac to display appropriate behavior and achieve success during math activities and tasks.

For this particular student, the focus for choice-making opportunities will be on academic activities related to math instruction and related IEP objectives. There are several ways to implement these opportunities into the existing curricula for Isaac, either before or during tasks, to provide environmental predictability and a sense of control for him. Note that the provision of choice does not alter the curricular objective for Isaac: accurately completing math worksheets.

Choices Before the Task Demand

To provide Isaac with predictability in his independent math seatwork period, Isaac's teacher may provide him with the opportunity to decide *when he will begin* his math worksheet. For example, many students are expected to perform a variety of tasks in the classroom that can be completed throughout the day. Such tasks may include watering the plants, returning library books, and picking up and returning lunch tickets. In Isaac's case, he was expected to straighten the workbook shelf and sharpen the pencils each day. His teacher could then state those two tasks along with the math task demand and provide Isaac with the choice of when to start his math: before he completes those two tasks or after completion of the two tasks. The choice of when to begin his worksheet may provide Isaac with a sense of predictability and a sense of control over his math routine and thus decrease his displays of inappropriate behaviors.

If Isaac were observed to request information regarding what events were scheduled for him after completing his math worksheets, it may indicate that the teacher was not following a consistent classroom routine or that Isaac's daily schedule was more complicated than he could effectively follow on his own. Providing Isaac with this information before or while giving him his task demand may influence his behavior based on whether the event is preferred (e.g., free time) or nonpreferred (e.g., spelling test).

> *Students may engage in inappropriate behavior to obtain a predictable response from the teacher.*

To promote appropriate behavior, his teacher may provide an opportunity for Isaac to *choose the event that will occur immediately following* completion of his math task, even if it is just for a few minutes, before another regularly scheduled class activity. For example, Isaac may select between a computer-simulated math game, a math card game with a peer, or a math board game. Thus, Isaac is rewarded for task completion with a selected event.

If the observation data suggested that Isaac's inappropriate behavior (e.g., out of seat behavior, disruption) increased because of his frustration with the math task, it may be helpful for his teacher to provide Isaac with *the choice of terminating the task* for brief periods of time (e.g., 30 seconds) so as to provide him with a "cooling off" period. Teaching Isaac to better regulate his own behavior within the context of a choice-making opportunity provides a functional and lifelong skill that most people could use.

Having opportunities to make choices in academic tasks can provide the environmental predictability needed to minimiize inappropriate behaviors of students, while strengthening appropriate responses and increased levels of engagement.

As the task is presented to Isaac, his teacher may remind Isaac that he has the option to take "mini-breaks" while working on the worksheet. For example, his teacher may ask Isaac how many problems he will attempt before choosing to take a break. Isaac may select three problems. The teacher then would remind Isaac: "After you work out three problems, you may choose to take a 30-second break before starting on your worksheet again." These mini-breaks are controlled by Isaac and provide him with the ability to self-regulate his behavior while still working on the task and may decrease his subsequent inappropriate behaviors.

The teacher can also allow Isaac to *select items* he feels he will need to complete his math task successfully. For example, the teacher may present Isaac with the math task and prompt him to prepare his work area. In this case, the teacher may ask him what type of writing utensil (e.g., pencil, pen, colored pencil), what kind of eraser (e.g., stuck on the pencil, hand-held eraser), and what color of scrap paper for his work (e.g., white, yellow, blue) he will need to complete his math task. By preparing his work area through choice-making opportunities, the teacher is minimizing Isaac's out-of-seat behavior—his selected supplies are at hand.

Choices During the Task Demand

To provide Isaac with predictability and consistency, as well as to give him perceived control *during* the task, his teacher may give him a variety of choice-making opportunities. For example, if Isaac is expected to complete more than one worksheet during the independent math period, his teacher may allow him to *select the order* in which to complete the worksheets. After presenting Isaac with all the worksheets he needs to complete, his teacher may ask him which worksheet he wants to complete first, second, and so on. Then the teacher (or Isaac) can write the numbers 1 and 2 on top of the worksheets to indicate his order preference.

To reinforce the order Isaac has chosen, the teacher may give Isaac one worksheet at a time and, on completion, give him the second or third worksheet while saying, "Good job! You are ready for the worksheet you chose to complete second."

Isaac may also have been observed to seek out assistance from his peers during independent math periods, thus affecting his peers' ability to complete their math tasks. No matter if Isaac is displaying these behaviors as a means to gain peer attention or to escape the math task–his teacher can manipulate the environment so that Isaac is appropriately interacting with his peers during this time. For instance, when the task is given to Isaac, he may be permitted to *select a peer with whom to work* on the task. Isaac may complete the even-numbered problems while his peer completes the odd-numbered problems, and then each can "check" the answers of the other. In this case, the task demand has not been changed; Isaac still needs to complete all the math problems (solving and check-

ing). Or Isaac may be permitted to *select the communication mode* with which to gain teacher attention (e.g., assistance). When the teacher gives Isaac a math task to work on at his desk, the teacher may prompt Isaac to select either raising his hand, holding up a red note card (provided by the teacher), or making a thumbs-up gesture to solicit assistance with the task. Such a choice provides Isaac with a means to appropriately gain teacher attention without disrupting his peers or leaving his seat.

In addition, Isaac may have been observed to wander around the room during seatwork periods, disrupting his peers who remain in their seats. While presenting Isaac with his math task, his teacher may provide him with an opportunity to *select where in the room* he wants to complete his math work-sheet(s). In many classrooms, empty desks or portions of large tables may be available as choices. If Isaac has a history of displaying increased levels of inappropriate behaviors when in close proximity to certain peers, then empty desks in that area would not be part of his choice. In that case, the teacher may limit the possible areas in the room that Isaac can select from.

When multiple math worksheets are not part of the task, nor are other choices involving peer partners or different locations feasible, Isaac's teacher may permit him to *choose the methods* in which he will complete the task. For example, Isaac could start at the bottom of the page and work to the top of the page, work from right to left, or randomly select the order of the problems from the worksheet. The teacher may also remind Isaac to be careful not to skip problems. Again, the task does not change, but how Isaac can complete the task has been manipulated.

In addition, Isaac may have occasionally asked his teacher for access to math manipulatives to use while he worked on his task. When appropriate, Isaac's teacher may provide him with opportunities to select the *type of manipulatives (materials)* he wants to use to complete the task. For example, he may select base-ten blocks, blocks, or beans. Or he may select a one-hundred chart, counting strip, or counting bracelet.

Benefits of Infusing Choice-Making Opportunities into the Classroom

Initial research in classrooms on the use of choice-making opportunities for students with EBD indicates that providing opportunities to make choices during ongoing academic activities is an effective, efficient classroom strategy (Cosden et al., 1995; Dunlap et al., 1994; Jolivette et al., 2001b). The following benefits may result:

- Providing a student with EBD an opportunity to choose among *already existing materials* may be a cost-effective-method to minimize some of the inappropriate behaviors typically displayed by these students during academic situations. Teachers can manipulate existing environmental conditions, materials, and natural consequences without using scarce time and money to create "new" instructional materials (e.g., where to sit in the room to complete a task, order of completion for existing tasks, methods to use to complete a given task).
- Providing choices may *promote more positive relations among all students, better teacher-student interactions, and a more focused classroom environment* (Shores et al., 1993). Providing opportunities to make choices can help teachers assign tasks in a more positive way, while providing predictability for the student in the current task situation.

For example, when a student selects to raise his or her hand to communicate "I need help," then the teacher reinforces the student's choice and comes over and offers assistance. And when the student completes the task with accuracy, the teacher provides the student a choice of what to do next (e.g., put a puzzle together, work on any home-work assignments, check out a book from the library).

- By providing the student with opportunities to make choices, *the teacher is relinquishing some of the decision-making power in the classroom*. Being able to make choices during academic tasks may provide students with skills needed

in other academically focused programs.

For example, a small group of students may have the task of creating a bulletin board as part of their report on the human body. Instead of the teacher telling the students that they will create a bulletin board on the digestive system and will highlight it with an interactive component, the teacher may allow the group to select the specific content for the bulletin board but provide parameters for their choice. These parameters may include (a) select one of the following body systems-nervous, digestive, circulatory; (b) provide a detailed visual with supporting information on the selected system; (c) incorporate an interactive activity; and (d) double check all information for accuracy and organization. Thus, the teacher has provided the small group with multiple opportunities to make choices while completing an academic task. This example would be appropriate for older students, but can be adapted for younger students like Isaac.

- The provision of choice-making opportunities may *simultaneously affect social and task-related behaviors of students with EBD*. Students with EBD seek opportunities to influence (control) their classroom environments; unfortunately they may do so by displaying inappropriate behaviors. Guess, Benson, and Siegel-Causey (1985) suggested that choice-making opportunities not only provide a student with the power to manipulate variables but the ability to exert control over environmental events through appropriate means. For students with EBD, this is significant given their use of inappropriate behavior as a means to create more preferred contexts. By adding the predictability to the tasks, as well as providing the student with "power" to manipulate those tasks through choices, the teacher may encourage students to display higher rates of appropriate social behavior while making academic improvement.

In Isaac's case, he was provided with opportunities to make choices within the context of his math tasks, which provided predictability in the math routine

and the ability to manipulate events within it.

Implications for Practice

When considering opportunities to infuse increased choice-making within the curriculum, consider the following issues:

1. Start small and think "manageable" in terms of successive steps. Instead of offering students with EBD opportunities to make choices throughout the entire school day, begin with one or two curricular areas or periods of time. A convenient place to start is during student free time or when students are finishing tasks on a varied schedule. For example, during free time, provide a student with EBD with three options from the classroom environment, such as access to the computer, a book from the teacher's bookshelf, or a puzzle with which to play. Once the student demonstrates the ability to make choices, combine choice-making opportunities. For instance, provide the student with choice options and, once an option is selected, allow the student a choice of where in the room to use the free-time option.

For students with EBD, predictability and control may be critical concepts and skills that are necessary for appropriately coping with the environment.

2. Begin infusing opportunities to make choices within the curricular area in which the student will gain the most. With Isaac, we suggested starting in math because he was experiencing high rates of both academic and social difficulties in that area, contributing to his school failure. When selecting the specific area, review existing student data (e.g., anecdotal records, grade summaries) to guide area selection.

3. View opportunities to make choices along a continuum. For example,

What Does the Literature Say About Choice-Making and Environmental Predictability and Control?

What are Choice-Making Opportunities? Providing students with EBD opportunities to make choices means that the student is provided with two or more options, is allowed to independently select an option, and is provided with the selected option. For example, before distributing a test, the teacher states that each student will complete 25 multiple-choice questions but may choose to either write two essay responses or five short-answer responses as the second part of the test. Each student is called to the teacher's desk to make a selection and is then provided with the selection and told to sit at his or her desk and complete the test. Once all students are at their desks, the teacher says, "When you finish the test, turn it in, take an enrichment folder, and follow the directions inside." This example highlights the provision of choice-making opportunities within naturally occurring classroom events and the connection between choice and environmental predictability.

What is Predictability? Predictability may be defined as a person's ability to accurately judge and interpret what environmental events precede or follow other specific environmental events. That is, the students are provided with an opportunity to make a choice, the choice option is honored, and the events after the test are known. Positive effects of choice-making opportunities may be due, in part, to this predictability once a choice is made (Brown, Belz, Corsi, & Wenig, 1993).

The ability to predict environmental relationships through choice-making opportunities provides the student with an opportunity to act in a manner that helps assure the occurrence of expected environmental events, such as positive interactions with others, cessation of tasks, or reinforcement for a behavior. In the test-taking *with choices*, the students knew what they were expected to do (make a choice and complete the test) and what event was going to occur after the test (work on tasks in enrichment folder). It is common, however, for students with EBD to have difficulty regulating their behaviors when environmental events are perceived to be unpredictable.

In the test-taking example, if the student selected the five short-answer responses but the teacher gave him or her the two essay questions instead, that would create unpredictability. In the student's search for a known or predictable environmental event, the student may consequently display high rates of inappropriate behaviors because he or she knows what the consequences of these behaviors will be. Although potentially undesirable, the consequences are, nevertheless, predictable. For example, a student may act out to gain teacher attention during independent seatwork if teacher attention does not occur when the student displays appropriate behavior and is consistently provided for inappropriate behavior during seatwork times. A student with EBD, however, with the skill to predict potential consequences of his or her own behavior, may display higher rates of appropriate behavior to help ensure the desired teacher attention.

The need for predictability may influence students' behavior even when the ability to exert control over the environment is unavailable (Gunter, Shores, Jack, Denny, & DePaepe, 1994). Given this need for predictability, it is important to assess and modify environments proactively to assist students in making positive choices that will result in both predictable and desirable outcomes (Brown et al., 1993).

How are Predictability and Inappropriate Behavior Linked? Current research in classrooms for students with behavior problems suggests that, unfortunately, predictability most often comes as the result of inappropriate behavior. For example, Van Acker, Grant, and Henry (1996) investigated the interactions that occurred between teachers and students at risk for EBD by conducting a study of 25 teachers and 206 students with mild levels of behavioral problems or higher levels of behavioral problems. These researchers found that most predictable teacher and student interaction patterns were that of teacher demand (academic or social)-to-student noncompliance behavior-to-teacher reprimand-to-student noncompliance behavior. When students engaged in appropriate behavior, however, there was less consistency in teacher responses to the student. Therefore, not surprisingly, if predictability in interactions were important, *students might engage in inappropriate behavior to obtain a predictable response from the teacher*.

The simultaneous effects of choice-making opportunities on both academic and social behaviors is an area that has been underexplored (Powell & Nelson, 1997) and will be an important area for future research and application of choice in the classroom for students with EBD.

How Do We Break the Cycle of Negative Responses? Providing opportunities for students with EBD to make choices related to academic tasks may disrupt the negative cycle of teacher-student interactions described by Van Acker et al. (1996), as well as provide consistency and predictability to academic contexts. For students with EBD, predictability and control may be critical concepts and skills that are necessary and required for appropriately interpreting and coping with the environment, as well as practicing new prosocial skills. When students with EBD perceive their environments to be less threatening and perceive themselves as able to predict and control events, they may increase appropriate kinds of behavior.

For example, in the test-taking scenario *with choices*, the test became more predictable through teacher direction and known events after completion of the test, and the students were able to control the type of written responses required—short answer or essay. Thus, the use of choice-making opportunities can provide the environmental predictability needed to minimize the characteristically inappropriate behaviors exhibited by students with EBD during task situations, while strengthening appropriate responses and increased levels of engagement.

the choices provided to Isaac were basic and concrete. That is, those choices were not significant to decisions he will need to make in the future (e.g., such as what job to train for) but still provided practice in choice-making critical to his proficiency and success in making more important choices.

4. Be consistent in both the presentation and follow-through with choice-making opportunities. For example, offer the same number of choice-making opportunities for the targeted area; and when a student makes a choice, reinforce the selection by providing him or her with the selected item.

By considering these four issues before infusing opportunities to make choices into the curricula for students with EBD, you may provide the appropriate environmental context for both student and teacher success.

Final Thoughts

Overall, research on classroom environments for students with EBD has suggested that punishing students (e.g., withholding rewards, denying choices) for inappropriate behavior only promotes negative and inconsistent interactions between teachers and students (Steinberg & Knitzer, 1992; Van Acker et al., 1996). These findings support the classroom components cited by Reitz (1994) as necessary for students with EBD to experience school success (e.g., high rates of social reinforcement and student academic involvement and achievement).

The provision of choice-making opportunities for students with EBD is a viable curricular modification that links student involvement with student decision making for social and academic suc-

cess (Mathur, Nelson, & Rutherford, 1998).

References

Brown, F., Belz, P., Corsi, L., & Wenig, B. (1993). Choice diversity for people with severe disabilities. *Education and Training in Mental Retardation, 28,* 318–326.

Cosden, M., Gannon, C., & Haring, T. G. (1995). Teacher-control versus student-control over choice of task and reinforcement for students with severe behavior problems. *Journal of Behavioral Education, 5,* 11–27.

Dunlap, G., DePerczel, M., Clarke, S., Wilson, D., Wright, S., White, R., & Gomez, A. (1994). Choice making to promote adaptive behavior for students with emotional and behavioral challenges. *Journal of Applied Behavior Analysis, 27,* 505–518.

Guess, D., Benson, H. A., & Siegel-Causey, E. (1985). Concepts and issues related to choice making and autonomy among persons with severe disabilities. *Journal of the Association of Persons with Severe Handicaps, 10,* 79–86.

Gunter, P. L., Shores, R. E., Jack, S. L., Denny, R. K., & DePaepe, P. (1994). A case study of the effects of altering instructional interactions on the disruptive behavior of a child identified with severe behavior disorders. *Education and Treatment of Children, 17,* 435–444.

Individuals with Disabilities Education Act Amendments of 1997, P. L. 105–17. 105th Congress, 1st Session.

Jolivette, K., Stichter, J., Sibilsky, S., Scott, T. M., & Ridgely, R. (2001a). *Naturally occurring opportunities for preschool children with and at-risk for disabilities to make choices.* Submitted for publication.

Jolivette, K., Wehby, J. H., Canale, J., & Massey, N. G. (2001b). Effects of choice making opportunities on the behavior of students with emotional and behavioral disorders. *Behavioral Disorders, 26,* 131–145.

Mathur, S. R., Nelson, J. R., & Rutherford, R. B. (1998). Translating the IEP into practice: Curricular and instructional accommodations. In L. M. Bullock & R. A. Gable (Eds.), *Implementing the 1997 IDEA: New challenges and opportunities for serving students with emotional/be-*

havioral disorders. Reston, VA: Council for Exceptional Children.*

Munk, D. D., & Repp, A. C. (1994). The relationship between instructional variables and problem behavior: A review. *Exceptional Children, 60,* 390–401.

Powell, S., & Nelson, B. (1997). Effects of choosing academic assignments on a student with attention deficit hyperactivity disorder. Journal of *Applied Behavior Analysis, 30,* 181–183.

Reitz, A. L. (1994). Implementing comprehensive classroom-based programs for students with emotional and behavioral problems. *Education and Treatment of Children, 17,* 312–331.

Shores, R. E., Jack, S. L., Gunter, P. L., Ellis, D. N., DeBriere, T. J., & Wehby, J. H. (1993). Classroom interactions of children with behavior disorders. *Journal of Emotional and Behavioral Disorders, 1,* 27–39.

Steinberg, Z., & Knitzer, J. (1992). Classrooms for emotionally and behaviorally disturbed students: Facing the challenge. *Behavioral Disorders, 17,* 145–156.

Van Acker, R., Grant, S. H., & Henry, D. (1996). Teacher and student behavior as a function of risk for aggression. *Education and Treatment for Children, 19,* 316–334.

Woodcock, R. W., & Johnson, M. B. (1989). *Woodcock-Johnson Psycho-Educational Battery-Revised.* Allen, TX: DLM.

Kristine Jolivette, *Assistant Professor, Department of Special Education and Rehabilitation Counseling, University of Kentucky, Lexington.* **Janine Peck Stichter** (*CEC Chapter #27*), *Associate Professor, Department of Special Education, Central Michigan University, Mt. Pleasant.* **Katherine M. McCormick** (*CEC Chapter #180*), *Assistant Professor, Department of Special Education and Rehabilitation Counseling, University of Kentucky, Lexington.*

Address correspondence to Kristine Jolivette, Department of Special Education and Rehabilitation Counseling, University of Kentucky, 119 Taylor Education Building, Lexington, KY 40506-0001 (e-mail: kjolive@uky.edu).

The Importance of Teacher Self-Awareness in Working With Students With Emotional and Behavioral Disorders

Brent G. Richardson & Margery J. Shupe

What are your primary concerns in the classroom? Are you constantly involved in power struggles with some students? Do you yearn for good relationships with all your students? Are you stressed out? This article may help.

The frequency and intensity of students' emotional and behavioral disorders have increased in the past several decades (Bartollas & Miller, 1998; Knitzer, 1993; Lerner, 1995; Long, Morse, & Newman, 1996). In surveys, teachers consistently reveal that disruptive student behavior and classroom discipline are their primary educational concerns (Long, 1996a). Teachers who work with students with emotional and behavioral disorders can enhance their effectiveness and job satisfaction, minimize power struggles, and build more positive relationships with children with disabilities by taking proactive steps to increase their own self-awareness. Gold and Roth (1993) identified teacher self-awareness as a key component for managing stress.

> ## Teachers revealed that disruptive student behavior and classroom discipline are their primary educational concerns.

Gold and Roth (1993) defined self-awareness as "a process of getting in touch with your feelings and behaviors" (p. 141). Increased self-awareness involves a more accurate understanding of how students affect our own emotional processes and behaviors and how we affect students, as well. Self-awareness is particularly important for teachers who work with students with emotional and behavioral disorders. Seldom are we unaffected by their behavior. Often, these students reflect the best and worst in ourselves (Richardson, 2001). Our development

as teachers depends on our willingness to take risks and regularly ask ourselves which of our own behaviors are helping or hindering our personal and professional growth. "If we could allow ourselves to become students of our own extraordinary self-education, we would be very well placed to facilitate the self-education of others" (Underhill, 1991, p. 79).

> ## Our development as teachers depends on our willingness to take stock of our own behavior.

This article identifies questions and strategies to help teachers become more self-aware regarding their interactions with students with behavioral and emotional disorders.

Five Key Questions to Increase Teacher Self-Awareness

1. Am I taking proactive steps to identify and defuse my own "emotional triggers"?

Cheney and Barringer (1995) asserted: "More than any other group, students with emotional and behavioral disorders appear to present problems that affect staff members on a very personal level" (p. 181). Unfortunately, teacher education does not always highlight the connection between a teacher's self-awareness and his or her ability to build and maintain meaningful relationships with youth with emotional and behavioral disabilities. Although teachers need to learn how to recognize signs of emotional distress in their students, it is equally important to acknowledge that teachers' own personalities, learned prejudices, and individual psychological histories have helped shape their attitudes and responses to certain behaviors (Long et al., 1996). Fritz Redl, a pioneer in working with students with emotional disturbances, emphasized that self-awareness is a key ingredient for succeeding with this population:

> As teachers we have a room, a group, equipment, materials, a curriculum, instructional methods, and grades, but most of all, we have ourselves. What happens to us emotionally in the process of teaching emotionally disturbed kids is the critical factor in determining our effectiveness. (cited in Long, 1996a, p. 44)

Helping youth with emotional and behavioral disabilities begins with understanding ourselves, particularly our own emotional processes that occur in the midst of conflict. Although psychological soundness and effective interpersonal skills are essential characteristics for teachers who work with this population (Kaufman, 1997; Webber, Anderson, & Otey, 1991), certain students can provoke even the most concerned, reasonable, and dedicated teachers to act in impulsive, acrimonious, and rejecting ways (Long, 1996a). Students experiencing stress have the capacity to locate and activate unresolved issues in our own personal lives. Few of us possess the inner peace to respond in a calm and professional manner without conscious effort. Awareness of our primary emotional triggers improves our chances of making rational decisions based on conscious choice, rather than unconscious emotional conditioning.

> *Helping youth with emotional and behavioral disabilities begins with understanding ourselves, particularly our own emotional processes that occur in the midst of conflict.*

Further, the psychological fit between a teacher's need to stay in control and a youth's inability to maintain control can lead to counterproductive power struggles (Long, 1996a). Long asserted that by taking ownership of "negative" feelings such as anger, frustration, and disdain, we are more likely to recognize the difference between having feelings and being had by our feelings. Teachers who are aware of their own emotional processes are more likely to minimize the frequency and intensity of these counterproductive power struggles (see box, "Strategy for Identifying and Defusing Emotional Triggers").

2. Am I paying attention to what I need to pay attention to?

Most teachers recognize the power and necessity of using positive reinforcement (Johns & Carr, 1995). By consciously noticing and reinforcing positive behavior, the classroom becomes a more positive environment—one in which the recognition of both academic and behav-

---

> ### Strategy for identifying and Defusing Emotional Triggers
>
> Take periodic "timeouts" before, during, or after both "negative" interactions with students. Ask yourself:
> - "What led me to respond this way?"
> - "Is this way of responding helping or hurting this relationship?"
> - "Is it helping me grow as an educator?"
> - "Is it helping the youth make better choices?"
>
> It is important to remember that we are often unaware of our primary emotional triggers. Actively seek consultation from colleagues and supervisors regarding behaviors and/or attitudes which are helping or hurting your effectiveness in the classroom.
>
> Ask a colleague or supervisor:
> - "What do you see as my biggesst strength in working with students with behavioral and emotional disorders?"
> - "What types of problems or student behaviors do I find the most difficult?"

ioral accomplishments leads to increased student self-esteem (Fagan, 1996). In an extensive study of effective teaching behaviors for students with disabilities, Larrivee (1982) found that "giving positive feedback" to be a behavior positively correlated with student performance measures. Johns and Carr recommended that at least 70% of comments teachers give students should be positive. Although researchers have found teacher praise to be linked to improved behavioral and academic outcomes of students with emotional and behavioral disorders, the use of praise in these classrooms is often low (Sutherland & Wehby, 2001).

> *Teachers often inadvertently neglect to recognize and build on students' positive behaviors and strengths.*

Good and Brophy (1984) found that teachers' perceptions of students can affect teaching outcomes. Teachers who work with students with emotional and behavioral disabilities can become so attuned to problem behaviors and perceived weaknesses, they inadvertently neglect to recognize and build on positive behaviors and strengths. A Minnesota youth poll by Hedin, Hannes, & Saito (as cited in Braaten, 1999) revealed that two thirds of respondents believed that they were perceived negatively by the significant adults in their lives. Only 25% believed that adults held positive images of them. Furthermore, a large proportion did not believe the adults' perceptions of them to be accurate. The researchers concluded that the youths believe that adults do not value or trust them and do not treat them with respect, and this belief increases as

Strategy for Shifting Your Focus (The Penny Transfer Technique)

Take five pennies and place them in your left pocket. Identify a student in your classroom who regularly needs to be redirected. Ideally, this should be a student whom you find difficult to engage. Every time you are able to verbally encourage that student for something he or she does well, transfer a penny to your right pocket. It is important to avoid phony or superficial affirmations (e.g., "I like your new jeans"). Your goal is to move all five pennies to the right pocket by the end of the day. Repeat this exercise each day for 2 weeks. (Note: You may need to use less pennies or extend the timeframe several days if you are only with the student one period.)

the youths grow older. In their study of teacher behaviors, Sutherland and Wehby (2001) found that ongoing teacher self-assessment had a positive impact on teacher praise.

People often expect teachers to assume not only academic roles, but also those of instructional model, disciplinarian, surrogate parent, social worker, and counselor.

The Penny Transfer Technique is one strategy teachers can use to help them shift their focus to more positive student behaviors and attributes (see box, "Strategy for Shifting Your Focus"). Richardson (2001) noted that professionals who have used the Penny Transfer Technique have found that (a) they began to automatically notice positive behaviors of problem students and (b) they were able to change their perceptions and thus improve their relationships with these youth.

3. Am I using effective strategies to reduce burnout and nurture my own mental health?

Teaching students with emotional and behavioral disorders is one of the most perplexing and challenging roles in education (Cheney & Barringer, 1995). These teachers are faced with enormous pressures and simultaneous challenges (Cheney & Barringer; Pullis, 1992) and report high levels of emotional exhaustion (Male & May, 1997). They are evaluated primarily on their ability to help students make tangible, academic improvements (Long, 1996b); yet they are also expected to assume multiple roles, such as model, disciplinarian, surrogate parent, social worker, and counselor.

Many teachers find it difficult to perform all these roles in the midst of decreasing budgets and increasing class sizes. Teachers find themselves struggling to find time to adequately cover each of the learning objectives while also attending to the emotional needs of their students. Teacher stress can adversely affect the teachers, their students, and the classroom climate. Cheney and Barringer (1995) found that stress "can be manifested as (a) a reluctance to consider factors beyond the immediately observable behavior of the student, and (b) a rigid focus on school rules as a way of coping with problematic social interactions" (p. 181).

We must develop effective strategies for regularly monitoring and managing our own stress.

To survive and thrive in the classroom, teachers who work with students with emotional and behavioral disabilities must develop effective strategies for regularly monitoring and managing their own stress.

Teachers need safe places to express their feelings and frustrations and recharge their emotional batteries. In a survey of special education teachers, Pullis (1992) found that talking with supportive colleagues is one of the most effective coping strategies. In fact, 96% of teachers rated collaborating and talking with special education colleagues as one of their most effective strategies for coping with stress (see box, "Strategy for Reducing Burnout and Nurturing Teacher Mental Health").

We need to recognize the difference, however, between the need to vent and a pattern of negativity and complaining. Assessing our results will help us make this distinction. Venting is only helping us if we are actually *venting* pent-up feelings. If this process only adds to our

Strategy for Reducing Burnout and Nurturing Teacher Mental Health

Recognize the difference between productive venting and an unproductive pattern of negativity and complaining. Take time to assess your conversations with friends and colleagues about your classroom and students. Ask yourself whether these conversations are helping to reduce or amplify your stress level. Periodically gauge your feelings and coping skills and seek out positive models.

Stop and ask yourself, "What is your vision for the children and youth that you teach?" If necessary, explore new strategies (e.g., exercising, seeking professional help, reframing student behavior, finding humor in potentially humorous situations, commending yourself for ways you are making a difference) for managing your stress and increasing your own morale.

stress level and frustration, we might want to employ a different strategy. A pattern of "unproductive venting" in the teacher's lounge, in the copy room, at lunch breaks, and at home is often the most foreboding precursor to burnout. We must regularly assess our coping skills and seek out positive colleagues and role models who will engage in supportive, constructive dialogue.

4. Am I using an appropriate sense of humor to build relationships, diffuse conflict, engage learners, and manage my own stress?

A number of educators have stressed that an appropriate sense of humor is absolutely essential for long-term success in working with youth with emotional and behavioral disorders (Richardson, 2001; Tobin, 1991, Webber et al., 1991). These students often are trying to make sense out of a variety of highly charged emotional stressors (e.g., poor reading skills, changing family structure, parental abuse and neglect) and will likely direct their hurt and frustration at teachers and peers. Students need to be held accountable for their behavior. If we take their actions personally or too seriously, however, we place ourselves at risk for both overreacting and burnout. Teachers want to approach their jobs diligently and sincerely; however, we need to recognize when we are taking ourselves, our students, or our jobs too seriously.

An appropriate sense of humor is an effective strategy for engaging students who seem to be disengaged.

While working as a high school counselor, one of the authors was informed that 80% of the disciplinary referrals to the assistant principal came from only 10% of the teachers. When asked if there were commonalities among those teachers, the assistant principal remarked,

> They all seem to take themselves and their jobs too seriously. They seem unhappy when they teach. Ironically, while they have very little tolerance for "acting-out" behaviors, students tend to act out more in their classrooms.

On the other hand, "teachers with a sense of humor are usually happy, relaxed, fun-loving, and reinforcing to others" (Webber et al., 1991, p. 291). A recent study supported these observations. Talbot and Lumden (2000) found that teachers who were more likely to use humor in their classroom reported lower emotional exhaustion and a higher sense of personal accomplishment.

Also, many writers have pointed out that an appropriate sense of humor is an effective strategy for engaging students who seem to be disengaged (Johns & Carr, 1995; Sommers-Flanagan & Sommers-Flanagan, 1997; Webb er et al., 1991). These authors also noted that humor is also one of the most effective means of de-escalating potential

crisis situations. Webber et al. observed that it is difficult for a student to continue to act aggressively or destructively while he or she is laughing. Crowley (1993) interviewed students with severe behavioral disorders regarding helpful teacher attitudes and behaviors and found that these students repeatedly talked about the relevance of humor in the classroom.

Victor Borge, the comedian, could have been talking about educators and students when he said, "Laughter is the shortest distance between two people." Sultanoff (1999) asserted, "One of the greatest potential gifts we can provide for children is to present ourselves as "humor beings." By living with a humorous perspective, we teach children to effectively manage life's challenges with far less stress" (p. 2).

Humor that heals is sensitive, is good natured, defuses difficult situations, and brings people closer together.

Having a sense of humor in the classroom is less about telling jokes and more about maintaining a relaxed and upbeat attitude and outlook about our jobs and life's bizarre twists. Teachers who have an appropriate sense of humor convey to their students that they

---

Strategy for Assessing Our Ability to Use an Appropriate Sense of Humor

To assess whether you might be incorporating an appropriate sense of humor into your classroom, periodically ask yourself the following questions:

- "How often do I laugh as I teach?"
- "Do students seem to enjoy learning in my classroom?"
- "For the most part, do I enjoy working with students with behavioral and emotional disorders?"
- "Do I use humor as a technique to defuse difficult situations or avoid potential power struggles?"
- "Does humor used in my classroom (by me or my students) tend to bring people closer together or push them further away?"

Based on your responses to these questions, it may be helpful to seek consultation or additional resources to more effectively incorporate humor into the classroom. Also, remember that qualifying language was used in these questions ("for the most part," "tend to"). You do not need to inject humor into every lesson plan or difficult situation. An honest self-assessment, however, will likely provide you with direction regarding areas where a change in attitude or behavior may be helpful.

enjoy their jobs, like their students, relish playful exchanges, and do not take themselves too seriously. Most importantly, they recognize the difference between humor that hurts and humor that heals. Richardson (2001) noted that humor that hurts is sarcastic, caustic, and pushes people away from one another, whereas humor that heals is sensitive, good natured, defuses difficult situations, and brings people closer together. As educators, we need to periodically assess our use of humor in the classroom and make adjustments when warranted (see box, "Strategies for Assessing Our Ability to Use an Appropriate Sense of Humor").

5. Do I regularly acknowledge significant ways I (and others) are making a difference in the lives of students?

In conducting workshops for professionals who work with youth with emotional and behavioral disabilities, one of the authors shared the following story of a young boy rescuing starfish on the beach:

> A young boy was walking along the beach in the middle of a sweltering, summer day. As the tide was retreating, he noticed thousands of starfish washed up on the dry sand. As the boy began throwing starfish back into the ocean, a man was passing by and said, "Son, look how many there are—you will never make a difference." Smiling, the boy looked at the starfish in his hand, threw it into the ocean, and declared, "I'll make a difference to that one."

The plight of students with disabilities is analogous to starfish washed up on the dry sand. It is easy to become paralyzed by the magnitude of the task and fail to recognize ways teachers are making a difference. It is easy to allow negative television newscasts, periodic setbacks, and seemingly unappreciative students and adults to discolor our perceptions and rob us of the idealism that propelled us to be a teacher. It is also easy to become so busy attending meetings and attending to students, we fail to attend to ourselves and our colleagues. Because of professional role demands, teachers of students with behavioral and emotional disabilities are frequently isolated from interaction with colleagues and particularly susceptible to this symptom of burnout (Zabel, Boomer, & King, 1984).

Kaufman and Wong (1991) found that teachers who perceive themselves as having the ability to bring about desired student results are more likely to perceive their students as teachable and worthy of their attention and effort. One study defined teacher efficacy as "the extent to which the teacher believes he or she has the capacity to affect student performance" (Bergman, McLaughlin, Bass, Pauly, & Zellman, 1977, p. 137). These teachers with a high sense of self-efficacy were also less likely to personalize the misbehaviors of students and more likely to maintain an attitude of tolerance for difficult students. Recognizing ways that they and others are making a dif-

---

Strategy for Recognizing Difference Makers: The Starfish Calendar

This technique is similar to the "Penny Transfer Technique"; however, the objective is to recognize the positive behavior of teachers. First, find a calendar. Draw and cut out pictures of yellow and orange starfish. When you recognize another educator making a difference (e.g., taking extra time after class, encouraging a student to talk to their counselor, using a creative intervention), communicate in some way that you appreciate their efforts.

Then, write a brief description of the behavior on a yellow starfish and paste it on the date in your Starfish Calendar. At the end of the day, identify a specific way you made a difference, and paste an orange starfish each day. This should only take a few minutes. If you happen to miss a day, try to find two the following day.

---

ference can affect the teachers' perceived self-efficacy (see box, "Strategy for Recognizing Difference Makers").

Although many teachers make a habit of overextending themselves, burnout is just as likely to result from a persistent feeling that they are not truly making a difference. The Starfish Calendar (see box) is one simple way to encourage ourselves and others to be proactive in acknowledging the contributions of teachers.

Final Thoughts

Many teachers have not received adequate training to recognize how their own psychological histories and personalities affect their interactions with youth with emotional and behavioral disabilities. Although the success of educators to reach and teach these young people depends on many factors (e.g., frequency and intensity of student behaviors, organizational structure, administrative support), this article focused on an important area in which teachers have more direct control— increasing their own self-awareness.

Many goals outlined here are challenging and may not be fully attainable. As vulnerable human beings, teachers will never discover all their emotional triggers, build positive relationships with every student, or completely avoid counterproductive power struggles. If teachers make conscious, ongoing efforts to increase their own self-awareness, they will likely enhance their effectiveness and their job satisfaction. Teachers who are willing to take prudent risks and try new strategies will inevitably make some mistakes. We need to view past conflict and unsuccessful interventions as helpful feedback, rather than personal failure. We must remember that the overall attitude of the teacher and the classroom climate affect students much more than most other techniques or interactions.

References

Bartollas, C., & Miller, S. J. (1998). *Juvenile justice in America* (2nd. ed.). Upper Saddle River, NJ: Prentice-Hall.

Bergman, P., McLaughlin, M., Bass, M., Pauly, E., & Zellman, G. (1977). *Federal programs supporting educational change: Vol. VII. Factors affecting implementation and continuation.* Santa Monica, CA: RAND. (ERIC Document Reproduction Service No. 335 341)

Braaten, J. L. (1999). Self-concept and behavior disorders. *Journal of Youth and Adolescence, 39*(1), 218-225.

Cheney, D., & Barringer, C. (1995). Teacher competence, student diversity, and staff training for the inclusion of middle school students with emotional and behavioral disorders. *Journal of Emotional and Behavioral Disorders, 3*(3), 174-182.

Crowley, E. P. (1993). Reflections on "A qualitative analysis of mainstreamed behaviorally disordered aggressive adolescents' perceptions of helpful and unhelpful teacher attitudes and behaviors." *Exceptionality, 4*(3), 187-191.

Fagan, S. A. (1996). Fifteen teacher intervention skills for managing classroom behavior problems. In N. Long, W. C. Morse, & R. G. Newman (Eds.), *Conflict in the classroom: The education of at-risk and troubled students* (5th ed., pp. 273-287). Austin, TX: Pro-Ed.

Gold, Y., & Roth, R. A. (1993). *Teachers managing stress and preventing burnout: The professional health solution.* Washington, DC: The Falmer Press.

Good, T. L., & Brophy, J. E. (1984). *Looking in classrooms* (3rd. ed.). New York: Harper & Row.

Johns, B. H., & Carr, V. G. (1995). *Techniques for managing verbally and aggressive students.* Denver: Love.

Kaufman, J. M. (1997). *Characteristics of behavior disorders of children and youth* (6th ed.). Columbus, OH: Merrill.

Kaufman, J. M., & Wong, K. L. (1991). Effective teachers of students with behavioral disorders: Are generic teaching skills enough? *Behavioral Disorders, 16*(3), 225- 237.

Knitzer, J. (1993). Children's mental health policy: Challenging the future. *Journal of Emotional and Behavioral Disorders, 1*(1), 8-16.

Larrivee, B. (1982). Identifying effective teaching behaviors for mainstreaming. *Teacher Education and Special Education, 5,* 2-6.

Lerner, R. M. (1995). *America's youth in crisis: Challenges and options for programs and policies.* Thousand Oaks, CA: Sage.

Long, N. (1996a). The conflict cycle paradigm on how troubled students get teachers out of control. In N. Long, W. C. Morse, & R. G. Newman (Eds.), *Conflict in the classroom: The education of at-risk and troubled students* (5th ed., pp. 244-265). Austin, TX: Pro-Ed.

Long, N. (1996b). Inclusion of emotionally disturbed students: Formula for failure or opportunity for new acceptance. In N. Long, W. C. Morse, & R. G. Newman (Eds.), *Conflict in the classroom: The education of at-risk and troubled students* (5th ed., pp. 116-126). Austin, TX: Pro-Ed.

Long, N., Morse, W. C., & Newman, R. G. (Eds.). (1996). *Conflict in the classroom: The education of at-risk and troubled students* (5th ed.). Austin, TX: Pro-Ed.

Male, D. B., & May, D. (1997). Stress, burnout and workload in teachers of children with special education needs. *British Journal of Special Education, 24*(3), 133-140.

Pullis, M. (1992). An analysis of the occupational stress of teachers of the behaviorally disordered: Sources, effects, and strategies for coping. *Behavioral Disorders, 17*(3), 191-201.

Richardson, B. G. (2001). *Working with challenging youth: Lessons learned along the way.* Philadelphia, PA: Brunner-Routledge.

Sommers-Flanagan, J., & Sommers-Flanagan, R. (1997). *Tough kids, cool counseling.* Alexandria, VA: American Counseling Association.

Sultanoff, S. M. (1999). President's column. *Therapeutic Humor, 13*(4), 2.

Sutherland, K. S., & Wehby, J. H. (2001). The effect of self-evaluation on teaching behavior in classrooms for students with emotional and behavioral disorders. *The Journal of Special Education, 35*(3), 161-171.

Talbot, L. A., & Lumden, D. B. (2000). On the association between humor and burnout. *Humor: International Journal of Humor Research, 13,* 419-428.

Tobin, L. (1991). *What to do with a child like this? Inside the lives of troubled children.* Deluth, MN: Whole Person Associates.

Underhill, A. (1991). The role of groups in developing teacher self-awareness. *English Language Teaching Journal, 46*(1), 71-80.

Webber, J., Anderson, T., & Otey, L. (1991). Teacher mindsets for surviving in BD classrooms. *Intervention in School and Clinic, 26,* 288-292.

Zabel, R. H., Boomer, L. W., & King, T. R. (1984). A model of stress and burnout among teachers of behaviorally disordered students. *Behavioral Disorders, 9*(3), 215- 221.

Brent G. Richardson, *Associate Professor; and* **Margery J. Shupe,** *Assistant Professor, Education Department, Xavier University, Cincinnati, Ohio.*

Address correspondence to Brent G. Richardson, Education Department, Xavier University, Cincinnati, OH 45207-6612 (e-mail: Richardb@xu.edu).

From *Teaching Exceptional Children,* November/December 2003. Copyright © 2003 by Council for Exceptional Children. Reprinted by permission.

Classroom Problems That Don't Go Away

Laverne Warner and Sharon Lynch

W*ade runs "combat-style" beneath the windows of his school as he makes his getaway from his 1st-grade classroom. It is still early in the school year, but this is the third time Wade has tried to escape. Previously, his teacher has managed to catch him before he left the building. Today, however, his escape is easier, because Mrs. Archie is participating with the children in a game of "Squirrel and Trees" and Wade is behind her when he leaves the playground area. She sees him round the corner of the school, and speedily gives chase. When she reaches the front parking lot of their building, however, she cannot find him. Wade is gone!*

Experienced and inexperienced teachers alike, in all grade levels, express concern about difficult classroom problems—those problems that don't ever seem to go away, no matter what management techniques are used. Wade's story and similar ones are echoed time and again in classrooms around the world as adults struggle to find a balance between correcting children's behavior and instructing them about self-management strategies.

Educators emphasize an understanding of appropriate guidance strategies, and teachers learn about acceptable center and school district policies. An abundance of books, videotapes, and other teacher resources are available to classroom practitioners to enhance their understanding of appropriate guidance strategies. Professional organizations such as the Association for Childhood Education International define standards of good practice. Textbooks for childhood educators define well-managed classrooms and appropriate management techniques (e.g., Marion, 2003; Morrison, 2001; Reynolds, 2003; Seefeldt & Barbour, 1998; Wolfgang, 2001).

Despite this preparation, educators daily face problems with guiding or disciplining children in their classrooms. Understanding the developmental needs of children and meeting their physical needs are two ingredients to happy classroom management. It is also important to look at the larger problems involved

when children's misbehaviors are chronic to the point that youngsters are labeled as "difficult." Are these children receiving enough attention from the teacher? Are they developing social skills that will help them through interactions and negotiations with other children in the classroom?

Mrs. Archie's guidance philosophy is founded on principles that she believes are effective for young children. Taking time at the end of the day to reflect on Wade's disappearance, Mrs. Archie concluded that she had done what she could, as always, to develop a healthy classroom climate.

She strives to build a classroom community of learners and act with understanding in response to antisocial behavior in the classroom, and she knows that the vast majority of children will respond positively. Mrs. Archie's classroom layout promotes orderly activity throughout the day and is well-stocked with enough materials and supplies to keep children interested and actively engaged in their learning activities. Although the activities she provides are challenging, many simple experiences also are available to prevent children from being overwhelmed by classroom choices.

Furthermore, Mrs. Archie's attitude is positive about children, like Wade, who come from families that use punitive discipline techniques at home. Her discussions with Wade's mother prior to his escape had been instructive, and she thought that progress was being made with the family. Indeed, when Wade arrived at home the day he ran off, his mother returned him to school immediately.

So what is the teacher to do about children, like Wade, with chronic and intense behavioral difficulties? If serious behavior problems are not addressed before age 8, the child is likely to have long-lasting conduct problems throughout school, often leading to suspension, or dropping out (Katz & McClellan, 1997; Walker et al., 1996). Since the window of opportunity to intervene with behavior problems is narrow, childhood educators must understand the nature of the behavior problem and design an educative plan to teach the child alternative approaches.

The ABC's of the Problem

The first step in analyzing the behavior problem is to determine the "pay-off" for the child. Challenging behaviors usually fall into one of the following categories: 1) behavior that gets the child attention, either positive or negative; 2) behavior that removes the child from something unpleasant, like work or a task; 3) behavior that results in the child getting something she or he wants, like candy or a toy; and 4) behavior that provides some type of sensory stimulation, such as spinning around until the child feels dizzy and euphoric.

To understand the pay-off for the child, it is important to examine the ABC's of the behavior: the antecedents, behaviors, and consequences associated with the problem. The *antecedent* requires a record, which describes what was happening just prior to the incident. The actual *behavior* then can be described in observable, measurable terms: instead of saying that the misbehaving child had a tantrum, detail that he threw himself to the floor, screamed, and pounded his fists on the floor for four minutes. Finally, we examine the pay-off (*consequences*) for the behavior.

Did the behavior result in close physical contact as the child was carried into the adjoining room and the caregiver attempted to soothe him? Did the behavior result in his being given juice so that he could calm down? Did the behavior result in scolding by the teacher, providing the kind of intense individual attention that some youngsters crave because it is the only demonstration of love and caring they have experienced? When teachers and caregivers examine the ABC's of the behavior, they are better able to understand the child's motivation, establish preventive strategies, and teach alternative social skills the child can use to meet his or her needs.

Prevention Strategies

Mrs. Archie knows that she needs to learn specific strategies that will help her work with "difficult" behaviors, like those of Wade, because these problems certainly don't seem to go away on their own. The following intervention methods are designed to preempt anti-social behaviors and often are referred to as prevention strategies. It is always better to prevent the behavior as much as possible.

Accentuate the Positive For the child who demonstrates inappropriate behavior to gain attention, the teacher should find every opportunity to give the child positive attention when he or she is behaving appropriately. Often, these opportunities to "catch the child being good" occur relatively early in the day. When children receive plenty of positive attention early in the day and the teacher continues to find opportunities for praise and attention as the day goes on, the child is not as likely to misbehave for attention as his need is already being met (Hanley, Piazza, & Fisher, 1997). This intervention is based on the principle of deprivation states. If the child is deprived of attention and is "hungry" for adult interaction, he will do anything to gain the attention of others, even negative attention.

Player's Choice When educators see a negative pattern of behavior, they can anticipate that the child is likely to refuse adult requests. This is often referred to as "oppositional behavior." A teacher may remark, "It doesn't matter what I ask her to do, she is going to refuse to do it." One successful strategy for dealing with this type of oppositional behavior is to provide the child with choices (Knowlton, 1995). This approach not only gives the child power and control, but also affords the child valuable opportunities for decision making. Example of choices include, "Do you want to carry out the trash basket or erase the chalkboard?," "Do you want to sit in the red chair or the blue chair?," or "Do you want to pick up the yellow blocks or the green blocks?"

The teacher must be cautious about the number of choices provided, however. Many children have difficulty making up their minds if too many choices are presented—often, two choices are plenty. Also, adults need to monitor their own attitude as they present choices. If choices are presented using a drill sergeant tone of voice, the oppositional child is going to resist the suggestions.

On a Roll When adults anticipate that a child is going to refuse a request, teachers can embed this request within a series of other simple requests. This intervention is based on the research-based principles of high-probability request sequences (Ardoin, Martens, & Wolfe, 1999). The first step in this procedure is to observe the child to determine which requests she consistently performs. Before asking the child to perform the non-preferred request, ask her to do several other things that she does consistently. For example, 8-year-old Morgan consistently resists cleaning up the dollhouse area. While she is playing with the dollhouse, her teacher could ask her to "Give the dolls a kiss," "Show me the doll's furniture," and "Put the dolls in their bedrooms." After she has complied with these three requests, she is much more likely to comply with the request to "Put the dolls away now" or "Give them to me."

Grandma's Rule This strategy often is referred to as the Premack Principle (Premack, 1959). When asking a child to perform an action, specifying what he or she will receive after completing it more often ensures its completion. Examples here include: "When you have finished your math problems, then we will go outside," "When you have eaten your peas, you can have some pudding," and "After you have rested awhile, we will go to the library."

A Spoonful of Sugar Helps the Medicine Go Down This principle involves pairing preferred and non-preferred activities. One particular task that is difficult for preschoolers, and many adults, is waiting. Most of us do not wait well. When asking a child to complete a non-preferred activity such as waiting in line, pairing a preferred activity with the waiting will make it more tolerable.

Businesses and amusement parks use the principle of pairing when they provide music or exhibits for customers as they wait in line. Similarly, with young children, teachers can provide enjoyable activities as children wait. Suggested activities that can be used during waiting periods include singing, looking at books, reading a story, or holding something special such as a banner, sign, or toy.

Another difficult activity for many young children is remaining seated. If the child is given a small object to hold during the time she must remain seated, she may be willing to continue sitting for a longer period. The principle of pairing preferred and non-preferred activities also gives the child increasing responsibility for her own behavior, instead of relying on teacher discipline.

Just One More This particular intervention is most effective when a child behaves inappropriately in order to escape a low-preference task. The purpose of the intervention is to improve work habits and increase time on task. The first step is to identify how long a particular child will work at a specific task before exhibiting inappropriate behavior. Once the teacher has determined how long a child will work on a task, the teacher can give the child a delay cue to head off misbehavior. Examples of delay cues are "Just one more and then you're finished," "Just two minutes and then you're finished," or "Do this and then you're finished."

In this intervention, a teacher sets aside preconceived ideas about how long children *should* work on a task and instead focuses on improving the child's ability to complete tasks in reference to his current abilities. As the children's challenging behaviors decrease, the adult gradually can increase the time on task, and the amount of work completed, before giving them the delay cue and releasing them from the task.

The More We Get Together Another way to improve task completion is by making the job a collaborative effort. If a child finds it difficult to complete non-preferred activities, then the instructor can complete part of the task with the student. For example, when organizing the bookshelf, the adult completes a portion of the task, such as picking up the big books as the student picks up the little books. She prefaces that activity by stating, "I'll pick up the big books, and you pick up the little books." As the child becomes more willing to complete her part of the task, the caregiver gradually increases the work expectations for the child while decreasing the amount of assistance.

Communication Development

In addition to preventing inappropriate behavior, another tactic is replacing the problem behavior by teaching the child alternative behaviors. The key to this process is "functional equivalence." Teachers must determine the *function* or pay-off for the inappropriate behavior and then teach an alternative *equivalent* action that will service the same purpose as the negative behavior. This often is referred to as the "fair pair" rule (White & Haring, 1976). Rather than punishing the behavior, teaching children a better way to behave assists in meeting their needs.

Bids for Attention The first step in addressing attention-seeking negative behaviors is to reduce their occurrence by providing plenty of attention for the child's appropriate behaviors. The next step is to teach the child appropriate ways to gain attention from others. Most children learn appropriate social skills incidentally from their family and teachers; some children, however, have learned negative ways to gain social attention. Some of the social skills that may need to be taught include calling others by name, tapping friends on the shoulder for attention, knowing how to join others in play, and raising one's hand to gain the teacher's attention. Numerous other social skills may require direct instruction. Any time a behavior is considered inappropriate, adults need to teach the child a better way to have his needs met.

When teaching social skills to chldren, break the skill into a maximum of three steps. Then model the steps and have the child demonstrate the skill. Provide positive and negative examples of the step and have the children label the demonstration as correct or incorrect. Use class discussion time to role-play and talk about when this particular social skill is appropriate. Throughout the day, set up situations that allow practice of the social skill and encourage the child to use the new skill. Finally, promote carry-over of the skill by communicating with the family about the social skills instruction in order for the child to practice the social skills outside of the classroom—on the playground, in the lunch room, and at home.

Ask for Something Else If we know that the child has disruptive behaviors when presented with tasks that are disliked, then the teacher can present the child with an alternative task or materials, something she likes, *before* the problem behavior occurs. Then the child can be taught to ask for the alternative activity or object. When the child requests the alternative, provide it and preempt the negative behavior. In this way, children can learn to communicate their needs and prevent the challenging behavior from occurring.

Ask for Help Many children behave disruptively because they are frustrated with a task. Teachers usually can determine when the child is becoming frustrated by observing and reading non-verbal communication signals. Possible signs of frustration might be sighing, fidgeting, reddening of the face, or negative facial expressions. Noticing these signs helps the teacher know that it is time to intervene. Rather than offering help when the child needs it, the teacher says, "It looks like you need some help. When you need help, you need to tell me. Now you say, 'I need help.'" After the child has responded by saying, "I need help," the teacher provides assistance. This strategy is much more effective if the group already has role-played "asking for help."

Ask for a Break This strategy is similar to the two listed above; in this case, educators teach the child to ask for a break during a difficult and frustrating task. Prior to presenting the task, the teacher can explain that she knows that the activity can be difficult, but that the child can have a break after spending some time working hard at it. Then, the child can be taught to request a break while other students are engaged in various tasks.

Although teachers would like to think that instruction and activities are always fun for children and that learning should be child-directed, certain important activities must be mastered if children are to become successful in school. Especially as children progress into the primary grades, teachers expect them to work independently on pencil-and-paper tasks. Teaching youngsters communication skills that will help them handle frustration and low-preference activities will improve their outcomes as learners in school and in life.

Reviewing Options

Mrs. Archie, in reviewing her options for working with Wade, is gaining confidence in her ability to work more carefully with the family and with Wade to ensure his successful re-entry to her classroom. Her resolve is to continue developing a "community of learners" (Bredekamp & Copple, 1997) by helping Wade become a functioning member of her group. She intends to teach him how to enter a play setting, negotiate for what he wants in the classroom, and learn how to make compromises, while nurturing him as she would any child. These are goals that she believes will help turn around Wade's negative behavior.

Mrs. Archie also knows that her administrator is a caring woman, and, if necessary, Wade could be placed in another classroom so that he could have a "fresh start" with his entry into school. Her hope is that this will be a last-resort strategy, because she understands how much Wade needs a caring adult who understands him and his needs. Her phone call to Wade's mother at the end of the day will be friendly and supportive, with many recommendations for how the school can assist the family.

A Long-Term Plan

Most children with chronic difficult behaviors did not learn them overnight. Many of these children experience serious ongoing problems in their families. As teachers, we cannot change home dynamics or family problems. Sometimes a parent conference or parent education groups can be helpful, as the family learns to support a difficult child at home. With others, we do well to teach the child socially appropriate behavior in the classroom. As a child learns socially appropriate behavior in school, she learns that the behavior is useful in other settings. Often, the school is the only place where the child has the opportunity to learn prosocial behaviors. Children's negative behaviors may have, in a sense, "worked" for them in numerous situations for a substantial period of time. When we work to teach the child a better way to get his or her needs met, we must recognize that this process takes time and effort. When we as educators invest this time and effort with children during childhood, we are pro-

viding them with the tools that can make the difference in their school careers and in their lives.

References

Ardoin, S. P., Martens, B. K., & Wolfe, L. A. (1999). Using high-probability instruction sequences with fading to increase student compliance during transitions. *Journal of Applied Behavior Analysis, 32*(3), 339–351.

Bredekamp, S., & Copple, C. (Eds.). (1997). *Developmentally appropriate practice in early childhood programs* (Rev. ed.). Washington, DC: National Association for the Education of Young Children.

Hanley, G. P., Piazza, C. C., & Fisher, W. W. (1997). Noncontingent presentation of attention and alternative stimuli in the treatment of attention-maintained destructive behavior. *Journal of Applied Behavior Analysis, 30*(2), 229–237.

Katz, L., & McClellan, D. (1997). *Fostering children's social competence: The teacher's role*. Washington, DC: National Association for the Education of Young Children.

Knowlton, D. (1995). Managing children with oppositional defiant behavior. *Beyond Behavior, 6*(3), 5–10.

Marion, M. (2003). *Guidance of young children* (3rd ed.). Englewood Cliffs, NJ: Prentice Hall.

Morrison, G. (2001). *Early childhood education today* (8th ed.). Englewood Cliffs, NJ: Prentice Hall.

Premack, D. (1959). Toward empirical behavior laws: I. Positive reinforcement. *Psychological Review, 66*, 219–233.

Reynolds, E. (2003). *Guiding young children* (2nd ed.). Mountain View, CA: Mayfield.

Seefeldt, C., & Barbour, N. (1998). *Early childhood education: An introduction* (4th ed.). Columbus, OH: Merrill.

Walker, H. M., Horner, R. H., Sugai, G., Bullis, M., Sprague, J. R., Bricker, D., & Kaufman, M. J. (1996). Integrated approaches to preventing anti-social behavior among school-age children and youth. *Journal of Emotional and Behavioral Disorders, 4*(4), 194–209.

White, O. R., & Haring, N. G. (1976). *Exceptional teaching*. Upper Saddle River, NJ: Merrill/Prentice Hall.

Wolfgang, C. H. (2001). *Solving discipline and classroom management problems* (5th ed.). New York: John Wiley and Sons.

Laverne Warner is Professor, Early Childhood Education, and Sharon Lynch is Associate Professor of Special Education, Department of Language, Literacy, and Special Populations, Sam Houston State University, Huntsville, Texas.

From *Childhood Education*, Winter 2002/2003, pp. 97-100. © 2002 by the Association for Childhood Education International.

UNIT 7
Vision and Hearing Impairments

Unit Selections

Key Points to Consider

- Looking back, what are the major accomplishments of a half-century of educating children with hearing impairments? Looking forward, what can we hope to accomplish in the next half-century?

- How can tactile strategies support learning for students with visual impairments and other severe disabilities?

 **Links: www.dushkin.com/online/**
These sites are annotated in the World Wide Web pages.

Info to Go: Laurent Clerc National Deaf Education Center
http://clerccenter.gallaudet.edu/InfoToGo/index.html

The New York Institute for Special Education
http://www.nyise.org/index.html

Earlier, more adequate prenatal care, preventive medicine, health maintenance, and medical technology have reduced the number of children born either blind or deaf. In the future, with knowledge of the human genome and with the possibility of genetic manipulation, all genetic causes of blindness and deafness may be eliminated. Now and in the future, however, environmental factors will probably still leave many children with vision and hearing impairments.

Children with visual disabilities that cannot be corrected are the smallest group of children who qualify for special educational services through the Individuals with Disabilities Education Act (IDEA). Legally, a child is considered to have low vision if acuity in the best eye, after correction, is between 20/70 and 20/180 and if the visual field extends from 20 to 180 degrees. Legally, a child is considered blind if visual acuity in the best eye, after correction, is 20/200 or less or if the field of vision is restricted to an area of less than 20 degrees (tunnel vision). These terms do not accurately reflect a child's ability to see or read print.

The educational definition of visual impairment focuses on what experiences a child needs in order to be able to learn. One must consider the amount of visual acuity in the worst eye, the perception of light and movement, the field of vision (a person "blinded" by tunnel vision may have good visual acuity in only a very small field of vision), and the efficiency with which a person uses any residual vision.

Public Law 99-457, fully enacted by 1991, mandated early education for children with disabilities between ages 3 and 5 in the least restrictive environment. This has been reauthorized as PL102-119. It requires individualized family service plans outlining what services will be provided for parents and children, by whom, and where. These family service plans (IFSPs) are up-

dated every 6 months. This early childhood extension of IDEA has been especially important for babies born with low vision or blindness.

In infancy and early childhood, many children with low vision or blindness are given instruction in using the long cane as soon as they become mobile. Although controversial for many years, the long cane is increasingly being accepted. A long cane improves orientation and mobility and alerts persons with visual acuity that the user has a visual disability. This warning is very important for the protection of persons with blindness/low vision.

Children with visual impairments that prevent them from reading print are usually taught to read braille. Braille is a form of writing using raised dots that are "read" with the fingers. In addition to braille, children who are blind are usually taught with Optacon scanners, talking books, talking handheld calculators, closed-circuit televisions, typewriters, and special computer software.

Hearing impairments are rare, and the extreme form, legal deafness, is rarer still. A child is assessed as hard-of-hearing for purposes of receiving special educational services if he or she needs some form of sound amplification to comprehend oral language. A child is assessed as deaf if he or she cannot benefit from amplification. Children who are deaf are dependent on vision for language and communication.

When children are born with impaired auditory sensations, they are put into a classification of children with congenital (at or dating from birth) hearing impairments. When children acquire problems with their hearing after birth, they are put into a classification of children with adventitious hearing impairments. If the loss of hearing occurs before the child has learned speech and language, it is called a prelinguistic hearing impairment. If the loss occurs after the child has learned language, it is called a postlinguistic hearing impairment.

Children whose hearing losses involve the outer or middle ear structures are said to have conductive hearing losses. Conductive losses involve defects or impairments of the external auditory canal, the tympanic membrane, or the ossicles. Children whose hearing losses involve the inner ear are said to have sensorineural hearing impairments.

In 1999 The Newborn and Infant Hearing Screening and Intervention Act in the United States provided incentives for states to test the hearing of newborns before hospital discharge. Thirty-four states now offer this test for a small fee. When an infant is diagnosed with deafness or hearing loss, an appropriate early education can begin immediately under the auspices of IDEA.

Students with vision or hearing impairments whose disabilities can be ameliorated with assistive devices can usually have their individualized needs met appropriately in inclusive classrooms. Students with visual or hearing disorders whose problems cannot be resolved with technological aids, however, need the procedural protections afforded by law. They should receive special services from age of diagnosis through age 21, in the least restrictive environment, free of charge, with semiannually updated individualized family service plans (IFSPs) until age 3 and annually updated individualized education plans (IEPs) and eventually individualized transition plans (ITPs) through age 21. The numbers of children and youth who qualify for these intensive specialized educational programs are small.

Many professionals working with individuals who are deaf feel that a community of others who are deaf and who use sign language is less restrictive than a community of people who hear and who use oral speech. The debate about what has come to be known as the deaf culture has not been resolved.

The first article in this unit deals with the progress that has been made in the last fifty years in the education of children with hearing impairments or deafness. Six areas are reviewed: use of American Sign Language (ASL), audiology, medicine, mental health, vocation and career preparation, and legislation which has facilitated the first five areas. Despite the improved quality of life for individuals with hearing impairments, the author argues that there is still a long way to go.

The second article discusses the importance of the sense of touch for students with visual impairments. They not only need instructional materials that provide tactile information, they also need the teacher to convey expectations, mood, and other social messages through physical contact. June Downing and Deborah Chen consider many issues for educating using the sense of touch.

A Half-Century of *Progress* for Deaf Individuals

By McCay Vernon

Merv Garretson, a highly respected leader in the deaf community (who is deaf himself) recently commented, "The past 50 years saw an amazing increase in the quality of life for people who are deaf."

This article will look at those 50 years of progress from the viewpoint of a person who is deaf. Six major areas will be considered: vocational rehabilitation and careers, American Sign Language, education, audiology, medicine, mental health and legislation.

Vocational Rehabilitation and Careers

What follows is a personal example of what vocational rehabilitation was like in the 1950s.

My late wife, Edith, was deaf. Early in the 1950s, she went to vocational rehabilitation in order to get help for a job or for education. The counselor she was sent to could not sign, declined to write to her and provided no interpreter. Instead, he chased her around his office and tried to seduce her. When she broke down crying, he gave her 25 cents and told her to leave.

This is an extreme example, but until the 1960s, there were no specialized counselors who could sign in the Division of Vocational Rehabilitation nor were vocational rehabilitation counselors trained to serve deaf clients. This was critical, because most deaf people had to depend upon vocational rehabilitation if they wanted to go to college or get vocational training after leaving

school. Subsequent legislation has greatly improved this situation. Most states now have specially trained counselors who sign and can serve deaf clients. If not, there are funds for interpreters. Today, many rehab counselors are deaf themselves.

In terms of careers, a half-century ago, residential schools for the deaf had strong vocational departments. They taught trades such as printing, barbering, shoe repair, cabinet making, upholstering, body and fender work, etc. Many graduates of these schools learned one of these trades while in school and applied what they had learned to earn decent livelihoods for the rest of their working days.

For example, the printing trade used to be one of the highest paid of all crafts. It was unionized, and there was a constant demand for printers—especially linotype operators. Once a deaf person became a printer and got a union card, he could go anywhere in the United States or Canada and find work. Assured of a job, many drifted all over, seeing the country. Because schools for the deaf—and industry in general—were resistant to hiring deaf college graduates into decent professional jobs, many of the deaf men graduating from Gallaudet worked as linotype operators as late as the 1950s.

Technology has changed all of this. Today for a bright, educated deaf person there are many career options available with good pay and excellent working conditions. For the lower 60 to 70 percent of deaf people who lack good edu-

cation, jobs that pay much more than minimum wage are hard to come by. Many of these individuals have turned to SSI and SSDI, which is unfortunate.

American Sign Language

By far, the major contribution made by linguists was that of the late William Stokoe. Until his book proving American Sign Language (ASL) was a bona fide language, it was thought to be only a gross, primitive set of unattractive gestures, mime, and ugly facial expressions. Educators, audiologists and other professionals in deafness, as well as some deaf professionals, perceived it in this way. Stokoe was reviled for his book on ASL by his colleagues at Gallaudet, where he was a professor. Initially, his work was rejected by his peers in deafness. However, other linguists—scholars such as Norm Chomsky—and a nucleus of Stokoe's deaf and hearing students recognized the tremendous significance of his contribution. Gradually and begrudgingly, as Stokoe continued his work and disciples—such as Ursula Bellugi and others—followed in his path, sign language gained in stature.

Today, ASL plays a major role in deaf education and deaf theater. Books on sign language are by far the best selling publications in the field of deafness. Thousands of hearing people study American Sign Language in colleges, universities and through non-credit courses. In theater, it has become almost a form of choreography. An entire profession—that of sign language interpreters—has grown, in part as a result of the pioneering work of Stokoe and his students.

Deaf people have been given access to hundreds more educational opportunities than ever before because of Stokoe's contributions and their implications relative to interpreting services. Today, sign language has a status that makes deaf people proud instead of ashamed, as was the case 50 years ago.

> The use of sign language in education… has improved educational achievement, but not to the levels that are needed for success in today's world.

Two examples illustrate the situation: In the 1950s, Gallaudet was the only college in the U.S. teaching signs. Even there, the only course offered related to sign language was called "dactology," in order to conceal the fact that Gallaudet was teaching sign language. At that time, such a stigma was attached to ASL that no academic institution wished to be associated with it. In the dactology class, fingerspelling was taught, as were signs, but not sign language (ASL). Students were taught to fingerspell and to sign a vocabulary of 150 to 200 words. No instruction was offered in the syntax of ASL—which, at that time, was still not thought to be a language.

Education

Unfortunately, when one looks at the bottom line, education has not made the progress that has been achieved in other areas. Today, 30 percent of deaf adults are still functionally illiterate. Average reading levels remain around fourth to fifth grade for most deaf school students.

However, there are pluses. Fifty years ago, the overwhelming majority of deaf youth attended classes in which sign language was forbidden. Few teachers even knew how to sign. Many schools forbid the use of sign language in classes, on playgrounds and in dormitories. However, starting in the late 50's and early 60's, research on the dismal educational results of oralism was being made

public. Coupled with the findings of linguists regarding sign language, educational methodology started to change. First, it went to simultaneous communication, known as "Total Communication." More recently, the bilingual-bicultural method is becoming widespread.

The use of sign language in the education of deaf students has improved educational achievement, but not to the levels that are needed for success in today's world.

At Gallaudet University in the 50's, deaf people wanting to teach were not permitted in the graduate program for teachers. Only hearing applicants were accepted. Whereas hearing students could practice teach at the Kendall Demonstration School on Gallaudet's campus, deaf would-be teachers were not allowed to practice teach at all, but could only do individual tutoring.

From the 1950's almost until the "Deaf President Now" movement at Gallaudet in 1988, deaf teachers were a relatively small minority in residential schools and only beginning to be accepted in mainstream programs. Those deaf teachers who were hired were usually given classes of very slow, difficult students and assigned additional time consuming activities, such as Boy Scout leader, coach, dormitory counselor, etc. There were no deaf school superintendents and only a few deaf lower level administrators. For many years, Tom Dillon in the New Mexico School was the only deaf educator to reach the level of principal.

This treatment of deaf educators, coupled with the stigma placed on sign language, bears considerable responsibility for the limited gains made in education over the last 50 years.

Currently, two trends in education are of concern: First is the lack of any national standards for mainstream programs. These programs are expanding rapidly, but in ways that are not always in the best interest of deaf youth. For example, most small mainstream programs are administered by school principals with no preparation or experience in deafness and often lacking interest in the field. This means that key decisions—such as those involving money, class size, psychological services, teacher

qualifications, educational curricula, interpreter standards, etc.—are often made by people who know little or nothing about deaf children. In large day schools, the situation is much better, but there are still no national standards, and key decisions are made by people who lack training and experience in deafness.

The other trend of concern is decreasing enrollments in residential schools. In the past, these schools educated the majority of deaf youth and have always hired the most deaf teachers and administrators. They are now in a fight for survival. There is a great need for national leadership on the part of the administrators of these schools if their schools are to survive as schools and not merely custodial facilities for severely multiply handicapped deaf youth.

On the positive side, educational opportunities are far better than ever before for bright, motivated deaf people. They can attend any college or university in the U.S. for which they are qualified and be provided an interpreter or CART service. Gallaudet continues to offer a fine liberal parts program. The National Technical Institute for the Deaf (NTID) provides excellent opportunities in technology and science. California State University at Northridge offers the same wide range of courses available in most large state universities, plus excellent support services for deaf students. There are also junior college programs in most states. These programs have both vocational and academic courses. Many also offer strong deaf support services.

This broad range of educational options was unheard of 50 years ago. At that time, it was essentially Gallaudet or nothing for a deaf person wanting to attend college.

Today, deaf individuals desiring to go into education have the opportunity to become teachers, principals, superintendents and state-level officials.

Audiology

For the last half century, audiology has been a bastion of oralism, and to some extent, still is. Through its influence in the powerful American Speech and Hearing Association (ASHA), it controlled many teacher preparation programs, all of which were oral and none of which hired deaf faculty or accepted deaf students.

In recent years, ASHA's position has modified some, but audiologists and speech therapists still have an influence on how deaf children are taught that far exceeds their knowledge of what deafness is all about.

On the plus side, audiologists have improved hearing aids dramatically. Fifty years ago, they were cumbersome instruments requiring the user to wear a box-like container in front with a wire attached to the ear mold. These devices were crude and tended to amplify as much noise as they did speech.

Today, hearing aids are so sophisticated that about 30 percent of the people who functioned as deaf 50 years ago are now "hard of hearing," meaning that with amplification they can converse orally, both expressively and receptively. For this, hearing impaired people owe audiologists a lot.

Medicine

The major contributions of medicine have been twofold; by discovering and perfecting antibiotics and vaccines, many major etiologies of deafness—such as scarlet fever, rubella, meningitis, whooping cough, mumps, etc.—have either been eliminated or greatly reduced as a cause of hearing loss.

Until the mid to late 1960s, complications of Rh factor caused a significant amount of childhood deafness. Half of these children were both deaf and had cerebral palsy. Through transfusion techniques and a vaccine, Rh factor is no longer a significant cause of deafness.

Currently, the major medical contributions have come from the invention and perfection of the cochlear implant and advances in genetics. Implants have proved a blessing to many individuals who were deafened adventitiously. Some have gone from being deaf to being able to understand speech. However, the procedure has also produced many failures. These tend to be covered up.

The use of cochlear implants with prelingually deaf children is far more controversial and has a lower rate of success. However, there is no question some

children born deaf have been helped by implants. Whether implants are significantly more effective than hearing aids for those born deaf remains a debatable issue.

Unfortunately, most of the published research on cochlear implants is being done by the surgeons, audiologists and speech therapists who are doing the surgery and rehabilitation—and making a fortune in the process. As a consequence, it is almost impossible to get any research published in audiological or medical journals that addresses the failures of cochlear implants. Many infants born with significant residual hearing are being implanted, despite laws to the contrary.

As indicated above, another new area of medical progress is genetics. About half of deafness is due to genetics. The locations of many of the genes causing different forms of deafness are being discovered; this offers the possibility for the future eradication of these particular causes of hearing loss.

Mental Health

Fifty years ago, there were about five psychologists in the United States and one psychiatrist who devoted as much as 20 percent of their time to the field of deafness. If a deaf person had a mental health problem, there were no outpatient clinical services that provided signing therapists or sign language interpreters. This meant there were no outpatient facilities that could offer meaningful help to patients who were deaf. Those who needed hospitalization were placed in mental hospitals where there were no staff who could sign, no interpreters, nor any other deaf patients. This was, in essence, anti-therapeutic custodial isolation, designed more for the convenience of society than for treatment of patients who were deaf. Consequently, deaf patients stayed in the hospital much longer than hearing patients.

Often they were misdiagnosed as mentally retarded by psychologists who used the wrong tests or by psychiatrists who confused their jumbled written syntax as being indicative of schizophrenia.

In the 1960s, a few pioneering psychiatrists—such as Rainer, Grinker, Alt-

shuler, Kallmann, and Robinson—took an interest in mentally ill deaf patients. They set up units for them in hospitals in New York, Chicago and Washington, D.C. Their research and publications led to other states establishing inpatient units for deaf patients and eventually to outpatient clinics. Gallaudet started programs to prepare school psychologists, school counselors and clinical psychologists. Both NTID and Gallaudet also established departments to train social workers. Many of the graduates of these programs are deaf.

As a consequence, today most deaf people have reasonable access to mental health services, except in rural areas. Most residential schools now have school psychologists and social workers, and some have school counselors and consulting psychiatrists. However, in the majority of mainstream programs, many of the psychologists responsible for working with deaf students have little or no experience with or preparation for evaluating youth who are deaf. This has led to a situation where misdiagnoses are common and the recommendations of these psychologists are often inappropriate and do damage to the deaf student.

Despite the "amazing increase in quality of life… there is still a long way to go."

In recent years, through the efforts of psychologists, such as Pollard and Marschark, and psychiatrists, such as Steinberg, work in mental health with deaf people has moved more into the mainstream of psychology and psychiatry. This is a very positive change from previous times, when deafness was of little interest to either the American Psychological Association or the American Psychiatric Association.

Legislation and Advocacy

Federal legislation—some facilitated by the Center for Law and Deafness—has been the basis for much of the progress made by deaf people over the last half century.

For several reasons, laws passed during the last 30 years have made possible what Merv Garretson referred to as "the amazing increase in the quality of life for people who are deaf." First, they guaranteed every deaf child an education up until 21 years of age. Second, they mandated affirmative action policies be implemented in all business, government and private agencies which receive any government funding. The Telecommunications Act is responsible for captioned TV and TDDs in essential places such as police stations, airports, fire stations, hospitals, etc.

The most sweeping law, the Americans with Disabilities Act of 1990, is intended to prevent discrimination in every aspect of society, including employment.

For example, it requires all state and local agencies, hotels, theaters, restaurants, etc. be accessible to those who are deaf.

The greatest progress made by people who are deaf has come from the political activism that has resulted in these revolutionary laws affecting deaf and hard of hearing people. Once this legislation started to be passed, the National Association of the Deaf—with the help of Gallaudet—set up the Law Center for the Deaf, and other advocacy law agencies came into being. These agencies brought test cases that established exactly what rights these laws provided for deaf people. More importantly, these test cases

facilitated the enforcement of these critically important laws.

Despite the "amazing increase in the quality of life for people who are deaf" referred to by Merv Garretson, there is still a long way to go, especially in the area of education. We also need to do much more for the 30–50 percent of deaf adults with educational levels at fourth to fifth grade or below.

McCay Vernon's career in deafness spans the 50 years he has written about in this article. He has worked as a psychologist, teacher, coach, professor and is an author of six books.

From *CSD Spectrum*, Summer 2002, pp. 12-15. © 2002 by CSD Spectrum, a publication of CSD, www.c-s-d.org.

Using Tactile Strategies With Students Who Are Blind and Have Severe Disabilities

June E. Downing • Deborah Chen

Vision is a primary sense for learning. Teachers use pictures, photographs, and a variety of color-coded materials in their instruction. They also use demonstrations and considerable modeling, which requires the students' visual attention. Many students with severe and multiple disabilities have considerable difficulty understanding verbal information and so rely heavily on visual information (Alberto & Frederick, 2000; Hodgdon, 1995; Hughes, Pitkin, & Lorden, 1998).

But what about students who cannot perceive visual cues—or access verbal information? When students have severe and multiple disabilities, teachers must resort to alternative teaching strategies to provide effective and accessible instruction.

If these students are also blind or have limited vision, however, they need instructional materials that provide relevant tactile information. This article describes specific tactile strategies to support instruction of students who have severe and multiple disabilities and who do not learn visually.

> **When students have severe and multiple disabilities, teachers must resort to alternative teaching strategies to provide effective and accessible instruction.**

Getting in Touch

A teacher's instructional style certainly influences what a student learns. Teachers engage their students by providing visual and auditory information. They convey their mood through facial expressions, body language, and tone of voice. They give directions by gestures, pointing, and spoken words. If students cannot receive or understand these modes of communication, the teacher must use alternative strategies. The primary alternatives are tactile. The teacher must convey his or her instructional expectations, mood, and information through physical

and direct contact with the student. Teaching through the sense of touch may be unfamiliar and uncomfortable for most teachers, including those with training in special education. Teachers should become aware of how they interact with the student through touch. To be most effective with tactile teaching, teachers must consider many issues:

- What impressions are conveyed to a student when he or she is touched?
- Do the teacher's hands convey different information depending on their temperature, tenseness of tone, speed of movement, and degree of pressure?
- Are teachers aware of the range of emotions that they can communicate through touch?
- Where do they touch the student (e.g., palms, back of hands, arms, legs, chest)?
- Do they touch the student's bare skin or clothing over the skin?
- How do students respond to different types of tactile input?

To be maximally effective, teachers must become aware of, interpret, monitor, and modify their tactile interactions from the student's perspective.

Tactile Modeling

Sighted students learn from demonstrations and through imitation. Students who are blind or have minimal vision need opportunities to feel the demonstrator's actions by touching the parts of the body or objects involved in the actions (Smith, 1998). For example, in a cooking class, a classmate demonstrates how to make meringue by whipping egg whites. The student who is blind can feel the peer's hand holding the bowl, the other hand grasping the electric mixer. This way, the student who is blind can "see" what his or her classmate is demonstrating. Like other tactile adaptations, the use of tactile modeling requires careful planning on the part of the teacher and extra time for the student to benefit from this instructional strategy.

Tactile Mutual Attention

Sighted students visually examine and make observations about something they are looking at together. The student with minimal or no vision should have opportunities for shared exploration with classmates through tactile mutual attention (Miles, 1999). For example, during a unit of study on masks, the student and a classmate may tactilely examine an African mask, placing their hands together as they explore the relatively smooth parts of the mask and find the leather strips, beads, and decorative feathers that border the mask. This way the student has a joint focus and shares observations with a classmate. Sighted classmates will have many creative ideas of ways to use tactile modeling and tactile mutual attention with peers who are blind and have additional disabilities (see Figure 1).

Tactile Learning and Teaching

When students with severe disabilities are unable to use their vision effectively for obtaining information, they require tactile information that is accessible to their hands or other parts of their body. Tactile information, however, has different characteristics from visual.

Unlike vision, touch provides a fragment of the whole; the student must put together a series of tactile impressions to understand what other students are looking at. For example, fourth-grade students are studying different aspects of life in the desert. One student, who is deaf and blind and does not know American Sign Language, is feeling a large desert tortoise. One hand is near the tail, and the other hand is feeling one edge of the shell near the tortoise's head. It will take this student considerable time and effort to tactilely examine and discover the physical characteristics of a tortoise, while his classmates can see that it is a tortoise in one glance.

> **Unlike vision, touch provides a fragment of the whole; the student must put together a series of tactile impressions to understand what other students are looking at.**

Certain concepts are easier to convey tactilely than others. Abstract concepts are much more difficult to adapt tactilely than more concrete facts. For instance, it is much easier to teach about helium using balloons than it is to teach historical events. The teacher must ensure that the tactile representation is truly representative of the concept and is relevant and meaningful to the student. For example, to teach that the solid state of water is ice, the use of raised (tactile) lines in waves to represent water and raised (tactile) straight lines to represent ice is not meaningful or understandable to most students with severe and multiple disabilities. In contrast, the use of water (wet, liquid) and ice (cold, solid) would clearly represent the critical aspects of the topic of study.

Figure 1. Considerations for Interacting Through Touch

1. Select the message that you want to communicate to the student (e.g., greeting, reassurance, encouragement, praise, redirection, demonstration).
2. Decide how best to communicate that message through the type of touch (i.e., duration, pressure, movement) and where to touch the student (e.g., back of hand, shoulder, or knee).
3. Identify how you will let the student know that you are close (e.g., by saying his name) before touching him or her (e.g., on the elbow).
4. Discuss whether and how to examine an item with the student (e.g., by having two students examine an African mask).
5. Decide whether and how to use tactile modeling (e.g., by asking a classmate to show the student how to blow up a balloon).
6. Observe the student's reactions to your tactile interactions and modify the interaction accordingly.
7. Identify how you will end the interaction (e.g., let the student know that you are leaving by giving him a double pat on the shoulder).

The educational team must decide what aspects of a lesson can be represented tactilely to make instruction most easily understood. At times, the best tactile representation may be tangential to the specific subject. For example, for a lesson on Lewis and Clark and their exploration of the West, artifacts of the Old West (e.g., pieces of clothing, fur, leather pieces, a whip, and tools) can be used to provide a tactile experience for the student with no usable vision. Such items would also benefit the entire class. Acting out the event using objects as props also adds clarity and interest to a seemingly abstract topic.

Obviously, students with different skills and abilities will develop different concepts of the topic of study. For example, whereas fifth-grade students without disabilities in geometry class learn how to find the area of a square, a student who has severe and multiple impairments, including blindness, may just be learning to sort square shapes from round ones. General and special educators need to understand such differences and still challenge students to learn what they can.

Presenting Tactile Information

You can provide visual (e.g., pictures or sign language) and auditory (e.g., speech) information to several students at once. These so called *distance senses* are quick and efficient. In contrast, tactile information requires individual physical contact and takes more time to understand. You must allow extra time for presentation of tactile information so the student has an opportunity to touch, handle, examine, and eventually synthesize and understand information (Downing & Demchak, 2002). Here are some reminders:

- Decide how to introduce an item to the student.

- The item should be accessible so the student can detect its presence and then manipulate it to determine its identity or relationship to familiar experiences.
- Touching the item to some part of the student's body (e.g., arm or side or back of hand) is less intrusive than manipulating the student's hand to take the item and therefore, such an approach is recommended (Dote-Kwan & Chen, 1999; Miles, 1999; Smith, 1998). Some students are timid about tactile exploration because they are wary and careful about handling unfamiliar or disliked materials.

> # Allow extra time for presentation of tactile information so the student has an opportunity to touch, handle, examine, and eventually synthesize and understand information.

A teacher or peer may introduce a new object to the student, by holding the object, and placing the back of his or her hand under the student's hand. The student is more likely to accept the touch of a familiar hand than that of an unfamiliar object. Slowly the teacher or peer can rotate his or her hand until the student is touching the object. This way the student has physical support while deciding whether to touch and examine the object (Dote-Kwan & Chen, 1999). After the student detects the presence of the item, he or she is more likely to take the item and explore it (if physically possible).

Ideally, students will use their hands to explore; however, some students have such severe physical disabilities that they may use touch receptors in their tongue, on their cheeks, or inside of their arms. In all cases, you need to encourage the student's active participation (even if only partial) in accessing information.

Providing Effective Tactile Representation

To determine whether tactile information is truly representative of a specific concept, the representation must be tactilely salient and meaningful. Because it is natural for sighted teachers to have a visual perspective, it is difficult to make tactile adaptations that make sense tactilely. For example, tactile outlines of items (e.g., string glued to a drawing of a house) may be used to represent different concepts but may not be recognized tactilely or understood by the student. Although miniatures are convenient because of their size and are easy to handle, they are based on visual characteristics of the objects they represent. For example, a small plastic dog has no tactile characteristics in common with a real dog. Similarly, a miniature of a house, while visually recognizable, does not resemble a house when examined tactilely. A key that the student has used to open the front door of his house will form a more accurate concept of "house."

Experiment with what can be perceived tactilely by blindfolding yourself and examining the adaptation using only your sense of touch. In addition, avoid misconceptions as much as possible. For example, in a kindergarten classroom, a student brought a glass paperweight with a rose in it for show and tell. He talked about the rose as he passed it around the class. When a classmate who has no vision and limited language was allowed to hold the paperweight, he was confused when told "it's a rose." More appropriate language should be used to describe what this student is experiencing (e.g., "round," "smooth," "heavy," and "glass"). If this student is to understand the meaning of "rose," then you need to provide a real rose, so the student can perceive its shape, texture, size, and scent (see Figure 2 for other considerations).

Hyperresponsivity to Touch

Some students demonstrate strong reactions to tactile information, even though this may be the best way for them to receive information. These reactions are often referred to as *tactile defensiveness* and treated as a negative characteristic of the student. Some people have a low sensory threshold and are hyperreactive or hyperresponsive to certain sensory stimulation (Williamson & Anzalone, 2001). Tactile responsivity is simply the degree to which an individual responds to tactile stimulation. Some individuals can tolerate considerable and varied amounts of tactile input without much reaction (e.g., tactile hyporesponsivity), while others are very sensitive to certain types of tactile input (tactile hyperresponsivity). These responses vary from person to person. Some people can wear certain fabrics next to their skin while others cannot.

Teachers must be aware of and respect these individual differences. Teachers should not take students' hands and physically make them touch materials if they are not willing to do so (Smith, 1998). If students are forced to have aversive tactile experiences, they are less likely to explore tactilely. The term tactile defensiveness has a nega-

---

Figure 2. Considerations for Developing Tactile Adaptions

1. Identify the objective of the lesson or the instructional concept.
2. Select the materials to convey this concept.
3. Close your eyes and examine the material with your hands.
4. Take a tactile perspective, not visual, when deciding how and what to present.
5. If the entire concept (e.g., house) is too complicated to represent through a tactile adaptation, then select one aspect of the concept (e.g., key) for the tactile representation.
6. Consider the student's previous tactile experiences. What items has he or she examined?
7. How does the student examine materials through the sense of touch?
8. Decide how the item will be introduced to the student.
9. Identify what supports the student needs to tactilely examine the item.
10. Decide what language input (descriptive words) will be used to convey the student's experience of the material.

tive connotation that may interfere with effective intervention. If the student has a sensory modulation problem that results in hyperresponsiveness, then the educational team should include an occupational therapist. Creative ways to bypass this problem and assist the student to handle tactile information are needed.

A Team Effort

Making appropriate tactile accommodations (instructional strategies or materials) cannot be left to one member of the team (i.e., the teacher certified in the area of visual impairment). A team effort is required, with different team members contributing their skills, knowledge, experiences, and ideas (Downing, 2002; Silberman, Sacks, & Wolfe, 1998). A special educator specifically trained in the area of visual impairments and blindness can be helpful with teaching ideas and tactile resources. Depending on this teacher's professional training and experiences, however, he or she may be unfamiliar with the types of accommodations a particular student may need. The student who is blind, has spoken language, and reads braille has very different learning needs from those of a student who does not speak, does not read braille, and has limited receptive language.

Relying on one specialist to meet the tactile needs of a student who is blind with additional severe disabilities should be avoided. The ideas of all members of the team are needed, including family members and classmates who do not have disabilities (Downing, 2002). This way tactile adaptations and strategies are more likely to be used at home and school and with peers.

Team members should consider how the student perceives information through touch, the student's best physical position, the student's ability to move different parts of his body, and past experiences with tactile information. Family members can provide insight on the student's tactile experiences and preferences. Occupational therapists can provide valuable information on the student's use of his hands, responsivity to tactile items, and strategies to decrease hyperresponsivity. Physical therapists can help with positioning considerations and adaptive equipment that support tactile exploration. In collaboration with the general educator, the teacher certified in visual impairments can provide ideas for making tactile adaptations to instructional materials. Classmates can be asked for their ideas on how to use tactile modeling or to gather objects and tactile materials that can make a lesson more meaningful.

The ideas of all members of the team are needed, including family members and classmates who do not have disabilities.

Final Thoughts

Meeting the learning needs of students who have severe disabilities and who do not have clear access to visual information is a significant instructional challenge. Teaching through touch is unfamiliar and perhaps awkward for most sighted people, but learning though touch is essential for students who are blind or have minimal vision. Effective use of tactile strategies must consider the individual student's needs and abilities, learning environment, and task. These strategies can best support students' learning when there is a concerted effort on the part of the educational team, additional time for the presentation of tactile information, and systematic evaluation of adaptations.

References

Alberto, P. A., & Frederick, L. D. (2000). Teaching picture reading as an enabling skill. *TEACHING Exceptional Children, 33*(1), 60-64.

Dote-Kwan, J., & Chen, D. (1999). Developing meaningful interventions. In D. Chen (Ed.), *Essential elements in early communication visual impairments and multiple disabilities* (pp. 287-336). New York: American Foundation for the Blind Press.

Downing, J. E. (2002). Working cooperatively: The role of team members. In J. E. Downing (Ed.), *Including students with severe and multiple disabilities in typical classrooms: Practical strategies for teachers* (2nd ed., pp. 189-210). Baltimore: Paul H. Brookes.

Downing, J. E., & Demchak, M. A. (2002). First steps: Determining individual abilities and how best to support students. In J. E. Downing (Ed.), *Including students with severe and multiple disabilities in typical classrooms: Practical strategies for teachers* (2nd ed., pp. 37-70). Baltimore: Paul H. Brookes.

Hodgdon, L. A. (1995). *Visual strategies for improving communication. Vol. 1: Practical supports for school and home.* Troy, MI: QuirkRoberts.

Hughes, C., Pitkin, S. E., & Lorden, S. W. (1998). Assessing preferences and choices of persons with severe and profound mental retardation. *Education and Training in Mental Retardation and Developmental Disabilities, 33,* 299-316.

Miles, B. (1999). *Talking the language of the hands to the hands.* Monmouth, OR: DBLINK, The National Information Clearinghouse on Children Who Are Deaf-Blind. (ERIC Document Reproduction Service No. ED 419 331)

Silberman, R. K., Sacks, S. Z., & Wolfe, J. (1998). Instructional strategies for educating students who have visual impairments with severe disabilities. In S. Z. Sacks & R. K. Silberman (Eds.), *Educating students who have visual impairments with other disabilities* (pp. 101-137). Baltimore: Paul H. Brookes.

Smith, M. (1998). Feelin' groovy: Functional tactual skills. Retrieved January 24, 2000, from http://www.tsbvi.edu/Outreach/seehear/summer98/groovy.htm

Williamson, G. G., & Anzalone, M. (2001). *Sensory integration and self regulation in infants and toddlers: Helping very young children interact with their environment.* Washington, DC: Zero to Three. (ERIC Document Reproduction Service No. ED 466 317)

Article 22. Using Tactile Strategies With Students Who Are Blind and Have Severe Disabilities

June E. Downing *(CEC Chapter #29), Professor; and* **Deborah Chen** *(CEC Chapter #918) Professor, Department of Special Education, California State University, Northridge.*

Address correspondence to June E. Downing, Department of Special Education, California State University, Northridge, 18111 Nordhoff St., Northridge, CA 91330-8265 (e-mail: june.downing@csun.edu).

The development of this article was supported by the U.S. Department of Education, Office of Special Education and Rehabilitative Services Grant # H3224T990025. The content, however, does not necessarily reflect the views of the U.S. Department of Education, and no official endorsement should be inferred.

UNIT 8
Multiple Disabilities

Unit Selections

Key Points to Consider

- What types of preplanning, and planning are required to develop IEPs for students with multiple disabilities being integrated into general education settings? Why is collaboration essential?

- Can paraeducators make a difference in the education of students with multiple disabilities? How can paraeducators be taught specialized skills quickly?

- Can teachers access state-of-the-art technology to assist in their education of students with multiple disabilities? How?

 **Links: www.dushkin.com/online/**
These sites are annotated in the World Wide Web pages.

Activity Ideas for Students With Severe, Profound, or Multiple Disabilities
http://www.palaestra.com/featurestory.html
Severe and/or Multiple Disabilities
http://www.nichcy.org/pubs/factshe/fs10txt.htm

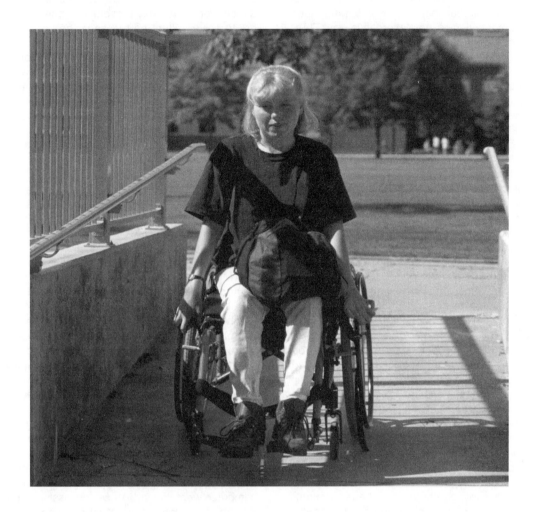

For most of the twentieth century, children with multiple disabilities (MD) were kept hidden in their parents' homes or put into institutions. Any father or mother presenting such a child at a public school for admission was ridiculed and turned away. The 1975 Individuals with Disabilities Education Act (IDEA) in the United States has turned this around. Such children may now be enrolled in general education classes if that is appropriate. They are entitled to a free education in the least restrictive environment that serves their needs. IDEA, in its years of existence, has allowed millions of students, who once would have been written off as "uneducable to be given some form of schooling."

A child placed in the category of multiple disabilities (MD) has two or more co-occurring areas of exceptionality. Each child with MD is very special and very needy. Consider the physicist, Steven Hawking, who has a brilliant mind but cannot communicate or move without augmentative technology. While many MD students have some cognitive disabilities, many have normal or above normal intellect. Their impairments may be developmental disabilities, speech and language impairments, autism, traumatic brain injuries, emotional and behavioral disorders, visual impairments, hearing impairments, orthopedic impairments, health impairments, or any combination of these.

The practice of deinstitutionalization (removing individuals from hospitals and large residential institutions and keeping them in their own homes) and the legal initiatives requiring free and appropriate public education in the least restrictive environment have closed some of the cracks through which these children once fell.

Schools are attempting to provide students with MD with the best education possible. Often, when schools fail, it is some condition(s) outside the school's control which share the onus of responsibility. Schools, when they fail to be effective, usually provide inadequate services due to lack of professional development. Without adequate teacher preparation and sufficient teaching support, education of all children in inclusive classrooms becomes infeasible. Professional development must be both improved and expanded to give regularized education a leg to stand on.

Another problem that looms large in the appropriate education for children with MD is lack of acceptance and preparation by the lay public and the macrosystem to accept their inclusion in public schools. Advocates for the rights of disabled individuals have used the term "handicapism" to describe this prejudice and discrimination directed at disabled students. The greater the disability, the greater the evinced prejudice. A disability (not able) is not the same as a handicap (hindrance, not at an advantage). The words should not be used interchangeably. A person who is not able to do something (walk, see, hear) has a disability but does not have to be handicapped. Schools and communities may impose handicaps (hindrances) by preventing the student with the disability from functioning in an alternative way. Thus, if a student who cannot walk can instead locomote in a wheelchair, he or she is not handicapped. If a building or classroom has no ramps, however, and is inaccessible to a wheelchair user, then the school has imposed a handicap by preventing access to that particular property of the environment. If a student cannot use vocal cords to communicate, and is provided with an augmentative and alternate communication (AAC) system, he or she is not handicapped. If a building or classroom has no power supply or other provisions for use of the AAC system, then the environment again has imposed a handicap. There are millions of ways in which properties of our environments and characteristics of our behavior prevent children with multiple disabilities from functioning up to their potentialities.

Some public schools have resisted the regular education initiative (REI) that calls for general education classes rather than special education classes to be primarily responsible for the education of students with more severe and multiple disabilities. The inclusive school movement, which supports the REI, would have special education teachers become consultants, resource specialists, or collaborative teachers rather than full-time special education teachers. While arguments for and against the REI have not been resolved, most educators agree that an appropriate education for each child with a disability may require a continuum of services. Some children, especially those with multiple disabilities, may require an environment more restrictive than a general education classroom for at least part of the day in order to get the type of assistance they need to function up to their potentialities. Teacher education typically does not offer comprehensive preparation for working with children with MD who require extensive special educational services. In addition, children with MD often require related services (for example, chemotherapy, physical therapy, psychotherapy, transportation) to enable them to learn in a classroom environment. Hopefully, teacher preparation, in-service education, and professional development sessions will address some of these concerns of service delivery in the near future.

Many children and youth with MD suffer from a lack of understanding, a lack of empathy, and handicapist attitudes that are directed at them. They present very special problems for teachers to solve. Often the message they hear is, "Just go away." The challenge of writing an appropriate individualized education plan (IEP) is enormous. Updating the IEP each year and preparing an individualized transition plan (ITP), which will allow the student with MD to function as independently as possible after age 21, is mandated by law. These students must be served. Teachers must be given the time and support needed to do so. Excuses such as no time, no money, and no personnel to provide appropriate services are unacceptable. Teachers can expect progress and good results, even with the most multiply disabled.

The first article in this unit, "Making Inclusion a Reality for Students with Severe Disabilities," emphasizes the how, when, and where of inclusion. The time for debating whether to include students with MD is past. Collaborative planning is essential for appropriate integration and education of students with MD. A cascade of integration options makes it possible for students with MD to be included even during content area instruction. The authors give suggestions for designing IEPs with workable instructional objectives.

The second article in this unit suggests that paraeducators can play a very important role in giving one-on-one services to students with MD in inclusive education settings, but it is necessary that in-service training be provided for paraeducators. This selection describes a one-day workshop that gives paraeducators an overview of effective methods of teaching adaptive skills to students with MD. Many highly successful teaching strategies can be learned quite quickly in this program.

The unit's final article discusses the uses of new technology to construct alternate portfolios for students with multiple disabilities. Four students with physical, cognitive, and behavioral characteristics of disability who were unable to learn on a standard computer were taught to use the assistive Intellikeys instead. They had a smorgasbord of other technological aids, and customized Intellikeys overlays. All four students showed increased achievement and independence.

Making Inclusion a Reality for Students With Severe Disabilities

Pamela S. Wolfe and Tracey E. Hall

Let's end the debate about *whether* to include students with severe disabilities in the general education classroom (see box, "What Does the Literature Say?"). Let's focus on *how* and *when* and *where*. This article provides helpful perspectives and suggestions for teachers, students, and parents in the struggle to provide an appropriate education for all students.

Here, we provide a cascade of integration options for inclusion. These integration options are based on the work of many researchers (Bradley, King-Sears, & Tessier-Switlick, 1997; Giangreco, Cloninger, & Iverson, 1998; Janney & Snell, 2000; Stainback & Stainback, 2000).

The social integration focus of inclusion negates the opportunity for the student with disabilities to receive instruction in content areas.

In these options, we have applied content area instruction to inclusive settings, using a case example. We have also outlined a system designed to facilitate collaborative planning between general and special education teachers, using a student's individualized education program (IEP) as a foundation for decision making. Use of the IEP ensures that educational programming is both individualized and integrated with the general classroom curriculum.

The Cascade of Integration Options

The Individuals with Disabilities Education Act (IDEA) promotes the concept of placement of students with disabilities into the least restrictive environment (LRE). The concept of LRE is based on the belief that educators must provide a range of placement options (Mastropieri &

Scruggs, 2000; Thomas & Rapport, 1998). A cascade of placement options can range from the home-school and general education class setting to institutional placements. This cascade of services highlights the need to individualize and base decisions for placement on the student's unique needs.

As noted, schools and districts are placing more students with severe disabilities in general education settings. But placement alone is insufficient to guarantee that the student with disabilities will benefit educationally. The optimal integration option is based on two factors:

- The type of activity undertaken in the general education setting.
- The objectives stated on the student's IEP.

Decisions about including a student with severe disabilities are frequently oriented toward fitting the student into the existing general education classroom activities and focus primarily on social integration (Scruggs & Mastropieri, 1996). The social integration focus negates the opportunity for the "included" student to receive instruction in content areas. Although we acknowledge the value of social integration, we advocate that programming should emanate from the student's IEP objectives. Teachers should consider content area coursework as a means by which the student may meet his or her IEP objectives. For example, teachers can address many objectives from the IEP in the general education setting by considering a range of adaptations and accommodations.

The Cascade of Integration Options illustrates a range of accommodations for students with severe disabilities who are included in general education settings (see box, "Cascade of Integration Options"). This cascade includes the following poles:

- The least restrictive inclusion option in which no changes are made (unadapted participation in the general education curriculum).

What Does the Literature Say About Inclusion for Students With Severe Disabilities?

The inclusion of students with severe disabilities into general education classrooms has become increasingly prevalent (Katsiyannis, Conderman, & Franks, 1995; Sailor, Gee, & Karasoff, 2000; U.S. Department of Education, 2000). Although IDEA '97 does not mandate the inclusion of students with disabilities, the legislation strongly encourages consideration of appropriate placement in general education settings.

Definition. The term *inclusion* has many interpretations. We have adopted the definition of inclusion noted by Mastropieri and Scruggs (2000) in which *students with disabilities are served in the general education classroom under the instruction of the general education teacher.* Specifically it involves providing support services to the student in the general education setting versus excluding the student from the setting and their peers. Inclusion requires the provision of adaptations and accommodations to classroom curriculum to ensure that the student will benefit from the placement. The definition, however, does not require that the student with special needs perform at a level comparable to peers without disabilities.

Benefits of Inclusion. Many research studies have shown that the inclusion of students with severe disabilities into general education settings is beneficial for all students (those with and without disabilities) particularly in relation to social acceptance, self-esteem, and social skills (Kennedy, Shukla, & Fryxell, 1997; Mu, Siegel, & Allinder, 2000). Although some research has indicated

academic gains, teachers are more challenged to appropriately include students with severe disabilities in the content areas (Heller, 2001). Content domain areas include social studies, sciences, health, and related academic subjects.

Role of IEP. Given that the goal of inclusion is to assure that *all* students benefit from instruction, educators must provide programming that meets the needs of *all* students including those with disabilities. For students with disabilities, the IEP serves as the document to guide program planning and instruction. Educators should use the IEP to determine *what* should be taught, *how* the content should be taught, and *who* can most appropriately provide instruction.

Roles of Professionals. There are many professions involved in providing services for students with severe disabilities in included settings. Two frequent members to this team of professionals are the general education and special education teachers. The collaboration of these teachers is essential to assure that the student with disabilities is successful in the placement both socially and academically (Jackson, Ryndak, & Billingsley, 2000; Salend, 2001; Salisbury, Evans, & Palombaro, 1997; Snell & Janney, 2000). Both teachers need to be aware of the student's IEP objectives and use this document to guide program planning decisions and data collection procedures. To meet the needs of students with disabilities in the general education classroom, changes in the curriculum may be necessary.

- A more restrictive option in which students with severe disabilities are temporarily removed from the setting (functional curriculum outside the general education classroom).

The cascade also includes a series of questions designed to help educators make decisions concerning the most appropriate integration options during content area instruction.

Collaborative Planning for Inclusion

As noted previously, the collaboration of educators involved with the student having severe disabilities is essential to ensure appropriate integration and educational programming. Special and general education teachers must share knowledge about teaching strategies when planning effective instruction. Through collaborative teaming, teachers set the stage for student achievement of goals.

We have identified two stages of planning for special and general education teachers when considering options for content area integration. Table 1 lists these stages as *preplanning* and collaborative *planning* activities.

- *In the preplanning stages,* the general education teacher reflects on the content area unit activities and conducts a task analysis to identify key components of the lessons. Once the general education teacher has identified components of the unit, the special education teacher is asked to reflect upon the individual student's IEP objectives and how those objectives can be addressed in the general education content area unit. This stage is a *thinking* or *reflection activity* before a meeting; or the teachers could hold a face-to-face meeting to think together.

- *In the collaborative planning stage,* the two teachers meet to determine the most appropriate integration options in relation to the IEP, what adaptations or accommodations will be re-

Cascade of Integration Options

Unadapted participation in the general curriculum
Same activities, same objectives, same setting
- Can student complete the activities as written for the general education classroom?
- Do one or more lesson objectives match the student's IEP?

Adaptations to the general curriculum
Same activities, different (related) objectives, same setting
- Can the student meet the lesson objectives with minor modifications (time, response mode)?

Embedded skills within the general curriculum
Similar activity, different (related) objectives, same setting
- Are there components of the activity that can be met by the students, even if not the central objective of the lesson but match an IEP objective?

Functional curriculum in the general education classroom
Different activities, different (related) objectives, same setting
- Are the class activities greatly unrelated to the student's IEP? Are there IEP? Are there IEP objectives that could be met in the same setting?

Functional curriculum outside general education classroom
Different activities, different (unrelated) objectives, different setting
- Are the class activities greatly unrelated to the student's IEP? Are IEP objectives better met in a different setting (require equipment, repetition, etc.)?

quired, what additional supports are needed, and how student progress will be monitored (see Table 1).

Case Study of Collaborative Planning

Table 2 shows a case example of the Cascade of Integration Options in operation, as educators implement accommodations for a student included in content area instruction. The example reflects the plan for a student named Billy, who is included in a sixth-grade classroom.

Billy's IEP contains instructional objectives in a variety of domain areas, including communication, functional academics, socialization, fine and gross motor skills, hygiene, and leisure and recreation. The teachers formed their instructional plan based on Billy's IEP objectives.

The teachers collaboratively determined how they could meet many of Billy's IEP objectives within the content area of social studies.

Critical to the successful application of the Cascade is a well-designed IEP with clearly stated instructional objectives

---

As Table 2 illustrates, the integration option varies across the activities and days of the instructional unit. Further, note that the teachers considered the need for additional support to implement instruction (adaptive equipment, additional personnel, technical support). In this case Billy was able to work on nearly all of his IEP objectives in the content area unit. The one exception is Billy's IEP objective related to hygiene; for programming related to showering and shaving, Billy is temporarily removed from the general education setting (functional curriculum outside the general classroom conducted during an adapted physical education class).

As Table 2 shows, teachers used a variety of integration options. Through the use of integration options, Billy was able to obtain instruction on important IEP objectives even though he did not always work on the general education social studies outcomes. Further, by employing the Cascade of Integration Options, Billy's teachers were able to provide Billy with the following:

- Social skills practice.
- Instruction on social studies information.
- Instruction on IEP objectives that focused on Billy's needs.

Although this article focused on the case of Billy, educators can apply the Cascade of Integration Options with most students and areas of instruction, throughout the school year. Critical to the successful application of the Cascade is a well-designed IEP with clearly stated instructional objectives.

Final Thoughts

Inclusion of students with disabilities requires the provision of curriculum and classroom adaptations. But inclusion does not require that the student with special needs perform at a level comparable to peers without disabilities. Students with disabilities may be included during content area instruction if teachers consider the Cascade of Integration Options.

If teachers collaborate to employ such options through carefully planned instruction, they can include students with severe disabilities in general education settings in meaningful ways—for *all* students.

Table 1. Stages of Planning for Curriculum Adaptations for Student With Disabilities in General Education Settings

Preplanning		Planning
General Education Teacher Unit Plan Analysis	*Special Education Teacher*	*General and Special Education Teacher Planning Meeting*
What are the objectives of my lessons? • What is the purpose of the unit? • What skills do I want students to obtain? What are the steps students must undertake to complete the unit? • What are the component activities within the series of lessons? (list in order) • Do the activities directly relate to the overall objective of the unit? • Are the steps logically sequenced? Will the completion of the unit include individual and/or group activities? • Cooperative Learning Groups • Individual • Group activities • Individual and Group What learner products are expected? • Written report • Oral Report • Tests • Computer Question • Concept maps/graphic displays What is the time frame to complete the activities for this unit? • Single day • Monthly • Weekly • Bimonthly • Longer term What are the required materials for the activities and/or unit? • Resource materials • Class text • Computer internet • Misc. materials (school, home) How will student progress be assessed throughout the unit? • End-of-unit test • Rubric • Performance or subjective evaluation	What are the IEP objectives for the included student(s)? What domain areas from the IEP can be addressed in the instructional unit? Does this student have characteristics that will require adaptations? Have I considered: • Cognitive skills • Motor skills • Communication skills • Social skills What levels of adaptations from the continuum are appropriate for this student for different activities within the unit? What required unit adaptations could be made for this student in terms of the following: • Materials • Time requirements • Product expectations	Based on the unit analysis, what IEP objectives can be worked on during content area instruction? What adaptations or accommodations will be required to work on these objectives? What other supports will the general education teacher need to successfully complete the activity? • Teaching assistant present • Adaptive equipment • Technical support • Materials adaptations • Co-teach with special education teacher Are the student's IEP objectives being addressed in this unit in a meaningful way? How will teachers communicate about student progress throughout the unit? • Informal discussion • Weekly meetings • Report from assistant • Communication journal How will progress toward attainment of IEP goal(s) be assessed?

Table 2. Case Example of Collaborative Planning in Content Area Instruction (Social Studies)

Preplanning

	Day 1	Day 2	Day 3	Day 4	Day 5
Activity	Assign to one of three map groups. • Political map • Geographic map • Natural resources map Start research for map information. Textbook, Encyclopedia. Newspaper, Library books, CD-ROM, Internet. 30-minute library time.	Continue research. Draw the map on 3' x 5' poster board, include scale, legend, major cities, and landmarks. Each student must draw and color a minimum of 10 features for specific map in appropriate location. 1-hour map making.	Continue map making: Draw the map on 3' x 5' poster board, include scale, legend, major cities, and landmarks. Draw or color features for specific map in appropriate location. 1-hour map making.	Final map construction. Preparation for oral presentation. Division of speaking roles. 30-minutes map work. 30-minutes presentation work.	Three groups orally present maps to class. 30-minute presentations for each group.
IEP Objective	**Communication:** Initiate conversation about map with group members using communication device. **Functional Academics Reading:** Identify parts of newspaper for peers to find map information. **Social Skills:** Take turns interacting with peers during research; maintain appropriate personal space. **Gross Motor:** Manipulate wheelchair to and within library.	**Fine Motor:** Cut out three pictures that represent resources on the map with adaptive scissors. **Functional Academics Math:** Count the number of resource features group members made (10 each). **Communication:** Initiative with peers if ready for them to count if number of items is correct using communication device.	**Fine Motor:** Paste the three objects on the map. **Functional Academics Math:** Alert the group when time is up map making. **Communication:** Initiate communication with peers using device.	**Functional Academics Reading:** While students are completing research information for presentation, student uses newspaper to identify leisure activities (movie section, TV guide). **Leisure:** Select preferred leisure activity for the weekend. **Functional Academics Math:** Practice time-telling in preparation for group presentation, day 5.	**Communication:** Introduce members of the working group to the class using communication device. **Functional Academics Math:** Keep time for the group. Notify members when half-hour period is over.

Planning

	Day 1	Day 2	Day 3	Day 4	Day 5
Level of Adaptation	Embedded skills within the general curriculum. Similar activities, different objectives, same setting.	Adaptations to the general curriculum. Same activities, different objectives, same setting.	Adaptations to the general curriculum. Same activities, different objectives, same setting.	Functional curriculum in the general education classroom. Different activities, different objectives, same setting.	Unadapted participation in the general curriculum. Same activities, same objective, same setting.
Support from Special Education Teacher	Co-teach presentation of the map assignment to class. Needed technical support.	Provide adapted scissors to general education room. Provide enlarged pictures for student to cut. Needed technical support.	Needed technical support.	Needed technical support.	None.

References

Bradley, D. F., King-Sears, M. E., & Tessier-Switlick, D. M. (1997). *Teaching students in inclusive settings.* Boston: Allyn & Bacon.

Heller, K. W. (2001). Adaptations and instruction in science and social studies. In J. L. Bigge, S. J. Best, & K. W. Heller (Eds.), *Teaching individuals with physical, health, or multiple disabilities* (4th ed., pp). Upper Saddle River, NJ: Merrill.

Giangreco, M. F., Cloninger, C. J., & Iverson, V. S. (1998). *Choosing outcomes and accommodations for children* (2nd ed.). Baltimore: Paul H. Brookes.

Jackson, L., Ryndak, D. L., & Billingsley, F. (2000). Useful practices in inclusive education: A preliminary view of what experts in moderate to severe disabilities are saying. *Journal of The Association for Persons with Severe Handicaps, 25*(3), 129–141.

Janney, R., & Snell, M. E. (2000). *Teachers' guide to inclusive practices: Modifying schoolwork.* Baltimore: Paul H. Brookes.

Katsiyannis, A., Conderman, G., & Franks, D. J. (1995). State practices on inclusion: A national review. *Remedial and Special Education, 16,* 279–287.

Kennedy, C. H., Shukla, S., & Fryxell, D. (1997). Comparing the effects of educational placement on the social relationships of intermediate school students with severe disabilities. *Exceptional Children, 64,* 31–47.

Mastropieri, M. A., & Scruggs, T. E. (2000). *The inclusive classroom. Strategies for effective instruction.* Upper Saddle River, NJ: Merrill.

Mu, K., Siegel, E. B., & Allinder, R. M. (2000). Peer interactions and sociometric status of high school students with moderate or severe disabilities in general education classrooms. *Journal of The Association for Persons with Severe Handicaps, 25*(3), 142–152.

Sailor, W., Gee, K., & Karasoff, P. (2000). Inclusion and school restructuring. In M. E. Snell & F. Brown (Eds.), *Instruction of students with severe disabilities* (5th ed.), *31–66.* Upper Saddle River, NJ: Merrill.

Salend, S. J. (2001). *Creating inclusive classrooms. Effective and reflective practices* (4th ed.). Upper Saddle River, NJ: Merrill.

Salisbury, C. L., Evans, I. M., & Palombaro, M. M. (1997). Collaborative problem-solving to promote the inclusion of young children with significant disabilities in primary grades. *Exceptional Children, 63,* 195–209.

Scruggs, T. E., & Mastropieri, M. A. (1996). Teacher perceptions of mainstreaming/inclusion 1958–1995: A research synthesis. *Exceptional Children, 63,* 59–74.

Snell, M. E., & Janney, R. (2000). *Teachers' guides to inclusive practices: Collaborative teaming.* Baltimore: Paul H. Brookes.

Stainback, S., & Stainback, W. (Eds.). (2000). *Inclusion: A guide for educators.* Baltimore: Paul H. Brookes.

Thomas, S. B., & Rapport, M. J. K. (1998). The least restrictive environment: Understanding the directions of the courts. *The Journal of Special Education, 32*(2), 66–78.

U.S. Department of Education. (2000). *Twenty-second annual report to Congress on the implementation of the Individuals with Disabilities Education Act.* Washington, DC: Author. (ERIC Document Reproduction Service No. ED 444 333)

Pamela S. Wolfe, *Associate Professor, Department of Educational and School Psychology and Special Education, The Pennsylvania State University, University Park.* **Tracey E. Hall** *(CEC Chapter #18), Senior Research Scientist/ Instructional Designer, Center for Applied Special Technology (CAST), Peabody, Massachusetts.*

Address correspondence to Pamela S. Wolfe, 212A CEDAR Building, The Pennsylvania State University, University Park, PA 16802 (e-mail; psw7@psu.edu).

Training Basic Teaching Skills to Paraeducators of Students with Severe Disabilities

A One-Day Program

Lakeisha beams at the teacher as she demonstrates her new skills at setting the table with plates, cups, forks, an napkins.

The new paraeducator can't wait to report that he successfully taught Jon to put on his coat independently.

Finally conquering the copy machine at her workplace, Susan proudly delivered 30 copies of the newsletter to her co-workers.

Marsha B. Parsons
Dennis H. Reid

Since the early 1970s, a technology for teaching students with severe disabilities has been evolving. Research behind the development of this teaching technology has indicated that the strategies for teaching students with severe disabilities are somewhat different from strategies used with students who have mild or moderate disabilities. Whereas the latter students may benefit substantially from teaching strategies based on verbal instruction, students with severe disabilities often require more individual instruction, using a high degree of physical guidance.

This article shows that when teachers and other staff members proficiently use physical guidance in conjunction with other teaching strategies, such as task analysis, prompting, reinforcement, and error correction, students with severe disabilities can learn useful skills (Parsons, Reid, & Green, 1993). And paraeducators can quickly learn to assist students with their learning.

The role of paraeducators is becoming even more important as greater numbers of students with severe disabilities receive their education in inclusive settings.

Paraeducators in Inclusive Settings

The valuable role paraeducators can play in teaching students with severe disabilities is currently well recognized and is becoming even more important as greater numbers of students with severe disabilities receive their education in inclusive settings. Whereas special education teachers often learn appropriate teaching strategies during their preservice training, paraeducators rarely have specific preservice training in how to use the teaching strategies that constitute "best practice" for these students. Hence, a major need in special education is to provide inservice training for paraeducators in effective methods of teaching adaptive skills to students with severe disabilities.

TSTP is efficient because the program can be conducted in one 8-hour workday.

Characteristics of Successful Staff Training Programs

Research has delineated four characteristics of successful staff training programs (Reid, Parsons, & Green, 1989). Each of these characteristics is particularly relevant in selecting a program for training paraeducators to teach students with severe disabilities.

1. Training focuses on *performance-based skills:* The training emphasizes what staff *do* when teaching their students. Although many programs provide interesting and *potentially* useful knowledge regarding teaching processes, such programs rarely train staff specifically how to apply the knowledge in actual teaching situations. How well paraeducators translate knowledge about the teaching process into the action of teaching directly affects the quality of education students receive.

2. Training is conducted *efficiently:* When paraeducators attend training away from the students' classrooms, schools and districts often must hire substitute personnel to assist with instruction, as well as with other essential routines, such as transportation and lunch. For school systems to have the resources to maintain well-trained paraeducators, cost factors must be contained by providing staff training as quickly as possible.

3. Training must be *effective:* In one sense, declaring that staff training should be effective seems to be asserting the obvious. School systems, however, frequently invest large sums of money in a staff training program with little, if any, verification of the program's effectiveness. Educators must examine the effectiveness of a training program from two perspectives:

- The program should result in staff mastery of the skills taught by the program. Staff should not complete the training until they achieve a criterion of satisfactory, hands-on teaching performance.
- The program is truly effective only if students learn when staff use their newly acquired teaching skills.

4. For long-term success of staff training programs, the training must be *acceptable* to staff. When staff dislike the training process, they are less willing to be involved in the training. Staff's negative reactions to training also result in unpleasantness for the staff trainer, which can cause the individual charged with staff training duties to become reluctant to conduct the training.

Teaching-Skills Training Program

We developed the Teaching-Skills Training Program (TSTP) to ensure that human service personnel are adequately prepared to teach people with severe disabilities. We conducted research over a 5-year period to meet each of four criteria for successful staff training (see box, "Characteristics of Successful Staff Training Programs"; Jensen, Parsons, & Reid, 1997; Parsons et al., 1993; Parsons, Reid, & Green, 1996; Reid & Parsons, 1996).

In initial research conducted to validate the program's effectiveness, we taught 9 direct-support staff and 4 supervisors in a residential program for people with severe disabilities to apply basic teaching strategies, with at least 80% proficiency (Parsons et al., 1993). In subsequent research, we trained 24 staff members, including group home personnel, paraeducators, and undergraduate teaching interns, to teach with 80% proficiency using TSTP (Parsons et al., 1996). Acceptability research has indicated that staff respond favorably to the training procedures (Parsons et al., 1993; Reid & Parsons, 1996). Finally, TSTP is efficient because the program can be conducted in one 8-hour workday (Parsons et al., 1996).

Since the initial validation research, educators have used TSTP to successfully train more than 300 paraeducators and other support personnel. Equally important, students with severe disabilities have made progress toward acquiring adaptive skills when their paraeducators have used the skills they learned during the program (Parsons et al., 1993).

To illustrate, graduates of TSTP have taught children with severe disabilities in an inclusive preschool program the following skills:

- Wash hands.
- Recognize numbers and letters of the alphabet.
- Operate a cassette player.
- Eat with a spoon.
- Respond to one-step directions.

In a school classroom for students with severe multiple disabilities, other graduates have taught students the following skills:

- Drink from a cup.
- Press a switch to activate a radio or TV.
- Use augmentative communication devices.

Other graduates have used the teaching strategies developed through TSTP to teach job skills to adults with severe disabilities—at the workplace.

Figure 1. Sample Activity Illustrating the Rationale for Using Task Analyses

Why Is a Task Analysis Important When Teaching a New Skill?

1. If you were asked to teach someone to prepare a place setting incorporating a plate, cup, napkin, knife, fork, and spoon, draw the placement of the items on a placemat. Assume that the placemat is already on the table in the appropriate place.

2. Compare what you have drawn to the drawings of others in the group. How many place settings among the group were exactly like yours?

3. Draw a place setting following the task analysis provided by the instructor.

4. Compare what you have drawn by following the task analysis to the drawings of others in the group. How many place settings were exactly like yours?

Task Analysis for Place Setting

1. Place the plate in the center of the placemat.
2. Place the napkin directly beside and to the left of the plate.
3. Place the fork on the napkin.
4. Place the knife directly beside and to the right of the plate.
5. Place the spoon directly beside and to the right of the knife.
6. Place the cup directly above the tip of the knife.

Teaching Skills

TSTP focuses on four basic teaching competencies: task analysis, least-to-most assistive prompting, reinforcement, and error correction.

Types of prompts range from mild forms of assistance, such as gesturing to the student, to more directive prompts, such as physically guiding the student through a skill.

Task Analysis

We teach staff that to use task analysis, they should list each specific behavior in performing a targeted skill sequentially, in the order the behavior should occur for the skill to be performed correctly. They teach the kinds of behavior, or steps, in the order specified in the task analysis to facilitate learning so that each step becomes a signal for the performance of each subsequent step in the task analysis. Figure 1 illustrates a task analysis for teaching students how to set a table for lunch or dinner.

Using the Least-to-Most Assistive Prompting Strategy

When teaching a student to put on her coat, the first step of the task analysis is to pick up the coat. If the student does not pick up the coat independently, the paraeducator might begin by saying to the student, "Pick up your coat."

If the verbal prompt does not result in the student's picking up the coat, the paraeducator might tell her to pick up the coat while simultaneously pointing to the coat.

Subsequently, if the combined verbal and gestural prompt as just described does not evoke the student's picking up the coat, the paraeducator might tell the student to pick up the coat while guiding her hand toward the coat (verbal and partial physical prompts).

Least-to-Most Assistive Prompting

Providing assistance on a continuum of least-to-most prompting involves giving a student only the assistance necessary to correctly complete each step of the task analysis. Types of prompts range from mild forms of assistance, such as gesturing to the student, to more directive prompts, such as physically guiding the student through a skill.

We teach staff that if the level of assistance they provide at first does not enable the student to correctly complete a step in the task analysis, they should gradually increase assistance—level of prompting—until the student successfully performs the step (see box, "Using the Least-to-Most Assistive Prompting Strategy").

Reinforcement and Error Correction

The third and fourth teaching competencies work together. *Reinforcement* is the means by which a paraeducator can increase the likelihood across successive teaching sessions that a student will perform the skill that the paraeducator is attempting to teach. We teach staff that a reinforcing consequence is more than a reward or provision of a preferred item. A consequence provided in the context of a teaching program can be regarded as a reinforcer only if student performance of the skill improves over time. Hence, one of the most important skills of paraeducators who teach people with severe disabilities is determining what constitutes reinforcement for a given student, and effectively providing that reinforcement to encourage student learning. Praise and attention are effective reinforcers for many students. Also, engaging in preferred activities following teaching sessions can function as a reinforcer.

TSTP focuses on four basic teaching competencies: task analysis, least-to-most assistive prompting, reinforcement, and error correction

---

When a student incorrectly performs a step within a skill, a staff member must deal with the *error* in a manner that promotes student learning. In essence, errors are opportunities for students to practice the wrong way of completing a skill and should be prevented whenever possible.

We teach paraeducators to prevent errors by increasing the assistance provided on a given step when they see that the student is about to make an error. When the staff member cannot prevent an error, he or she immediately stops the student and has the student repeat the step of the task while providing enough assistance to prevent the error from occurring a second time. For example, when a student who is learning to use a copier loads the paper incorrectly, the paraeducator should stop the student, remove the paper, and provide more assistance so that the student loads the paper a second time with no mistake.

Training Format

For paraeducators in our program, we use a training format consisting of classroom-based instruction, on-the-job monitoring and feedback, and follow-up supervision.

Classroom-Based Component

The primary purpose of the classroom-based training is to familiarize paraeducators with the *rationale* for each teaching competency (task analysis, prompting, and so forth) and the terminology used in describing the teaching process.

For example, using the activity shown in Figure 1, we show the rationale for using a *task analysis* to ensure that staff members teach students a skill in a consistent way. When several staff trainees draw a place setting without the task analysis, almost invariably the placement of cups, plates, and other items will differ across the staff trainees. Thus, if each trainee were teaching a student the task, the task would differ each time it was taught, so that a student with severe disabilities would find it difficult to learn to perform the task. If all trainees follow the task analysis when drawing the place setting, however, the completed drawings should look the same.

A second purpose of the classroom-based training is to begin training staff in the *performance skills* necessary to teach students with severe disabilities by having trainees practice the skills in a role-play situation. We limit the group size of classroom-based training to six trainees. Working with a small group allows the instructor sufficient time for the instruction, observation, and feedback necessary to ensure that each trainee acquires the teaching competencies.

During classroom-based training, we teach prospective paraeducators the skills of task analysis, prompting, reinforcement, and error correction, one at a time. We provide a rationale for using each skill to teach people with severe disabilities, and we demonstrate both correct and incorrect applications of each skill. Trainees practice and receive feedback about their performance from the instructor until each trainee can perform each respective teaching skill proficiently in a role-play situation (see box, "Modeling, Practice, and Feedback").

On-the-Job Monitoring and Feedback

The primary purpose of on-the-job monitoring and feedback is to ensure that trainees can apply the teaching skills learned during the classroom-based component in an actual teaching situation with their students. The instructor observes the trainee's teaching in the classroom and provides feedback regarding the trainee's application of the teaching skills. Through monitoring, the instructor determines the trainee's proficiency in applying each of the teaching competencies.

Modeling, Practice, and Feedback

Instructor demonstration of a teaching skill, followed by trainee practice of the skill with subsequent feedback from the instructor, is the most important aspect of classroom-based training.

Modeling. When training paraeducators how to use a least-to-most assistive prompting strategy, the instructor first demonstrates a prompting sequence in a teaching program with a staff trainee who plays the role of a student.

Practice. Each trainee practices implementing the prompting strategy, with another trainee playing the role of the student.

Feedback. After the trainee practices the prompting strategy, the instructor provides the paraeducator feedback regarding the accuracy of his or her prompting.

Using an Observation Form. To facilitate the instructor's job in this respect, we use the form shown in Figure 2, in conjunction with the criteria listed in Table 1. The form in Figure 2 guides the instructor in focusing on whether or not the trainee performs each of the teaching skills proficiently.

To use the observation form, the observing instructor lists steps of the task analysis (e.g., steps for setting a table) in the appropriate order along the left side of the form. As illustrated in Figure 2, the observer scores each teaching skill under the column labeled for the respective skill on the line corresponding to the designated step of the task analysis. The observer scores each performed skill as being either correct (+) or incorrect (-). Nonapplicable (NA) is scored if there is no opportunity to perform one of the teaching skills for a given step of the task analysis. Table 1 shows the specific criteria for scoring a teaching skill as correct.

In small groups, paraeducators role-play effective teaching strategies.

Providing Feedback. Following observation of the student-teaching session, the instructor provides the trainee with feedback by explaining the teaching skills that were correctly and incorrectly performed. For those teaching skills that the trainee performed incorrectly, the instructor describes or demonstrates how the skill should have been performed.

The trainee's teaching proficiency is calculated by dividing the total number of *correctly* implemented teaching skills across all program steps by the *total* number of all skills taught, and multiplying by 100%. This calculation results in a percentage of correct teaching skill application, as illustrated in Figure 2. We consider a staff trainee *proficient* when he or she scores at least 80% correct during two separate observations of student teaching.

Follow-up Supervision

We designed the final component of TSTP, follow-up supervision, to ensure that paraeducators maintain their teaching skills at the 80% proficiency level. Establishing maintenance procedures is essential for the long-term success of staff training programs (Reid et al., 1989, Chapter 4). This part of the program, of course, lasts longer than 1 day!

Follow-up supervision entails implementing a schedule for continued observation of staff teaching and provision of feedback. The frequency of follow-up sessions is determined by how proficiently a given paraeducator continues to teach—the more proficient the teaching skills, the

less frequently observations with feedback are needed, and vice versa.

Role of Special Education Teachers and Administrators

We have successfully implemented TSTP using two different staff training models: direct training and pyramid training.

Direct Training

A model that works well in settings where fewer than 10 staff require training involves having one instructor directly train all staff. The instructor is responsible for the classroom-based training, on-the-job observations, and follow-up supervision for all staff in a school or agency. The instructor may be a principal, supervising teacher, or educational consultant—essentially, anyone with experience using the teaching strategies, observing staff performance, and providing feedback. The *Teaching-Skills Training Program Instructor's Manual*, available from the authors, serves as a guide in implementing the program (Reid & Parsons, 1994).

Pyramid Training

In school systems where a large number of staff require training, other researchers have successfully used the *pyramid* staff training model (Demchak & Browder, 1990). Using the pyramidal model, one instructor initially trains all *supervising teachers*, who, in turn, directly train the paraeducators whom they supervise. The type of training teachers should receive is twofold:

- Teachers may need to complete TSTP to ensure that the teachers themselves are proficient in the skills they will be training to paraeducators.
- Teachers should be trained in the supervisory skills of systematically observing the teaching skills of others and providing feedback to improve the teaching process. This focused supervisory training for teachers is often essential to the successful training of paraeducators because, although teachers are expected to supervise paraeducators, few teachers have had training in effective strategies for supervision.

Figure 2. Sample of a Completed Form for Observing Teaching Proficiency

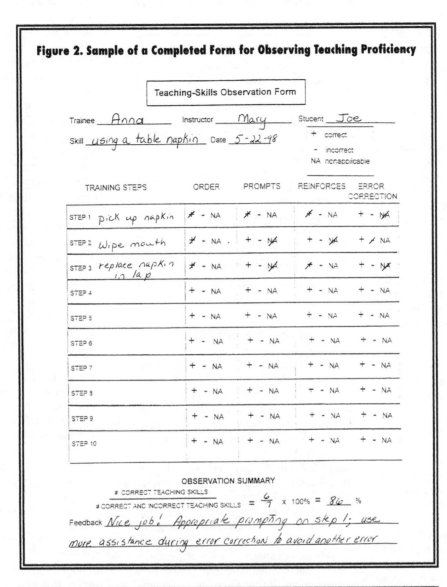

Teaching-Skills Observation Form

Trainee **Anna**   Instructor **Mary**   Student **Joe**

Skill **using a table napkin**   Date **5-22-98**

+ correct
− incorrect
NA nonapplicable

TRAINING STEPS	ORDER	PROMPTS	REINFORCES	ERROR CORRECTION
STEP 1 pick up napkin	⊕ − NA	⊕ − NA	⊕ − NA	+ − N⊘
STEP 2 wipe mouth	⊕ − NA .	+ − N⊘	+ − ⊘A	+ ⊘ NA
STEP 3 replace napkin in lap	⊕ − NA	+ − N⊘	⊕ − NA	+ − N⊘
STEP 4	+ − NA	+ − NA	+ − NA	+ − NA
STEP 5	+ − NA	+ − NA	+ − NA	+ − NA
STEP 6	+ − NA	+ − NA	+ − NA	+ − NA
STEP 7	+ − NA	+ − NA	+ − NA	+ − NA
STEP 8	+ − NA	+ − NA	+ − NA	+ − NA
STEP 9	+ − NA	+ − NA	+ − NA	+ − NA
STEP 10	+ − NA	+ − NA	+ − NA	+ − NA

OBSERVATION SUMMARY

$$\frac{\text{\# CORRECT TEACHING SKILLS}}{\text{\# CORRECT AND INCORRECT TEACHING SKILLS}} = \frac{6}{7} \times 100\% = \underline{86}\ \%$$

Feedback _Nice job! Appropriate prompting on step 1; use more assistance during error correction to avoid another error_

Table 1. Definitions for Correct Application of the Basic Teaching Skills

Teaching Skill	Definition for Correct Application
Order	The steps of the task analysis are taught in sequence so that each step taught is preceded by the specific step listed in the task analysis.
Prompt	Each successive prompt (if more than 1 prompt is used) provided for a given step in the task analysis involves more assistance than the previous prompt.
Reinforcement	A positive consequence is provided following the last correct step of the task analysis and is not provided following any incorrectly performed step. Reinforcement could be provided following any correctly performed step but must be provided following the last correctly performed step.
Error Correction	When the student incorrectly performs a step of the task analysis (i.e., a behavior incompatible with the step), the student is required to repeat the step; and a more assistive prompt is provided on the second trial. The prompt on the second trial should provide sufficient assistance so the student completes the step without another error.

Focused supervisory training (in observation and feedback methods) for teachers contributes to the successful training of paraeducators

Supervisory training for teachers should include practice in observing another staff member teach, completing the observation form, and giving feedback in a role-play situation. A protocol for teachers to use as a guide for giving diagnostic feedback is presented in Figure 3. Once a teacher is competent in observing and providing feedback in a role-play situation, the instructor observes the teacher on the job as the teacher observes the paraeducator conduct a teaching session. When the teacher can provide accurate feedback to the paraeducator regarding the latter's teaching skills, then the teacher independently observes and provides feedback to the paraeducator several times each week until the paraeducator can perform the basic teaching skills.

Research has indicated that when teachers complete TSTP, as well as the additional supervisory training, they can train paraeducators to implement the basic teaching skills through observation and feedback in the classroom and *without the paraeducators participating in the classroom-based component* (Jensen et al., 1997). Moreover, these researchers found that the supervisory training improved the teacher's *own teaching skills* when those skills were below the 80% proficiency criterion prior to training. The supervising teacher provides follow-up supervision for paraeducators through intermittent observations and feedback.

Figure 3 shows a checklist that supervising teachers can use to guide their feedback sessions. This form actually constitutes a "task analysis" for providing feedback, beginning with setting a positive tone and ending with making a positive statement.

Figure 3. Protocol for Giving Diagnostic Feedback to a Staff Member Following the Observation of a Teaching Session

Supervisor's Feedback Checklist

Staff Trainee _____ Student _____ Skill _____

Supervisor _____ Location _____ Time _____ Date _____

Feedback Components

Check each component included in your feedback to the trainee. Check NA (nonapplicable) for components 4 and 5 if no teaching errors were made.

	Yes	No	NA
1. Set a positive tone for feedback session			
2. Began diagnostic feedback with positive feedback			
3. Gave appropriate positive feedback.			
4. Identified each skill category with teaching errors			
5. For each category with teaching errors, described how the teaching skill should have been performed correctly			
6. Solicited questions for feedback from trainee			
7. Referenced current training status			
8. Ended feedback session with a positive statement			

Student and Parent Input

The highly effective teaching strategies espoused by the Teaching-Skills Training Program require brief teaching sessions involving one student at a time. Individual instruction, however, is only one component of a quality educational experience for students with severe disabilities. Students and family members should have significant input into which skills warrant teaching in this manner and how much time should be directed to individual teaching services versus other valuable educational supports.

When individualized teaching, embedded within the daily routine, is deemed necessary, the TSTP provides paraeducators with the requisite teaching skills to improve student achievement.

References

Demchak, M., & Browder, D. M. (1990). An evaluation of the pyramid model of staff training in group homes for adults with severe handicaps. *Education and Training in Mental Retardation, 25*, 150–163.

Jensen, J. E., Parsons, M. B., & Reid, D. H. (1997). *Multiple effects of training teachers to improve the data recording of teacher aides.* Manuscript submitted for publication.

Parsons, M. B., Reid, D. H., & Green, C. W. (1993). Preparing direct service staff to teach people with severe disabilities: A comprehensive evaluation of an effective and acceptable training program. *Behavioral Residential Treatment, 8*, 163–185.

Parsons, M. B., Reid, D. H., & Green, C. W. (1996). Training basic teaching skills to community and institutional support staff for people with severe disabilities: A one-day program. *Research In Developmental Disabilities, 17*, 467–485.

Reid, D. H., & Parsons, M. B. (1994). *Training to teach in a day: The teaching skills training program instructor's manual.* Morganton, NC: Carolina Behavior Analysis and Support Center, Ltd.

Reid, D. H., & Parsons, M. B. (1996). A comparison of staff acceptability of immediate versus delayed verbal feedback in staff training. *Journal of Organizational Behavior Management, 16*(2), 35–48.

Reid, D. H., Parsons, M. B., & Green, C. W. (1989). *Staff management in human services: Behavioral research and application.* Springfield, IL: Charles C Thomas.

Marsha B. Parsons, *Associate Director, Carolina Behavior Analysis and Support Center, Ltd., Morganton, North Carolina.* **Dennis H. Reid,** *Associate Professor, Louisiana State University Medical Center, New Orleans.*

Address correspondence to Marsha B. Parsons, Carolina Behavior Analysis and Support Center, Ltd., P.O. Box 425, Morganton, NC 28680.

Using Technology to Construct Alternate Portfolios of Students with Moderate and Severe Disabilities

Anne Denham

Elizabeth A. Lahm

The 1997 Amendments to the Individuals with Disabilities Education Act (IDEA '97) require that all states include students with disabilities in their measures of account-ability. Such measures may be part of the statewide and districtwide general education assessment programs through appropriate accommodations or through alternate assessments for those who cannot complete the general education assessment (Kleinert & Kearns, 1999).

Inclusion in Statewide Assessments

Since 1992, Kentucky has been including all students in the statewide assessment and going beyond federal regulations by including all students in the accountability system. Students receiving special education services are assessed in one of three ways:
- Through participation in the general education assessment program.
- Through participation in the general assessment program with accommodations.
- Through participation in the alternate portfolio system.

This article shares how the students in one classroom achieved "Distinguished" ratings, the highest of ratings, on their alternate portfolios, using assistive technology (see box, "What Is an Alternate Portfolio?").

Student Profiles

We conducted multiple case studies in one Kentucky classroom for students with moderate to severe cognitive disabilities to explore the process of using the IntelliKeys keyboard as an alternative computer input device for the production of the alternate portfolio. The classroom is located in a small elementary school (430 fourth- and fifth-grade students) in rural Kentucky. The students receive instruction in the general education classroom, the community, and a special class. The teacher has 12 years' experience servicing students in both the general and special education environment, is a recent graduate of an assistive technology educational specialist degree program, and holds an Assistive Technology Practitioner certificate. The students use a selection of assistive technology devices commensurate with their needs, to include single communication aids; a variety of switches to access tape recorders, electric kitchen mixer, and television through an environmental control; and an adaptive keyboard with custom overlays to access the computer.

How do we provide alternate assessments for those who cannot complete the general education assessment?

Four of the seven students in the class were in the age groups of students in the fourth and eighth grades and were thus required to participate in the Kentucky assessment program. Three were 9-year-old females, and one was a 13-year-old male. Two students were classified as having severe cognitive disabilities and two as having multiple disabilities. Table 1 describes these students further, according to physical, cognitive, and behavioral domains. The teacher determined that they qualified to participate in the assessment by completing an alternate portfolio.

What Is an Alternate Portfolio?

The alternate portfolio showcases student work where educators can assess learning across life domain activities in a comprehensive way. It represents performance-based evaluation, using a multidisciplinary approach, and models the use of holistic scoring. As with the general education portfolio scoring system, educators score alternate portfolios on four different levels: novice, apprentice, proficient, and distinguished. To qualify for a distinguished score, the highest level, the student must show the following:

- Progress on specifically targeted skills that are meaningful in current and future environments.
- Planning, monitoring, and evaluating self progress.
- Evaluation used to extend performance.
- Extensive evidence of Kentucky Academic Expectations in all entries.
- Natural supports.
- Use of adaptations, modifications, and/or assistive technology to evidence independence.
- Performance occurring in a variety of integrated settings, within and across all entries.
- Clearly established mutual friendship(s) with peers without disabilities.
- Choice and control in age-appropriate portfolio products within and across all entries.

The alternate portfolio assessment was designed by Kentucky educators specifically for those students whose limitations in cognitive function prevented completion of the standard assessment program (see below "Alternate Portfolios in Kentucky"). Eligibility is determined by the IEP committee, by considering cognitive function, adaptive behavior, cause of limited function, application skill level, use of community-based instruction, and level of performance with supports. Kleinert, Kearns, and Kennedy (1997) stated that between 0.5% and 1.0% of the public school students meet such requirements.

In addition to becoming part of the school's accountability indexes, alternate portfolios serve as "an 'instructional organizer' to give clarity and focus to the student's daily educational program, and as a teaching tool for students to learn higher order self-management, planning, and self-evaluation skills" (Kleinert, Haigh, Kearns, & Kennedy, 2000, p. 24). Such organizers provide teachers with a solid framework from which to work.

Alternate Portfolios in Kentucky

For more information about alternate portfolios, as implemented in Kentucky, visit the following Web sites:
Kentucky Alternate Portfolio Online
http://www.ihdi.uky.edu/projects/KAP/
Kentucky Alternate Portfolio Assessment Teacher's Guide (PDF format)
http://www.ihdi.uky.edu/projects/KAP/downloads/ap%20book99.pdf

Each of the four students was required to produce five entries for their alternate portfolio, in addition to demonstrating their use of a daily schedule and writing a letter to the reviewers. Table 2 shows the activities selected for these students to illustrate Kentucky's academic expectations within four content areas. Statements in black are target skills, and statements in italic are questions they had to respond to in order to demonstrate that skill. For example, Amanda demonstrated her computation skills by responding to the question "Did I count the cans?" on her activity sheet for loading the soda machine. One curricular area entry for each student was the focus of the study and is used to demonstrate the assessment process.

Students used a smorgasbord of assistive technology: single communication aids; a variety of switches to access tape recorders, electric kitchen mixer, and television through an environmental control; and an adaptive keyboard with custom overlays to access the computer.

All four students were unable to use the standard computer keyboard effectively. The teacher determined that the IntelliKeys keyboard was an appropriate adaptation for each. Three of the students used switches plugged into the IntelliKeys, in addition to the IntelliKeys keyboard itself. The switches were used to highlight and read text on the activity sheet with the use of text reading software.

The teacher constructed a custom overlay for each student, using Overlay Maker (IntelliTools, 1996) to support each student's individual needs. The overlay provided response choices to be used in the completion of a data sheet that was displayed on the computer (see Figure 1). By pressing a response choice on the overlay, the student caused the text programmed into that cell to be entered into the data sheet. The amount of text in the response depended on the student's level of functioning. For example, one student was able to record a complete sentence by sequencing three response choices, whereas another had only "yes" or "no" programmed as response choices. Color and location were used on the overlays to provide visual cues as to which response choices should be used for each of the assessment questions. Figure 2 is an example of one student's overlay.

The teacher provided a short training session for each student and one peer buddy on all components of the assessment process. For each student, the IntelliKeys with a custom overlay was used to respond to the assessment

Table 1. Profile of the Students in the Study				
Subject	*Physical Characteristics*	*Cognitive Characteristics*	*Behavioral Characteristics*	*Disability*
Sandra: Age 9	Hearing impaired; hyperactive; impaired speech	Exceedingly low academic ability compared with typical peers	Noncompliant; resists authority	Multiple: hearing impaired and severe cognitive disability
Christine: Age 9	Low to fluctuating tone; nonambulatory; verbal though not clearly understood by anyone other than parent	Exceedingly low academic ability compared with typical peers	Friendly but demanding; persistent presence	Multiple: physical and severe cognitive disability
Amanda: Age 9	Small, ample stamina to function well with peers	Very low academic ability; beginning academics; delayed language skills	Friendly, predominantly smiling; enjoys being the center of attention; loud; silly behaviors	Severe cognitive disability
Brent: Age 13	Very small and thin; exhibits self-stimulatory behaviors; nonverbal; ambulatory but resistant	Nonparticipatory	Self-stimulatory behaviors; little response to peers or adults; very little interaction with others	Severe cognitive disability

questions. The teacher created an activity data sheet using a word processor with table capabilities (Microsoft, 1997). Figure 1 shows one of these activity data sheets. The text-to-speech feature of the software (textHELP! 1999) was used to read each assessment question to the student. The student responded using the custom overlay, and their answer was read back to them so they could confirm the correctness of the answer.

The teacher provided a short training session for each student and one peer buddy on all components of the assessment process.

Each student had content area tasks for which they were responsible. One student was in charge of filling the soda machine; another, shopping for ingredients for a cooking activity. After the activities were completed, they rated and commented on their performance using the activity data sheet. With a peer, they sat at the computer workstation. They responded to the assessment questions that were read aloud by the computer, using the activity-specific IntelliKeys overlay to "type" their response to each question. The peer provided prompts and assistance when needed. On the activity sheet, independent responses were recorded in blue and assisted responses

were recorded in red. Based on that record, each student's level of independence was determined across four trials. Table 3 (page 14) shows the increase in independence across the trials for each student.

Examples of Student Use of Portfolio Entries

Amanda

We used Amanda's math entry for this study with the following activities: (a) filling the soda machine with a peer, (b) taking cans to the recycling center, and (c) purchasing items at the store. Targeting improvement in computation and money skills, Amanda planned, monitored, and evaluated her activities by using the IntelliKeys and the custom overlay to respond to the questions on the activity sheet. The activity sheets and overlays were designed to allow Amanda to read the text with the text-reading software and construct a variety of sentences in response to the questions posed on the activity sheet. The response keys on the custom overlay were grouped according to color and use to facilitate correct choice (Figure 3).

On the first trial activity sheet, 48% of Amanda's responses were made independently. By the fourth trial, Amanda had increased her independence to 88%. Figure 4 illustrates how on one response item, the quality of her responses also improved. Before using the IntelliKeys, Amanda was limited to handwriting her response, which was painstakingly slow. The IntelliKeys system allowed her to write 56 words in 20 minutes, a feat she could not have accomplished without it. Amanda's reaction to the IntelliKeys system was, "This is neat."

Table 2. Student Evidence of Performing Each of the Nine Criteria for a "Distinguished" Rating

Assessment Dimension and Requirements of the Alternate Portfolio	Amanda-Math • Loading soda machine • Recycling cans • Shopping at the store	Christine-Lang.Arts • Cooking • Purchasing items for cooking	Sandra-Soc.Studies • Art activity • Shoping for art supplies	Brent-Science • Pet care • Purchase items at the store
Performance:				
Progress on specifically targeted skills which are meaningful in current and future environments	Increased accuracy by 20% or more in computation and coin values Did I count the cans?	Increased accuracy by 20% or more in visual scanning ability Did I scan my pictures?	Increased frequency of requesting assistance in an appropriate manner by 20% or more Did I follow directions?	Increased accuracy by 20% or more in selecting the correct object Did I touch the correct object?
Planning, monitoring, and evaluating self progress	Evaluating performance Did I say I am ready?	Reporting and following a sequence of tasks What will I do first?	Following a sequence of tasks Do I know what to do?	Following a sequence of tasks Did I wash my hands when I finished?
Evaluation used to extend performance	Developing a goal for the next session Next time I will try harder with...	Making a quality choice using visual scanning Did I try harder with...	Making a quality choice related to a targeted skill Next time I will try harder with...	Making a quality choice related to a targeted skill Did I try harder with...
Extensive evidence of Kentucky Academic Expectations in all entries	**E.G. Quantifying,** How many cans did we need? **Classifying,** Did I put the soad in the right space?	**E.g. Reading,** Did I use pictures to read the recipe? **Production,** What am I making	**E.g. Accessing information,** Did I ask for help if I needed it? **Democratic principles,** Did I have good manners in class?	**E.g. Constancy,** Did I follow my schedule? What do I plan to do first? **Speaking,** Did I use my switch to ask for food?
Supports:				
Natural support	Peers working on estimation and mental math skills Who worked with me today?	Peers working on math skills wihtin the cooking activity What friend cooked with me today?	Peers exploring a variety of media within the art activity Who did I sit with today?	Peers learning about domestic animals within the pet care activity Which friend helped me today?
Use of adaptations, modifications, and/or assistive technology to evidence independence	Big key calculator; IntelliKeys to record performance on the computer	Switch controlled electric mixer; IntelliKeys to record performance on the computer	Modified goals; IntelliKeys to record performance on the computer	Auditory switch device; IntelliKeys to record performance on the computer
Settings:				
Performance occurring in a variety of integrated settings, within and across all entries	Teacher's lounge, office, stockroom, recycle center, store Where did I go?	Classroom, kitchen, store, office, other classrooms Where did I go?	Art room, classroom, cafeteria, store Where did I go?	Classroom, kitchen, restroom, store, recycle center Where did I go?
Social Relationships:				
Clearly established mutual friendship(s) with non-disabled peers	Time spent in activities with peers to facilitate friendships Who helped me today?	Time spent in activities with peers to facilitate friendships What friend cooked with me today?	Time spent in activites with peers to facilitate friendships Who did I sit with today?	Time spent in activities with peers to facilitate friendships Which friend helped me today?
Context:				
Choice and control in age-appropriate portfolio products within and across all entries	Multiple opportunities for choice and decision making Did I make a choice?	Multiple opportunities for choice and decision making Did I say I was ready?	Assuming personal responsibility Did I ask for help correctly?	Multiple opportunities for choice and decision making What do I plan to do first?

Table 3. Level of Independent Performance During Completion of Activity Sheets

		Percentage of Responses Made Independently				
Student	**Activity**	**Trial 1**	**Trial 2**	**Trial 3**	**Trial 4**	**Overall Gain**
Amanda	Soda	48	56	72	88	25%
	Recycle	55	66	82	71	
	Store	62	72	85	82	
Christine	Cooking	25	54	60	75	43%
	Store	35	53	71	--	
Sandra	Art class	4	24	16	35	22%
	Store	18	22	31	30	
Brent	Pet care	7	25	44	56	32%
	Store	40	40	50	56	

Figure 1. Soda Machine Activity Sheet

Prompt	Response			
Date				
Did I use my schedule?				
Did I say I am ready?				
What will I do first?				
Did I use my sheet so I know what to do next?				
Where did I go?	Office Lounge	Office Lounge	Office Lounge	Office Lounge
Did I write what sodas were needed?				
Did I use my list to say what sodas were needed?				
Did I count the cans?				
Did I make a choice?				
How many cans did we need?				
Did I put the can in the right place?				
Did I do a good job?				
Did I try harder?				
Next time I will do better at …				
Who helped me today?				
What did my friend do?				

sheets. That was accomplished with physical assistance from a peer or adult to assist in stamping and reading the questions. The overlay was designed to be simple, with large keys outlined in black. The keys were arranged by color and location to facilitate correct responses. The overlay keys also directly addressed her individualized education program (IEP) objectives—to visually scan pictures or objects from left to right or from top to bottom. Christine also used two color-coded single switches plugged into the IntelliKeys, to highlight activity sheet cells on the computer and to have it read each question.

> **Sandra's initial trial with the art class activity showed that 4% of her responses were made independently. By the fourth trial she increased her independence to 35%.**

As with Amanda, by the fourth trial Christine had increased her performance level substantially, achieving 75% of her responses independently with the cooking activity sheet. Christine attended well to the reporting activity and appeared to enjoy the print output. She asked to take it home with her.

Christine

Christine's alternate portfolio activities targeted her language arts objectives. She engaged in two activities to demonstrate her achievements: cooking and buying items from the store. Before using the IntelliKeys for recording responses. Christine was limited to using a rubber stamp to indicate a yes/no response to questions on the activity

Sandra

Sandra's portfolio demonstrated her achievements in social studies. She participated in two activities: shopping for art supplies, and participating in a general education art class. Sandra's overlays were simple, using color coding and

Figure 2. Amanda's IntelliKeys Overlay

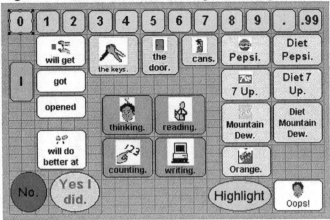

Figure 3. Amanda's Additional IntelliKeys Overlay

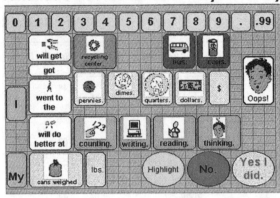

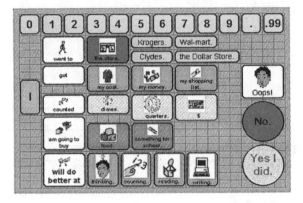

location, to facilitate correct responses. When using the IntelliKeys, Sandra listened to the peer who cued her verbally and with gestures, as necessary. She also used switches to highlight and read the text. Sandra responded well to peer cues, tolerating their guidance, following their directions, and remaining seated during the activity. Sandra's initial trial with the art class activity showed that 4% of her responses were made independently. By the fourth trial she increased her independence to 35%. A similar gain was found in the shopping activity. She apparently enjoyed working on the computer with the IntelliKeys. She grinned and clapped as each entry was keyed into the cell, and read with the text reader as it was typed. She anxiously waited for the printed output so she could take it from the printer's paper tray.

The design of the custom overlay is an important consideration in the success of student use of the IntelliKeys.

Brent

Brent's example is for his science entry. Two custom overlays were used—one overlay was restricted to two cells demonstrating a yes/no response to the activity sheet questions, and the other with five keys giving Brent the opportunity to document a high-quality independent choice over his area of improvement (Figure 5). Two

switches were used to highlight and read the text as with the other students.

Brent averaged a 32% gain in independent performance. Brent's responses were more erratic than the others, but this is typical for Brent. He requires consistent cueing and often hand-over-hand instruction with physical cues. Brent is nonverbal and at present has an inconsistent system of communication. He required physical guidance to be seated and consistent cueing to remain seated. Brent's response to the question regarding improved performance was generated through activation of two out of five keys linked to his IEP goals and targeted skills. He consistently chose either the "choose the right one" or "look" key, both located at the bottom of the overlay toward the left (Figure 6 on page 16). It is not clear if the location of the activated keys on the overlay was a factor.

Figure 4. Example of Amanda's Responses to One Activity Question

Prompt	Student Response			
	Day 1	Day 2	Day 3	Day 4
Did I use my money?	Yes I did.	Yes I did. 1 $	Yes I did.	Yes I did. I counted $ 1.

External Review

Each alternate portfolio in this study was scored at the regional level by trained teams of scorers using a double-blind method. Table 4 presents the two scores awarded each portfolio. Out of a total of 40 possible scores when including each dimension, the portfolios carried 36 distinguished ratings and 4 proficient ratings. This results in a 90% distinguished rating when considering each dimension separately. The alternate portfolio is scored holistically, however, assigning one score to each complete portfolio. These four students received a rating of "distinguished."

The design of the custom overlay is an important consideration in the success of student use of the IntelliKeys.

Figure 5. Brent's IntelliKeys Overlay

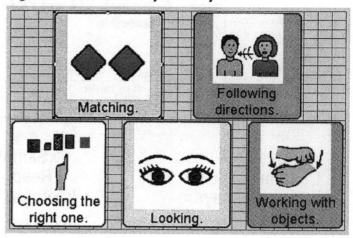

Overlay Design

The design of the custom overlay is an important consideration in the success of student use of the IntelliKeys. Thorough knowledge of student need and capabilities of the device is essential to use the customizing features and maximize student potential. As a result of this study, we can share several design tips (see box "Design Tips for Customizing IntelliKeys Overlays"). Experimentation based on observation, however, is the most important element.

First, overlay design must be student centered. Motor and cognitive abilities guide the spatial arrangement of the overlay. Range of motion and reach are considerations for the placement of buttons. Items that will be needed more frequently should be easily within reach to avoid fatigue and frustration. Fine motor abilities are factored into button size. For students with cognitive impairments, color and clustering can facilitate use. Buttons in close proximity should be related to a single task and may be highlighted in

a specific color to provide cues to the student for their use. These design considerations are especially useful with more complex overlays.

Cognitive abilities play a role in the number of buttons or response options, and the design of the button depends on the student's cognitive level (for example, contrast Amanda's overlay in Figure 2 with Brent's in Figure 5). Type of graphic representation of a response option is critical. Pairing the written word with the picture will be beneficial for some students, but detrimental to others.

If using different layouts for different tasks, it is important to maintain as much consistency across the layouts as possible. For example, you may always put program commands (e.g., enter, space, delete) in the upper left quadrant and task-specific content keys in the lower right. In doing so, you reduce the cognitive load on the students as they complete each response. Taking both cognitive and motor abilities into account, you facilitate increased accuracy and reduction of time, which both contribute to fatigue.

Table 4. Scores Received from Two Reviewers on the Alternate Portfolio Dimensions

Student	Amanda	Christine	Sandra	Brent
Performance	Distinguished Distinguished	Distinguished Distinguished	Distinguished Distinguished	Distinguished Distinguished
Support	Distinguished Distinguished	Distinguished Distinguished	Proficient Distinguished	Distinguished Distinguished
Settings	Distinguished Distinguished	Distinguished Distinguished	Distinguished Distinguished	Distinguished Distinguished
Social relationships	Proficient Distinguished	Distinguished Distinguished	Distinguished Proficient	Proficient Distinguished
Contexts	Distinguished Distinguished	Distinguished Distinguished	Distinguished Distinguished	Distinguished Distinguished

---

Figure 6. Example of Brent's Responses to One Science Activity Question

	Student Response			
Prompt	Day 1	Day 2	Day 3	Day 4
Next time I will try harder with …	Choose the right one.	Choose the right one.	Look.	Look.

Design Tips for Customizing IntelliKeys Overlays

- Student needs and functioning level must drive the content and format.
- Use voice output to read the prompt and read the response back to the user.
- Group keys according to color to facilitate correct responses.
- Enable the "nonrepeat" function to ensure only one entry per response.
- Use left-to-right formats to naturally facilitate sentence construction.
- Size the text and the keys to match the visual abilities of the user.
- Program whole words and phrases into the keys to speed responses.
- Match the programmed responses to the student's cognitive ability (e.g., single-word responses limit the construction of complete sentences).
- Outline keys in black to improve contrast.
- Place frequently used keys on the user's dominant side of the keyboard.
- Include graphics on the keys with the text for the nonreader.
- Consider the complexity of training issues when choosing keys (e.g., arrow keys for directional movement are very difficult to teach).
- Place keys that are common across overlays in a consistent location on each.

Sample Peer Responses to Interview Questions

Six general education peers helped the students use the IntelliKeys during recording sessions. The overwhelming consensus was that the peers liked using the IntelliKeys with the students, primarily because it enhanced the student level of performance and increased their independence. The following are some of their responses:

- One peer appeared quite shocked at Amanda's performance within her math entry, and remarked that he did not know "she could do all that."
- Most peers were surprised with work that the students were able to produce with the IntelliKeys, and admitted that it elevated their opinion of the students' ability.
- Observations indicated that the peers enjoyed the process of working with the students, though this was in the form of a peer-tutor relationship.
- Each peer reported that working with a student helped him or her to get to know the student better, since they spent more time together. Spending time with one another provided the opportunity for relationships to develop, an important element within the social relationships dimension of the alternative portfolio.

Sample Student Responses Recorded in Observation Notes

- "Amanda appears to enjoy the technical aspects of the program; perhaps it gives her a sense of independence that she cannot get from other methods of reading and writing."
- "Amanda appears pleased with her work. At no time does she appear hurried or anxious to get finished. The teacher does not have to remind her to remain on task."
- "Christine was compliant in coming to the computer. She appears to enjoy computer tasks since it does give her an avenue for written expression and she likes to take things home."
- "Christine's mother came into the classroom when she was completing the activity sheets and Christine became animated and demanded that her mother watch what she was doing."
- On her first trial with the IntelliKeys, Sandra "grinned and clapped as each entry was keyed into the cell and read with the text-to-speech software as she typed."
- During Brent's first trial completing the science activity sheet, "Brent voiced and resisted being seated in the chair by the computer. He looked upwards at all times and avoided contact with the IntelliKeys and the monitor."
- Brent "does better on the computer than he does with the stamps since he is selecting the key and is the cause of the entered text."

Final Thoughts

In addition to the data showing the achievements of the students with disabilities, observations of the students working with their peers on these tasks confirmed other benefits of the program. Overall, the peers gained a better perspective on the students' abilities, and the students responded positively to their accomplishments and interactions with their peers (see boxes, "Sample Student Responses," for student observations and peer interviews).

This series of case studies denotes a beginning level of research, and is an indication for further definitive research at a critical time when states are looking to include students with moderate and severe disabilities in their accountability indexes. Studies of a more rigorous method of inquiry and more reliable data collection in the area of student support and assistive technology and assessment are essential. Kentucky is the only state fully including the assessment of this population in their school accountability indexes, and thus provides an excellent base for research.

Another area of focus for future research is on overlay design issues, because it is apparent that they influence output. Researchers and practitioners might look at overlay design and attempt guidelines to facilitate increased independence, increase output, and minimize the potential for student error.

References

IntelliTools. (1996). Overlay maker. [Computer software]. Novato, CA: Author.

Kleinert, H., Haigh, J., Kearns, J., & Kennedy, S. (2000). Alternate assessment. Lessons learned and roads not taken. *Exceptional Children, 67,* 51–66.

Kleinert, H., & Kearns, J. (1999). A validation study of the performance indicators and learner outcomes for Kentucky's alternate assessment for students with significant disabilities. *Journal of the Association for Persons with Severe Handicaps, 24*(2), 100–110.

Kleinert, H., Kearns, J., & Kennedy, S. (1997). Accountability for all students: Kentucky's alternate portfolio assessment for students with moderate and severe cognitive disabilities. *Journal of the Association for Persons with Severe Handicaps, 22*(2), 88–101.

Microsoft Corporation. (1997). WORD 97. [Computer software]. Redmond, WA: Author.

textHELP! (1999). Read & write. [Computer software]. Antrim, N. Ireland: Author.

Anne Denham *(CEC Chapter #5), Teacher, Mason County Public Schools, Maysville, Kentucky.* **Elizabeth A. Lahm** *(CEC Chapter #180), Assistant Professor, Department of Special Education and Rehabilitation Counseling, University of Kentucky, Lexington.*

Address correspondence to Elizabeth A. Lahm, Department of Special Education and Rehabilitation Counseling, University of Kentucky, 229 Taylor Education Building, Lexington, KY 40506-0001 (e-mail: ealahm1@pop.uky.edu).

From *Teaching Exceptional Children,* May/June 2001, pp. 10-17. © 2001 by The Council for Exceptional Children. Reprinted with permission.

UNIT 9

Orthopedic and Health Impairments

Unit Selections

Key Points to Consider

- What is the importance of giving young children with orthopedic disabilities mobility instruction within the context of typical daily activities? Describe the MOVE program.

- What kinds of accommodations are appropriate for students with health impairments (e.g., cancer, asthma, epilepsy)?

- Why is ADHD considered a health disorder? Are medications for ADHD justified?

 **Links: www.dushkin.com/online/**
These sites are annotated in the World Wide Web pages.

Association to Benefit Children (ABC)
http://www.a-b-c.org
An Idea Whose Time Has Come
http://www.boggscenter.org/mich3899.htm
Resources for VE Teachers
http://www.cpt.fsu.edu/tree//ve/tofc.html

Try using the word "handicapped" on a computer with a spell check. Today's computers are programmed to advise you that this is a derogatory term when applied to any individual. Older dictionaries defined "handicapped" as inferior and in need of an artificial advantage. People were described as handicapped if they were encumbered by physical limitations. Today, handicapped means limited by something in the environment. Handicap is synonymous with hindrance. If a property of the environment prevents a person with an orthopedic or health impairment from functioning to the best of his or her abilities, then the environment has imposed a handicap.

Children and youth with orthopedic and health impairments can be divided into classifications of mild, moderate, and profound. Within most impairments, the same diagnosis may not produce the same degree of disability. For example, children with cerebral palsy may be mildly, moderately, or profoundly impaired.

Orthopedic impairments are usually defined as those that hinder physical mobility or the ability to use one or more parts of the skeletomuscular system of the body. Orthopedic problems may be neurological (brain or spinal cord) or skeletomuscular (muscles or skeletal bones). Regardless of etiology, the child with an orthopedic impairment usually has a problem with mobility. He or she may need crutches to walk or may be in a wheelchair.

Health impairments are usually defined as those that affect stamina and predominantly one or more systems of the body: the cardiovascular, respiratory, gastrointestinal, endocrine, lymphatic, urinary, reproductive, sensory, or nervous systems. Children with health impairments usually have to take medicine or follow a medical regimen in order to attend school. The degree of impairment (mild, moderate, profound) is usually based on limitations to activity, duration of problem, and extent of other problems.

Attention-deficit hyperactive disorder (ADHD) is formally recognized as a health impairment, as well as a learning disability. Often children with ADHD are also assessed as gifted or as emotionally-behaviorally disordered. It is possible for a child with ADHD to have characteristics of all of these categories. ADHD will be covered in this unit.

Orthopedic and health impairments are not always mutually exclusive. Many times a child with an orthopedic impairment also has a concurrent or contributing health impairment, and vice versa. In addition, children with orthopedic and health impairments may also have concurrent conditions of educational exceptionality.

Some children with orthopedic and health impairments have only transitory impairments; some have permanent but non-worsening impairments; and some have progressive impairments that make their education more complicated as the years pass and may even result in death before the end of the developmental/educational period.

Each of the dimensions defined in the preceding paragraphs makes educational planning for children with orthopedic and health impairments very complicated.

The reauthorization of IDEA mandated that schools must pay for all medical services required to allow orthopedically or health impaired students to attend regular education classes. The only exceptions are the actual fees for physician-provided health services. Thus, if children need ambulances to transport them to and from school, the schools must pay the tab. Federal appropriations for special educational services only pay about 10 percent of the bills. Thus high-cost special needs students can quickly drain the funds of state and local education departments.

Teachers may resent the need to spend teacher time giving medications or providing quasi-medical services (suctioning, changing diapers) for students with health impairments in the many U.S. schools that no longer have school nurses.

Resentment is common in parents of nondisabled students who feel that the education of high-cost disabled students robs their children of teacher time, curriculum, and supplies to which they should be entitled. More than 95 percent of special needs students attend regular schools today. About 3 percent attend separate schools and about 2 percent are served at home, in hospitals, or in residential facilities.

When orthopedic or health impairments are diagnosed in infancy or early childhood, an interdisciplinary team usually helps plan an individualized family service plan (IFSP) that includes working with parents, medical and/or surgical personnel, and preschool special education providers.

When the orthopedic or health impairment is diagnosed in the school years, the school teachers collaborate with outside agencies, but more of the individualized educational planning (IEP) is in their hands. Children who have orthopedic or health impairments need psychological as well as academic support. Teachers need to help them in their peer interactions. Teachers should also work closely with parents to ensure a smooth transition toward a lifestyle that fosters independence and self-reliance. By middle school, individualized transition plans (ITPs) should be developed. They should be implemented throughout high school and until age 21 when the students move to adult living, and they must be updated every year. Schools are held accountable for their success in helping students with orthopedic and health impairments to make smooth transitions to maturity.

The first article emphasizes the importance of giving young children with orthopedic disabilities mobility instruction within the context of typical daily activities. Keith Whinnery and Stacie Barnes recommend the MOVE curriculum, an integrated therapy with high expectations that supports and motivates children. A case study of 4-year-old Breanna, who has cerebral palsy, illustrates how it works.

The second selection for this unit suggests some of the accommodations that school systems must make to ensure that students with orthopedic and health impairments receive an appropriate education. It explains the 504 plans required under the Americans with Disabilities Act. MaryAnn Byrnes points out that the teaching profession is about allowing students to learn. Removing barriers will do that.

In the last selection Michael Fumento questions the veracity of the diagnosis of attention deficit hyperactive disorder (ADHD). Many persons have declared the label a hoax, and the use of medication to treat it a conspiracy to make boys more like girls. The article presents evidence that it is a neurological disorder which can usually be successfully treated with medicine.

Mobility Training Using the MOVE® Curriculum

A Parent's View

Keith W. Whinnery, Stacie B. Barnes

Breanna is a 4-year-old girl who loves playing outside. Today she and her mom, Trellis, are taking a walk to feed the dogs, chase the chickens, and pick flowers. Though this might seem like a fairly common scenario for a parent and young child, it is quite extraordinary for Breanna and Trellis. Breanna contracted meningitis and encephalitis at 3 1/2 weeks of age, resulting in cerebral palsy with a mixture of high and low muscle tone, limited strength for standing or sitting upright, and difficulty holding her head upright. Since that time, life for Breanna and her family has consisted of numerous doctors' appointments, regular therapy sessions at a child development center, and constant strengthening and stretching exercises at home.

This article presents an interview with Trellis, Breanna's mother, who is using a new mobility curriculum with her daughter. The interview provides a glimpse into Trellis's concerns and expectations for Breanna's future independence, as well as her feelings about the use of the curriculum. The article also provides an overview of the curriculum and discusses Breanna's mobility progress.

A Parent's Search for Help

Despite continuous therapy sessions and Trellis's diligent home therapy program, Breanna still required significant physical assistance and was at risk for eventual hip dislocation. High muscle tone in her legs was causing "scissoring," which was increasing the degree of separation in her hip joints. Recently one of Breanna's doctors had recommended surgery to resolve the problem.

As with many parents of children with disabilities, Trellis was constantly searching for ideas and programs to help Breanna. After reading about the MOVE program (see section "How MOVE Works") in a Rifton Company catalog (1999), Trellis requested information on the program. She was sent literature and videotapes and was also given the names of two university professors in her area who were involved with training and research on the program.

Mobility instruction should occur within typical daily activities that are functional for the child.

A Find: How to Facilitate Mobility

After an introduction to MOVE, Trellis went through a 2-day training program to better understand the curriculum and how to implement it. As part of the MOVE program at home, Trellis was encouraged to think of activity-based instruction opportunities. It was explained that mobility instruction should occur within typical daily activities that were functional for Breanna. Initially, Trellis selected activities if Breanna enjoyed them, and if mobility skills could be embedded within them. This included daily dressing, eating, bathing, and playing activities. Although Breanna was able to participate only partially in these activities and needed extensive physical support, Trellis continued to be interested and participate because of the motivation of the activity.

The physical supports or prompts used in the MOVE curriculum are designed to *facilitate* the use of mobility skills, not to *replace* them. In this case, prompts to help support weight, provide balance, and guide the legs for reciprocal steps were provided. These prompts were fre-

Figure 1. Breanna's Mobility Progress

First Week--11/8/99 to 11/15/99	Last week*--4/16/00 to 4/23/00 *end of data collection and recording
Mean Number of Steps Taken (with adult assistance)	**Mean Number of Steps Taken** (with adult assistance)
15	509
Mean Number of Steps Taken (with gait trainer)	**Mean Number of Steps Taken** (with gait trainer)
0	125
Mean Time Standing	**Mean Time Standing**
45 seconds	4.02 minutes

quently provided by the mother and sometimes by the use of a gait trainer. The curriculum provides a guide for the use of prompts; however, as soon as prompts are implemented, a systematic plan for their removal is also developed.

In these activity-based learning opportunities, Trellis took every opportunity to let Breanna physically participate to the fullest degree possible.

Some of the activities Trellis selected to teach Breanna walking skills included feeding the dogs, feeding the chickens and checking for eggs, walking across the yard to Grandma's house, and picking flowers in the yard. Activities that required standing included washing hands at the sink, playing at the sink, and standing at the blackboard to play letter and number games. In these activity-based learning opportunities, Trellis took every opportunity to let Breanna physically participate to the fullest degree possible. For example, when learning games were to be played in the bedroom, the activity might start with Trellis helping Breanna to transfer from a sitting position to a standing position in the living room. Breanna would then walk with support to the bedroom and stand at the board while playing the game. Although it would have been easier for Trellis to have picked her up and carried her to the bedroom, the anticipation of playing the games motivated Breanna to participate in the mobility practice.

The MOVE Curriculum is typically used in school settings, where the team can measure and chart the students'

progress. During this home-based implementation of MOVE, we asked Trellis to keep records of the progress that Breanna made while using the MOVE Curriculum. She recorded the number of steps taken during activities that required walking inside and outside. She also recorded the number of seconds of weight-bearing during standing activities throughout the day (see Figure 1). In addition, we conducted an interview with Trellis to present her perspectives on MOVE. A portion of the interview follows.

A Concerned Parent's Words

We know you were doing a lot with Breanna before MOVE. What made you want to try MOVE?

After I watched the tape of *Kids on the MOVE* (Barnes, 1997) and saw how much they were able to do, I was willing to try just about anything. It seemed like those kids were able to do so much after MOVE; and I thought, if they can do it, then so could Breanna.

Was this approach, the MOVE Program, different from what you were doing?

They [the people on the video] were doing things I wasn't doing. After I saw it, I thought, this makes a lot of sense. Before, I was getting Breanna to stand up and sit down from a chair and walk, but it was just a lot of therapy exercises. The kids in the video were doing these things in regular activities. Now I can have Breanna stand up and sit down from the potty chair—she's being potty trained now! I was just moving her, but now we do these things all through the day in our regular routine. It's so much easier now that it is just part of what we do during the day, and we can practice standing and walking while playing.

We know that in the past you were discouraged because you were doing so much for Breanna and you were worried about the future.

I had gotten frustrated because it's like I told my husband: I said that I don't want to sit here and hold Breanna for the rest of her life. I want her to get up and walk; I want her to be independent. I want to have a little time to do something I want to do, and that's the reason I'm pushing her now and doing what I do. I don't want to do this for the next 20 years. I got discouraged and talked to the doctor about it one time, and she told me I needed to just take a little break and find a hobby or do something.

Did you follow the doctor's advice?

I have backed off, and I don't do as much as I did before; and the reason is last year I got really stressed out. I just wore down. We were doing so much on weight-bearing a day and so much of this and so much of that. By night if I didn't do everything I had planned, I would just almost freak out because I didn't do what I wanted to do; and I just thought the more I do, the better she's going to be. I guess that's true to a point, but I've also realized that after speaking with a therapist and a doctor, I've got to let her be a little girl too and let her have some free play time. So now I try to incorporate training when she's having a fun activity; I make her walk to it, I don't push her, and we take our time a little more. I just don't rush her from place to place like I did before, because I had these goals set that by a certain time I would have this done or that done, and I was just wearing myself out.

So maybe now you're accomplishing as much but enjoying it more?

I think so; I don't feel guilty now—I feel better. I used to have my list of exercises and practice to do, and if I didn't do my list, I felt frustrated. I just wanted a break, but now the practice is like playing. It's more enjoyable for the whole family. My husband, Jeff, has always wanted to be involved with this, but he wasn't sure what to do. Now we go outside and play hide and seek. We've found that one thing she likes is our pond. We can go catch fish in the pond, and we'll drive th golf cart down because it's a pretty good ways down the hill. Jeff will drop us off at one point, and he'll go somewhere else. We'll have to walk to where he is to help get the fish off [the hook], and she thinks that's fun. So she's getting in walking while we have fun and play together.

Now that you've been through the MOVE training and after you've been using the MOVE Curriculum, what are your thoughts about the program? Do you think it has helped you accomplish any of your goals?

Oh, I know it has. For instance, like the steps in front of the sink. You know, I never thought about putting steps in front of a sink and making her walk up the steps to wash her hands. Normally, what I would have done is pick her up and hold her over the sink and wash her as best I could. Now if she wants to go somewhere, you know, I'll stand her up, and instead of just picking her up, I'll make her push up with her legs and use her muscles to stand up; and then we'll walk to where she wants. If she wants to go to her room, I make her walk. I don't just pick her up and carry her like I did most of the time, and I think that's why she's developed the strength that she has in her legs because she's using them more.

Can you give us an example of one thing that she wasn't doing before starting the MOVE program that she is doing now?

When we first started her measurements in the hallway, like with me holding her arms, her most steps when we first started was about 20. Then I remember when it got up to 50 and 60, the length of the hallway; and we were running out of space to measure. So now we measure outside, and she has gone 500 steps without stopping for more than 20 seconds.

"I want her to know that I know she's going to do it, and I push her and challenge her to do it."

—Breanna's mother

In the year that we have known you and have worked with you, we have become aware of your expectations for your daughter. In general, do you think adult expectations of a child's success or failure has an effect on the child's overall performance?

I do. I say that I have high hopes for Breanna. She's already successful in moving from where she was to where she is now. She's done nothing but improve. I don't ever see her getting any worse, or I hope I don't. Because I see her improving, I push her. I want her to know that I know she's going to do it, and I push her and challenge her to do it. If I thought she wasn't able to do it, then we wouldn't even attempt it; and then, who would know? She might not ever do it.

Has this project made you change your expectations?

I still have high expectations for Breanna, and I always wanted her to walk independently without any supports. I guess I had too many expectations a year or a year and a half ago, because I thought she would walk by age 5 or 6; but I really don't think now that that is a realistic goal. She has progressed, but more slowly. Now I think it will be later. That's changed, but I don't think it's because of the MOVE program. It's just that I think I was expecting too much. I wanted too much too early.

Do you feel okay with this slower rate of progress?

Yes, I'm fine with that. I want her to be as independent as possible, and if she never walks without supports—I mean if she has to walk with a walker, or crutches, or a cane—that's fine because I don't want her to always have to rely on me to hold her. I want her to get around and be the most that she can. If she's 10, that's fine; I mean, she has many years after 10, I hope, to live and enjoy life.

You've mentioned in past conversations that a few people have tried to discourage you. Can you think of anything specific that anyone has said that has discouraged you or that has made you...

Mad?

Yes.

Yes, one of her orthopedists. He told me this child would never walk; and I said, "No, you're wrong, and one day I'm going to bring her to your door; and you're going to see her walk to the opposite end of the room." I don't take that lightly. No, every child is different, and she may not walk without supports; but if she's able to walk at all independently and in any shape or form, she's walking.

Did he say why he thought that?

He said that from his experience, and he said that he could tell by his experience that she would never walk, comparing her with all the other kids. That was basically what he told me. He said that she would not be able to sit up independently, and he sat her up on his table. Well, for one thing, she was crying and screaming her head off, and she was so upset that she just reared back and she wouldn't even try to do anything for him. And he just said, "Well, I tell you, she's never going to walk."

When we started this process you had switched doctors. The doctor that you were seeing at that time was thinking that surgery might be needed.

Yes, let me tell you, we went back to the doctor, and when she went, she had subluxation on her right hip at 28%. That's what it was calculated at. When we went to the doctor in March, it was down to 23%; and it's actually gone back in a little into her socket.

That's wonderful. Did the doctor comment about that?

He said it was because she was up and mobile and getting weight through her legs and hips. He said that she was improving.

That's great

So he told us that because her hip was doing well, we wouldn't need another visit for 6 to 8 months.

So now he's not considering surgery this time?

No.

Good. So all of that walking that you have been making her do seems to be helping. What was it like trying to get Breanna to walk more when she had been used to being carried?

I think it was hard for her, and she wouldn't try as much; but now because she is so much stronger and her muscles are not as tight, she's got more control. Weight shifting is easier for her, so she's going to do more. Now, she knows she can.

> ## "If it's something that she wants to do, like play hide and seek, or go outside and pick something, or chase a ball, or chase a rooster, she'll do it"
>
> — Breanna's mother

And does she seem to enjoy walking more now?

Oh, yes, she likes to do things she's not supposed to. If it's something that she wants to do, like play hide and seek, or go outside and pick something, or chase a ball, or chase a rooster, she'll do it. One day, when we were walking down the road, she started looking in the direction of my parents' house, so I asked her if she wanted to go; and she gave me a kiss for yes. I said okay, we'll go and walk down there (about 600 feet). So we did. She was very determined, and she got almost all the way—she got to their yard before she gave out. But she wanted to go.

You have found that there are more things that she wants to do now. Do you think motivation plays a role in her accomplishments?

If she doesn't want to do something, there's really no competition. That's why I've got to find things that are fun and motivating. Because if I tell her, let's walk to your room, we're going to get on the bolster and wedge to exercise, she's not going to go. And I know she's not. But if I tell her to go to her room because we're going to paint, she'll go.

You have mentioned that she seems to have better head and trunk control now. Has this made it easier to do other things around the house?

Yes, I can… just hold her. I mean, if we're standing and not walking, I have let her go and not helped her; and she has stood on her own for a couple of seconds. I can just barely have my arms on her, and she's fully supporting herself. I mean she's supporting herself even when I have my arms wrapped around her; but if I just let go and loosely touch her just so she knows I'm there, she'll stand. She's got so much more strength and control and balance.

Now that Breanna is more mobile, do you see changes in her relationships with other people?

I know I've told you before that Breanna is hard to handle physically. I mean, she has her special needs; and other people didn't know how to do her therapy. They would just carry her, but now they can walk with her because she can stand upright more. They can stand her on the ground and hold her arms rather than just carry her.

What would you recommend to other parents who have children with similar disabilities?

I think all parents ought to know that the more they do for their children when they are young, the more independent they're going to be and be able to do. Breanna's improved a lot since you first met her. I want parents to know that if they worked with their children, they can do better, and they will improve.

Trellis, this is wonderful information. Is there anything else that comes to your mind?

Well, you gave me some ideas when we started the [MOVE] program, and I thank you both for helping her and helping us. You gave me a lot to think about. Before, I was more interested in saving time, and that's maybe why I would pick her up and carry her instead of waiting for her to walk. But I found that she got so much more out of it when I helped her to walk from here to there. Instead of trying to save 9 minutes of time, we were better off taking the 10 minutes. Before I started the program, I didn't make her walk as much because I would carry her a lot to quickly get to the place where we would do our exercises. Now I make her go that extra distance and I think that's why she's improving like she is.

The MOVE Curriculum helps to provide the support, the motivation, and the high expectations to facilitate the development of functional motor skills.

Another example of what she is doing now happened just the other day at my sister's house. I had to run to the bathroom before lunch to wash up. My mom and my sister were in the kitchen fixing us some sandwiches. I put Breanna on the couch with Jordan, her cousin, I told Jordan to sit beside Breanna and not to let her fall off. She wouldn't fall off anyway because she can sit on a couch by herself now. So I went to the bathroom, and the next thing I knew my mom and sister were hollering, "Come here, come here, look at Breanna!" She had gotten off the couch and was standing holding the couch and just laughing. And they swore up and down that they did not help her, and Jordan had gotten down and come to the kitchen. When she did, they looked to make sure Breanna was still okay, and she was sitting on the couch. And the next time they looked, she had gotten off by herself. I think she must have seen Jordan getting off, and she did it, too. I put her on the couch and told her to do it again, and she wouldn't do it. But, she's done it once, she's going to do it again.

That's like when she walked from here to my parents'—she can do it again. It may not be today, and it may not be tomorrow. It may take her a few days, but she will do it again.

How MOVE Works

The MOVE Curriculum helps to provide the support, the motivation, and the high expectations to facilitate the development of functional motor skills. Although this can be accomplished in a variety of settings, such as the home, the curriculum is ideally suited for the school environment (see box, "MOVE Foundations").

Team Approach

Adopting the MOVE Curriculum allows the school team to develop a common focus based on the family's goals and dreams. Related services, such as occupational therapy and physical therapy are then embedded into meaningful activities that incorporate the skills needed to achieve the goals. MOVE uses data-based instruction in which repeated measures are taken on both student progress and the level of support required. Physical support from adults or equipment is provided to allow partial participation in the activity; and the support is reduced as skills increase. In this approach, eating lunch may change from a daily routine to a daily instructional opportunity, as follows:

- Transitioning from sitting to standing.
- Bearing weight (to wash hands at sink).
- Taking reciprocal steps (walking to and from table).
- Maintaining balance in a traditional classroom chair (while eating).

Within the structure of meaningful activities, the team can also incorporate functional academic, communication, and socialization goals. This allows educational teams to write integrated goals that focus on the needs of the individual, rather than on the isolated skills of specific disciplines.

Integrated Curriculum

MOVE is a top-down, activity-based curriculum designed to teach people with physical disabilities the basic, functional motor skills needed for greater participation within home, school, and community environments (Kern County Superintendent of Schools, 1999). The curriculum was developed by Linda Bidabe, a teacher in Bakersfield, California, who was frustrated with the lack of progress of many of her students who had severe disabilities. She recognized that small developmental gains in motor skills frequently gave way to growing bodies and that many of these students remained in wheelchairs, or returned to them, before they ever achieved independent mobility.

Bidabe's solution to this situation was to focus on the functional skills of standing, walking, and sitting, as opposed to prerequisite or developmental skills, such as raising head from a prone position, rolling over, and crawling. In this "top-down" approach to program planning, the team selects instructional activities and basic skills, based on functional outcomes, and incorporates events dispersed throughout the day. Assessment, planning, and instruction are accomplished through transdisciplinary teams that include parents, educators, and therapists who work together to achieve the family's goals for the student.

MOVE was developed on the following foundations:

- *Functional Curriculum*—Learning occurs within meaningful activities.

- *Natural Environments*—Skills are practiced where they will be used.

- *Family Centered*—Family priorities are an essential part of MOVE.

- *Integrated Therapy*—Team collaboratively plans, sets goals, and intervenes in students' natural environments.

- *Partial Participation*—Students participate in meaningful activities to the greatest degree possible.

MOVE uses motivating activities to teach functional mobility skills that

- Are age-appropriate.

- Increase independence.

- Increase access to the community.

- Reduce custodial care.

- Promote communication, social, and daily-living skills.

Final Thoughts

When working with individuals with limited mobility, it is important that the adults who are facilitating learning have high expectations and provide multiple opportunities for practice. This task can be challenging.

As an integrated, engaging, and motivating approach to education for students with mobility and other needs, MOVE holds great promise for teams of educators, students, and families. As Breanna and her mother discovered, learning independent skills can be fun and can lead to great strides in learning and improvement.

References

Barnes, S. B. (Producer). (1997). *Kids on the MOVE: Holm elementary* [Video]. (Available from MOVE International, 1300 17th Street, City Centre, Bakersfield, CA 93301-4533.)

Barnes, S. B., & Whinnery, K. W. (1997). Mobility Opportunities Via Education (MOVE): Theoretical foundations. *Physical Disabilities: Education and Related Services, 16*, 33–46.

Barnes, S. B., & Whinnery, K. W. (in press). Effects of functional mobility training for young students with physical disabilities. *Exceptional Children.*

Bidabe, D. L., Barnes, S. B., & Whinnery, K. W. (2001). M.O.V.E.: Raising expectations for individuals with severe disabilities. *Physical Disabilities: Education and Related Services, 19*, 31–48.

Campbell, S. K., Vander Linden, D. W., & Palisano, R. J. (2000). *Physical therapy for children* (2nd ed.). Philadelphia: W. B. Saunders.

Dunn, W. (1991). Integrated related services. In L. H. Meyer, C. A. Peck, & L. Brown (Eds.), *Critical issues in the lives of people with severe disabilities* (pp. 353–377). Baltimore: Paul H. Brookes.

Heriza, C. (1991). Motor development: Traditional and contemporary theories. In M. J. Lister (Ed.), *Contemporary management of motor control problems: Proceedings of the II Step Conference* (pp. 99–126). Alexandria, VA: Foundation for Physical Therapy.

Horak, F. B. (1991). Assumptions underlying motor control for neurologic rehabilitation. In M. J. Lister (Ed.), *Contemporary management of motor control problems: Proceedings of the II Step Conference* (pp. 11–27). Alexandria, VA: Foundation for Physical Therapy.

Kern County Superintendent of Schools. (1999). M.O.V.E.: Mobility Opportunities Via Education. Bakersfield, CA: Author.

Orelove, F. P., & Sobsey D. (1996). *Educating children with multiple disabilities* (3rd ed.). Baltimore: Paul H. Brookes.

Rainforth, B., & York-Barr, J. (1997). *Collaborative teams for students with severe disabilities: Integrating therapy and educational services.* Baltimore: Paul H. Brookes.

Rifton: Community Playthings. (1999). *Rifton equipment* (catalog). Rifton, NY: Community Products LLC.

Snell, M. E., & Brown, F. (2000). *Instruction of students with severe disabilities* (5th ed.). Upper Saddle River, NJ: Prentice-Hall.

Vockell, E. L., & Asher, J. W. (1995). *Educational research* (2nd ed.). Englewood Cliffs, NJ: Merrill.

Keith W. Whinnery (CEC Chapter #770), Associate Professor; and **Stacie B. Barnes**, (CEC Chapter #770), Assistant Professor, Special Education Department, University of West Florida, Pensacola.

Address correspondence to Keith W. Whinnery, Special Education Department, University of West Florida, 11000 University Parkway, Pensacola, FL 32514 (e-mail: kwhinner@at;uwf.edu).

From *Teaching Exceptional Children*, January/February 2002, pp. 44-50. © 2002 by The Council for Exceptional Children. Reprinted by permission.

Accommodations for Students with Disabilities: Removing Barriers to Learning

Secondary school principals frequently encounter questions about educating students with disabilities. Sometimes the questions revolve around seeking a deeper understanding of the disability and the best way to meet student needs. Other times, the questions focus on all the changes that must be made to ensure students receive an appropriate education. What questions do teachers ask about accommodations for students with a disability?

By MaryAnn Byrnes

Think about taking a driver's test without wearing glasses (if you do, that is). Not fair, you say; you need the glasses to see. You have just identified an accommodation that you need. Wearing glasses does not make a bad driver better or make driving easier; rather, wearing glasses makes driving possible. Glasses are so much a part of our lives that we do not even consider that they remove a barrier caused by a disability.

Secondary school teachers encounter students every day on an Individualized Education Plan (IEP) or 504 Plan, both of which address programs for students with disabilities. Most likely, the person charged with monitoring this plan has indicated that particular students need changes in teaching style, assignments, or testing strategies.

It is usually easy to understand the need for glasses or wheelchairs or hearing aids. These sound like changes the student must make. Other adjustments, modifications, or accommodations on these plans, such as extended time, may not be as clear.

What is an accommodation?

An accommodation is an adjustment, to an activity or setting, that removes a barrier presented by a disability so a person can have access equal to that of a person without a disability. An accommodation does not guarantee success or a specific level of performance. It should, however, provide the opportunity for a person with a disability to participate in a situation or activity.

Think of that pair of glasses, or the time you broke your leg and could not drive. Think of how your life was affected by these conditions. Your competence did not change. Your ability to think and work did not change. Your ability to interact with (have access to) the reading material may be very limited without your glasses. Your ability to get to (have access to) work or the grocery store may be very limited without someone to transport you. The support provided by the glasses—or the driver—made it possible for you to use your abilities without the barrier presented by less than perfect vision or limited mobility.

An accommodation is an adjustment, to an activity or setting, that removes a barrier presented by a disability so a person can have access equal to that of a person without a disability.

The accommodations in IEPs or 504 Plans serve the same purpose. They identify ways to remove the barrier presented by a person's disability.

Why do we need to provide accommodations?

Accommodations are required under Section 504 of the Federal Rehabilitation Act of 1974 as well as the Americans with Disabilities Act. Both these federal laws prohibit discrimination against individuals who have a disability. Situations that limit access have been determined to be discriminatory.

Accommodations must be provided not just by teachers to students, but by employees for workers and governments for citizens. Curbs have been cut to provide access. Doors have been widened and door handles altered to provide access to people for whom the old designs posed a barrier. Employers provide computer adaptations or other adjustments in work schedules and circumstances.

For employers and schools, individuals with disabilities may have a document called a 504 Plan, which details the types of accommodations that are required. Students who have a 504 Plan will not require special education services, just changes to the environment or instructional situation.

Students who have a disability and require special education services in addition to accommodations will have this information contained in an IEP, which also details the types of direct services that need to be provided and the goals of these services. Accommodations will be listed within this IEP.

With the recent changes in IDEA '97, the federal law governing special education, you will be addressing accommodations that must be made so a student with a disability can participate in large-scale districtwide or statewide assessment systems as well as classwork and school life.

Who needs accommodations?

According to Section 504, an individual with a disability is any person who has "a physical or mental impairment that limits one or more major life activities." IDEA '97, the federal special education law, lists the following disabilities: autism, deaf-blindness, deafness, hearing impairment, mental retardation, multiple disabilities, orthopedic impairment, other health impairment, serious emotional disturbance, specific learning disability, speech or language impairment, traumatic brain injury, and visual impairment.

Students who have a 504 Plan will not require special education services, just changes to the environment or instructional situation.

Some conditions are covered by Section 504, but not special education. These can include attention deficit disorder—ADD, (also attention deficit hyperactivity disorder—ADHD); chronic medical conditions (such as cancer, Tourette Syndrome, asthma, or epilepsy); communicable diseases; some temporary medical conditions; physical impairments; and disorders of emotion or behavior. To qualify, there must be a demonstrated and substantial limitation of a major life activity.

Students (or adults) who have disabilities may require accommodations to have equal access to education. Not every student with a disability will require accommodations, and not every student with a disability requires the same accommodation all the time.

Think of Jim, a student who has limited mobility in his hands, affecting his ability to write. This disability will present a barrier in a class that requires the student to take notes quickly or write long essays in class. In a class that does not require either of these activities, no barrier may be present. Equal access is possible without accommodation. The student can learn and demonstrate what he knows and can do unaffected by his disability.

What kind of accommodations are there?

Just as there is no limit to the range of disabilities, there is no limit to the range of accommodations. The point is to understand disability and determine if it presents a barrier to equal access. If so, decide whether an accommodation can be identified to remove the barrier— and make sure the accommodation is implemented.

Not every student with a disability will require accommodations, and not every student with a disability requires the same accommodation all the time.

Think of the student described above. The limited mobility in Jim's hands presents a barrier in a class that requires rapid note taking or the writing of long essays in class. There are several accommodations that can result in equal access. Jim might tape the lesson and take notes later. These notes could be written or dictated into a computer. Essays could be composed verbally at a computer workstation or dictated into a tape recorder or to a scribe. A computer might be adapted so typing becomes an effective way to record information on paper. In yet another type of accommodation, essays could be replaced by oral reports.

Are there some accommodations that should not be used?

Like many difficult questions, the answer depends on the context. An accommodation should not alter the essential purpose of the assignment. If the skill you want to measure is the ability to make multiple rapid hand movements, then there is probably no accommodation that is appropriate. Jim will not do well because of his disability. Alternately, if the purpose of a task is to see if someone has perfect vision without glasses, using those glasses is not an appropriate accommodation. If the purpose is to see if you can read, the glasses become a reasonable accommodation.

Who decides about accommodations?

The team that writes IEPs and 504 Plans reviews the disability and determines what accommodations, if any, are necessary. These are then written into the EIP or 504 Plan.

Once more, return to Jim. As you consider the requirements of your class, think of the most appropriate way to remove the barrier that is presented by the limited mobility Jim has in his hands.

If we use accommodations, how will the student ever be prepared for independent life in college or the world of work?

Some people are concerned that the supports provided in school will result in the student being unable to work productively when he or she leaves school. As a matter of fact, Section 504 applies to colleges and employers as well. Colleges offer support centers and provide accommodations upon documentation that a disability exists. Employers are required to provide reasonable accommodations to any person who is otherwise qualified to fulfill the elements of the job.

If companies remove barriers at the workplace, educators should be willing and able to take barriers out of the school activities that prepare a student for the workplace. Teachers can help a student identify the type of accommodation that will be the least cumbersome for everyone, and those that will permit the student to be most independent.

Don't accommodations just make school easier?

That depends on how you view the world. Does wearing glasses make driving easier? Not really—for a person with limited vision, wearing glasses makes driving *possible*. With or without glasses, you need to be able to drive to pass the test. The same is true of an academic accommodation; whether or not the accommodation is provided, the students still must demonstrate that they know required material.

An accommodation should not alter the essential purpose of the assignment.

Think about the important elements of your class: Is it more important that Jim take notes in class or understand the material? Is it more important that Jim demonstrate good handwriting or the ability to communicate thoughts in print? Often, when you identify the main purpose of your assignments and consider the skills and abilities of a student, you will see that an accommodation lets you determine more clearly what a student knows, understands, and can do.

Does a student need to follow the IEP accommodations in all classes?

The IEP or 504 Plan needs to address any area in which the student's disability affects life in school. Sometimes this means in all classes, but not always. For example, a student who was blind would need to use Braille in all classes dealing with written material. Jim, our student with limited mobility in his hands, might not require accommodations in world languages or physical education.

Can we make accommodations without having students on an IEP?

Many accommodations are just different ways of teaching or testing. You should be able to have this freedom in your classes. In some cases, the way in which a class is taught makes accommodations unnecessary. Accommodations change the situation, not the content of the instruction. However, accommodations on standardized tests must be connected to IEP's or 504 Plans.

May teachers give different assignments on the same content as a way to meet the needs of different learning styles without lowering standards?

Absolutely. The point is to remove the barrier of the disability; this is one way to accomplish that. Some teachers find they tap student knowledge best in active projects; others find that written work is best. Many secondary schools are using portfolios or performance activities to document student learning.

These assessment activities can be very compelling and they do tap different methods of expression. A student like Jim, for example, might communicate depth of understanding and analysis to a social studies debate with a disability in the area of speech or language might find barriers in the performance activities that do not exist on a paper-and-pencil task.

. . . educators should be willing and able to take barriers out of the school activities that prepare a student for the workplace.

What if accommodations are not implemented?

Since accommodations allow equal access, refusing to provide them can be viewed as discrimination. Individuals who knowingly refuse to implement accommodations make themselves personally liable for legal suit.

This sounds serious, and it is serious. Once the accommodations are found to be necessary, everyone must implement them in situations where the student's disability poses a barrier that prevents equal access.

If no barrier exists in your class, the accommodation is not necessary. No one has the option, however, of deciding not to implement a necessary accommodation. Telling students they could not wear glasses or use a hearing aid is unthinkable. Just as inappropriate is a decision not to allow Jim to use accommodations to remove the barrier posed by his disability, even though it means making some changes to your own work.

Questions About Specific Accommodations

Now that the issues underlying accommodations have been addressed, it is time to talk about frequently-encountered accommodations that raise questions and concern. All these questions have come from secondary school faculty members in a variety of school systems.

Why is it fair to read material aloud to some students?

Some students have a learning disability that makes it difficult for them to decode print. They can understand the concepts; they can comprehend the material when they hear it; they can reason through the material. They just can't turn print into meaning. If the task is to determine if the student can read, you already know they will have difficulty. If the task is to determine if the student has content knowledge, reading material aloud removes the barrier of the learning disability. Reading material aloud to a student who does not understand the material will not result in a higher grade.

Why is it fair to give some students extra time on tests?

Some students have motor difficulties that make writing an enormous challenge. They may not be able to form the letters correctly. They may not be able to monitor their thoughts while they work on the physical act of writing. They understand the material, and they know what they want to respond; it just takes longer to write the answer. If the task is to determine how quickly the student can respond, you already know they will have difficulty. If the task is to determine if the student has the knowledge, providing extra time removes the

barrier of the motor disability. Providing extra time to a student who does not understand the material will not result in a higher grade.

Why is it fair to permit some students to respond orally to tests?

Think about the example above. For some students, responding orally would be a comparable accommodation. In this case, allowing an oral response will not result in a higher grade if the student does not know the material.

A student with a disability in the area of speech or language might find barriers in the performance activities that do not exist on a paper-and-pencil task.

The Bottom Line

It all comes down to deciding what is important. Think about your assignment and expectations. Think about the disability. If the disability provides a barrier, the accommodation removes it. The accommodation does not release a student from participating or demonstrating knowledge—it allows the student to be able to participate and demonstrate knowledge. And isn't that what school is all about?

References

Americans with Disabilities Act of 1990, P.L. 101–336, 2, 104 Stat. 328.1991.
Individuals with Disabilities Education Act Amendments of 1997, P.L. 105–17, 20 U.S. Code Sections 1401–1486.
Livovich, Michael P. *Section 504 of the Rehabilitation Act of 1973 and the Americans with Disabilities Act. Providing access to a free appropriate public education: a public school manual.* Indianapolis, Ind.: 1996.
Vocational Rehabilitation Act of 1973, 29 U.S.C. 794.

*MaryAnn Byrnes (**byrnes@mediaone.net**) is assistant professor at the Graduate College of Education, University of Massachusetts-Boston.*

Trick Question

A liberal 'hoax' turns out to be true.

By MICHAEL FUMENTO

IT'S BOTH RIGHT-WING and vast, but it's not a conspiracy. Actually, it's more of an anti-conspiracy. The subject is Attention Deficit Disorder (ADD) and Attention Deficit Hyperactivity Disorder (ADHD), closely related ailments (henceforth referred to in this article simply as ADHD). Rush Limbaugh declares it "may all be a hoax." Francis Fukuyama devotes much of one chapter in his latest book, *Our Posthuman Future*, to attacking Ritalin, the top-selling drug used to treat ADHD. Columnist Thomas Sowell writes, "The motto used to be: 'Boys will be boys.' Today, the motto seems to be: 'Boys will be medicated.'" And Phyllis Schlafly explains, "The old excuse of 'my dog ate my homework' has been replaced by 'I got an ADHD diagnosis.'" A March 2002 article in *The Weekly Standard* summed up the conservative line on ADHD with this rhetorical question: "Are we really prepared to redefine childhood as an ailment, and medicate it until it goes away?"

Many conservative writers, myself included, have criticized the growing tendency to pathologize every undesirable behavior—especially where children are concerned. But, when it comes to ADHD, this skepticism is misplaced. As even a cursory examination of the existing literature or, for that matter, simply talking to the parents and teachers of children with ADHD reveals, the condition is real, and it is treatable. And, if you don't believe me, you can ask conservatives who've come face to face with it themselves.

MYTH: ADHD ISN'T A REAL DISORDER.

The most common argument against ADHD on the right is also the simplest: It doesn't exist. Conservative columnist Jonah Goldberg thus reduces ADHD to "ants in the pants." Sowell equates it with "being bored and restless." Fukuyama protests, "No one has been able to identify a cause of ADD/ADHD. It is a pathology recognized only by its symptoms." And a conservative columnist approvingly quotes Thomas Armstrong, Ritalin opponent and author, when he declares, "ADD is a disorder that cannot be authoritatively identified in the same way as polio, heart disease or other legitimate illnesses."

The Armstrong and Fukuyama observations are as correct as they are worthless. "Half of all medical disorders are diagnosed without benefit of a lab procedure," notes Dr. Russell Barkley, professor of psychology at the College of Health Professionals at the Medical University of South Carolina. "Where are the lab tests for headaches and multiple sclerosis and Alzheimer's?" he asks. "Such a standard would virtually eliminate all mental disorders."

Often the best diagnostic test for an ailment is how it responds to treatment. And, by that standard, it doesn't get much more real than ADHD. The beneficial effects of administering stimulants to treat the disorder were first reported in 1937. And today medication for the disorder is reported to be 75 to 90 percent successful. "In our trials it was close to ninety percent," says Dr. Judith Rapoport, director of the National Institute of Mental Health's Child Psychiatry Branch, who has published about 100 papers on ADHD. "This means there was a significant difference in the children's ability to function in the classroom or at home."

Additionally, epidemiological evidence indicates that ADHD has a powerful genetic component. University of Colorado researchers have found that a child whose identical twin has the disorder is between eleven and 18 times more likely to also have it than is a non-twin sibling. For these reasons, the American Psychiatric Association (APA), American Medical Association, American Academy of Pediatrics, American Academy of Child

Adolescent Psychiatry, the surgeon general's office, and other major medical bodies all acknowledge ADHD as both real and treatable.

MYTH: ADHD IS PART OF A FEMINIST CONSPIRACY TO MAKE LITTLE BOYS MORE LIKE LITTLE GIRLS.

Many conservatives observe that boys receive ADHD diagnoses in much higher numbers than girls and find in this evidence of a feminist conspiracy. (This, despite the fact that genetic diseases are often heavily weighted more toward one gender or the other.) Sowell refers to "a growing tendency to treat boyhood as a pathological condition that requires a new three R's—repression, re-education and Ritalin." Fukuyama claims Prozac is being used to give women "more of the alpha-male feeling," while Ritalin is making boys act more like girls. "Together, the two sexes are gently nudged toward that androgynous median personality… that is the current politically correct outcome in American society." George Will, while acknowledging that Ritalin can be helpful, nonetheless writes of the "androgyny agenda" of "drugging children because they are behaving like children, especially boy children." Anti-Ritalin conservatives frequently invoke Christina Hoff Sommers's best-selling 2000 book, *The War Against Boys*. You'd never know that the drug isn't mentioned in her book—or why.

"Originally I was going to have a chapter on it," Sommers tells me. "It seemed to fit the thesis." What stopped her was both her survey of the medical literature and her own empirical findings. Of one child she personally came to know she says, "He was utterly miserable, as was everybody around him. The drugs saved his life."

MYTH: ADHD IS PART OF THE PUBLIC SCHOOL SYSTEM'S EFFORTS TO WAREHOUSE KIDS RATHER THAN TO DISCIPLINE AND TEACH THEM.

"No doubt life is easier for teachers when everyone sits around quietly," writes Sowell. Use of ADHD drugs is "in the school's interest to deal with behavioral and discipline problems [because] it's so easy to use Ritalin to make kids compliant: to get them to sit down, shut up, and do what they're told," declares Schlafly. The word "zombies" to describe children under the effects of Ritalin is tossed around more than in a B-grade voodoo movie.

Kerri Houston, national field director for the American Conservative Union and the mother of two ADHD children on medication, agrees with much of the criticism of public schools. "But don't blame ADHD on crummy curricula and lazy teachers," she says. "If you've worked with these children, you know they have a serious neurological problem." In any case, Ritalin, when taken as prescribed, hardly stupefies children. To the extent the medicine works, it simply turns ADHD children into normal children. "ADHD is like having thirty televisions on at one time, and the medicine turns off twenty-nine so you can

concentrate on the one," Houston describes. "This zombie stuff drives me nuts! My kids are both as lively and as fun as can be."

MYTH: PARENTS WHO GIVE THEIR KIDS ANTI-ADHD DRUGS ARE MERELY DOPING UP PROBLEM CHILDREN.

Limbaugh calls ADHD "the perfect way to explain the inattention, incompetence, and inability of adults to control their kids." Addressing parents directly, he lectures, "It helped you mask your own failings by doping up your children to calm them down."

Such charges blast the parents of ADHD kids into high orbit. That includes my Hudson Institute colleague (and fellow conservative) Mona Charen, the mother of an eleven-year-old with the disorder. "I have two non-ADHD children, so it's not a matter of parenting technique," says Charen. "People without such children have no idea what it's like. I can tell the difference between boyish high spirits and pathological hyperactivity…. These kids bounce off the walls. Their lives are chaos; their rooms are chaos. And nothing replaces the drugs."

Barkley and Rapoport say research backs her up. Randomized, controlled studies in both the United States and Sweden have tried combining medication with behavioral interventions and then dropped either one or the other. For those trying to go on without medicine, "the behavioral interventions maintained nothing," Barkley says. Rapoport concurs: "Unfortunately, behavior modification doesn't seem to help with ADHD." (Both doctors are quick to add that ADHD is often accompanied by other disorders that are treatable through behavior modification in tandem with medicine.)

MYTH: RITALIN IS "KIDDIE COCAINE."

One of the paradoxes of conservative attacks on Ritalin is that the drug is alternately accused of turning children into brain-dead zombies and of making them Mach-speed cocaine junkies. Indeed, Ritalin is widely disparaged as "kiddie cocaine." Writers who have sought to lump the two drugs together include Schlafly, talk-show host and columnist Armstrong Williams, and others whom I hesitate to name because of my long-standing personal relationships with them.

Mary Eberstadt wrote the "authoritative" Ritalin-cocaine piece for the April 1999 issue of *Policy Review*, then owned by the Heritage Foundation. The article, "Why Ritalin Rules," employs the word "cocaine" no fewer than twelve times. Eberstadt quotes from a 1995 Drug Enforcement Agency (DEA) background paper declaring methylphenidate, the active ingredient in Ritalin, "a central nervous system (CNS) stimulant [that] shares many of the pharmacological effects of amphetamine, methamphetamine, and cocaine." Further, it "produces behavioral, psychological, subjective, and reinforcing effects similar to those of d-amphetamine including increases in rating of euphoria, drug liking and activity, and decreases in sedation." Add to this the fact that the Controlled Substances Act lists it as a

Schedule II drug, imposing on it the same tight prescription controls as morphine, and Ritalin starts to sound spooky indeed.

What Eberstadt fails to tell readers is that the DEA description concerns methylphenidate *abuse*. It's tautological to say abuse is harmful. According to the DEA, the drugs in question are comparable when "administered the same way at comparable doses." But ADHD stimulants, when taken as prescribed, are neither administered in the same way as cocaine nor at comparable doses. "What really counts," says Barkley, "is the speed with which the drugs enter and clear the brain. With cocaine, because it's snorted, this happens tremendously quickly, giving users the characteristic addictive high." (Ever seen anyone pop a cocaine tablet?) Further, he says, "There's no evidence anywhere in literature of [Ritalin's] addictiveness when taken as prescribed." As to the Schedule II listing, again this is because of the potential for it to fall into the hands of abusers, not because of its effects on persons for whom it is prescribed. Ritalin and the other anti-ADHD drugs, says Barkley, "are the safest drugs in all of psychiatry." (And they may be getting even safer: A new medicine just released called Strattera represents the first true non-stimulant ADHD treatment.)

Indeed, a study just released in the journal *Pediatrics* found that children who take Ritalin or other stimulants to control ADHD cut their risk of future substance abuse by 50 percent compared with untreated ADHD children. The lead author speculated that "by treating ADHD you're reducing the demoralization that accompanies this disorder, and you're improving the academic functioning and well-being of adolescents and young adults during the critical times when substance abuse starts."

MYTH: RITALIN IS OVERPRESCRIBED ACROSS THE COUNTRY.

Some call it "the Ritalin craze." In *The Weekly Standard*, Melana Zyla Vickers informs us that "Ritalin use has exploded," while Eberstadt writes that "Ritalin use more than doubled in the first half of the decade alone, [and] the number of schoolchildren taking the drug may now, by some estimates, be approaching the *4 million mark*."

A report in the January 2003 issue of *Archives of Pediatrics and Adolescent Medicine* did find a large increase in the use of ADHD medicines from 1987 to 1996, an increase that doesn't appear to be slowing. Yet nobody thinks it's a problem that routine screening for high blood pressure has produced a big increase in the use of hypertension medicine. "Today, children suffering from ADHD are simply less likely to slip through the cracks," says Dr. Sally Satel, a psychiatrist, AEI fellow, and author of *PC, M.D.: How Political Correctness Is Corrupting Medicine.*

Satel agrees that some community studies, by the standards laid down in the APA's *Diagnostic and Statistical Manual of Mental Disorders (DSM)*, indicate that ADHD may often be over-diagnosed. On the other hand, she says, additional evidence shows that in some communities ADHD is *under*-diagnosed and *under*-treated. "I'm quite concerned with children who need the medication and aren't getting it," she says.

There *are* tremendous disparities in the percentage of children taking ADHD drugs when comparing small geographical areas. Psychologist Gretchen LeFever, for example, has compared the number of prescriptions in mostly white Virginia Beach, Virginia, with other, more heavily African American areas in the southeastern part of the state. Conservatives have latched onto her higher numbers—20 percent of white fifth-grade boys in Virginia Beach are being treated for ADHD—as evidence that something is horribly wrong. But others, such as Barkley, worry about the lower numbers. According to LeFever's study, black children are only half as likely to get medication as white children. "Black people don't get the care of white people; children of well-off parents get far better care than those of poorer parents," says Barkley.

MYTH: STATES SHOULD PASS LAWS THAT RESTRICT SCHOOLS FROM RECOMMENDING RITALIN.

Conservative writers have expressed delight that several states, led by Connecticut, have passed or are considering laws ostensibly protecting students from schools that allegedly pass out Ritalin like candy. Representative Lenny Winkler, lead sponsor of the Connecticut measure, told *Reuters Health*, "If the diagnosis is made, and it's an appropriate diagnosis that Ritalin be used, that's fine. But I have also heard of many families approached by the school system [who are told] that their child cannot attend school if they're not put on Ritalin."

Two attorneys I interviewed who specialize in child-disability issues, including one from the liberal Bazelon Center for Mental Health Law in Washington, D.C., acknowledge that school personnel have in some cases stepped over the line. But legislation can go too far in the other direction by declaring, as Connecticut's law does, that "any school personnel [shall be prohibited] from recommending the use of psychotropic drugs for any child." The law appears to offer an exemption by declaring, "The provisions of this section shall not prohibit *school medical staff* from recommending that a child be evaluated by an appropriate medical practitioner, or prohibit school personnel from consulting with such practitioner, with the consent of the parent or guardian of such child." [Emphasis added.] But of course many, if not most, schools have perhaps one nurse on regular "staff." That nurse will have limited contact with children in the classroom situations where ADHD is likely to be most evident. And, given the wording of the statute, a teacher who believed a student was suffering from ADHD would arguably be prohibited from referring that student to the nurse. Such ambiguity is sure to have a chilling effect on any form of intervention or recommendation by school personnel. Moreover, 20- year special-education veteran Sandra Rief said in an interview with the National Education Association that "recommending medical intervention for a student's behavior could lead to personal liability issues." Teachers, in other words, could be forced to choose between what they think is best for the health of their students and the possible risk of losing not only their jobs but their personal assets as well.

"Certainly it's not within the purview of a school to say kids can't attend if they don't take drugs," says Houston. "On the other hand, certainly teachers should be able to advise parents as to problems and potential solutions.... [T]hey may see things parents don't. My own son is an angel at home but was a demon at school."

If the real worry is "take the medicine or take a hike" ultimatums, legislation can be narrowly tailored to prevent them; broad-based gag orders, such as Connecticut's, are a solution that's worse than the problem.

THE CONSERVATIVE CASE FOR ADHD DRUGS.

There are kernels of truth to every conservative suspicion about ADHD. Who among us has not had lapses of attention? And isn't hyperactivity a normal condition of childhood when compared with deskbound adults? Certainly there are lazy teachers, warehousing schools, androgyny-pushing feminists, and far too many parents unwilling or unable to expend the time and effort to raise their children properly, even by their own standards. Where conservatives go wrong is in making ADHD a scapegoat for frustration over what we perceive as a breakdown in the order of society and family. In a column in *The Boston Herald*, Boston University Chancellor John Silber rails that Ritalin is "a classic example of a cheap fix: low-cost, simple and purely superficial."

Exactly. Like most headaches, ADHD is a neurological problem that can usually be successfully treated with a chemical. Those who recommend or prescribe ADHD medicines do not, as *The Weekly Standard* put it, see them as "discipline in pill-form." They see them as pills.

In fact, it can be argued that the use of those pills, far from being liable for or symptomatic of the Decline of the West, reflects and reinforces conservative values. For one thing, they increase personal responsibility by removing an excuse that children (and their parents) can fall back on to explain misbehavior and poor performance. "Too many psychologists and psychiatrists focus on allowing patients to justify to themselves their troubling behavior," says Satel. "But something like Ritalin actually encourages greater autonomy because you're treating a compulsion to behave in a certain way. Also, by treating ADHD, you remove an opportunity to explain away bad behavior."

Moreover, unlike liberals, who tend to downplay differences between the sexes, conservatives are inclined to believe that there are substantial physiological differences— differences such as boys' greater tendency to suffer ADHD. "Conservatives celebrate the physiological differences between boys and girls and eschew the radical-feminist notion that gender differences are created by societal pressures," says Houston regarding the fuss over the boy-girl disparity among ADHD diagnoses. "ADHD is no exception."

But, however compatible conservatism may be with taking ADHD seriously, the truth is that most conservatives remain skeptics. "I'm sure I would have been one of those smug conservatives saying it's a made-up disease," admits Charen, "if I hadn't found out the hard way." Here's hoping other conservatives find an easier route to accepting the truth.

MICHAEL FUMENTO is a senior fellow at the Hudson Institute in Washington, D.C., where he is completing his latest book, tentatively titled *Bioevolution: How Biotechnology Is Changing our World*, due this spring from Encounter Books.

UNIT 10
Giftedness

Unit Selections

Key Points to Consider

- How can significant adults identify children with exceptional gifts and talents? What types of assessment are valid and reliable? What guidelines are important for their individualized education programs?

- Do children from minority cultures with exceptional gifts and talents hide their creative potentials? Why? How can their special gifts be identified and enhanced?

- What types of instruction are effective for students who have both giftedness and learning disabilities?

 **Links: www.dushkin.com/online/**
These sites are annotated in the World Wide Web pages.

The Council for Exceptional Children
http://www.cec.sped.org/index.html

National Association for Gifted Children (NAGC)
http://www.nagc.org/home00.htm

The individuals with Disabilities Education Act (IDEA) mandates special services for children with disabilities, but not for children with exceptional gifts or talents. The monies spent to provide special services for three children with high-cost disabilities could pay for accelerated lessons for a classroom full of college-bound students with intellectual giftedness. Should schools in the twenty-first century be more egalitarian? IDEA mandates appropriate education but not sameness of quantity or degree of knowledge to be imported to every child. Are we inclined to push compensatory education of students with shortcomings in learning, while leaving students with a gift for learning to cope for themselves to counterbalance the equation? Do we want educational parity?

Since many textbooks on exceptional children include children with special gifts and talents, and since these children are exceptional, they will be included in this volume. Instructors who deal only with the categories of disabilities covered by IDEA may simply omit coverage of this unit.

The Omnibus Education Bill of 1987 provided modest support for gifted and talented identification and the education of students with giftedness in the United States. It required, however, that each state foot the bill for the development of special programs for children with exceptional gifts and talents. Some states have implemented accelerated or supplemental education for the gifted. Most states have not.

Giftedness can be viewed as both a blessing and a curse. Problems of jealousy, misunderstanding, indignation, exasperation, and even fear are often engendered in people who live with, work with, or get close to a child with superior intelligence. Are children with giftedness at a disadvantage in our society? Do their powerful abilities and potentialities in some area (or areas) leave them ridiculed or bored in a regular classroom? Children with special gifts and talents are deprived of some of the opportunities with which less exceptional children are routinely provided.

Students who are gifted tend to ask a lot of questions and pursue answers with still more questions. They can be incredibly persistent about gathering information about topics that engage them. They may, however, show no interest at all in learning about topics that do not. They may be very competitive in areas where they are especially skilled, competing even with teachers and other adults. They may seem arrogant about their skills, when in their minds they are only being honest.

Many children and youth with special gifts and talents have extraordinary sensitivity to how other people are reacting to them. As they are promoted through elementary school into middle school and high school, many such children learn to hide their accomplishments for the secondary gain of being more socially acceptable or more popular. Because they have not been challenged or have been discouraged from achieving at their highest potentialities, underachievement becomes a problem. They have poor study habits as a result of not needing to study. They are unmotivated, intensely bored, and discouraged by the educational programs available to them.

Researchers who have studied creative genius have found that most accomplished high achievers share one childhood similarity. Their parents recognized their special abilities early and found tutors or mentors who would help them develop their skills. This is true not only of mathematicians and scientists but also of world-class sports players, musicians, artists, performers, writers, and other producers of note.

Educational programs that refuse to find tutors or mentors, to encourage original work, or to provide special education in the skill areas of students with gifts are depriving the future of potential producers.

The earlier that children with special gifts and talents are recognized, the better. The sooner they are provided with enriched education, the more valuable their future contributions will become. Children from all ethnic backgrounds, from all socioeconomic levels, and from both sexes can have exceptional gifts and talents. Researchers have reported that parents of gifted persons seldom have any special creative skills or talents of their own.

The assessment of children with special gifts and talents, especially in the early childhood years, is fraught with difficulties. Should parents nominate their own children when they see extraordinary skills developing? How objective can parents be about their child's ability as it compares to the abilities of other same-aged children? Should measures of achievement be used (recitals, performances, art, reading levels, writings)? Many parents are embarrassed by their child's extraordinary aptitudes. They would rather have a popular child or a child more like his or her peers.

The first article in this unit suggests resources for parents and teachers of young gifted children. Guidelines are given for understanding the uniqueness of each preschooler with special gifts and talents. They are often described as "4 going on 40." In fact, each one has different areas of acceleration. Helping them understand themselves and their environments can be a challenging task. Many persons, unaccustomed to working with children with advanced talents, may misinterpret their unique behaviors. If unattended, they may learn to camouflage their giftedness in order to "fit in" with their peers. While peer tutoring can make children with advanced abilities feel needed, if used excessively it can lead to problems. Finding and reinforcing areas of giftedness, while attending to their social needs, and their self-esteem, are areas addressed in this article.

The second article, "Cultivating Otherwise Untapped Potential" warns that allowing special talents to lie dormant may lead to their demise. Our society can benefit greatly from identifying creative potential and developing it early. The article includes a discussion of the pros and cons of acceleration for children with exceptional potential.

In the last article Susan Winebrenner describes students who are twice-exceptional: both exceptionally gifted and learning-disabled or ADHD, a not uncommon phenomenon. They usually do not receive gifted education. Their school work may be patronizingly simple. Ms. Winebrenner cautions us not to take time away from their strengths to focus on their weaknesses. She gives 9 suggestions for educating them more appropriately.

Understanding the Young Gifted Child:
Guidelines for Parents, Families, and Educators

Young children who are gifted or talented share special characteristics that impact on the way they learn and develop. Teachers and parents need to consider the unique needs of each child as they plan ways to nurture and educate these youngsters. Concerns such as uneven development, the need for acceleration and/or enrichment, appropriate socialization and peer interactions, and modification of the curriculum are some of the topics discussed. Suggestions for teachers and parents are included along with a variety of resources.

KEY WORDS: gifted; talented; acceleration; enrichment; socialization.

Jennifer V. Rotigel

INTRODUCTION

Much has been written about the development of children, and it is generally agreed that early development has profound consequences for later development. However, the social, emotional, and intellectual development of young *gifted* children has received little attention outside of the journals that deal specifically with gifted and talented children. The net result is that teachers and parents are often uninformed or misinformed regarding the social and emotional development of young gifted children, particularly in relation to intellectual development and schooling. This article describes characteristics of young gifted children, focuses on typical concerns voiced by parents and teachers, and provides suggestions for appropriately meeting the needs of the young gifted child through curricular modification and enhanced understanding.

WHAT DOES IT MEAN TO BE GIFTED AND TALENTED?

Gifted and talented children are usually identified by schools in the early grades when they are referred for evaluation by either the teacher or the parents. The child may be evaluated through the consideration of a constellation of factors, such as scores on an intelligence test, grades in school, classroom achievement, and teacher and parent input. For example, some schools require that the child demonstrate achievement of at least two grade levels above their current grade placement in reading or mathematics. The identification process varies from district to district and state to state, but the outcome should be that the gifted child receives necessary modifications to the school's curriculum so that she can be appropriately challenged in school.

It is important to realize that when a child is gifted and talented, all aspects of the child's experience are affected. Young gifted children are gifted all day, not just when they are in school or in a "pull-out" program. The cluster of traits that are characteristic of gifted and talented individuals encompasses intellectual, social, emotional, and physical aspects of the child's life. Not all gifted children demonstrate all traits, of course, but there is a commonality that allows for some description of the gifted individual. For example, gifted children often become deeply absorbed in a topic and need to know all there is to know about it, while high achieving children may be satisfied with a more superficial understanding and are then ready to move on. Gifted individuals are often perfectionists, and they grasp new information with little or no repetition. Many gifted children have advanced vocabularies and seek to understand and be involved in world events, even at a young age.

Research in the area of emotional and social adjustment of gifted children has produced overwhelmingly positive results. Children who are gifted are, in general, as well adjusted and emotionally mature as other students (Howley, Howley, & Pendarvis, 1995). As noted by Clark (1997), gifted children need to be given the opportunity to understand themselves and experience positive educational opportunities.

Helping young gifted children understand themselves and their world can be a challenging task for teachers and parents. Many gifted children strive to understand at an early age why they do not seem to fit in with their peers, and it is important that their questions be answered truthfully and carefully. Too many children misunderstand the interactions that they experience and draw conclusions that may be harmful to their development. For example, a young gifted child may be frustrated by his inability to guess the "right" answer that the kindergarten teacher is looking for. Often this is because he is thinking more deeply about a topic than the other children or than the teacher expects and therefore does not supply the simple answer to a simple question. Since he fails to have the answer that the teacher rewards, he may conclude that he is stupid or inadequate.

WHAT ARE TYPICAL CONCERNS REGARDING GIFTED YOUNG CHILDREN?

The information that a child has been identified as being gifted is not always welcomed by adults or even by the child. Teachers are sometimes intimidated by the news and fearful of the demands that may be made of them in terms of providing an appropriate education for the child. Teachers may lack specific information that would assist them in meeting the child's educational needs, and they may be uninformed regarding the social and emotional factors that must be considered in planning for the child. Teachers with little experience in educating gifted children may misinterpret a child's behavior. For example, at a meeting between the parents and the first-grade teacher of a gifted child, the teacher assured the parents that the child was being appropriately challenged in school. The parents reported that their daughter often complained that she was bored in school. The teacher countered with her observation that the child seldom participated in class, so she must not really know the material. When they got home, the parents asked their daughter about her reported lack of participation in class. She responded, "Well, I don't want the other kids to know that I know all of the answers. I do put up my hand when the teacher is really stuck, because I feel like I should help her out when no one else has the answer."

Schools that are already under fire for low performance in academic areas may not have the resources to devote to children who are already able to perform well on required state assessment tests. As school funding becomes increasingly problematic, programs for gifted children are among the first to go, thereby placing an increased burden on the classroom teacher.

Parents sometimes greet a diagnosis of giftedness with relief, as they may feel that there should be some explanation of their child's differences. Along with the information that the child is gifted, however, comes the expectation that somehow the child's educational experiences will improve. Unfortunately, this is not always the case, as school districts vary widely in their provisions for gifted children. This can lead to struggles between the school and the parents who advocate for their children. In many cases, the teachers and parents are in agreement regarding what would be best for the child, but the school administrators are unable to commit financial resources or are fearful of setting a precedent of service that they may not be able to provide for other gifted children.

Some parents, however, are upset by the news that their child is gifted, as they feel overwhelmed by the responsibility of raising a child who seems to be so different from anyone that they know. Many parents have little understanding of what giftedness really means and have heard some of the myths that surround giftedness. For example, on receiving the news of her 3-year-old child's high score on a screening test, a mother burst into tears because she believed that her child would grow up to be "weird" or "like Einstein." If parents are told that their child scored in the top 2% of the population, they may fear that they will need to send the child to a boarding school for very bright children.

Although to the uninitiated it might seem to be a blessing to be a gifted child, many children do not view their life experience as particularly lucky. Many will go to great lengths to camouflage their giftedness in order to "fit in" with their peers (Roedell, 1988). For example, one young gifted child who learned to read at an early age tried to hide this newfound skill from everyone. His mother overheard him confiding to his younger brother, saying, "It's not my fault that I can read, the words just keep jumping out at me!" This same child tried to conceal his reading abilities from his mother because he was afraid that she would stop reading aloud to him. He was, emotionally speaking, a young child who really enjoyed the closeness of the time that he spent each day sitting in his mother's lap as they shared books together.

HOW DO YOUNG GIFTED CHILDREN DEVELOP?

Gifted children sometimes demonstrate uneven development that can be problematic (Tolan, 1989). For example, gifted children often have interests that are unusual for their age. A 4-year-old who is interested in the Civil War is unlikely to find someone among his age mates who is interested in exploring this topic with him. Unfortunately, it is sometimes difficult to find reading material that is suitable for such a child and similarly difficult to find an adult who wants to discuss Civil War events with a young child.

Because of their advanced vocabulary skills and unusual interests, gifted children sometimes seem to be more mature than their age mates. In fact, since they spend so much time conversing with adults about their shared interests, these young gifted children may seem to be 4 years old, going on 40. This can lead to difficulties, as often there is a gap between their emotional development and their intellectual development that is not as obvious as is the difference between their physical and intellectual development.

There are many ways to describe the differential that may occur between the physical, intellectual, social, and emotional development of gifted children. Researchers have called this differential "internal dyssynchrony" and use the term to describe areas of development that are not "in sync" with other areas within a particular child (Callahan, 1997; Roedell, 1988). Internal dyssynchrony may be a significant problem for some gifted children, yet it is poorly understood and seldom addressed by parents or teachers. A young gifted child may be able to function intellectually at a much higher level than her age mates and thus finds that sometimes she needs to discuss ideas with older children or adults who share her interests. But if a 6-year-old child is able to read at the fourth grade level, it may be very inappropriate to place her in a fourth-grade class because of physical, social, and emotional factors.

The level of dyssynchrony varies with each individual and is felt more severely by highly gifted children. For example, the 7-year-old child who is interested in the war on terrorism and how it relates to his understanding of religion is likely to have difficulty engaging a classmate in a conversation of this type. On the other hand, he may not have the emotional development that would allow him to participate in viewing the CNN reports on this subject, so his information must come from secondary sources. This child may be very concerned about what he hears adults discussing but lack the social development to understand that this is not a topic that can be adequately addressed in school. With no one to help him make sense of this, the child may become frightened and withdrawn, unable to explore ideas that have captured his imagination.

One of the most important aspects of socialization for gifted children is having peers who share similar interests. Because of the dyssynchrony they experience, many gifted children will need several different peer groups. One group may satisfy their intellectual needs and be able to discuss topics of mutual interest. Another group may fit better emotionally, and yet a third group may be the social solution that the child needs. The gifted child may have to hide her intellectual ability from the social group and her emotional development from the intellectual group. This role-playing can be difficult for the young child to understand, and she will need to talk with understanding adults who can help her to cope.

Gifted children are sometimes teased about their abilities and interests. One of the most common strategies is for someone to ask a very difficult question of the child. If the gifted child admits that they do not know the answer, the person may respond, "What's the matter, you should know since you are so smart!" Such exchanges are bound to cause the gifted child to resolve that they will no longer appear to know the answers to anything, if that would be the way to avoid such cruel teasing. In this way, abilities that cause very bright children to be so out of step with their classmates can come to be regarded by the child a poor gift, indeed.

WHAT ARE THE IMPLICATIONS FOR TEACHING AND CURRICULUM?

Many people have criticized programs for gifted children on the grounds that providing programs for them is elitist, since the gifted and talented child already seems to have so much. Although it is certainly true that enrichment programs such as trips to the museum or the opera can and should be provided to all children who are interested in them and can benefit from them, it is equally true that gifted children deserve to learn something of value in school each and every day, just as we think all children should.

Gifted children are as different from the norm as are children with other special needs, and the range of abilities covered by the gifted label is wide. Gifted children are not necessarily gifted in all academic areas, either. The child who may absolutely zoom in math may be an average reader. Unfortunately, schools often attempt to treat gifted children as though they all possess the same strengths and weaknesses (Fiedler, 1993).

The curriculum in most schools is designed to meet the needs of the "average" student, so the assumption is made that most children benefit from that curriculum. However, many gifted children begin a school year having mastered most of the content that will be presented that year. Few schools provide routine pretesting of content mastery, so gifted children are expected to march in place for a large portion of their days, waiting for their classmates to grasp the material. This situation causes gifted children to waste much of their instructional time, unless their educational programs are modified to better meet their needs. Gifted children who are forced to waste much of their time in school sometimes resort to misbehavior in order to combat boredom. In addition, when schoolwork is always too easy, children do not learn how to study and are robbed of the opportunity to feel satisfaction in the accomplishment of a project that challenged them intellectually. Researchers have pointed out that when we reward children for doing tasks that are too easy, their self-esteem is not enhanced (Tomlinson, 1994).

For highly gifted children, the question of whether to provide acceleration or enrichment programs may come up very early in their schooling. Of course, the answer to this question is that both acceleration and enrichment should be provided as needed. According to Boatman, Davis, and Benbow, "the goal of acceleration is curricular flexibility or curricular access without regard to age" (1995, p. 1085). An appropriate education for gifted children is one that allows the learners to make progress at their own pace. Since one of the hallmarks of giftedness is an increased rate of acquisition, this means that children who are gifted and talented naturally accelerate themselves. Allowing a kindergarten child to have access to third-grade materials is appropriate if he is reading on the third-grade level and comprehending the content well.

If a young gifted child needs to receive modifications in the school program, it is important to explain to the child why this is being done. One young 6-year-old whom I met was upset when he was told that he had been chosen to attend the special class. He concluded that he must have fallen far behind his classmates if he needed so much special help.

One of the surest ways to foster an unrealistic view of the world is to isolate a gifted child in a classroom where he has no intellectual peers. It is very important for gifted children to interact with each other so they can see that they are not the only ones with lots of answers, lots of questions, and perhaps some unusual hobbies and interests.

One difficulty that is sometimes ignored is the problem of providing reading material of an appropriate social and emotional level for a precocious reader (Halstead, 1990). For example, a third grader who reads on the college level cannot be expected to read only the third-grade text and elementary level chapter books. But finding college-level novels that have an appropriate theme and content for a young child can be a challenge to teachers and parents. Young children should not be exposed to the inappropriate language and adult content that are so often found in popular literature. It is also essential that the child have someone with whom to discuss his reading, and this can be problematic. Gifted children have lots of time to read and often can read faster than the adults who are trying to keep up. Local reading groups seldom welcome a young gifted child since they may indulge in gossip or adult conversation along with their discussion of the book of the week. If a child has no one to share his reading with, it can reinforce his feelings of isolation and limit his understanding of the content.

One of the inappropriate solutions that are sometimes employed is giving children three books to read while the other students are only expected to read one. This is referred to as "more of the same, piled higher" and often serves to make gifted children feel that they are being punished for their ability, especially if all of the books are at an inappropriately low level. The curriculum needs to be modified to meet a gifted child's needs, and this can only be done by assessing the child's needs and carefully planning strategies and content that will allow her to interact with challenging and appropriately difficult materials.

In school, group work may be assigned with a mixed-ability group. Unfortunately, the gifted child sometimes ends up "carrying" the group. Even when gifted children resent this, they are often trapped because they do not want to receive a bad grade or disappoint the teacher or the other group members. Gifted children are often asked to teach other children. Within reason, this can be beneficial to both parties, but if the strategy is used excessively, it can lead to problems. For example, when does the gifted child get a chance to learn something new if his time is spent tutoring his classmates? Additionally, simply because someone has ability in a particular area or understands a concept does not mean that he will be able to teach it to classmates. Some children do not want to be viewed as the teacher's aide, or worse, the teacher's pet. The child is often asked to tutor others in an area of content in which he excels. If the gifted child's progress is hampered by too much time spent tutoring others, he may lose interest in the subject completely.

CONCLUSION

Parents and teachers need to develop a more complete understanding of the gifted child so that they can truly be helpful (Table I). Nurturing young gifted children requires sensitivity to the special challenges that gifted children face and a willingness to work together with other adults who are involved with the child. Adults must clearly define giftedness, understand how it develops in children, and recognize the impact that it has on curriculum and instruction. When all of this is in place, a gifted and talented child is not likely to say, as one 8-year-old did, "school must be made for someone else, because it just doesn't work for me."

Table I. How Can Teachers and Parents Help?

- View each gifted child as an individual. Make clear assessments of the child's social, emotional, physical, and educational needs.
- Group children according to ability, achievement, or interest. Flexible group strategies can be powerful tools in assisting children to find appropriate intellectual, social, and emotional peer groups.
- Guard against unrealistic and unfair expectations. Do not ignore the social and emotional development of the child when setting goals.
- Talk with children to discover their level of understanding regarding their giftedness. Children are not always able to articulate the reasons they do certain things.
- Ensure that the gifted child has intellectual peers who are also age mates.
- Encourage hobbies and interest. Mentors can be a wonderful help, as they can share their expertise in the area of interest.
- Remember that although children may interact with adults in a seemingly mature way, their emotional development may be more closely matched with that of their age mates.
- Make sure that the educational program is appropriate. Each gifted child needs to have an individual assessment and the curriculum needs to be modified in order to meet the child's needs.
- Do not expect the gifted child to spend too much time tutoring his classmates. All children need to be able to learn new things every day, not just repeat lessons already learned.
- Search out reading materials that are age appropriate as well as challenging, and make sure that the child has someone with whom to discuss his reading.

APPENDIX: RESOURCES FOR TEACHERS AND PARENTS

National Association for Gifted Children
http://www.nagc.org

American Association for Gifted Children
http://www.aagc.org/index.html

Hoagies Gifted Education Page
http://www.hoagiesgifted.org/

National Research Center on Gifted and Talented,
    University of Connecticut
http://www.gifted.uconn.edu

Gifted Development Center
http://www.gifteddevelopment.com

Gifted and Talented Resources
http://www.Gtworld.org/links.html

Center for Talent Development
Northwestern University
617 Dartmouth Place
Evanston, IL 60208
(847) 491-3782

The Council for Exceptional Children
1920 Association Drive
Reston, VA 22091-1589
(703) 620-3660

Gifted Child Society, Inc.
Ms. Gina Ginsberg Riggs, Ex. Dir.
190 Rock Rd.
Glen Rock, NJ 07452
(201) 444-6530

Institute for the Academic Advancement of Youth
    (IAAY)
Johns Hopkins University–IAAY
Office of Public Information
3400 N. Charles Street
Baltimore, MD 21218
(410) 516-0245

National Association for Gifted Children
Suite 550
1707 L Street, NW
Washington, DC 20036
(202) 785-4268

National Research Center on the Gifted and Talented
The University of Connecticut
2131 Hillside Road, Unit 3007
Storrs CT 06269-3007
(860) 486-4676

REFERENCES

Boatman, T. A., Davis, K. G., & Benbow, C. P. (1995). Best practices in gifted education. In A. Thomas & J. Grimes (Eds.), *Best practices in school psychology-III* (pp. 1083–1095). Washington, DC: The National Association of School Psychologists.

Callahan, C. M. (1997). Giftedness. In G. Bear, K. Minke, & A. Thomas (Eds.), *Children's needs II* (pp. 431–448). Bethesda, MD: National Association of School Psychologists.

Clark, B. (1997). *Growing up gifted* (5th edition). Upper Saddle River, NJ: Merrill.

Fiedler, E. (1993). Square pegs in round holes: Gifted kids who don't fit in. *Understanding Our Gifted, 5*(5A), 1, 11–14.

Halstead, J. W. (1990). *Guiding the gifted reader.* Reston, VA: ERIC Clearinghouse on Handicapped and Gifted Children.

Howley, C. B., Howley, A., & Pendarvis, E. D. (1995). *Out of our minds: Anti-intellectualism and talent development in American schooling.* New York: Teachers College Press.

Roedell, W. C. (1988). "I just want my child to be happy." Social development and young gifted children. *Understanding Our Gifted, 1*(1), 1, 7–11.

Tolan, S. S. (1989). Helping your highly gifted child (ERIC Digest #477). Reston, VA: ERIC Clearinghouse on Handicapped and Gifted Children. (ERIC Document Reproduction Service No. ED321482 90)

Tomlinson, C. A. (1994). The easy lie and the role of gifted education in school excellence. *Roeper Review, 16*(4), 258–259.

Jennifer V. Rotigel, Department of Professional Studies in Education, Indiana University of Pennsylvania.

Correspondence should be directed to Jennifer V. Rotigel, D.Ed., Professional Studies in Education, 312 Davis Hall, Indiana University of Pennsylvania, Indiana, PA 15705; e-mail: jrotigel@iup.edu.

From *Early Childhood Education Journal*, Summer 2003, pp. 209-214. © 2003 by Human Sciences Press.

Cultivating otherwise untapped potential

Psychologists are developing programs to identify gifted children earlier—and to ensure their success.

BY DEBORAH SMITH
Monitor staff

Psychologist Frank Worrell, PhD, has seen countless adolescents develop into highly talented college students in the Academic Talent Development Program at the University of California, Berkeley—a program that offers summer enrichment and acceleration classes to children in kindergarten through 11th grade. Students who struggle with introductory courses when they enter the program can earn As in the program's most difficult classes by the end, says Worrell, the program's lead researcher.

> Dr. Frank Worrell is the lead researcher of the Academic Talent Development Program, which uses a broad range of assessments, such as teacher recommendations and work samples, to boost minority participation in its summer enrichment programs.

But that talent doesn't flourish on its own, he says: "People have talents in various areas, but if those talents aren't developed, they're not going to mean anything."

Without extra supports, many children with potential are left behind, agrees James Gallagher, PhD, professor emeritus at the University of North Carolina at Chapel Hill, who has written extensively on educating gifted children. "When you have a youngster brought up in poverty with no stimulation and little language development, you often will lose a youngster who might have been gifted," he explains. "With the proper environment and the proper education, you can increase the number of high-ability youngsters and adults."

Psychologists are working in schools and through their own independent programs to provide youth with that kind of environment. They're casting wide to find and nurture potentially gifted children and also increasing the achievement and creative productivity of exceptional performers, says Rena Subotnik, PhD, director of APA's Esther Katz Rosen Center for Gifted Education Policy.

"This second effort is viewed as more selective and elite, yet is also an essential component of gifted education," says Subotnik. The hope, she explains, is that students of all backgrounds will have equal access to the heights of talent development if schools do an effective job of nurturing potential talent.

However, some public schools' gifted supports are in danger, say psychologists in the field. In an era of mandated, high-stakes testing, schools with limited resources are being forced to focus on raising the scores of low performers—instead of on raising the achievement of all students, including gifted ones.

"There is a myth in our country that gifted children don't need any special help, that they'll make it on their own," says psychologist James T. Webb, PhD, who is founder of the nonprofit group Supporting Emotional Needs of the Gifted. "Some will, sure, but a lot will not."

> "Students need to be in the right place at the right time. For some students, this means that high school would offer very little."
>
> *Nancy M. Robinson,*
> *University of Washington*

Indeed, gifted students may be teased for their abilities, hide their talents to avoid being singled out and have difficulty establishing true friendships. The problems arise when there is a mismatch between gifted students and the education system or family, says Webb. "There is really little inherent in being a gifted child that creates emotional problems," he explains.

Acceleration: Is moving ahead the right step?

When many people hear talk of a 15-year-old student heading to college, their gut reaction is to wonder how a teen could miss out on high school football games and dances, or how a teen could ever fit in with students so much older.

But some psychologists' research shows that acceleration—skipping grades or working ahead in a particular subject—can be one of the best methods to meet the needs of gifted youth. While not a panacea, acceleration gives students access to true peers and challenging work, say a number of experts.

"Students need to be in the right place at the right time," explains psychologist Nancy M. Robinson, PhD, of the University of Washington and former director of the Halbert and Nancy Robinson Center for Young Scholars. "For some students, this means that high school would offer very little."

However, many schools are hesitant to accelerate students out of concern for their emotional development. While research by Robinson and others finds accelerated students who receive appropriate support don't suffer adverse social or emotional effects from moving ahead, others note that most of this research has been conducted with gifted students who are already achieving—not underachieving or unidentified students. Indeed, says Robinson, students can struggle when they are accelerated without effective study habits, access to similarly talented peers and a supportive family or encouraging mentor, such as a teacher or counselor.

That's why acceleration decisions should be made on a case-by-case basis, say experts such as Susan Assouline, PhD, and Nick Colangelo, PhD, who have developed the Iowa Acceleration Scale, a tool to help parents and educators make such decisions.

For example, acceleration may not be right for a gifted student who is also a stand-out football player or isn't socially mature. And others may need acceleration in only one area, since many gifted children develop asynchronously.

Moreover, some caution against looking at acceleration as just moving ahead. Talented students—whether they skip grades, work ahead in one subject or stay with their peers—need enriching experiences, says Joseph S. Renzulli, EdD, director of the University of Connecticut's National Research Center on the Gifted and Talented.

"It's not just how far and fast one can run," he explains, "but rather what one can do to apply the material that one has learned in an environment that allows them to generate hypotheses, gather data, to write a play, poem or song."

But gifted students who don't receive some kind of enrichment—whether it's acceleration or a supplemental program—are less likely to excel. For instance, many gifted children spend 25 to 50 percent of class time waiting for other students to catch up. To make up for the boredom, gifted students may engage in self-stimulating behavior, such as counting their teeth with their tongue, tapping a foot or entertaining themselves by distracting other students—actions that look like problem behaviors to a teacher.

"From the child's point of view, it's an attempt to make an unendurable situation endurable," explains psychologist James T. Webb, PhD, founder of the nonprofit group Supporting Emotional Needs of the Gifted. "The very characteristics that make these children what they are—curiosity, advanced intellect, intensity, sensitivity—can become problems at school or at home if they're not understood."

When teachers, parents and even mental health professionals mistake common attributes of giftedness for social and emotional problems, students can end up with misdiagnoses of attention-deficit hyperactivity disorder, Asperger's disorder oppositional-disorder and other problems, instead of an enriching education, says Webb.

And boredom has other consequences. If gifted students never meet a challenge in school, they may not develop the coping skills necessary to persevere through challenges later in life, notes Paula Olszewski-Kubilius, PhD, director of the Center for Talent Development at Northwestern University.

—D. SMITH

Who is gifted?

Because the school environment plays such a key role in fulfilling the potential of gifted students, many psychologists are looking for different ways to identify talented students.

"We need to start working at the kindergarten level to start, in fact, preparing kids well so that those who do have potential gifts actually get those gifts developed sufficiently," says Worrell, who is also an associate school psychology professor at Penn State University.

For example, since an academic-achievement gap between whites and minorities still exists, Worrell's program recruits youth from traditionally under-represented groups using a broad range of criteria: test scores, teacher recommendations, grades, interest inventories and a work sample of the student's choice, such as a short story.

Other psychologists are advocating for different kinds of tests to identify gifted students. For example, Jack Naglieri, PhD, of George Mason University, has developed tests to measure nonverbal reasoning ability without the influence of achievement or knowledge. Children who speak English as a second language or don't have the benefit of educated parents can still be smart, he reasons, but because they're not knowledgeable, they are often overlooked for gifted programs.

APA President Robert J. Sternberg, PhD, is studying how measures of creative and practical thinking, such as writing cartoon captions and doing practical math, in addition to the SAT, predict college students' success. He and his colleagues at Yale University have found that the tests predict freshman-year performance substantially better than the SAT alone, and also close the gap between ethnic groups.

Such efforts to close the gap are critical, many say, because gifted programs are taking a hit over diversity concerns. The reductions could be felt all the more sharply in the current economic climate as financial pressures will force many middle-class gifted children from more challenging private programs back into public school, say Subotnik and Nancy M. Robinson, PhD, professor emerita at the University of Washington and former director of the Halbert and Nancy Robinson Center for Young Scholars.

"Programs for gifted kids are being dropped or weakened in many cases because [they are] in many cases over-weighted with white and Asian middle-class-and-above kids," says Robinson. "But the fault doesn't lie with the programs nor with those kids. It lies within our society and the burdens that are put on families who don't have financial resources or who are marginalized."

The concern, say psychologists, is that children and adolescents who have great potential—whether they're unidentified minority students or attending a school that's cutting gifted programs—will flounder without support.

Gifted students with disabilities are especially at-risk. It's not uncommon for these "multiexceptional" youth to be passed over for both gifted and academic support programs because their talents and disabilities often mask each other, says school psychologist Ron Palomares, PhD, of APA's Practice Directorate. For example, a girl's learning disability hides her math talent, and the math talent compensates for her learning disability—so she gets passing, but mediocre, math grades.

"To receive services, there has to be an education need, and when the issues are masked, they go without help," Palomares explains.

Developing talents

Because gifted students are a diverse group with varying needs, experts in the field agree that there's no one way to help them flourish.

"We need to be much more explicit about examining the individual child and his or her needs, and then structuring program services around those needs," says Richard Olenchak, PhD, president-elect of the National Association for Gifted Children and director of the Urban Talent Research Institute at the University of Houston. The institute's research has found

that gifted students' social and emotional adjustment is moderately correlated with whether they receive personalized program opportunities.

Psychologists are also working with educators and parents to provide gifted youth with a host of options that will develop their particular skills and abilities. Besides advanced placement courses, online classes and magnet schools, many students can enroll concurrently in a local community college or university. The program Worrell helps run at Berkeley offers students intensive summer programs and access to the university's libraries and laboratories.

Other programs provide students with year-round academics, substituting for all or part of high school and sending adolescents to college at 15 or 16 years old. For example, the Center for Talent Development at Northwestern University, directed by psychologist Paula Olszewski-Kubilius, PhD, supplements students' high school coursework by offering intensive courses that pack a typical year's worth of material into several weeks.

Mentoring from experts is another option. APA's Center for Gifted Education Policy teams talented adolescents with top thinkers in an array of fields, from music to psychology, through its Pinnacle Project and Young Scholars Social Science Summit. The programs also provide students with an opportunity to meet similarly talented peers.

"Kids who don't have access to true peers, particularly among the highly gifted, tend to have significant ongoing problems," says Montana clinical child psychologist Maureen Neihart, PhD, explaining that gifted children need interaction with others who share the same interests, abilities and drive—qualities they seldom find in 'normal' same-age peers.

FURTHER READING

- Friedman, R.C., & Rogers, K.B. (1998). *Talent in context: Historical and social perspectives on giftedness*. Washington, DC: American Psychological Association.
- Friedman, R.C., & Shore, B. (2000). *Talents unfolding: Cognition and development*. Washington, DC: American Psychological Association.
- Heller, K.A., Mönks, F.J., Sternberg, R.J., & Subotnik, R.F. (Eds.). (2000). *International handbook of giftedness and talent* (2nd ed.). Oxford, United Kingdom: Pergamon.
- Horowitz, F.D., & O'Brien, M. (Eds.). (1985). *Gifted and talented: Developmental perspectives*. Washington, DC: American Psychological Association.
- Neihart, M., Reis, S.M., Robinson, N.M., & Moon, S.M. (2002). *The social and emotional development of gifted children*. Waco, TX: Prufrock Press.

Teaching Strategies for Twice-Exceptional Students

For many years, parents and teachers have been perplexed about youngsters who have dramatic learning strengths in some areas and equally dramatic learning weaknesses in others. These students appear to defy accurate labeling: Are they gifted or learning disabled? Finally, the debate has stopped, and educators are now recognizing these students as "twice-exceptional." Rather than trying to use evidence from their weak learning areas to prove they are not "truly gifted," savvy teachers are now learning how to allow these students to experience the same opportunities available for gifted students when they are learning in their strength areas. When students are learning in their areas of weakness, teachers are learning to provide the same compensation strategies used by other students with learning disabilities. This article offers specific instruction to empower teachers to effectively teach twice-exceptional students.

SUSAN WINEBRENNER

Can you visualize the well-known Far Side (Larson, 2000) cartoon that depicts a boy pushing a door with all his might to get into a school for gifted? The problem is, the door is clearly marked "PULL." Many in my audience laugh when I show this picture. Some nod ruefully, recognizing themselves or a child they know. In gifted education over the years, students like this have caused great frustration for their teachers and parents because their obvious exceptional abilities in some areas of learning seem overshadowed by their painfully apparent weaknesses, particularly in the areas of organizational or social skills and just plain common sense.

At the workshops I present for teachers, I often hear statements of extreme frustration with students who seem to defy accurate description. In some ways, their clearly exceptional abilities are apparent. But in many other ways, their learning deficiencies seem to make it nearly impossible for learning success to occur, even in their areas of greatest strength, because they often skip important steps as they make intuitive leaps toward answers or problem solutions. Sometimes, these students impress their teachers and peers with highly creative stories and scenarios, but when their teachers ask them to write their great ideas, the students contend, "I can't write!" Teachers are caught between belief and disbelief, as they wonder if the student actually cannot do a task or simply is "too lazy" to exert the required effort. Teachers have often used evidence of the student's learning weaknesses to prove to a parent or administrator that the child is not "truly gifted," by which they usually mean gifted in all learning areas. Sometimes, students' learning difficulties depress their gifted potential into very average performance. Teachers may wonder how the parents of such kids could claim their children are exceptionally capable when their perfectly average performance should satisfy.

When we add to these facts the reality that some gifted students are extremely active and nonconforming, we can predict that many of them have been or will be diagnosed as having an attention-deficit/hyperactivity disorder (ADHD) or a learning disability (LD), and they probably will not receive services in gifted education during their years in public school (Webb & Latimer, 1993).

Slowly but surely, educators have come to acknowledge the dichotomy of abilities that characterize students we now refer to as *twice exceptional:* youngsters who have clearly exceptional abilities in some areas and weaknesses in others. Sadly, most classroom time and attention is focused on student weaknesses, with little or no attention to their remarkable strengths. Are these kids gifted? Do they have learning disabilities? Yes … and yes!

Working together, educators in gifted and special education are discovering ways to create and maintain optimum learning conditions for twice-exceptional students. More important than understanding how each specific learning challenge manifests itself is that educators encourage twice-exceptional students to use proven strategies that will allow them to compensate for their areas of weakness while simultaneously experiencing opportunities gifted students appreciate in their areas of learning strength. Twice-exceptional students cannot improve by simply "trying harder." Their learning challenges often emanate from a series of neurological twists and turns as messages try to make their way to the brain from the original stimulus. By the same token, many students already labeled as having LD do not actually have neurological implications. Such students would better be labeled as "learning strategy disabled" because their academic outcomes can improve dramatically when they learn to use appropriate compensation techniques. This article describes specific teaching and learning methods that teachers and parents can use to facilitate significant learning progress for twice-exceptional students in areas of both strengths and weaknesses.

Teach Them the Way They Learn

While planning and teaching compensation strategies, educators must acknowledge the need for teaching the same concepts in many different ways: If students are not learning the way we teach them, teach them the way they learn. When we keep trying to teach something to a child in a way in which he or she has repeatedly failed, discouragement and self-blame quickly become a self-fulfilling prophecy. If learners assume that their failures to learn are caused by stupidity or laziness, their primary purpose in the classroom is to hide their ineptness from peers and teachers. Clowning and other misbehaviors, they believe, can obfuscate their perceived lack of ability. When they are in the classes of teachers who can "teach them the way they learn," they can begin to gather evidence that learning success is probable when they can use methods that capitalize on their strengths and compensate for their weaknesses.

Beware of creating a situation that Landfried (1989) has designated as "educational enabling." His work documented that our tendency is often to make learning tasks as easy as possible so students can feel successful. However, the more evidence students get that their teachers do not expect them to handle grade-level work, the more convinced these students become that no one believes they can handle more challenging content. Instead of implying there is something wrong with the students themselves because of their repeated failures, we can demonstrate that we will help students try as many different methods as necessary until we find the "fit" that allows the students to experience learning success with material that is close to grade-level standards.

Recently, I was in a conversation with a friend whose learning challenges sometimes interfere with his speech fluency. As hesitations, repetitions, backtracking, and loss of memory about what he was trying to say became ever more frustrating, I offered a suggestion. I asked him to straighten his arm, use his hand to trace an imaginary infinity sign lying on its side, and allow his eyes to follow his hand as it traced that sign in large arches that crossed the center of his body. After a few moments of this exercise, he resumed his story with remarkable fluency. The method comes from a program called Brain Gym, which was created by Dennison (1989). It is based on the concept that specific kinesiology exercises can facilitate cross-over between brain hemispheres and improve fluency and competence in learning tasks. It is just one dramatic example of ways in which simple compensation strategies may facilitate learning for persons with learning difficulties, including those who fit the profile of the twice-exceptional learner.

The rule to follow when teaching twice-exceptional students is simple. When teaching these students in their areas of strength, offer them the same compacting and differentiation opportunities available to other gifted students. When teaching in their areas of challenge, teach them directly whatever strategies they need to increase their learning success. *Never* take time away from their strength areas to create more time to work on their deficiencies.

Are these kids gifted? Do they have learning disabilities? Yes . . . and yes!

The first twice-exceptional student I recall having in my class was a fifth grader named Eric. He had serious difficulty with any written task, which was compounded by almost illegible handwriting. His math skills were weak; he had great trouble writing coherent sentences and appeared to be very frustrated when asked to recall skill work he had "mastered" a short time ago. When we started a unit on maps, Eric really shined. He had always been in charge of mapping his family's summer auto trips and could remember in incredible detail the routes of trips they had taken since he was 7 years old. He also had an almost photographic memory of information about national parks and monuments. Eric asked if he could demonstrate what he knew about these subjects in order to be excused from "learning" it all over again. I agreed and simply offered the end of the unit test to anyone who wanted to take it, explaining that anyone who earned an A would be allowed to work on extension activities instead of the regular content.

Eric and several other students met the required criteria, but I then faced a serious dilemma. I was sorely tempted to use some of Eric's social studies time to remediate his glaring weaknesses. However, the truth was that he was exceptionally capable in the content his classmates were just beginning to learn. Therefore, I decided that he was as entitled as anyone else to engage in differentiated learning during the length of this map unit. Remediation could wait for the appropriate class period.

From a menu of activities, Eric chose to create a country from papier mâché and was expected to demonstrate the placement in his imaginary country of the same geographic features the class was studying. He was also expected to explain why he placed elements where he did as well as the relationships between elements. The other students did not resent Eric's freedom to work in this manner because everyone in the class had a similar opportunity to take the pretest. Watching Eric work sparked interest from other students to create a country also. Creating group countries became the culminating activity for all students. During their work on this project, Eric became the "create a country consultant." The status he earned from this experience significantly improved classmates' perception of Eric's ability, and he felt good about the experience as well. So remember the rule: Never remediate students' weaknesses until you first teach to their strengths!

Tips for Teachers When Addressing Students' Learning Challenges

The following strategies provide a framework for addressing the specific learning needs of children who are twice exceptional.

1. Teach students to appreciate individual differences. For all students in a class to accept the presence of differentiation opportunities, teachers need to be willing to spend time helping all students understand and appreciate individual differences. This is an area in which I think our schools fall short. Schools support programs of multicultural diversity appreciation yet fail to understand how short-sighted it is to limit teachers' efforts for

the benefit of children from other cultures. Why not use the same type of techniques to help students become more accepting of all individual differences?

Take time at the beginning of every school year to help all your students appreciate, respect, and support individual differences in everything from observable physical differences to apparent differences in learning abilities. When teachers can consistently demonstrate that diversity is a positive and desirable condition, students will follow their lead, and acceptance of individual differences becomes the modus operandi. Many students who have committed violence in schools have a history of being teased mercilessly for their noticeable differences. Efforts to facilitate respect for learning differences should continue throughout the school year and should become a schoolwide initiative. Teachers and schools must enforce policies that simply do not allow teasing, name calling, or other harassment practices that demonstrate rejection of kids for any reason.

This is a very tall order, given the assumption that "kids will be kids." Is it possible that students can learn to be more tolerant instead of so demanding of conformity? I believe it is, in much the same way as U.S. citizens have changed their attitudes about the acceptability of driving while under the influence of addictive substances. Twenty years ago, jokes about drunken behavior were ubiquitous. Now, the humor seems less politically correct than a national effort to save lives that may be lost to drunk drivers on our highways. If a nation can change its culture in a positive way, so can schools. If students could learn to cheer when someone learns something a different way, soon they would become conditioned to celebrate diversity.

I further believe this can be accomplished even without apparent support from parents. Although it is best to have parental support, it is not always possible. The mores of classrooms reflect wide discrepancies compared with what is found in some students' homes. This respect for diversity could simply be one more area in which students understand that "We do things differently at school, and that's the way it is." The only arena in which teachers can have real influence is at school. If teachers believe they must wait for families to communicate only helpful values to their children, they will be waiting a long time in some cases. Let's consider the classroom as the place for these reforms to begin.

2. Be aware that many students who have learning difficulties are global learners who prefer visual and tactile-kinesthetic formats for learning success. Some students with learning problems may have sensory challenges. They may be uncomfortable in absolutely quiet places, prefer soft light to brightly lighted areas, appreciate multiple opportunities for movement, or prefer relaxed postures (Carbo, Dunn, & Dunn, 1986). Teachers should offer these students choices of different work areas. They should be free to choose the place in which they will do their work as long as they follow three simple rules:

- Do not bother anyone while you are working, including the teacher.
- Do not call attention to yourself or the fact you are doing something different than other students.
- Do the work you are supposed to do.

Students who follow these expectations are allowed to choose where they will work. Students who do not follow these guidelines will have their working area chosen by the teacher, one day at a time (Winebrenner, 1996).

3. Always teach content by teaching concepts first and details second. Make sure students see the big picture before they try to learn its pieces. Strategies that are helpful include the Survey and Question strategies from SQ3R (Robinson, 1970), watching a video before and after studying a novel or other unit of work, hearing a story read aloud before reading it individually, and working from graphic organizers that fit on one page so that students can see the entire unit content. All skills should be integrated into meaningful content rather than taught as separate learning activities.

4. Teach students how to set realistic short-term goals and to take credit for reaching those goals, even if they represent only a partial amount of the entire task. This technique is highly effective in helping discouraged learners become positively motivated to put more effort into their work because it makes larger assignments feel more manageable. Both in-class assignments and homework should be designated in terms of the amount of time these students are expected to work rather than as a prescribed number of problems or specific amount of work to be completed. Parents can help by monitoring that the designated time was spent. This is preferable to having students spend several painful hours trying to complete an arbitrary amount of work. When teachers feel frustrated by students who do not do their homework, the issue of whether students *can* do the work must be taken into consideration. This means that teachers must be sure students have learned enough during class time to have the skills to complete their assignments at home. It also means that parents or caretakers need to provide an appropriate place at home to work on school assignments.

5. Teach in a way that ties past learning to new content. In order for students to learn and generalize new skills, they must be able to connect the new learning to something they already know. Many students with learning difficulties prefer making everything visual so they can see the patterns and connections they need to assimilate new learning. Use graphic organizers, charts, graphs, timelines, semantic maps, vocabulary maps, and similar tools that condense words into pictures or graphics. If you lecture, supplement your words with visual organizers as you talk. Stop frequently to check for understanding with group signals and other group response methods rather than simply accepting one or two verbal responses from volunteers as evidence that all students have learned the content.

6. Immerse all the senses in learning activities. Use musical chants, raps, rhymes, or rhythms for students who respond to those methods. Companies that stock teaching and learning aids will often carry such products. For many students, the simple act of singing or chanting the content makes mastery much easier to achieve.

Build movement into learning tasks. Recognize the validity of needing to move as an actual learning style, and observe how movement helps some students learn specific content. Ask students to stand or jump to indicate their responses to questions. Use team games where students can walk to different areas of the room to indicate a response. Allow them to hold squeezeable objects, such as Kush Balls®, that enable them to keep moving their hands. Guard against the impulse to automatically label highly kinesthetic learners as having ADHD.

Understand that twice-exceptional students often prefer hands-on and experiential learning situations. Such opportunities meet students' needs to learn from the concrete to the abstract. Actual manipulation of objects often helps these students better understand concepts when they are transferred to more abstract applications within content areas. Include projects, models, and visual representations as assignments because students can often understand concepts better when they are encouraged to "do" rather than to hear or see. Unfortunately, teachers sometimes prevent this type of learning activity because it is thought to be more difficult to manage classroom behavior. The irony is that acceptable behavior is much more likely to occur when students are vitally interested and involved in what they are learning.

Allow struggling readers to listen to the books on tape before the class reads a designated story or novel. Listening to one chapter at a time allows many students to become more active participants in class discussions and activities. An agency called Recording for the Blind and Dyslexic (see Resources) has recordings of almost every book used in U.S. classrooms and allows schools or individual families to borrow taped books for a nominal fee. All that is required is a letter from a medical or educational professional indicating that the child has some learning difficulty.

7. Provide specific instruction in organizational techniques. Provide color-coded notebooks by subject areas and two sets of texts, one that can be kept at home. Teach students to organize their lockers, desks, and supplies. Help students learn to use an assignment notebook or personal desk assistant to keep track of assignments and long-term projects. Use any other methods that work.

8. Find and use any available technology that will improve a student's productivity. Students are not "cheating" by using calculators, tape recorders, word processors, and spell-check programs if not using such aids would contribute to the continuation of the learning weaknesses. These aids help students concentrate on conceptual content instead of forcing them to focus on less important details such as spelling. In addition, teaching students to use technology provides them with a useful life skill.

9. Allow students to take tests in separate, supervised environments so they can either read the test aloud to themselves or have someone else read it to them. Some students have difficulty concentrating on tests when typical classroom noise occurs. A quiet place allows a student to focus. Furthermore, listening to a voice read the questions aloud helps the student better understand the questions.

Tips for Teachers to Accommodate Gifted Abilities in Students Who Are Twice Exceptional

It is often difficult for teachers to understand that students with learning difficulties might also be gifted in some areas of learning. However, if we remember that the essential definition of twice exceptional is exactly that, we can see such learners from a different perspective. Allow these students to experience the same compacting and differentiation opportunities available to other students. Offer pretests to allow them to document previous mastery of upcoming content. Allow opportunities for students to move through new content at a faster pace and to use allocated worktime on projects related to topics in which they have a particular interest (Winebrenner, 2000).

Compacting is the process of allowing highly capable students to demonstrate their previous mastery of some of the required curriculum. Compacting also occurs when students are allowed to demonstrate that they need less time than their peers to learn new material (Renzulli, 1977). When the evidence of the need for compacting is present, differentiation follows. Thus, when students demonstrate that the general curriculum or pacing does not provide an appropriate challenge, they can gain access to more challenging topics or activities. Gifted students deserve these opportunities, not simply because they are gifted but because all students are entitled to experience the promises of the school's mission statement. If it promises that students are supposed to be able to achieve learning to the highest levels of their potential, gifted students must be allowed access to activities that are personally challenging. If giftedness im-

plies a learning ability that exceeds expectations for same-age peers, it is natural to understand the need for differentiated curriculum.

> # The most serious challenge is that the giftedness will go unnoticed and unaccommodated in favor of attending to learning deficits.

Teachers often cannot be convinced of the real need for differentiation until they know the value of challenging all students to move into uncharted waters. Gifted students often do not come close to their learning potential, especially when they are "given" high grades for work they know took little to no effort. Although most teachers believe that all students should have their self-esteem needs met as part of their learning experience, few realize that self-esteem actually is enhanced when success is attained through tasks an individual considers challenging (Rimm, 1986). Development of high self-esteem requires that students be allowed to challenge themselves in an environment in which their mistakes and struggles, as well as their successes, will be allowed and appreciated.

When students receive high grades and other acknowledgements for assignments or projects they know required little or no effort, their self-confidence may be undermined. These students may learn to always find the easiest way out or creatively postpone their exposure to challenges. Others students fear that if they try something challenging and do not instantly master content with little or no effort, others might conclude that they are not really very smart after all.

To assume that gifted students are learning by virtue of the fact that they demonstrate minimum standards on state assessments is ludicrous. When appropriate compacting and differentiation opportunities are regularly available, gifted students can spend considerable class time working on differentiated activities while their classmates are preparing for these high-stakes assessments.

Compacting and differentiation efforts should revolve around the following guidelines. Many children who are twice exceptional have very uneven standardized test scores. This profile paints an accurate picture of the very definition of this condition—strong highs and significant lows. Often, the learning disability depresses the gifted ability so the child scores in the average range.

All learning activities, including thematic, interdisciplinary units, should have preassessment opportunities available for students who volunteer to demonstrate prior knowledge and mastery of concepts, ideas, and skills. Whatever method has been planned for assessing student progress during or at the end of a particular unit of study is the same method that can be used for the preassessment.

Whether the preassessment takes the form of a written test, measuring student response as the class brainstorms all they know about an upcoming topic, or performance on a designated task, any student who chooses to participate in the designated task should be encouraged to do so. When the preassessment tasks are available to all who think they could demonstrate the required degree of mastery, there should be little resentment from students who are unable to do so, particularly if the "regular" activities are interesting and challenging.

Students who qualify for differentiation after the preassessment spend much of their class time working on extension activities, some designed by the teacher and some reflecting student choice. These students are required to pay attention to direct instruction only when the teacher is presenting material the students have not mastered.

In subjects where pretesting is not feasible because the content is new for all students, teachers compact the amount of time students have to spend learning the designated content. Students who can and want to are allowed to work with study guides to learn the designated content at their own pace without actually being required to do the actual activities other students are doing. Their class time is spent instead on becoming resident experts on a topic related to the unit content. When they share what they have learned with the class, the unit content is enriched for everyone. During the duration of the unit, students take the same assessments at the same time as others in the class, which helps the teacher document that they are learning the required material. When students can do this, they are allowed to continue work on their projects. If the students indicated through the assessments that they are not keeping up with the required content, they must rejoin their classmates for the duration of the unit and do the required activities from that point on.

When students need acceleration of content in addition to or in place of extensions, such as in subjects that are very sequential like reading or math, acceleration opportunities should be made available, even if the student is working below grade level in other subjects. Students might be allowed to work with a group of students from a higher grade for the subject areas in which they are significantly advanced. In rare cases, where a youngster's entire learning level is significantly advanced from that of same-age peers, radical acceleration or double promotion is another option.

Don't worry about the fairness issue. If you are concerned that other students will resent the options available for your gifted students or students with learning challenges, simply allow any students who are interested to participate for a short period of time. When assessments are required at regular intervals, it is easy to identify students who should not continue with the compacting and who need to return to direct instruction. It is also a good idea to allow all class members to choose extension activities from time to time, even though they would spend less time on these activities than time spent by the "resident expert."

Summary

Teaching children who are twice exceptional is very challenging. The most serious challenge is that the giftedness will go unnoticed and unaccommodated in favor of attending to learning deficits. Any efforts teachers can direct toward understanding and teaching the whole child will go a long way toward creating optimum learning conditions for these very interesting and challenging youngsters. Happily, there are many more resources available now than at any time in the past to aid teachers in their quest for making educational plans that will challenge and enrich students' school experiences.

ABOUT THE AUTHOR

Susan Winebrenner, MS, is the author of two books: *Teaching Gifted Kids in the Regular Classroom* and *Teaching Kids with Learning Difficulties in the Regular Classroom.* She has consulted with school districts in more than 40 states and in several foreign countries, helping teachers learn how to meet the needs of twice-exceptional students in heterogeneous classes. Address: Susan Winebrenner, PO Box 667, San Marcos, CA 92069.

REFERENCES

Carbo, M., Dunn, R., & Dunn, K. (1986). *Teaching students to read through their individual learning styles.* Englewood Cliffs, NJ: Prentice Hall.

Dennison, P. (1989). *Brain gym.* Ventura, CA: Edu-Kinesthetic. (Web site: www.braingym.org)

Landfried, S. E. (1989, November). "Enabling" undermines responsibility in students. *Educational Leadership, 47*(3), 79-83.

Larson, G. (2000). *The far side.* Seattle: Farworks.

Renzulli, J. (1977). *The enrichment triad model.* Mansfield Center, CT: Creative Learning Press.

Rimm, S. (1986). From a class at the University of Wisconsin.

Robinson, F. (1970). *Effective study* (4th ed.). New York: Harper & Row.

Webb, J., & Latimer, D. (1993). *ADHD and children who are gifted.* Reston, VA: Clearinghouse on Disabilities and Gifted Education.

Winebrenner, S. (1996). *Teaching kids with learning difficulties in the regular classroom.* Minneapolis: Free Spirit.

Winebrenner, S. (2000). *Teaching gifted kids in the regular classroom* (2nd ed.). Minneapolis: Free Spirit.

Winebrenner, S. (2002). Strategies for teaching twice exceptional students. *Understanding Our Gifted, 14*(2), 3-6.

RESOURCES

Freed, J. (1998). *Right brained children in a left brained world: Unlocking the potential of your ADD child.* New York: Simon & Schuster.

Hoagies Gifted Education: An excellent resource for information about gifted education and twice-exceptional issues. Web site: www.hoagiesgifted.com

Kay, K. (Ed.). (2000). *Uniquely gifted: Identifying and meeting the needs of the twice-exceptional student.* Gilsum, NH: Avocus Publishing.

LaVoie, R. *How Difficult Can This Be?* and *Last One Picked—First One Picked On.* PBS Video (800/344-3337).

LD Online: An excellent resource for information about all types of learning disabilities. Web site: www.ldonline.com

Levine, M. (1990). *Keeping a head in school: A student's book about learning abilities and learning disorders.* Toronto: Educator's Publishing Service.

Recording for the Blind and Dyslexic. (800/221-4792); Web site: www. rfbd.org

Willard-Holt, C. (1999). *Dual exceptionalities.* Reston, VA: Clearinghouse on Disabilities and Gifted Education.

UNIT 11
Transition

Unit Selections

Key Points to Consider

- What are some of the collaborative efforts needed to help students with severe disabilities make the transition from a sheltered setting to the outside world?

- What services are needed to make the transition smoother from middle school to high school for students with disabilities?

- What are the eight curricular components of a self-determination curriculum?

 **Links: www.dushkin.com/online/**
These sites are annotated in the World Wide Web pages.

National Center on Secondary Education and Transition
http://www.ncset.org

Transitional services help young children with disabilities who have been served by individualized family service programs (IFSPs) before school, make a smooth passage into the public school system. Transitional programs help modulate the next stages when students with special needs transfer from elementary to middle school, from middle school to high schools, from special classes into inclusionary classes, or from one school district to another. The special services link the educational changes which take place.

Special educational services are also required by law for students from the completion of their public school education through age 21 if they have a diagnosed condition of disability. The U.S. Individuals with Disabilities Education Act (IDEA), when it was reauthorized in 1997, made terminal transitional services mandatory. Services are to help them transfer from their relatively protected life as students into the more aggressive world of work, driven by forces such as money and power.

The terminal services that the educational system needs to give to students with disabilities to help them prepare for the world of work start with an assessment of their interests, abilities, and aptitudes for different types of work. Career counseling about what they need to do to prepare for such employment, and its feasibility, comes next. Counselors must remember to allow students to dream, to think big, and to have optimistic visions of themselves. They also need to inculcate the idea that persistence pays: It takes a lot of little steps to achieve a goal.

The implementation of transitional services has been slow. The U.S. government defined transitional services as outcome-oriented, coordinated activities designed to move students with disabilities from school to activities such as college, vocational training, integrated employment, supported employment, adult education, adult services, independent living, and community participation. Choices are not either/or but rather multiple: to help students with disabilities move from school to successful adulthood. While some students may only be able to achieve partial independence and supported employment, others may achieve professional degrees and complete self-sufficiency.

Every student with a disability should have an individualized transition plan (ITP) added to his or her individualized education plan (IEP) by age 16, the upper limit for beginning transition planning. Transitional services are more difficult to design than educational plans because of the nearly unlimited possibilities for the rest of one's life compared to the defined academic subjects it is possible to learn while in school.

The first step is to determine an appropriate individualized transition plan (ITP) for each unique student. Many teachers, special educators, vocational counselors, and employment mentors (job coaches) are not sure what kind of vocational preparation should be given in the public schools or when. Should children with disabilities start planning for their futures in elementary school, in middle school, in high school, throughout their education, or just before they finish school? Should there be a trade-off between academic education and vocational education for these students? Should each student's vocational preparation be planned to meet the kind of needs and abilities of the individual, with no general rules about the wheres and whens of transitional services? Should students with disabilities be encouraged to seek out post-secondary education? The choices are legion. The need to rule out some possibilities and select others is frightening. Nobody on a team wants to make a mistake. Often the preferences of the student are quite different from the goals of parents, teachers, counselors, or significant others. Compromises are necessary but may not please everyone, or anyone.

The transition to the world of work may take the form of supported employment (mobile work crew, clustered or enclave placement, on-site training and supervision by a job coach, group providing a specific service product) or sheltered employment (in a workshop). Many students with disabilities can make a transition from school to competitive employment. If they will eventually work side-by-side with nondisabled coworkers, they may need transitional services such as assertiveness training, conflict resolution, negotiating skills, and personal empowerment counseling.

Just a few years ago, adults with disabilities were expected to live in institutions or with parents, siblings, or extended family members. This is no longer considered appropriate. Each individual with a disability should be encouraged to be as autonomous as possible in adulthood. Self-sufficiency is enhanced by providing education in life skills such as meal preparation and cleanup, home deliveries (for example, mail) and delivery pickups (for example, trash), using money and paying bills, making household repairs, and following home safety precautions.

The transition from noncommunity participant to fully participating member of society requires ITP modifications quite different from IEP academic goals. Students with exceptional conditions may need more than the usual amount of assistance in learning to drive a car or to use public transportation. They need to know how to read maps and schedules. They must be able to assert their right to vote in secret (for instance, ballot in braille or computerized for their software) and to marry, divorce,

reproduce, sue, defend themselves, or even run for public office. They should know social conventions (greetings, conversation skills, manners), grooming fashions, and clothing styles. They deserve to have the same access to health settings, religious locales, social activities, and information services (telephone, television, computer networks) as do persons without disabilities.

The first article in this unit offers insights into the collaborative efforts required of administrators, staff, regular and special education teachers, employment specialists, and students with severe disabilities. The authors emphasize the need for rigorous employment-training programs. Students who lack communication skills and academic skills pose special challenges. The development of partnerships with potential employers of disabled students in the area surrounding the school can make each ITP voyage a smoother sail.

In the second article, Theresa Letrello and Dorothy Miles address the problems which occur when students with disabilities change school programs and schools, while also undergoing the vast physical transitions of puberty. The article gives suggestions for making this period of time less traumatic.

The last article in this transition unit deals with self-determination. This is one of the most important considerations for any ITP, yet one that is often forgotten as experts (parents, teachers, counselors, and so on) debate what would be most appropriate for a student with a disability. This selection describes a project whose goal was to promote each student's self-determination.

Transition Planning for Students with Severe Disabilities:

Policy Implications for the Classroom

Christy Holthaus Stuart and Stephen W. Smith

The reauthorization of the Individuals with Disabilities Education Act Amendments (IDEA, 1997) is the cornerstone for disability legislation entitling students to a free appropriate public education. Within the law, students with disabilities are afforded an Individualized Education Program (IEP) that provides an appropriate education in the least restrictive environment. The reauthorization of IDEA included several specific components addressing transition issues (e.g., career planning, job training, functional skill development) beginning at age 14 for students receiving special education services. The transition components for students with disabilities included (a) a coordinated set of activities (e.g., real work experience) specific to the individual, (b) activities for movement from school to postschool environments (e.g., supported employment, adult services), (c) assessment of students' individual needs, (d) identification of student preferences and interests, and (e) development of employment objectives.

The IDEA transition components are intended for all students with disabilities; however, some professionals may disregard students with more severe disabilities, such as profound mental retardation and deaf-blindness. Under the Rehabilitation Act (1973), when students with severe disabilities leave school, they are entitled to continued services for supported living and employment services. The Rehabilitation Act promotes individuals with severe disabilities and their rights to gainful employment. Specifically, the Act defines *a person with a severe disability* as an individual whose ability to function independently in family or community or whose ability to become gainfully employed is limited due to the severity of his or her disability. Both the IDEA and the Rehabilitation Act are equally important in providing support, such as supported employment and educational training programs, for individuals with disabilities, yet for individuals with severe disabilities there continue to be significant problems.

Individuals with severe disabilities have unique learning characteristics, such as difficulty in generalizing learned skills to new work situations. Further, individuals with more significant disabilities learn more slowly, which in turn means that they learn less and have difficulty generalizing learned skills to other settings, putting together isolated activities that make a skill, and maintaining what they have learned over time (Ryndak & Alper, 1996). These learning characteristics may lead some people to believe that persons with severe disabilities are incapable of learning necessary job skills. Consequently, persons with severe disabilities are caught in a difficult cycle. They have difficulty learning the job skills, resulting in perceptions of being incapable of successful employment, which causes them to be further stigmatized and reduces the possibility that employers will hire them. Despite the legislative support that has evolved over the years, outcome data such as long-term employment continue to show poor results for individuals with severe disabilities.

Educator's General Role

Teachers of secondary students with severe disabilities play a significant role in developing and implementing effective transition plans to help students plan for the future and obtain gainful employment. For example, a student may indicate that following school, he or she wishes to live in an apartment with friends and have a job that involves sports. The student's interests can be gathered from a variety of sources, such as student, parents, and family members, and used as a stepping stone to prepare the student for the skills necessary to achieve future goals. Specifically, exposing the student to a variety of sport jobs (e.g., greeter/usher using a communication device or an equipment manager paired with a peer) and encouraging the student to develop goals assists the student in eventually maintaining employment and living as independently as possible. Because of poor outcomes, such as low full-time employment rates, and decreased competitive wages and hours, policymakers need knowledge and direction from practitioners at the implementation level (i.e., school-based vocational programs) to compose effective policies that, in turn, promote effective practice.

Promoting Employment Skills Through Transition Planning

Secondary educators must do their part in facilitating a meaningful transition for their students with severe disabilities to create a link between school setting services and services provided in the postschool employment setting. McDonnell, Mathot-Buckner, and Ferguson (1996) emphasized the need for an effective and rigorous employment-training program that would identify the skills students need to participate successfully in the postschool employment setting. Students need

- work experience and work-related behaviors,
- work interests and preferences, and
- supports necessary to ensure success in employment settings.

Because common work and work-related behaviors are necessary for success in every job, the goal for every student during high school is to develop employment skills (e.g., manage one's time, stay on task, complete step-by-step directions), communicate effectively, demonstrate social and interpersonal skills, and tend to personal hygiene. The behaviors that accompany the skills are paired with a successful transition for the student with disabilities.

Employment training must incorporate a job sampling process that provides students with the basis for determining their work interests and preferences. Exposure to a wide range of employment options is a key component for the future job matching process (Chadsey-Rusch & Heal, 1995). Students with severe disabilities who may lack adequate communication and academic skills pose a special challenge because the information traditionally gathered (student interests and preferences) regarding career alternatives must be gathered from sources other than the student (e.g., parents, peers, service coordinators from agencies).

Identifying the nature and amount of supports depends on the individual needs of the student, but coordinating the supports to be as least restrictive as possible is the challenge. During the employment-training phase, a variety of supports can be tested. For example, a student with severe disabilities may respond more effectively with supports from a peer rather than a paraprofessional. This information may be used for future interactions with service agencies that use peers on the job versus job coaches from an agency.

Obtaining meaningful employment is crucial to the successful transition of students from school to community/employment life. This outcome is achieved most effectively when an educational program is designed to develop skills and routines that better prepare individuals with disabilities for life after school. It is up to secondary educators to develop and implement meaningful training programs that equip their students with skills and prepare them for employment and community involvement outside the educational arena. Several guidelines are recommended for secondary education teachers to follow while developing individual transition programs:

- Promote individual choice and self-determination activities (e.g., self-directed IEPs);
- include a variety of participants who have contact with the student (special education and general education) in the development of the transition IEP;
- develop partnerships with community establishments and potential job training or employment sites;
- extend agency collaboration as part of the transition process;

- make significant changes to traditional prevocational training programs to include job training in natural work environments and to include all students, especially those with the most severe disabilities in the program; and
- incorporate placement models at the secondary level to ease the transition to postschool employment activities (individual placement model, clustered placement model, mobile crew model, and the entrepreneurial model).

Summary

The increase in responsibility for educators to collaborate and develop effective transition plans should also empower educators to become stakeholders in the transition process (Kohler, 1998). As stakeholders, the secondary educators should be encouraged to

- participate in program-level planning;
- serve on curriculum development teams;
- participate in teacher or family training, technical assistance, and staff development activities; and
- play a role in strategic planning and resource allocation.

Although transition planning is to be included on a student's IEP, all professionals, otherwise known as stakeholders (general education teachers, special education teachers, transition specialists, employment specialists), need to be prepared to participate in an ongoing process that begins in secondary schools and continues in the postschool environment. This process needs to be collaborative in nature. Feedback from stakeholders proves to be an effective tool in making changes or improvements to current practices. The expertise of those individuals at the grass roots level, in this case the educators themselves, should prove to be a source of knowledge and information that will drive best practice in transition planning.

References

Chadsey-Rusch, J., & Heal, L. (1995). Building consensus from transition experts on social integration outcomes and interventions. *Exceptional Children, 62(3)*, 165–187.

Individuals with Disabilities Education Act Amendments of 1997, 20 U.S.C. § 1401 (26).

Kohler, P. D. (1998). Implementing a transition perspective of education. In F. R. Rusch & J. G. Chadsey (Eds.), *Beyond high school: Transition from school to work* (pp. 179–205). Boston: Wadsworth.

McDonnell, J., Mathot-Buckner, C., & Ferguson, B. (1996). *Transition programs for students with moderate/severe disabilities.* Baltimore: Brookes.

Rehabilitation Act of 1973, 29 U.S.C. § 701 *et seq.*

Ryndak, D. L., & Alper, S. (1996). *Curriculum content for students with moderate and severe disabilities in inclusive settings.* Boston: Allyn & Bacon.

Christy Holthaus Stuart, MS, is a doctoral candidate in the Department of Special Education at the University of Florida. **Stephen W. Smith**, PhD, is a professor in the Department of Special Education at the University of Florida. Address: Christy Holthaus Smart, Dept. of Special Education, G315 Norman Hall, University of Florida, Gainesville, FL 32611.

From *Intervention in School and Clinic,* March 2002, pp. 234-236. © 2002 by Pro-Ed, Inc. Reprinted by permission.

The Transition from Middle School to High School

Students with and without Learning Disabilities Share Their Perceptions

By THERESA M. LETRELLO and DOROTHY D. MILES

The move to high school by eighth grade students can be a traumatic experience, especially for students with learning disabilities. Because this transition can have an impact on students' success in high school, we felt that it was an important subject to investigate. We explored how students perceived this transition period and whether there was a difference in the perceptions of students with learning disabilities and those without.

As students in eighth grade prepare to enter ninth grade, they are experiencing significant physical growth and change. Wiles and Bondi (2001) said that the middle school years for ten to fourteen-year-olds are characterized by emotional instability. Erratic and inconsistent behavior is present; anxiety and fear are also common and contrast with reassuring false security. Dealing with physical changes, striving for independence from family, and acquiring new methods of intellectual functioning are all emotional issues for emerging adolescents. "Students have many fears real and imagined. At no other time in development is a student likely to encounter such a diverse number of problems simultaneously" (Wiles and Bondi 2001, 35). Students experience a transition in their physical environment in the move from one school to another, as well as different academic requirements, larger school size, and new social interactions.

Although for some the transition from middle school to high school can be easy, many young adolescents experience a decline in grades and attendance (Barone, Aguirre-Deandreis, and Trickett 1991); they begin to view themselves more negatively and experience an increased need for friendships (Hertzog et al. 1996). The change can overwhelm the coping skills of some students, lower self-esteem, and decrease motivation to learn (Mac Iver 1990). For some students, the singular and unsettling act of changing from one school in eighth grade to a new school in high school may be a precipitating factor in dropping out (Roderick 1993).

Students with learning disabilities making the move to high school face even more challenges (Smith and Diller 1999). A crisis often develops when the student enters high school because the students' compensating efforts are no longer adequate (Smith and Diller 1999). Wagner (1993), in a report from the National Longitudinal Transition Study of Special Education Students (NLTS) (which studied a nationally representative sample of 8,000 students aged 15 to 23 in secondary special education classes), found that the school programs for students with disabilities in the ninth and tenth grades were strenuous. Because of the heavy load of academic requirements, students with disabilities were more likely to experience problems in these years.

With the heavy academic focus in high school, the predominance of regular education placements, and the lower level of support services provided, it is not surprising that ninth and tenth grade students were more likely to receive failing grades than were students in the upper grades. By failing classes, students with disabilities may fall behind their peers in progress toward graduation. Marder (1992) reported that students with learning disabilities had a dropout rate of 30 percent, one of the highest for students with disabilities.

Students in eighth grade usually begin to prepare for the move to the high school during their last semester. To do so, most students experience transition activities that acquaint them with the high school. Transition programs should address all aspects of the transition—academic and social—so that the students have the greatest opportunity to succeed (Hertzog and Morgan 1998). Typical transition activities consist of registration, high school principal talks, peer panels, high school visits, and pairing with upperclassmen. Students with learning disabilities experience these activities also, but often more is involved in their transition process. According to their Individual Education Programs (IEPs), learning-disabled students are usually followed more closely by parents and special educators. These special educators track the progress of learning disabled students and make sure they are placed in classes where they will receive needed assistance.

Interviews

The first researcher did individual interviews of twelve ninth grade students—six with learning disabilities and six without learning disabilities—about their transition to high school. All students attended the same Midwestern high school at the time of the interviews. The school, located in a suburban district, had a total of 1,200 students in grades 9-12. In the eighth grade, all students had attended the local middle school with a total population of 1,150 students in grades 6-8. All interviews took place at the high school in a private room. To assure confidentiality, all participating students were identified by codes and not names. After all interviews were completed, we divided the interview data into two groups for study: students with learning disabilities and students without learning disabilities. We then analyzed the data for emerging themes or concepts.

The major research question was, "What transition activities did the students find helpful, and were there differences between the experiences of those with learning disabilities and those without?" We used the following interview questions:

1. What were some of your fears about going to high school when you were in eighth grade?

2. As an eighth grader, what were some of your expectations of high school?

3. What major differences between middle school and high school have you observed?

4. What do you feel was the most difficult aspect of moving to high school?

5. What do you feel was the easiest aspect of moving to high school?

6. What activities have you been involved in at high school?

7. While in eighth grade, you were introduced to the high school with various activities, such as counselor and principal visits. What activities helped you get acquainted with the high school?

8. If you had a chance to talk to current eighth graders, what advice would you give them as they prepare for the move to ninth grade?

Results

When we analyzed the interviews, it was apparent that both groups gave extremely similar responses to the questions. Both groups expressed that as eighth graders they were fearful of high school, especially of the size of the school, of older students, of not having enough friends, and of not being able to find all their classes. Students in both groups expected that high school would be "hard," that they wouldn't see their friends, that they would have difficult classes and difficult and demanding teachers, and that high school students would be more mature than those in middle school.

Major differences that students in both groups described were that the high school was bigger, that they had more freedom in high school, that they participated in more extracurricular activities, and that high school students were more accepting of student differences. The students said that the most difficult aspects of moving to high school included getting accustomed to the block schedule, high expectations of the teachers, managing time, and lack of time for social activities because of the demands of homework. Students with learning disabilities indicated that they relied more heavily on help from peers and teachers to be successful in the ninth grade year than did students without learning disabilities.

The easiest aspect of moving to the high school, expressed by students in both groups, included making friends, getting involved in extracurricular activities, and having more fun and freedom. All of the students were involved in extracurricular activities such as sports, band, drama productions, and student council, but students with learning disabilities were involved in fewer such activities than students without. Activities that helped both groups get acquainted with the high school as eighth graders included talking to their academic counselors and friends. Many students in both groups felt that just talking to older friends and siblings helped them understand life in high school. Some students in both groups also said they learned about the high school by visiting the school on their own and attending athletic events. Students in both groups said they would advise future ninth graders to use good study habits, to get involved in extracurricular activities, complete homework, and be prepared to meet new and different people.

The interview data revealed two major recurring themes—social interaction and activity involvement. Students in both groups talked frequently about interaction with friends and other students. This demonstrates that social interaction, particularly with peers, was important for them in their transition to high school. Moreover, even though students with learning disabilities engaged in fewer activities, participation was important for students in both groups during the transition.

Recommendations

From this study, we have produced the following recommendations to enhance the transition from eighth grade to ninth grade:

1. Middle schools should have as many activities as possible to prepare students for the change to high school. These activities should include high school visits and explanation of activities as well as curricula.

2. Transition teams should be formed at the middle school and the high school to plan activities for the transition to ninth grade. These teams should work together with planned activities starting in eighth grade.

3. Students' needs and fears regarding the move to high school should be assessed and addressed in eighth grade.

4. Because social interaction proved to be an important facet of satisfaction with high school, high school students should be trained to facilitate groups at the middle school to discuss concerns with eighth graders and should also become peer mentors to the students when they move to the high school.

5. Students with learning disabilities should have continuous support from teachers and staff during the transition and after they have entered high school.

6. Students entering ninth grade should be encouraged to get involved in extracurricular activities.

Key words: learning disabled, transition activities, middle school, high school

References

Barone, C., A. J. Aguirre-Deandreis, and E. J. Trickett. 1991. Means - end problem solving—solving skills, life stress, and social support as mediators of adjustment in the normative transition to high school. *American Journal of Community Psychology* 19:207-25.

Hertzog, C. J., and P. L. Morgan. 1998. Breaking the barriers between middle school and high school: Developing a transition team for student success. *National Association of Secondary School Principals Bulletin* 82:94-98.

Hertzog, C., P. L. Morgan, P. A. Diamond, and M. J Walker. 1996. Making the transition from middle level to high school. *The High School Magazine* 3(1): 28-30.

Mac Iver, D. J 1990. Meeting the needs of young adolescents: Advisory groups, interdisciplinary teaching teams, and school transition programs. *Phi Delta Kappan* 71:458-64.

Marder, C. 1992. Education after secondary school. In Wagner, M., *next? Trends in post school outcomes of youth with disabilities. The second comprehensive report from the National Longitudinal Transition Study of Special Education Students.* Menlo Park, CA: SRI International

Milligan, P. 1995. The fast lane to high school: Transitions from middle school/junior high school to high school. Salt Lake City, UT: *Systematic transition of Utah's disabled youth.* ERIC, ED 389105.

Roderick, M. 1993. *The path to dropping out. Evidence for intervention.* Westport, CT: Auburn House.

Smith, J. and H. Diller. 1999. *Unmotivated adolescents.* Dallas, TX: Apodixis Press.

Wagner, M. (Ed) 1993. *The secondary school programs of students with learning disabilities: A report from the National Longitudinal Transition Study of Special Education Students.* Menlo Park, CA: SRI International.

Wiles, J., and J. Bondi 2001. *The new American middle school: Educating preadolescents in an era of change* (3rd ed.). Upper Saddle River, NJ: Prentice-Hall, Inc.

Theresa M. Letrello is a language arts and history teacher at Parkway West Middle School, in Chesterfield, Missouri. Dorothy D. Miles is an associate professor of educational psychology, disabilities studies, and research and statistics at Saint Louis University, in Missouri.

From *The Clearing House,* March/April 2003. Reprinted by permission of the Helen Dwight Reid Educational Foundation. Published by Heldref Publications, 1319, Eighteenth St., NW, Washington, DC 20036-1802. Copyright © 2003.

Choosing a Self-Determination Curriculum

PLAN *for the Future*

David W. Test • **Meagan Karvonen** • **Wendy M. Wood** • **Diane Browder** • **Bob Algozzine**

Self-determination. In almost every special education publication, conference, or inservice workshop, someone mentions "self-determination." The popularity of this term is not surprising, considering the urgent need to improve postsecondary outcomes for students with disabilities (see box, "What Does the Literature Say About Self-Determination?"). Self-determination is certainly a factor in the success of all students.

This article describes a project to help educators improve the self-determination of students with disabilities. We conducted this project with support from the U.S. Department of Education, Office of Special Education Programs, to gather, evaluate, and disseminate information about curriculum/ assessment materials and strategies on promoting self-determination. In addition, we suggest a process other educators can use to select materials and curricula.

The Self-Determination Synthesis Project

The Self-Determination Synthesis Project (SDSP) has the objective of synthesizing and disseminating the knowledge base and best practices related to self-determination for students with disabilities. To this end, the purpose of the project was to improve, expand, and accelerate the use of this knowledge by the professionals who serve children and youth with disabilities; parents who rear, educate, and support their children with disabilities; and the students themselves.

We found 60 curricula
designed to promote self-determination skills.

As part of the SDSP effort, we have conducted a comprehensive literature review of self-determination interventions research, visited school systems that exhibited exemplary self-determination outcomes, and gathered and catalogued published self-determination curricula. For more information on our exemplary sites and literature review visit our Web site at http://www.uncc.edu/sdsp.

Existing Self-Determination Curricula

To identify existing self-determination curricula, we reviewed the literature, conducted Web searches, asked experts in the area, and advertised in newsletters and at conferences. As a result, we found 60 curricula designed to promote self-determination skills. Table 1 shows a sampling of these curricula; other reviews are available from the authors (see Table 1). We compiled the name of each curriculum, the publisher, telephone number, and cost information for each curriculum. Further, we identified, for each curriculum, which of the eight self-determination components the curriculum included, based on the most commonly identified components of self-determination found in the literature (e.g., Field & Hoffman 1994; Mithaug, Campeau, & Wolman, 1992; Ward, 1988; Wehmeyer, 1996). The eight curricular components are as follows:
- Choice/decision-making.
- Goal setting/attainment.
- Problem-solving.
- Self-evaluation, observation, and reinforcement.
- Self-advocacy.
- Inclusion of student-directed individualized education programs (IEP).
- Relationships with others.
- Self-awareness.

Finally, we listed the materials included in each curriculum and the appropriate student audience identified by the author, and noted whether the curriculum had been field-tested.

Table 1. A Sample of Self-Determination Curricula and Components (For a complete listing, see http://www.uncc.edu/sdsp)								
TITLE	Choice/ Decision Making	Goal Setting/ Attainment	Problem Solving	Self Eval	Self Advocacy	IEP Plan	Relationships w/Others	Self Awareness
Next S.T.E.P.: Student transition and educational planning **Product Info:** Pro-Ed (800) 897-3202 Price: $144	X X	X		X		X		X
Contents: Video, Teacher manual, Student workbook **Audience:** Transition aged students with and without disabilities, and students at-risk **Other:** Adjustment, Employment, Education, Housing, Daily living, Community *Field Test* X								
Self-advocacy strategy for education and transition planning **Product Info:** Edge Enterprises (785) 749-1473 Price: $15	X X				X	X		X
Contents: Instructor's manual **Audience:** Audience: Primary and secondary students with mild disabilities, and high risk students **Other:** Employment, Education, Housing, Daily living, Personal, Community *Field Test* X								
Take action: Making goals happen [Choicemaker] **Product Info:** Sopris West Inc. (800) 547-6747 Price: $95	X X	X		X				
Contents: Teacher's manual, Reproducible lesson masters, Video **Audience:** Not specified **Other:** Adjustment, Employment, Education, Housing, Daily living, Personal, Community *Field Test* X								
TAKE CHARGE for the future **Product Info:** OHSU Center on Self-Determination (503) 232-9154 Price: $45	X X	X		X	X	X		X
Contents: Student guide, Companion guide, Parent guide, Class guide **Audience:** Sophomores and juniors with disabilities **Other:** Adjustment, Employment, Education, Housing, Daily living, Personal, Community *FieldTest* X								
Whose future is it anyway? A student-directed transition process **Product Info:** The Arc National Headquarters (888) 368-8009 Price $20	X X	X		X	X	X		X
Contents: Student manual with coach's guide **Audience:** Middle school and transition aged students with mild to moderate cognitive, developmental, or learning disabilities **Other:** Employment, Education, Housing, Daily living, Personal, Recreation, Community *Field Test* X								

Choosing the Right Curriculum

We found many curricula that address the different components of self-determination. Some curricula teach specific skills, such as decision making or goal setting. Others include content intended to increase students' knowledge about their disabilities or about disability rights. Still others include learning approaches or processes by which students take greater ownership of their IEP planning process. With the variety of materials available, how do teachers know what will be most effective for use with their students? We suggest that the process begin with a careful review of the sampling in Table 1 to become familiar with the variety of resources that are available. In addition, you might want to gather other published descriptions/reviews of self-determination curriculum (see Field, 1996; Field et al., 1998).

What Does the Literature Say About Self-Determination?

Here are the current trends in self-determination research:

- Current research has referred to self-determination as the ultimate goal of education (Halloran, 1993).
- Research has demonstrated a positive relationship between self-determination and improved postsecondary outcomes. These outcomes include a higher rate of employment and higher wages 1 year after graduation for students with mild mental retardation and learning disabilities (Wehmeyer & Schwartz, 1997).
- Classroom teachers are recognizing that self-determination is an important skill to teach students (Agran, Snow, & Swaner, 1999; Wehmeyer, Agran, & Hughes, 2000).

Definition of Self-Determination. Beginning with the "normalization" movement in the early 1970s, many researchers, educators, and self-advocates have developed definitions of self-determination. According to a consensus definition by Field, Martin, Miller, Ward, and Wehmeyer, 1998, self-determination is

a combination of skills, knowledge, and beliefs that enable a person to engage in goal-directed, self-regulated, autonomous behavior. An understanding of one's strengths and limitations together with a belief in oneself as capable and effective are essential to self-determination. When acting on the basis of these skills and attitudes, individuals have greater ability to take control of their lives and assume the role of successful adults. (p. 2)

Conceptual models of self-determination have included knowing and valuing oneself (Field & Hoffman, 1994); skills and knowledge on topics such as choice and decision making, goal setting and attainment, problem-solving, and self-advocacy (Martin & Marshall, 1995; Wehmeyer, 1999); and recognition of the environment's role in supporting self-determination for people with disabilities (Abery & Stancliffe, 1996).

Need for Instruction in Self-Determination. Unfortunately, so far all the rhetoric, research, and recognition is not being translated into classroom instruction. For example, Agran et al. (1999) found that whereas over 75% of middle and secondary teachers rated self-determination skills as a high priority, 55% indicated that self-determination goals were either not included in their students' IEPs or only in some students' IEPs. This finding is supported by: (a) Wehmeyer and Schwartz (1998) who found no self-determination skills in 895 IEP transition goals; and (b) Wehmeyer et al. (2000) who found 31% of secondary-level teachers reported writing no self-determination goals in student IEPs, 47% reported writing self-determination IEP goals for some students, and only 22% reported writing self-determination IEP goals for all students.

Although many explanations may exist for why self-determination skills are not included in student IEPs, we believe a major reason is that teachers are unaware of what resources exist to help with the task. This is supported by Wehmeyer et al. (2000), who reported that 41% of teachers with secondary-aged students indicated that they did not have sufficient training or information on teaching self-determination, and 17% were unaware of curriculum/assessment materials/strategies.

> **Promoting self-determination also requires training those without disabilities to encourage and respect the decisions made by self-determining individuals with disabilities.**

Figure 1 shows a curriculum materials review checklist that we have found useful when deciding what curriculum might be most appropriate. The information included in Figure 1 is summarized in the following set of questions:

Does the intended audience match my students?

Are the materials age-appropriate? Are they designed for use with students who have mild, moderate, or severe disabilities? Some materials that may have been originally designed for use with a specific group of students may have to be modified for use with other groups (including students without disabilities). Check the introductory section of the teacher's manual to see what the authors say.

Do the skills covered in this curriculum meet my students' needs?

You may find that your students are perfectly capable of setting goals, but they do not know enough about their rights under current legislation such as the Individuals with Disabilities Education Act or the Americans with Disabilities Act to be able to ask for reasonable accommodations in their postsecondary setting, or maybe they need a better understanding of how to run their IEP meeting. In some cases, the introduction or overview section of the teacher's manual will state the goals of the curriculum. For example, the Take Action curriculum states: "Students learn to act on their plans, evaluate their plan and results, and make any necessary adjustments" (Marshall, et al., 1999, p. 9). Do the goals of the curriculum match your instructional objectives?

Does the curriculum require prerequisite skills?

Some curricula may require relatively sophisticated reading levels, or assume that the students will already understand how to make choices for themselves. Both the teacher's manual and the student activities will give you a sense of what skill level is required for students to begin using the curriculum.

Figure 1. Curriculum Materials Review Checklist

CURRICULUM MATERIALS REVIEW CHECKLIST

Title:_____

Author:_____

Publisher's name contact/information:_____

Date of publication:_____ Cost of materials:_____

For what type of student is the curriculum designed (e.g., age, disability)?

_____

What types of materials are included (e.g., instructor manual, student workbook, video, alternate formats)

_____

Do the components of self-determination match my students' needs

Students' Needs	Included in Curriculum		Comments
Choice-making	YES	NO	
Decision-making	YES	NO	
Goal setting/attainment	YES	NO	
Problem solving	YES	NO	
Self-evaluation	YES	NO	
Self-advocacy	YES	NO	
Self-awareness	YES	NO	
Person-centered IEP Planning	YES	NO	
Relationship with Others	YES	NO	
Other:_____			

Rate each of the following on a scale from 1 (Excellent) to 4 (Poor) based on your students and yourself as a teacher.

	1 Excellent	2 Good	3 Fair	4 Poor	5 Can't tell
How easy is it to get materials?					
How well do the cost of materials fit my budget?					
Are the materials available in alternative formats?					
Are support materials provided?					
Are the instructions "teacher friendly"?					
Are the prerequisite skills delineated?					
Are there sufficient opportunities for practice?					
How relevant/motivating is the content for my students?					
How age-appropriate is the content for my students?					
How well do the materials match the academic level of my students?					
Is a system for assessing student progress included?					
Is the content based on research/field testing?					
How appealing are the videos and other materials?					
How well does the instructional time (number and length of sessions) fit with my schedule?					
Additional Comments:					

What types of materials are provided?

If you work with students who are visually or hearing impaired, does the curriculum have audiotape, closed-captioned, or Braille formats? Are the materials durable and easy to use? Do they provide enough variety or hold the interest of students? Is an assessment tool included?

How easy is it to follow the lesson plans?

Are the objectives for each lesson clearly stated? Is it easy to tell what materials you will need and how much time each lesson will require? Is the text formatted so you can easily find prompts? Is there flexibility in the order of the lesson plans?

Were the materials field-tested?

Has anyone collected information about whether students who used this curriculum improved their self-determination knowledge, skills, or behaviors? Just because someone is selling a product doesn't mean that it works. Many of the curricula we listed have been field-tested, but not all of them report the results of those tests. Sometimes authors report field-test results in a journal article or book chapter instead of the manual.

What are the time and financial obligations associated with this curriculum?

The costs of materials sampled in Table 1 range from nothing to more than $1,000. The time commitments also vary extensively. Is the financial cost of the curriculum appropriate to the length of instructional time you have available to teach the skills?

Important questions include: Are the materials age-appropriate? Are they designed for use with students who have mild, moderate, or severe disabilities? Do they provide enough variety or hold the interest of students? Is an assessment tool included?

Sample Curricula

We have selected five curricula which have published research documenting their effectiveness to describe in more detail here.

The Self-Advocacy Strategy for Education and Transition Planning

This curriculum was developed using a modified version of the Strategies Intervention Model (Ellis, Deshler, Lenz, Schumaker, & Clark, 1991) at the University of Kansas. The

Article 34. Choosing a Self-Determination Curriculum

Self-Advocacy Strategy is a motivation strategy that teachers can use to help students prepare for any type of educational or transition planning meeting. The strategy, called I-PLAN, consists of five steps:
- *I*nventory your strengths, areas to improve, goals, needed accommodations, and choices for learning.
- *P*rovide your inventory information.
- *L*isten and respond.
- *A*sk questions.
- *N*ame your goals.

The instructor's manual contains step-by-step lesson plans and cue cards that you can use as transparencies, handouts, or worksheets. Finally, the Self-Advocacy Strategy has been field-tested with students with learning disabilities ages 14–21 (Van Reusen & Bos, 1994; Van Reusen, Deshler, & Schumaker, 1989).

Next S.T.E.P. (Student Transition and Education Planning)

Developed by Andrew Halpern and his colleagues at the University of Oregon, the purpose of the Next S.T.E.P. curriculum is to teach high school students how to begin planning for their lives after they leave school. Materials include a teacher's manual with lesson plans and necessary forms, a student workbook, and a videotape that contains an overview of the curriculum, as well as vignettes that address important issues from specific lessons. The Next S.T.E.P. curriculum has been field-tested with students with mild mental retardation ages 14–19 (Zhang, 2000).

Take Action: Making Goals Happen

Take Action is the last of the three strands of the Choice-Maker Self-Determination Curriculum designed by Laura Huber Marshall and Jim Martin and their colleagues at the University of Colorado at Colorado Springs. The first two strands are Choosing Goals and Expressing Goals (or Self-Directed IEP). Take Action is designed to provide teachers with a set of lessons to teach students a generalizable process for attaining their goals. Materials include a teacher's manual with reproducible lesson masters and a student instructional video. Take Action was field-tested with six students with mild or moderate mental retardation ages 16 to 18 (Jerman, Martin, Marshall, & Sale, 2000). Results indicated that all six students accomplished all goals set during maintenance.

TAKE CHARGE for the Future

This multicomponent curriculum was designed by Laurie Powers and her colleagues at Oregon Health Sciences University to assist students to become more involved in their transition planning process. The four components are coaching, mentorship, parent support, and staff training. Materials include a student guide, companion guide, parent guide, and class guide. TAKE CHARGE for the Future was field-tested with 43 students with specific learning disabilities, emotional disabilities, other health impairments, or orthopedic impairments ages 14–17 years (Powers, Turner, Matuszewski, Wilson, & Phillips, in press). Results indicated significant differences in education planning, transition awareness, family empowerment, and student participation in transition planning.

41% of teachers with secondary-aged students indicated that they did not have sufficient training or information on teaching self-determination.

Whose Future Is It Anyway? A Student-Directed Transition Planning Process

Developed by Michael Wehmeyer and his colleagues at the Arc National Headquarters, this curriculum is designed for middle school and transition-aged students with mild or moderate disabilities. The curriculum consists of a student manual, which includes a cut-out Coach's Guide. While the manual is written for students to read and work through at their own pace, the teacher's role is three part:
- To facilitate student success.
- To teach information requested by students.
- To advocate for a successful transition for students.

This curriculum was field-tested with 53 students with mild or moderate mental retardation ages 15–21 (Wehmeyer & Lawrence, 1995). Results indicate significant increases in self-efficacy and outcome expectancy measures.

For more information on our exemplary sites and literature review visit our World Wide Web site at http://www.uncc.edu/sdsp.

Final Thoughts

Self-determination develops over the life span as students gain self-awareness and learn to make increasingly important decisions about their lives with the guidance of their parents, teachers, and other adult mentors. Because traditionally other people (professionals) have made most major life decisions for them, students with disabilities often require instruction on the skills needed to be self-determining citizens. Promoting self-determination also requires training those without disabilities to encourage and respect the decisions made by self-determining individuals with disabilities.

Fortunately, many self-determination curricula are available from which to choose. We hope that the suggestions provided in this article will help you decide which

curriculum will best promote self-determination for your students.

References

Abery, B., & Stancliffe, R. (1996). The ecology of self-determination. In D. J. Sands & M. Wehmeyer (Eds.), *Self-determination across the lifespan: Independence and choice for people with disabilities* (pp. 111–145). Baltimore: Paul H. Brookes.

Agran, M., Snow, K., & Swaner, J. (1999). Teacher perceptions of self-determination: Benefits, characteristics, strategies. *Education and Training in Mental Retardation and Developmental Disabilities, 34*, 293–301.

Ellis, E. S., Deshler, D. D., Lenz, B. K., Schumaker, J. B., & Clark, F. L. (1991). An instructional model for teaching learning strategies. *Focus on Exceptional Children, 23*(4), 1–24.

Field, S. (1996). Self-determination instructional strategies for youth with learning disabilities. *Journal of Learning Disabilities, 29*, 40–52.

Field, S., & Hoffman, A. (1994). Development of a model for self-determination. *Career Development for Exceptional Individuals, 17*, 159–169.

Field, S., Martin, J., Miller, R., Ward, M., & Wehmeyer, M. (1998). *A practical guide for teaching self-determination*. Reston, VA: Council for Exceptional Children.

Halloran, W. D. (1993). Transition service requirements: Issues, implications, challenge. In R. C. Eaves & P. J. McLaughlin (Eds.), *Recent advances in special education and rehabilitation* (pp. 210–224). Boston: Andover.

Jerman, S. L., Martin, J. E., Marshall, L. H., & Sale, P. R. (2000). Promoting self-determination: Using *Take Action* to teach goal attainment. *Career Development for Exceptional Individuals, 23*, 27–38.

Marshall, L. H., Martin, J. E., Maxson, L., Hughes, W., Miller, T., McGill, T., & Jerman, P. (1999). *Take action: Making goals happen*. Longmont, CO: Sopris West.

Martin, J. E., & Marshall L. H. (1995) Choicemaker: A comprehensive self-determination transition program. *Intervention in School and Clinic, 30*, 147–156.

Mithaug, D., Campeau, P., & Wolman, J. (1992). *Research on self-determination in individuals with disabilities*. Unpublished Manuscript.

Powers, L. E., Turner, A., Matuszewski, J., Wilson, R., & Phillips, A. (in press). TAKE CHARGE for the future: A controlled field-test of a model to promote student involvement in transition planning. *Career Development for Exceptional Individuals*.

Van Reusen, A. K., & Bos, C. S. (1994). Facilitating student participation in individualized education programs through motivation strategy instruction. *Exceptional Children, 60*, 466–475.

Van Reusen, A. K., Deshler, D. D., & Schumaker, J. B. (1989). Effects of a student participation strategy in facilitating the involvement of adolescents with learning disabilities in Individualized Education Program planning process. *Learning Disabilities, 1*, 23–34.

Ward, M. J. (1988). The many facts of self-determination. *NICHCY Transition Summary: National Information Center for Children and Youth with Disabilities, 5*, 2–3.

Wehmeyer, M. L. (1996). Self-determination in youth with severe cognitive disabilities: From theory to practice. In L. E. Powers, G. H. S. Singer, & J. Sowers (Eds.), *On the road to autonomy: Promoting self-competence for children and youth with disabilities* (pp. 17–36). Baltimore: Paul H. Brookes.

Wehmeyer, M. L. (1999). A functional model of self-determination: Describing development and implementing instruction. *Focus on Autism and Other Developmental Disabilities, 14,* 53–61.

Wehmeyer, M. L., Agran, M., & Hughes, C. A. (2000). A national survey of teachers' promotion of self-determination and student directed learning. *The Journal of Special Education, 34,* 58–68.

Wehmeyer, M., & Lawrence, M. (1995). Whose future is it anyway? Promoting student involvement in transition planning. *Career Development for Exceptional Individuals, 18,* 69–83.

Wehmeyer, M. L., & Schwartz, M. (1997). Self-determination and positive adult outcomes: A follow up study of youth with mental retardation or learning disabilities. *Exceptional Children, 63,* 245–255.

Wehmeyer, M. L., & Schwartz, M. (1998). The self-determination focus of transition goals for students with mental retardation. *Career Development for Exceptional Individuals, 21,* 75–86.

Zhang, D. (2000). The effects of self-determination instruction on high school students with mild disabilities. *Louisiana Education Research Journal, 25*(1), 29–54.

David W. Test *(CEC Chapter #147), Professor, Special Education Program;* **Meagan Karvonen,** *Project Coordinator, Special Education Program;* **Wendy M. Wood,** *Associate Professor, Special Education Program;* **Diane Browder,** *Snyder Distinguished Professor, Special Education Program; and* **Bob Algozzine,** *Professor, Department of Educational Administration, Research, and Technology, College of Education, University of North Carolina at Charlotte.*

Address correspondence to David Test, Special Education Program, University of North Carolina at Charlotte, 9201 University City Blvd., Charlotte, NC 28223 (e-mail: dwtest@email.uncc.edu; URL: http://www.uncc.edu/sdsp).

Index

Index

mobility training, using MOVE curriculum, 170–175

MOVE program, for mobility training, 170–175

movement: differences in, and understanding inarticulate students, 100, 101; mobility training and, 170–175; twice-exceptional students and, 198

multidisciplinary approach, use of, for performance-based evaluation, 160

multidisciplinary teams, determining language disabilities from language differences in second-language students and, 70–77

Murphy v. United Parcel Service, 97

music, in inclusive environment, 29–32

O

O'Connor, Sandra Day, 97

obsessions, 111

obsessive-compulsive disorder, 111, 112

oppositional defiant disorder, 108. *See also* emotional and behavioral disorders

organizational techniques, twice-exceptional students and, 198–199

orthopedic impairment, accommodations for, 177

P

P.A.L.S. center, 38

paraprofessionals, 153, 155–156, 158

Participation Model, of assessment, and African Americans, 81

peer-interaction play centers, 38

Penny Transfer Technique, teacher self-awareness in working with students with emotional and behavioral disorders and, 124

pervasive developmental disorder, 113

phonetic awareness, reading disabilities and, 51

Player's Choice, as classroom management technique, 129

positive reinforcement, classroom management and, 123–124, 129

posttraumatic stress disorder, 111–112

Premack Principle, 129

Preproduction stage, of second-language acquisition, 73

principals: attitudes of elementary school, toward inclusion, 13–21; collaboration and, 24, 25

psychiatric disorders, 107–115

punishment, relationship building and, 34

pyramid training, for special education teachers, 156

R

reading disabilities, brain and, 51–54

recognition, disability rights and, 96–97

redistribution, disability rights and, 96–97

Redl, Fritz, 123

refusals, understanding inarticulate students and, 101–102

Rehabilitation Act of 1974, 176, 177, 178

reinforcement: positive, and classroom management, 123–124, 129; as teacher competency, 154, 155

resistance, understanding inarticulate students and, 101–102

Ritalin, 109, 180, 181–183

S

Satel, Sally, 182, 183

scaffolded instruction, supporting independence through, 45–50

schizophrenia, 112–113

Schlafly, Phyllis, 180, 181

second-language acquisition, stages of, 72–73

second-language students, determining language disabilities from language differences in, 70–77

Section 504, of Rehabilitation Act, 176, 177, 178

selective serotonin reuptake inhibitors (SSRIs), 110

self-advocacy skills, promoting through LEAD group, 55–62

Self-Advocacy Strategy, for education and transition planning, 213

self-awareness: self-advocacy and, 55–62; teacher, and working with students with emotional and behavioral disorders, 122–127

Self-Determination Synthesis Project (SDSP), 209

self-determination: curriculum, 209–215; student transition and, 55–62

self-management strategies, classroom management and, 128

separation anxiety disorder, 111

service delivery, trends in special education teaching force and, 7, 9–10

severe disabilities, 153; inclusion of students with, 147–152; transition planning for students with, 205–206

Silent stage, of second-language acquisition, 73

social interaction, transition from middle school to high school and, 208

social skills: group intervention for improving, 63–67; itinerant teachers and, 36–41; music in inclusive environments and, 30, 31

Sommers

Sommers, Christina Hoff, 181

Sowell, Thomas, 180, 181

spoken language, reading disabilities and, 51

staff training programs, characteristics of success of, 154

standard-based lessons, for diverse learners, 3–5

S.T.E.P. (Student Transition and Education Planning), 213

stress, augmentative and alternative communication systems and, 79

structured social-skills groups, 38, 39

student-directed transition planning process, 214

supervisory training, 158

support groups, promoting self-advocacy and, 58

Supreme Court, U.S., on Americans with Disabilities Act, 97

Sutton v. United Airlines, Inc., 97

T

tactile defensiveness, 141–142

tactile modeling, 139

tactile mutual attention, 140

tactile strategies: for blind and severely disabled students, 139–143; twice-exceptional students and, 197–198

Take Action, 213

Take Charge for the Future, as multicomponent curriculum, 213–214

task analysis, as teacher competency, 154, 155

teacher diversity, trends in special education teaching force and, 6, 7–9

teacher preparation, trends in special education teaching force and, 6–7, 9

Teacher-Skills Training Program (TSTP), 153–158

teaching assignments, trends in special education teaching force and, 6, 7, 8

teaching force, trends in special education, 6–12

technology, use of, to construct alternative portfolios of students with moderate to severe disabilities, 159–167

Telecommunications Act, 138

Telegraphic stage, of second-language acquisition, 73

testing, identification of giftedness and, 193–194. *See also* assessment

titration, 109

touch. *See* tactile strategies

Tourette Syndrome, 113; accommodations for, 177

transition planning: self-advocacy training and, 213; for students with severe disabilities, 205–206

twice-exceptional students, 195–201

Test Your Knowledge Form

We encourage you to photocopy and use this page as a tool to assess how the articles in *Annual Editions* expand on the information in your textbook. By reflecting on the articles you will gain enhanced text information. You can also access this useful form on a product's book support Web site at *http://www.dushkin.com/online/*.

NAME:

DATE:

_____

TITLE AND NUMBER OF ARTICLE:

_____

BRIEFLY STATE THE MAIN IDEA OF THIS ARTICLE:

_____

LIST THREE IMPORTANT FACTS THAT THE AUTHOR USES TO SUPPORT THE MAIN IDEA:

_____

WHAT INFORMATION OR IDEAS DISCUSSED IN THIS ARTICLE ARE ALSO DISCUSSED IN YOUR TEXTBOOK OR OTHER READINGS THAT YOU HAVE DONE? LIST THE TEXTBOOK CHAPTERS AND PAGE NUMBERS:

_____

LIST ANY EXAMPLES OF BIAS OR FAULTY REASONING THAT YOU FOUND IN THE ARTICLE:

_____

LIST ANY NEW TERMS/CONCEPTS THAT WERE DISCUSSED IN THE ARTICLE, AND WRITE A SHORT DEFINITION:

We Want Your Advice

ANNUAL EDITIONS revisions depend on two major opinion sources: one is our Advisory Board, listed in the front of this volume, which works with us in scanning the thousands of articles published in the public press each year; the other is you—the person actually using the book. Please help us and the users of the next edition by completing the prepaid article rating form on this page and returning it to us. Thank you for your help!

ANNUAL EDITIONS: Educating Exceptional Children 05/06

ARTICLE RATING FORM

Here is an opportunity for you to have direct input into the next revision of this volume.
We would like you to rate each of the articles listed below, using the following scale:

1. **Excellent: should definitely be retained**
2. **Above average: should probably be retained**
3. **Below average: should probably be deleted**
4. **Poor: should definitely be deleted**

Your ratings will play a vital part in the next revision.
Please mail this prepaid form to us as soon as possible.
Thanks for your help!

RATING	ARTICLE
	1. Standards for Diverse Learners
	2. Trends in the Special Education Teaching Force: Do They Reflect Legislative Mandates and Legal Requirements?
	3. Attitudes of Elementary School Principals Toward the Inclusion of Students With Disabilities
	4. An Interview With Dr. Marilyn Friend
	5. Music in the Inclusive Environment
	6. Building Relationships With Challenging Children
	7. The Itinerant Teacher Hits the Road: A Map for Instruction in Young Children's Social Skills
	8. Providing Support for Student Independence Through Scaffolded Instruction
	9. Reading Disability and the Brain
	10. Successful Strategies for Promoting Self-Advocacy Among Students With LD: The LEAD Group
	11. Group Intervention: Improving Social Skills of Adolescents with Learning Disabilities
	12. Language Differences or Learning Difficulties
	13. Young African American Children With Disabilities and Augmentative and Alternative Communication Issues
	14. The Secrets of Autism
	15. Citizenship and Disability
	16. Inscrutable or Meaningful? Understanding and Supporting Your Inarticulate Students
	17. Psychiatric Disorders and Treatments: A Primer for Teachers
	18. Making Choices—Improving Behavior—Engaging in Learning
	19. The Importance of Teacher Self-Awareness in Working With Students With Emotional and Behavioral Disorders
	20. Classroom Problems That Don't Go Away
	21. A Half-Century of Progress for Deaf Individuals
	22. Using Tactile Strategies With Students Who Are Blind and Have Severe Disabilities
	23. Making Inclusion a Reality for Students With Severe Disabilities

RATING	ARTICLE
	24. Training Basic Teaching Skills to Paraeducators of Students With Severe Disabilities
	25. Using Technology to Construct Alternate Portfolios of Students With Moderate and Severe Disabilities
	26. Mobility Training Using the MOVE Curriculum: A Parent's View
	27. Accommodations for Students With Disabilities: Removing Barriers to Learning
	28. Trick Question
	29. Understanding the Young Gifted Child: Guidelines for Parents, Families, and Educators
	30. Cultivating Otherwise Untapped Potential
	31. Teaching Strategies for Twice-Exceptional Students
	32. Transition Planning for Students With Severe Disabilities: Policy Implications for the Classroom
	33. The Transition from Middle School to High School
	34. Choosing a Self-Determination Curriculum

(Continued on next page)

BUSINESS REPLY MAIL
FIRST CLASS MAIL PERMIT NO. 551 DUBUQUE IA

POSTAGE WILL BE PAID BY ADDRESEE

McGraw-Hill/Dushkin
2460 KERPER BLVD
DUBUQUE, IA 52001-9902

NO POSTAGE
NECESSARY
IF MAILED
IN THE
UNITED STATES

ABOUT YOU

Name _____ Date _____

Are you a teacher? ☐   A student? ☐
Your school's name _____

Department _____

Address _____ City _____ State _____ Zip _____

School telephone # _____

YOUR COMMENTS ARE IMPORTANT TO US!

Please fill in the following information:
For which course did you use this book?
_____

Did you use a text with this ANNUAL EDITION?   ☐ yes ☐ no
What was the title of the text?
_____

What are your general reactions to the *Annual Editions* concept?
_____

Have you read any pertinent articles recently that you think should be included in the next edition? Explain.
_____

Are there any articles that you feel should be replaced in the next edition? Why?
_____

Are there any World Wide Web sites that you feel should be included in the next edition? Please annotate.
_____

May we contact you for editorial input?   ☐ yes ☐ no
May we quote your comments?   ☐ yes ☐ no